INCREASE YOUR WORD POWER

Using Your Senses to Improve Your Vocabulary

by

Dorothy A. Fontaine, Ph.D.

Head of Middle School
Wakefield School
The Plains, Virginia

BARRON'S

Dedication
To two souls who make life's journey both
the thrill ride
and the gentle walk in the country
that it is meant to be—
my tenacious research assistants
and homegrown cheering section
John and Ian.

All inquiries should be addressed to:
Barron's Educational Series, Inc.
250 Wireless Boulevard
Hauppauge, New York 11788
http://www.barronseduc.com

Library of Congress Control Number 2006034341

ISBN-13: 978-0-7641-3429-6
ISBN-10: 0-7641-3429-9

Library of Congress Cataloging-in-Publication Data
Fontaine, Dorothy A.
    Increase your word power : using your senses to improve your vocabulary / by Dorothy A. Fontaine.
        p. cm.
    Includes index.
    ISBN-13: 978-0-7641-3429-6
    ISBN-10: 0-7641-3429-9
    1. Vocabulary—Study and teaching (Secondary) 2. Multiple intelligences.   I. Title.

LB1631 .F636 2006
428.1071'2—dc22

2006034341

10%
POST-CONSUMER WASTE
Paper contains a minimum of 10% post-consumer waste (PCW). Paper used in this book was derived from certified, sustainable forestlands.

Table of Contents

Introduction

This book is designed primarily for the student and only secondarily for the teacher. Based on ideas introduced by Dr. Howard Gardner in 1983, this book is designed to help you learn vocabulary in ways that you, personally, best learn vocabulary. Based on on-going research on multiple intelligences, this book will help you discover study techniques that will work well for you according to how you learn.

Whether or not followers of Dr. Gardner's "Multiple Intelligences" theory, master teachers have known for a long time that different students learn material different ways. One of the traits exhibited by master teachers is the ability to adapt their teaching styles to the needs of the students sitting before them in the classroom. Multiple Intelligences theory is one structure through which this differentiation can be understood and implemented. Many educators have been looking at research on multiple intelligences to help them create lessons that are useful and meaningful to their students. While this is a serious area of study, multiple intelligences can be explored quite easily by members of the general public through the Internet or from widely-available books.[1]

Basically, the theory holds that there are at least eight different "intelligences" or ways that people express and create knowledge. One can learn best by doing (bodily/kinesthetic), through music (musical/rhythmical), in groups (interpersonal), by oneself (intrapersonal), through contact with the natural world (naturalist), by sight and perspective (visual/spatial), through language (verbal/linguistic), or through patterns and logic (logical/mathematical). While each person may have a particular strength in one or more areas, it is important to remember that we all have all of these intelligences to varying degrees. As our lives progress, we need to nurture the obvious strengths we have while we work on our less-obvious intelligences to make them more available to us on a daily basis.

Using This Book

This book is organized into eight sections, one for each intelligence currently recognized. If you don't know which intelligences are your greatest assets right now, you may want to begin by taking the inventory at the end of this introduction and then reading the opening of each section where the intelligences are discussed. When you find the intelligences that sound the most like you, look over the techniques recommended there for vocabulary study. Although some may sound odd at first, if you incorporate these techniques into your study process as you work through all eight sections, you will see how they can help you retain information longer and in more detail.

---

[1] See the bibliography at the end of this book for more information about multiple intelligences.

Structure

While each section introduces a particular intelligence, the vocabulary in *all* eight sections is designed for *all* learners. There are 125 words introduced in each chapter for a total of approximately 1,000 new words. These words have been chosen for their usefulness on standardized tests but also, more importantly, for their usefulness in the everyday life of an educated adult.

Each word is first introduced in a narrative. There are five narrative chapters in each section and each chapter introduces twenty-five new words. Following each narrative, the words are defined *as they are used in the narrative* with two example sentences to help cement the meaning in context. In some cases, the word in the narrative will also be used in its secondary or tertiary meaning to help you learn alternative uses of familiar words.

Each chapter contains two interesting facts to provide insight into the fun and complexity of the English language. These fun facts might have to do with a common spelling problem, an interesting etymology, or even a joke or two. Have fun reading through these bits of language trivia.

Finally, each full section ends with a writing exercise related to the section's theme to help you practice using your newfound vocabulary in a directed way. These writing activities are meant to be a relaxing and entertaining way to put these words to good use right away.

Pronunciations

The pronunciations in this book are based on those accepted by *Merriam-Webster's Collegiate Dictionary, Eleventh Edition*. There are marked differences in the pronunciation of the same word in different English-speaking countries and even within regions of the same country. Feel free to check with others in your area to confirm how a particular word may be pronounced and understood in your region.

Parts of Speech

English is marvelously flexible in its use of words. Because of that, a single word may be used as both a noun and a verb, or a noun and an adjective, or in any number of possible combinations depending on the sentence in which it is being used. In Appendix 1 there is a chart that lists several parts of speech variations of each of the words treated in this book; it is by no means the complete list of all variations! I am sure that you, too, will find additional words to add to some of the columns on this chart as you develop your vocabulary skills.

A Note on Participles. Throughout the lessons, the participial form of a word is often used as an adjective and is labeled as such. This may cause confusion for some people. When in doubt about a word's part of speech (i.e., noun, verb, adjective, adverb, and so on), look at how the word is used in the specific sentence. A participle is nothing more than a verb form being used as an adjective. For example, the words *embarrassed* and *embarrassing* are both participial forms of the verb *to embarrass*. So you might encounter sentences like:

The *embarrassed* girl looked at her feet for most of the evening.

or

The most *embarrassing* thing happened to me yesterday!

In the first sentence, *girl* is a noun and *embarrassed* tells us more about the girl, so it is being used as an adjective. In the second sentence, *thing* is a noun and *embarrassing* tells us more about that noun, so it is also being used as an adjective. The rule to remember is:

If it looks like a verb
And sounds like a verb
But it acts like an adjective—
It's a participle!

A Final Note

This book is intended to help you help yourself to expand your knowledge of, and comfort with, a variety of words in English. A book like this is very useful for intensive study when you have specific vocabulary-building goals in mind. The experts all agree, though, that the very best way to improve your vocabulary over the long term is to become a devoted and eclectic reader; that is, a reader who often reads for pleasure and information (devoted), and who reads a wide variety of subjects in a number of formats (eclectic), such as novels, poetry, nonfiction books, magazines, and Web sites. Reading is a lifetime habit I strongly encourage—and personally recommend!

Acknowledgments

I have developed a number of these techniques in my own classroom but that does not preclude their having been developed by others who came before me as well—teachers are a creative and adaptable group. If you see a technique that I have not acknowledged properly, I apologize and ask that you provide me with the reference to the published text so that I may correct the oversight in future editions.

I want to thank learning specialists who have offered me their time and expertise, most particularly Amrit Kasten-Daryanani, Ph.D., Roz Sarmiento-Anderson, and Susan Danker at Wakefield School in The Plains, Virginia.

I am not a Lewis and Clark scholar, but a report on National Public Radio about these two explorers caught my interest when it focused on a Newfoundland dog that accompanied the two on their epic journey across the American west. I was intrigued with this dog's-eye-view of history and incorporated this dog into my section on visual/spatial learners. It was not until after the book was completed that a stray comment from a Lower School teacher let me know that a number of other writers had been intrigued by the same story element. I feel I would be remiss if I didn't offer references to these writers and their books for those who might want to read more about Seaman, this remarkable dog.

Eubank, Patti Reeder. *Seaman's Journal: On the Trail with Lewis and Clark.* Nashville, TN: Ideals Children's Books, 2002.

Karwoski, Gail. *Seaman: The Dog Who Explored the West with Lewis and Clark.* Atlanta, GA: Peachtree Jr., 2003.

Myers, Laurie. *Lewis and Clark and Me: A Dog's Tale.* New York: Henry Holt and Co., 2002.

Pringle, Laurence P. *Dog of Discovery: A Newfoundland's Adventures with Lewis and Clark.* Honesdale, PA: Boyds Mills Press, 2004.

Smith, Roland. *The Captain's Dog: My Journey with the Lewis and Clark Tribe.* Orlando, FL: Harcourt, 2000.

The following are some of the sources I used in putting this book together:

Armstrong, Thomas. *The Multiple Intelligences of Reading and Writing: Making the Words Come Alive.* Alexandria, VA: Association for Supervision and Curriculum Development, 2003.

This is only one of Armstrong's useful books on Multiple Intelligences. He has written well on other subjects, too, and I recommend his work highly. His chapter on "Grooving with the Rhythms of Language" was particularly useful to me for the study techniques in "Section 1: Life as a Symphony."

Caddy, John. *Morning Earth: Field Notes in Poetry*. Minneapolis, MN: Milkweed Editions, 2003.

My thanks for permission to use two of his poems in "Section 6: The Rhythm of the Earth."

Gentile, William W. Sr. *Daily Warm-Ups: Commonly Confused Words*. Portland, ME: Walch Publishing, 2003.

I have found the *Daily Warm-Ups* series very handy for classroom use, as well as for reminding myself of certain problem elements and words in English.

Lansky, Bruce. *Baby Names Around the World*. New York: Meadowbrook Press/Simon and Schuster, 1999.

I wanted to honor the tradition of multi-culturalism in North American society, and Lansky's book helped me spell names whose cadences had already captured me aurally.

McKenna, Michael C. "Teaching Vocabulary to Struggling Older Readers." *Perspectives*, Winter, 2004. Baltimore, MD: The International Dyslexia Association, p. 134–136.

This publication was most useful for the word line appearing in Section 7: The Great Cell Phone Caper. I have used a variation of a word line before, but this line is particularly clear.

McKenzie, Walter. *http://surfaquarium.com*

For his Multiple Intelligences Inventory, used in the Introduction of this book.

Rice, Ruth. *Daily Warm-Ups: Prefixes, Suffixes, & Roots*. Portland, ME: Walch Publishing, 2004.

Roget, Peter Mark. *Roget's International Thesaurus, Third Edition*. New York: Thomas Y. Crowell Co., Inc., 1962.

This older edition of a long-standing reference text continues to be a great book through which to browse on a quiet afternoon.

Shaw, Harry. *Dictionary of Problem Words and Expressions*. New York: McGraw-Hill, 1987.

This reference book was useful for reminding me of certain problem elements and words in English.

Stahl, Steven A. "Audacious? Debris? Salubrious? Vocabulary Learning and the Child with Learning Disabilities." *Perspectives*, Winter, 2004. Baltimore, MD: The International Dyslexia Association, pp. 6–12.

This article provides a fine overview of techniques for all vocabulary learners.

I used four different dictionaries for checking myself, but any errors are solely mine and not to be laid at the doorstep of any of these fine reference works:

Barnhart, Robert K. *The Barnhart Concise Dictionary of Etymology*. New York: W. H. Wilson/Harper-Collins, 1995.

Brown, Lesley, ed. *The New Shorter Oxford English Dictionary on Historical Principles.* Oxford, UK: Clarendon Press, 1993.

Mish, Frederick C., ed. *Merriam-Webster's Collegiate Dictionary, Eleventh Edition.* Springfield, MA: Merriam-Webster, Inc., 2004.

Pronunciations in this text are based on this dictionary's guidance.

Soukhanov, Anne H., ed. *The American Heritage Dictionary of the English Language, Third Edition.* New York: Houghton-Mifflin, 1992.

Multiple Intelligences Inventory[2]

Take this inventory as a way of assessing what your Multiple Intelligences relative strengths and weaknesses are right now. This is not a test but a way to help you take charge of your own learning. There are no wrong or right answers, so be as honest as you can be with yourself.

Part I

Complete each section by placing a "1" next to each statement you feel accurately describes you. If you do not identify with a statement, leave the space provided blank. Then total the column in each section.

Section 1

_____ I enjoy categorizing things by common traits.
_____ Ecological issues are important to me.
_____ Classification helps me make sense of new data.
_____ I enjoy working in a garden.
_____ I believe preserving our National Parks is important.
_____ Putting things in hierarchies makes sense to me.
_____ Animals are important in my life.
_____ My home has a recycling system in place.
_____ I enjoy studying biology, botany, and/or zoology.
_____ I pick up on subtle differences in meaning.

_____ **TOTAL** for Section 1

Section 2

_____ I easily pick up on patterns.
_____ I focus in on noise and sounds.
_____ Moving to a beat is easy for me.
_____ I enjoy making music.
_____ I respond to the cadence of poetry.
_____ I remember things by putting them in a rhyme.
_____ Concentration is difficult for me if there is background music.
_____ Listening to sounds in nature can be very relaxing.
_____ Musicals are more engaging to me than dramatic plays.
_____ Remembering song lyrics is easy for me.

_____ **TOTAL** for Section 2

Section 3

_____ I am known for being neat and orderly.
_____ Step-by-step instructions are a big help.
_____ Problem solving comes easily to me.
_____ I get easily frustrated with disorganized people.
_____ I can complete calculations quickly in my head.
_____ Logic puzzles are fun.
_____ I can't begin an assignment until I have all my "ducks in a row."
_____ Structure is a good thing.
_____ I enjoy troubleshooting something that isn't working properly.
_____ Things have to make sense to me or I am dissatisfied.

_____ **TOTAL** for Section 3

Section 4

_____ I learn best interacting with others.
_____ I enjoy informal chat and serious discussion.
_____ The more the merrier.
_____ I often serve as a leader among peers and colleagues.
_____ I value relationships more than ideas or accomplishments.
_____ Study groups are very productive for me.
_____ I am a "team player."
_____ Friends are important to me.
_____ I belong to more than three clubs or organizations.
_____ I dislike working alone.

_____ **TOTAL** for Section 4

Section 5

_____ I learn by doing.
_____ I enjoy making things with my hands.
_____ Sports are a part of my life.
_____ I use gestures and non-verbal cues when I communicate.
_____ Demonstrating is better than explaining.
_____ I love to dance.
_____ I like working with tools.
_____ Inactivity can make me more tired than being very busy.
_____ Hands-on activities are fun.
_____ I live an active lifestyle.

_____ **TOTAL** for Section 5

Section 6

_____ Foreign languages interest me.
_____ I enjoy reading books, magazines, and Web sites.
_____ I keep a journal.
_____ Word puzzles like crosswords or jumbles are enjoyable.
_____ Taking notes helps me remember and understand.
_____ I faithfully contact friends through letters and/or e-mail.
_____ It is easy for me to explain my ideas to others.
_____ I write for pleasure.
_____ Puns, anagrams, and spoonerisms are fun.
_____ I enjoy public speaking and participating in debates.

_____ **TOTAL** for Section 6

Section 7

_____ My attitude affects how I learn.
_____ I like to be involved in causes that help others.
_____ I am keenly aware of my moral beliefs.
_____ I learn best when I have an emotional attachment to the subject.
_____ Fairness is important to me.
_____ Social justice issues interest me.
_____ Working alone can be just as productive as working in a group.
_____ I need to know why I should do something before I agree to do it.
_____ When I believe in something I give more effort towards it.
_____ I am willing to protest or sign a petition to right a wrong.

_____ **TOTAL** for Section 7

Section 8

_____ Rearranging a room and redecorating are fun for me.
_____ I enjoy creating my own works of art.
_____ I remember better using graphic organizers.
_____ I enjoy all kinds of entertainment media.
_____ Charts, graphs, and tables help me interpret data.
_____ A music video can make me more interested in a song.
_____ I can recall things as mental pictures.
_____ I am good at reading maps and blueprints.
_____ Three-dimensional puzzles are fun.
_____ I can visualize ideas in my mind.

_____ **TOTAL** for Section 8

Part II

Now carry forward your total from each section and multiply by ten below:

Section	Total Forward	Multiply	Score
1		× 10	
2		× 10	
3		× 10	
4		× 10	
5		× 10	
6		× 10	
7		× 10	
8		× 10	

Part III

Now plot your scores on the bar graph provided:

100								
90								
80								
70								
60								
50								
40								
30								
20								
10								
0	Sec 1	Sec 2	Sec 3	Sec 4	Sec 5	Sec 6	Sec 7	Sec 8

Part IV

Key:
Section 1:   This reflects your Naturalist strength.
Section 2:   This suggests your Musical strength.
Section 3:   This indicates your Logical strength.
Section 4:   This shows your Interpersonal strength.
Section 5:   This tells your Kinesthetic strength.
Section 6:   This indicates your Verbal strength.
Section 7:   This reflects your Intrapersonal strength.
Section 8:   This suggests your Visual strength.

Remember:

- Everyone has all of the intelligences.
- You can strengthen each intelligence.
- This inventory is meant as a snapshot in time; it can change.
- Multiple Intelligences are meant to *empower*, not *label*, learners.

SECTION 1: LIFE AS A SYMPHONY

Learning Style: The Musical/Rhythmical Learner

If you find yourself moving to the beat of the music in your head, one of your primary intelligences is likely that of the Musical/Rhythmical learner.

Are you someone who hums, sings, or taps your way through life? Do you love singing or playing a musical instrument? Are you the one everyone asks when they have a question about a song on the radio? Are you aware of sounds and noises in general—how they fit together, how they cancel each other out, how they distract or attract you? Do you sometimes catch yourself noticing (and maybe moving along with) the tapping rhythm of windshield wipers and turn signals when you're in the car?

If you have answered "yes" to several of the above, this is one of your stronger intelligences.

Possible Approaches

- **Rhythmic Clapping.** Use vocabulary words and paraphrased definitions of those words in a rhythmic clapping exercise or a chant; try clapping or tapping louder on the stressed syllables in the words than on the unstressed for variation in rhythm. Rehearse these repeatedly.
- **Combine Chants.** Create a group exercise in which students pool their chants and learn one another's. Tap or slap on the desks in the rhythm of what everyone has written. Try to combine chants into longer ensemble pieces.
- **Rap.** Write a rap using the vocabulary words in sentences (and/or sentence fragments) that clearly show you understand the words' definitions and how to use them.
- **Popular Songs.** Put vocabulary words and sentences that define them well to the tunes of popular songs. Share these songs with one another.
- **Poetry.** Let the music in poetry help you: rhyme, assonance, and alliteration can all help you learn vocabulary. Write lines of poetry (or entire poems) that use these techniques with specific vocabulary words so that you can "hear" the vocabulary in your mind when you see these words again.
  - Rhyme: When two words, often at the ends of lines of poetry, end with the same sound. For example, cat/hat; rude/attitude.
  - Assonance: When the same vowel (*a, e, i, o, u, y*) sound repeats itself in neighboring words or at the ends of lines in poetry. (Words with assonance do not quite rhyme since some of the consonant sounds are not usually the same.) For example, cud/cut; open/broken; warm/gone.

1

- Alliteration: The repeated use of the same beginning consonant sound in words that are close together. For example, Kelly's corporate car; two twilight tickets. When the consonant sound is "*s*" (snowy silver slippers), the technique is referred to as "sibilance."
- Try studying with quiet music on in the background. You may find that music with lyrics is distracting (I can't resist singing along and I'll bet you can't either), so you will want to use only instrumental music in the background when you are working on vocabulary.

Chapter 1: Falling Apart?

The *meager* amount of work they had gotten done during that afternoon's rehearsal nagged at Nick. He felt he had been more than *accommodating* listening to everyone's differing points of view on the key change at the end of the first verse of the song, but the *fruitless*—and endless—discussion had gone on long enough.

"I'm willing to *concede* that the song needs some sort of 'umpff' there," he said, searching in *vain* for just the right word, "but when we met today we swore we would not end the rehearsal until we had run through all of our songs at least once. I remain *adamant* that a full rehearsal is our first *priority*; let's *table* this key change issue until the next time we get together."

Georgia, who had been the most *vociferous* critic of the song's current form, was unwilling to give up the argument without getting in the last word.

"The way the song sounds now is so *trite*!" she declared *vehemently*, *reiterating* the same argument that had been running them around in circles for an hour already. Nick could see Wan Ju was warming up to her *corresponding* argument so he *interjected* quickly and brightly, "Fine, then, let's get on with the next piece!"

Once again Nick managed to *avert* a serious *clash* between the two girls and get the rehearsal on track, but his role as peacemaker was taking its *toll* on his nerves. Chuy, as usual, said almost nothing.

Walking to class the next day, Nick *confided* his frustration to Joaquin. "Get rid of the weaker musician of the two," *shrugged* Joaquin, as though the solution were *self-evident*. Nick sighed, wishing it were that *straightforward*. Georgia might be *volatile* but she could play a little bit on several different instruments; her *versatility* could be a great *asset* to the band. Wan Ju, on the other hand, had been the driving force in forming the band in the first place; kicking her out would be *demoralizing* for the entire group.

accommodating (uh-kah-ma-DAY-ting) (adjective) helpfully going along with something; obliging.

> Although the music store didn't have facilities for people to listen to CDs before buying them, the clerk wanted to be *accommodating* so he played his own copy of that CD for the customers.

> "I generally like to be *accommodating*," said his mother, "but the band may not practice here after 9 P.M. because it's just too loud."

adamant (A-duh-munt) (adjective) unwilling to bend or change; stubborn; unyielding.

> Wan Ju was *adamant* about her argument at first, but she gradually became more flexible and open to Georgia's point of view as they talked things over.

> Because their parents were so *adamant* about homework, the band didn't get to practice much during the week.

asset (A-set) (noun) a person, trait, or item that gives an advantage or adds value in a given situation.

> Chuy's creativity with musical styles was beginning to become a tremendous *asset* to the band.

> While Joaquin's skill with lyrics would have been an *asset* to Nick's songwriting, it was clear Joaquin was no singer!

avert (uh-VERT) (verb) to avoid or prevent (usually something that is just about to happen).

> Hoping to *avert* problems with copyright on published music, the band wrote all of their own songs.

> Nick narrowly *averted* a break-up of the band by asking for professional advice.

Easy Errors   ***would have* vs. *would of***

This is one of those times that pronunciation might make you slip up in your writing. You know that *would have* can be made into a contraction because we do it all the time when we're talking. Be careful in your writing not to spell this contraction as *would of*—which is how it might sound when said quickly. Spell it properly as: *would've*.
(would + have − ha = would've)

---

clash (KLASH) 1. (noun) an argument or personality conflict between two people or groups; strongly-opposing disagreement. (plural: clashes); 2. (verb) to express opposition, often through an argument.

> Chuy avoided any hint of argument, preferring to create a compromise rather than a *clash* of wills.

> Normally the band members agreed on most musical issues, but they *clashed* over the arrangement of one song.

concede (kun-SEED) (verb) to accept the argument or point of view of another in a reluctant way; to give in.

> Nick wanted the song to end on an upbeat, but he had to *concede* that the band sounded slightly better on a downbeat.

> I say I don't like country music, but I have to *concede* that there are certain country artists whose work I really like.

confide (kun-FIDE) (verb) to tell one's secrets to someone trusted.

> Despite their artistic differences, Wan Ju and Georgia are good friends who *confide* in each other and trust the other to keep their secrets.

Nick *confided* in Joaquin, confident that his friend would not spread rumors about the band's problems.

corresponding (ko-ri-SPAHN-ding) (adjective) refers to an item or idea that is normally paired with another item or idea; going along with another.

To advertise the band, Wan Ju put an advertisement in her local paper. Nick, who lived in the next county, put a *corresponding* ad in his local paper to do the same.

When working on a two-part harmony, Nick started his part and then Georgia joined in with her *corresponding* part.

demoralizing (dee-MOR-uh-lize-ing) (adjective) describes a situation in which positive spirit has been replaced with discouragement; causing a loss of morale.

All of them found it *demoralizing* when two of them were at odds.

It was *demoralizing* for Chuy to spend all afternoon working on a song only to find that the others didn't like it.

fruitless (FROOT-lus) (adjective) unproductive; unsuccessful.

It was *fruitless* to rehearse after a particularly long, hard week at their studies, so the band skipped a rehearsal and went home to sleep.

Trying to practice with two broken guitar strings was both laughable and *fruitless*; they decided to try again tomorrow.

interject (in-tur-JEKT) (verb) to put an item or speech in the middle of two others; to insert.

Chuy tried to *interject* a guitar riff in the middle of the song but Georgia and Wan Ju sang right over it.

"Wait, wait, don't go yet!" he *interjected*. "We still have decisions to make."

meager (MEE-gur) (adjective) a small amount; too little of something.

While famous bands make a lot of money, many professional musicians get by on a *meager* amount of money.

Nick and Wan Ju had a *meager* amount of experience with organization, but they still wanted to run a successful band.

priority (pry-OR-uh-tee) (noun) something with a high level of importance or urgency; when ranking items, the most important or urgent. (plural: priorities)

Wan Ju made it her first *priority* to get Nick into her new band.

While rehearsals were a high *priority*, the band members' first job was keeping up with their school work.

reiterate (ree-I-tu-rayt) (verb) to say the same thing or idea again.

When the student didn't understand, the band teacher picked up a flute and demonstrated what she meant rather than *reiterating* it.

Feeling that she had been misunderstood, Georgia had *reiterated* her opinion repeatedly.

self-evident (self-EH-vu-dunt) (adjective) clear without further explanation; requiring no further proof.

It seemed *self-evident* to Wan Ju that since she had started the band, everyone should do what she wanted.

That the band was having problems was *self-evident* to any observer.

Similar Sounds   *colonel* and *kernel*

Watch your spelling with this odd combination. We pronounce the word *colonel* (an officer in the armed forces) the same way we pronounce *kernel* (a small piece of corn from a corn cob). A *colonel* may tell a corny joke but that won't make him a *kernel*!

---

shrug (SHRUG) (verb) to move the shoulders in an upward fashion to imply doubt or dismissal.

The next day when Nick asked Georgia if she was feeling better, she just *shrugged*.

When they asked Chuy which version he preferred, he *shrugged*.

straightforward (strayt-FOR-wurd) (adjective) direct; to the point; with no hidden motives.

Georgia was absolutely *straightforward* about her resistance to the song's current form.

Nick preferred to be *straightforward,* but at times he could see the wisdom of listening rather than speaking his mind.

table (TAY-bl) (verb) to set aside an issue for discussion at a later date.

The student council decided to *table* the issue of which band to hire for the prom based on their need for more information.

Rather than decide on whether to hire a DJ or a band before they had all the facts, the discussion was *tabled* until a later date.

toll (TOLE) (noun) the feeling of weariness from an emotionally or physically demanding situation or significant loss (as in "to take a toll" on someone or something). (plural: This word is not used in the plural for this meaning.)

> Trying to start a new band and keeping up with her homework at the same time was taking a physical *toll* on Wan Ju; she had little time to sleep.

> Neither of the girls enjoyed conflict, and their argument was taking a *toll* on their friendship.

trite (TRITE) (adjective) predictable in a boring way; overused.

> Georgia felt the song was *trite* and repetitive whereas Wan Ju liked the way its rhythm fit into the pattern of modern music.

> It is *trite* to say that artists (including musicians) can be touchy, but Chuy was beginning to think that that just might be very true.

(in) vain (VAYN) (adverb) to no useful purpose; without success.

> The band seemed to be searching in *vain* for just the right combination of sounds.

> Nick tried in *vain* to keep the girls from arguing during rehearsal.

vehemently (VEE-uh-munt-lee) (adverb) in a forceful and direct manner; with great emotional intensity.

> That Georgia spoke so *vehemently* was proof of her passionate opinion about the song.

> Rather than make his point forcefully and *vehemently*, Nick preferred to talk people into agreeing with him.

versatility (vur-su-TIL-uh-tee) (noun) the ability to do a variety of things well. (plural: This word is not used in the plural.)

> Because they had a small group, it was important that each member could show some *versatility* in performance by both singing and playing an instrument.

> Chuy could only play the guitar, but he was beginning to show great *versatility* in working with different playing styles.

vociferously (vo-SI-fur-us-lee) (adverb) in a direct, loud, insistent, and forceful manner.

> Wan Ju *vociferously* defended early country and western music whenever someone criticized the old style.

> Whenever someone *vociferously* challenged Chuy, he had a quiet way of fading into the background until voices and emotions died down again.

volatile (VAH-lu-tl) (adjective) suddenly changeable, often implying violent change or inconsistency.

> With her artist's personality, Georgia's emotions had a tendency to be a bit *volatile*.

> When oiling the wood on his guitar, Chuy was very careful since the wood oil was *volatile* and likely to start a fire if used near a spark.

Quick Match 1

Match each word to its definition.

1. ____ confide	A.	a small amount; too little of something
2. ____ reiterate	B.	helpfully going along with something
3. ____ demoralizing	C.	with great emotional intensity
4. ____ straightforward	D.	something that gives an advantage
5. ____ (in) vain	E.	suddenly changeable; inconsistent
6. ____ accommodating	F.	feeling of weariness at a demanding time
7. ____ interject	G.	to tell one's secrets to someone trusted
8. ____ versatility	H.	to set aside for later discussion
9. ____ corresponding	I.	in a direct, forceful, insistent manner
10. ____ trite	J.	to avoid or prevent something
11. ____ asset	K.	something with a high level of urgency
12. ____ table	L.	to no useful purpose
13. ____ self-evident	M.	to insert in the middle of something
14. ____ vehemently	N.	to move the shoulders in an upward way
15. ____ volatile	O.	requiring no further proof; clear
16. ____ adamant	P.	ability to do a variety of things well
17. ____ fruitless	Q.	describes an item or idea paired with another
18. ____ vociferously	R.	to give in; to accept another's argument
19. ____ priority	S.	predictable in a boring way; overused
20. ____ toll	T.	direct; to the point; no hidden motives
21. ____ clash	U.	unwilling to bend or change; stubborn
22. ____ shrug	V.	unproductive; unsuccessful
23. ____ meager	W.	to say the same thing or idea again
24. ____ avert	X.	causing a loss of morale
25. ____ concede	Y.	strongly-opposing disagreement

Sentence Completions 1

Choose the proper word or pair of words for each of the sentences below.

1. It probably seems _____ to most people that a new band has little chance of major success, but new band members don't see such a lack of success as inevitable.

    (a) volatile   (b) fruitless   (c) self-evident   (d) corresponding   (e) meager

2. It is difficult to _____ any voice of reason into an argument when the parties involved are particularly angry; it's best to wait until tempers have cooled.

    (a) table   (b) clash   (c) demoralize   (d) confide   (e) interject

3. The band responded forcefully and _____ to any suggestion that they didn't have a shot at doing well in the music business.

    (a) vehemently   (b) in vain   (c) tritely   (d) meagerly   (e) confidently

4. For a band that would like to appeal to a broad audience with a variety of tastes, _____ should be a major _____.

    (a) toll . . . volatility   (b) confidence . . . asset   (c) reiteration . . . clash
    (d) versatility . . . priority   (e) corresponding . . . interjection

5. Chuy would rather simply _____ and turn away to _____ an argument than become involved and possibly cause one.

    (a) interject . . . clash   (b) shrug . . . avert   (c) reiterate . . . table
    (d) confide . . . concede   (e) trite . . . toll

Chapter 2: Working It Out

Later in the day, Joaquin *flagged* Nick down between classes.

"I was thinking about your *dilemma*," he said, "and I have the perfect solution—talk to a school counselor."

Nick's heart sank. He shook his head.

"Look, Joaquin, I don't have emotional problems or anything; this is an issue with the band." He *protested*, "Besides, I don't want anyone to see me going to the counselor."

Joaquin grinned.

"Let's see," he *mused*, "You have a problem and it involves emotions—and that isn't an emotional problem?" He *smirked*, "See you after biology."

The more Nick thought about it, the less *unlikely* a solution it seemed. At the end of his next class, he *strode* purposefully to the office and made an appointment for the following day.

At their next band rehearsal, even Chuy seemed nervous. Wan Ju's mood was *sullen* and Georgia was *abnormally terse*; each girl had convinced herself that it was time for the other to *surrender* her position in the band for the good of the group. Nick had a different idea.

"I think our root problem is that fact that we haven't established a sound for ourselves yet," he began *buoyantly*, startling the two *adversaries* who had expected an *ultimatum* on their behavior. "I've come to the *conclusion* that we need to *distinguish* between what we can and can't do well."

With help, Nick had *drafted* a plan to both *curb* the arguments and *imbue* the band with new energy. He *proposed* that for the next two months the band would totally *immerse* itself in a different style of music each week. Wan Ju offered to lead the band through a history of country-and-western music for the first week. Georgia groaned, knowing what an *aficionado* Wan Ju was of the early twang of country music that she herself *loathed*. Nick reminded everyone of the importance of an open *attitude* and then, just for fun, ran a light rehearsal of *cacophonous* jamming before they all headed home for the night.

abnormally (ab-NOR-muh-lee) (adverb) done in a way that is not typical; outside of the expected.

> When Nick saw her in the hall, Wan Ju was *abnormally* quiet and that reminded him of Chuy.

> The humidity was *abnormally* high and everyone's instruments needed to be tuned repeatedly because of the damp air.

adversary (AD-vur-sayr-ee) (noun) opponent or enemy. (plural: adversaries)

> It was unusual for Wan Ju and Georgia to be *adversaries* since they had been great friends for a very long time.

11

Sometimes musicians can get jealous of other musicians' talent but there is really no point in creating an *adversary* of another artist; all artists learn from one another, so any great talent is a help to all.

aficionado (uh-fi-shee-uh-NAH-doe) (noun) a great fan of a particular art or subject. (plural: aficionados)

> Nick wasn't really an *aficionado* of any particular style of music; he liked a little of everything.

> Chuy was a great *aficionado* of classic guitar riffs and played with that art form whenever he had a chance.

attitude (A-tu-tood) (noun) 1. a way of looking at things; a feeling. 2. a body position or posture. (plural: attitudes)

> Chuy had a very relaxed *attitude* toward life.

> Hands on her hips, the girl's physical *attitude* showed her anger.

buoyantly (BOY-unt-lee) (adverb) in a lighthearted or happy way; bouncy.

> It was tough for Wan Ju to be sad or angry for very long. She generally lived her life *buoyantly*, finding the positive in all things.

> Whenever Georgia heard a new song that she liked, she would bounce around school *buoyantly*, singing it for days on end.

cacophonous (ka-KAH-fu-nus) (adjective) describes sounds that are irritating, jarring, noisy, or discordant.

> When writing songs, Wan Ju took her inspiration from other artists and the natural world with a tendency to focus on interesting, *cacophonous* combinations instead of predictable note patterns.

> When tuning their instruments at the beginning of a concert, an orchestra sounds chaotic and *cacophonous*.

conclusion (kun-KLEW-zhun) (noun) the end of something; the final, proven result of a persuasive argument. (plural: conclusions)

> At the *conclusion* of the concert, the audience rose to a standing ovation.

> Nick came to the *conclusion* that he had to do something to save the band.

curb (KURB) (verb) to slow down or stop something; to control or restrain.

> Wan Ju and Georgia tried to *curb* Chuy's appetite for guitar riffs by singing right through them.

To ease this problem between them, Georgia may need to *curb* her temper and Wan Ju may need to relax her control a bit.

dilemma (duh-LE-muh) (noun) a problem that has two or more options or possible solutions that seem equally good or bad. (plural: dilemmas)

Wan Ju felt her *dilemma* was whether to drop out of the band herself or to ask Georgia to leave.

Nick had five new songs to give to Chuy to work on. His only *dilemma* was which song to give to Chuy first.

distinguish (di-STIN-gwish) (verb) to tell the difference between two or more items; discern.

The counselor helped Nick *distinguish* between a permanent break-up of the band and a temporary problem.

The girls seemed to be having a problem *distinguishing* the difference between an artistic disagreement and their friendship.

draft (DRAFT) (verb) to create an initial version of a plan or composition.

To reduce arguments, perhaps the band would do well to *draft* an agreement of what each person's duties would be within the band.

As upsetting as the argument had been, Nick found himself *drafting* some really great poetry for his songs that week.

International   ***draft*** and ***draught***

There are a number of differences in spelling (as well as pronunciation and word use) between American usage and international usage of English. The word *draught* in British English is used—and pronounced—the same way as *draft* in American English. Watch for other spelling differences such as *colour/color*, *honour/honor*, *centre/center*, and *theatre/theater*. In all of these examples, the pronunciation remains the same.

---

flag (FLAG) 1. (verb) to get someone's attention, often by waving. 2. to lose energy or to lessen in interest.

Late for the rehearsal, Chuy had to *flag* down the bus that had already left his stop.

Her interest *flagging*, Wan Ju was ready for the rehearsal to be over.

imbue (im-BYOO) (verb) to completely fill with something (often, to fill with inspiration).

> Unhappy and tense, Wan Ju tried to *imbue* herself with calm and inspiration by listening to some of her favorite music.

> Nick *imbued* all his poems with low-key, honest emotion.

immerse (i-MURS) (verb) 1. to completely cover with liquid. 2. to become totally involved in some activity or area of study.

> Georgia *immersed* her hands in the sink to wash them and became absorbed in the sounds of the splashing and the rhythms she could create with them.

> Chuy was sometimes late to school because it was easy for him to become *immersed* in a song he was working on and forget about time.

loathe (LOWTHE) (verb) to hate; to detest.

> Georgia didn't know what she *loathed* more: fighting with Wan Ju, or having to listen to country-and-western music for a week.

> Chuy *loathed* conflict and did his very best to stay away from it.

muse (MYOOZ) (verb) to think dreamily on a topic; to work through an idea or concept in one's head; to meditate.

> Sometimes working hard on a song is not as effective as letting it play through your mind as you *muse* on it.

> As she *mused* on the problem between her and Georgia, Wan Ju realized that it was more important to work that out than it was to have a successful band.

propose (pru-POZE) (verb) to put forth an idea; to suggest; to recommend.

> Nick didn't want to *propose* a change of band members, just a change of attitude.

> At first, Wan Ju *proposed* an old-style, country-and-western band, but the others wanted to be free to work with a variety of musical styles.

protest (PRO-test) 1. (verb) to argue against or to object to something. 2. (noun) a formal objection to a particular policy or point of view, often from a group and often expressed publicly. (plural: protests)

> Although Georgia did *protest* against Wan Ju's opinion on a particular song, the girls usually got along well.

The school had issued a ban against certain kinds of music being played on campus and the band members had all signed a student petition as a *protest* against this decision.

smirk (SMURK) 1. (verb) to smile in a way that shows you understand more than the person you are talking with; to smile in a knowing, self-satisfied, offensive way. 2. (noun) an offensive, knowing smile. (plural: smirks)

> Chuy used to have a fellow band member who *smirked* in a very superior way every time Chuy made a mistake. Chuy quit that band.

> Sometimes it's hard to hide a *smirk* when you have predicted a bad outcome for an unwise action and your worst predictions come true.

stride (STRYD) (verb) to walk with purpose with long steps and great energy. ("Strode" is the past form.)

> Georgia could be a little shy and, to hide this, she generally tried to *stride* into a room confidently with her head high so that others wouldn't suspect her secret.

> Angry and frustrated, he *strode* out of the building ahead of the others to give himself a little private time to think things through.

Pieces and Parts   *phon-* or *phono-*

This root means "sound" or "voice." *Cacophonous* is formed from the Greek *kakós* (bad) + *phono* (sound). Its opposite or antonym, *euphonious*, is formed from the Greek *eu* (good) + *phono* (sound). Other words that we use regularly with the *phon-* root in them are: *telephone*, *phonics*, and *phonology* (the study of speech sounds in a language).

---

sullen (SU-lun) (adjective) describes a facial expression and/or body attitude showing resentment; sulky.

> Wan Ju felt that she had every right to be *sullen* since it was her band and she felt Georgia should do as she was told in this case.

> Some people thought of Chuy as *sullen* when they first met him and saw how quiet he was, but he was really very pleasant and happy inside.

surrender (su-REN-dur) (verb) to give up (something), often because of force; to give up control over something to another.

> Nick felt ready to *surrender* to everyone else's emotions and quit the band almost before it really got started.

> Wan Ju did not want to *surrender* control of the band to anyone else, but it was clear that Nick was trying to be a leader in settling the dispute.

terse (TURS) (adjective) using few words; brief; concise.

> While Chuy was naturally *terse*, Georgia usually had plenty to say.

> Sometimes to show her unhappiness over something, though, Georgia had a tendency to become *terse* in her speech.

ultimatum (ul-tu-MAY-tum) (noun) a final choice offered to someone that has permanent consequences. (plural: ultimatums)

> Nick wanted to avoid a situation in which an *ultimatum* was issued and someone had to accept it or leave the band.

> Both Georgia and Wan Ju knew they had been a bit unreasonable and neither was really certain how to reply to an *ultimatum* if the other insisted on one.

unlikely (un-LIKE-lee) (adjective) unexpected; liable to fail.

> These four strong personalities might have seemed an *unlikely* combination for success but each was also committed to music as an art.

> When Nick first started piano lessons at a young age, it seemed *unlikely* that he would ever become a competent musician.

Quick Match 2
Match each word to its definition.

1. ___ aficionado	A.	to tell the difference between two items
2. ___ dilemma	B.	in a lighthearted or happy way; bouncy
3. ___ loathe	C.	to think dreamily on a topic; to meditate
4. ___ adversary	D.	the end of something; final proven result
5. ___ muse	E.	brief, concise
6. ___ ultimatum	F.	in a way that is not typical
7. ___ curb	G.	an offensive, superior, knowing smile
8. ___ protest	H.	an initial version of a plan or composition
9. ___ draft	I.	a way of looking at things or a body position
10. ___ stride	J.	to put forth an idea; to recommend
11. ___ terse	K.	to get someone's attention, often by waving
12. ___ immerse	L.	unexpected; liable to fail
13. ___ distinguish	M.	to become totally involved in some activity or study
14. ___ abnormally	N.	to give up, often because of force
15. ___ unlikely	O.	opponent or enemy
16. ___ smirk	P.	to walk with purpose and long steps
17. ___ propose	Q.	to completely fill with something
18. ___ sullen	R.	hate, detest
19. ___ cacophonous	S.	a great fan of a particular art or subject
20. ___ surrender	T.	a formal objection to a particular policy
21. ___ imbue	U.	to control or restrain; to slow or stop
22. ___ attitude	V.	a final choice with permanent consequences
23. ___ conclusion	W.	a problem with two or more possible solutions
24. ___ flag	X.	showing resentment; sulky
25. ___ buoyantly	Y.	describes sounds that are irritating or jarring

Sentence Completions 2

Choose the proper word or pair of words for each of the sentences below.

1. If you don't have a good ear for music, you may find it difficult to _____ between certain notes when they are played.

    (a) draft   (b) stride   (c) imbue   (d) distinguish   (e) propose

2. The sound of the crows squawking in the yard every morning was _____, but the noise did give Chuy an idea for a guitar riff.

    (a) flagging   (b) unlikely   (c) cacophonous   (d) sullen   (e) terse

3. Georgia believes that she _____ country-and-western music but, if she gave it a chance, she might find pieces that she really enjoys.

    (a) curbs   (b) muses   (c) distinguishes   (d) imbues   (e) loathes

4. It was a big _____ for Wan Ju as a leader: should she _____ against Georgia's strong opinion or accept the open discussion as good for the band?

    (a) ultimatum . . . smirk   (b) conclusion . . . muse
    (c) aficionado . . . curb   (d) dilemma . . . protest   (e) adversary . . . stride

5. The easily-discouraged drummer decided to _____ his usual negative _____ and try to be optimistic about his chances to join the band.

    (a) immerse . . . protest   (b) surrender . . . attitude   (c) imbue . . . smirk
    (d) curb . . . adversary   (e) distinguish . . . dilemma

Chapter 3: Feelin' Your Pain

From his viewpoint, Joaquin felt that the first week of his friend's experiment was borderline *catastrophic*. Assigned different singers to listen to every day, the band members were *inundated* with broken hearts and despair starting with artists from the 1940s and 1950s. When the others *balked* at this *chronological* approach, Wan Ju *chided* them that "they couldn't understand the present if they hadn't experienced the past." Nick seemed to feel the *chasm* was widening between the girls as Georgia grudgingly *deferred* to Wan Ju's lead when they were together but bitterly *disparaged* her music choices when she was alone with Nick. Nick *doggedly* stuck with the experiment, but Joaquin was *cognizant* of his friend's doubts and personal *dejection*. Since he wasn't a member of the band, Joaquin was *empathetic* but felt powerless to *intervene* in what he saw simply as excessive *egotism* in various band members. When Wan Ju had first *intimated* that she would like to start a band with him and Chuy, Nick had begged Joaquin to join them, *citing* his skill in writing *lyrics*. Joaquin assured Nick of the huge potential he had for a *deleterious* effect on a *nascent* band.

"I only sing in the shower," he had laughed, "and I really am tone-deaf. If we were out of key, I would never know."

He did promise, however, to *collaborate* on song lyrics from time to time and Nick had to be satisfied with that. In *retrospect*, Nick saw the wisdom of Joaquin's decision; Nick heard him singing to himself in the car one time—*discordant* sounds to say the least! Still, he *heeded* his good friend's advice.

Unwilling to *interfere* with Nick's *tentative* experiment, Joaquin decided to keep his opinion to himself for a week or two.

balk (BAWLK) (verb) to resist something or a situation stubbornly.

> Joaquin *balked* at the idea of joining the band.

> The entire band *balked* at the notion that they were forming a band to become "famous and rich." They all considered themselves artists first.

catastrophic (ka-ta-STRAH-fik) (adjective) describes an event or situation that results in a sudden disaster.

> Wan Ju felt that if the band didn't listen to a range of musical periods, their first attempts of making their own music would be *catastrophic*.

> Joaquin sensed *catastrophic* results if certain band members' egos were not held in check.

chasm (KA-sm) (noun) 1. a deep gorge in the earth. 2. a wide emotional or intellectual separation between people. (plural: chasms)

> Whenever Georgia heard a Neil Diamond song on the radio, she always thought of the Grand Canyon since her parents were playing his music in the car as they drove to the edge of that great *chasm*.

Wan Ju and Georgia were just as anxious as Chuy and Nick about the increasing distance between them; they didn't really want this emotional *chasm* to widen either.

chide (CHYD) (verb) to gently correct someone's behavior verbally; to reprimand.

Occasionally Wan Ju would *chide* Chuy for playing out of tune.

Nick *chided* the band members for not putting in enough rehearsal time.

chronological (krah-nu-LAH-ji-kul) (adjective) arranged in order by time.

The group played various tunes from each music era in *chronological* order.

To really know a composer's work, it's best to start listening from the beginning of his or her career and listen to all of that composer's works in *chronological* order.

cite (SYT) (verb) to offer (an expert) as support or proof in an argument; to quote as an authority.

Chuy would often *cite* the Beatles' guitar chord changes in musical discussions.

During some practice sessions, Georgia *cited* music theory textbooks to support her opinions.

cognizant (KAHG-ni-zunt) (adjective) knowing or understanding thoroughly.

When Chuy first became *cognizant* of his musical talent he was eager to learn all he could about music.

During the first few practice sessions, the band was *cognizant* of the constant need to improvise to create a fresh, new sound.

Similar Sounds   *cite, site,* **and** *sight*

Cite is a verb that means "to quote as an authority of some piece of information or thought"; *site* is a noun that means "the precise location of something (often a building)"; and *sight* is a noun that means "something that you see." Therefore, you may "*cite* your *sight* of the blueprints of a building to prove you know its future *site*."

---

collaborate (ku-LA-bu-rayt) (verb) to work together on a project or idea; to cooperate in a work situation.

Sometimes it is easier to work individually than to *collaborate* on a particular musical composition.

When the band was *collaborating* well, each individual instrument began to sound as one connected whole.

defer (di-FUR) (verb) to give in to someone else, usually out of politeness or recognition of their experience rather than by force.

It wasn't difficult for Chuy to *defer* to Georgia's opinions on chord changes because he usually found he agreed with the final product when he did so.

Nick was often skeptical of Wan Ju's ideas during rehearsal, but he usually *deferred* to her leadership of the band.

dejection (di-JEK-shun) (noun) a feeling of sadness and discouragement. (plural: This word is not usually used in the plural.)

The *dejection* that Wan Ju felt over the growing problems in her band was increasing with each day.

When asked how the band was going, Nick tried to hide his *dejection* and be upbeat and positive about it.

deleterious (de-lu-TI-ree-us) (adjective) having a negative effect on something or someone.

Many aspects of the life of a touring musician—fast-food meals, late nights, the stress of travel—can be *deleterious* to the artist's health.

It can be *deleterious* to a band's reputation for them to accept the offer of a public performance before they are really ready.

discordant (dis-KOR-dnt) (adjective) 1. describes a harsh mixture of sounds. 2. describes an interpersonal relationship that is unhappy or tense.

Some composers like to combine musical rhythms and notes that are unpredictable, prompting some listeners to say that they find the music *discordant* and unpleasant to listen to.

After years of harmony as friends, the girls were unhappy over the *discordant* elements that had emerged in their relationship since they had begun to work together in the band.

disparage (di-SPA-rij) (verb) to criticize in a way that makes something or someone seem less worthy of respect; to belittle.

Wan Ju mistakenly believed that when people criticized her taste in music they meant to *disparage* her personally.

A couple of their classmates *disparaged* Nick and Chuy for spending time on a band when they could have been on the basketball team instead.

doggedly (DAW-ged-lee) (adverb) describes doing something with perseverance, without giving up.

> Georgia *doggedly* maintained that her opinion on the key change was the only way for the band to proceed.

> Old-fashioned music wasn't really to Nick's taste either, but he *doggedly* listened to everything Wan Ju had recommended.

egotism (EE-gu-ti-zum) (noun) a strong focus on oneself, often to the point of being negative; the state of being conceited or very self-involved. (plural: This word is not usually used in the plural.)

> A professional musician must almost have excessive confidence in herself, to the point of *egotism*, to be able to keep going in the face of so much rejection that often occurs early in her career.

> Joaquin observed that part of the band's problem was excessive *egotism* in two of the members rather than valid differences of opinion.

empathetic (em-pu-THE-tik) (adjective) describes one who puts himself or herself in another person's position emotionally, and who understands that person and situation well.

> In her more rational moments, Georgia could be *empathetic* of Wan Ju's position as leader of the band and recognized the responsibility that involved.

> As he worked with the band, Nick became more *empathetic* with his friends about their personality conflicts on their sports teams at school.

heed (HEED) (verb) to listen to or pay attention to.

> After an hour or so of listening to Wan Ju's music, Chuy began to *heed* the rhythms of it and began to get excited about their possibilities for his own music.

> Although he still wasn't sure how things would turn out, Nick was glad he had *heeded* Joaquin's advice.

interfere (in-tur-FEER) (verb) to put oneself in the middle of a situation to try to control its outcome; to involve oneself in a situation so that one gets in the way.

> Georgia's parents were tempted to *interfere* in the band's quarrel since they both really liked Wan Ju and wanted the girls to remain friends.

> Georgia's tendency to criticize Wan Ju in front of Nick was beginning to *interfere* with his ability to be neutral in their disagreement.

intervene (in-tur-VEEN) (verb) to involve oneself in a negative situation or an argument in the hopes of improving the situation.

> Even though they wanted to *intervene* in their daughter's disagreement with her friend, Georgia's parents stayed out of it.

> Nick's faith in his plan was beginning to fail, and he was tempted to ask the school counselor to *intervene* more actively in the situation.

Pieces and Parts   *inter-*

This prefix (a prefix is something added to the beginning of a word to change the meaning) is used to mean *within, between,* or *shared*. Thus, *interfere* is *inter* (come between) + *ferir* (to strike or hit). *Interfere* then means "to put oneself in the middle of a situation"—or maybe even the middle of a fight!

---

intimate (IN-tu-MAYT) (verb) to hint to someone; to let someone know something indirectly.

> Joaquin didn't want to tell Nick directly that he had doubts about Nick's strategy, but he tried to *intimate* to him in subtle ways that it might not be working.

> Rather than insult Georgia directly in front of Chuy and Nick, Wan Ju tried to *intimate* her displeasure with more indirect comments.

inundate (I-nun-dayt) (verb) 1. to completely cover with water, often to overflowing. 2. to overwhelm (someone or something).

> Chuy's first guitar was ruined when a hurricane came through the area and his basement practice area was *inundated* with flood water.

> On top of the difficulty within the band, all of the band members were also *inundated* with school work that week and overwhelmed with everything that had to be done.

lyrics (LIR-iks) (noun) the words to a song. (plural: For this meaning, this word is always used in the plural; "lyric" is an adjective in English.)

> Joaquin was famous at school for knowing song *lyrics* to old and obscure songs.

> When Georgia wrote songs, she usually wrote the music first and fit the *lyrics* in later; Wan Ju worked in the reverse order.

nascent (NA-snt) (adjective) newly-born; just getting started.

> The idea of the band was just barely *nascent* when Wan Ju approached Nick about it.

Nick was a *nascent* songwriter, getting his inspiration to try his skills at it by watching his band mates.

retrospect (RE-tru-spekt) (noun) a look at things from the past. (plural: This word is not usually used in the plural.)

In *retrospect*, Georgia wondered if accepting a spot in Wan Ju's band was a good idea in view of the resulting strain on their friendship.

Calculus was a very demanding subject this year and Chuy wondered in *retrospect* if he should have finished this school year before diving into his music so thoroughly.

tentative (TEN-tu-tiv) 1. (adjective) describes a first draft of a plan or idea, not completely thought-out or finished. 2. hesitant.

Nick and the school counselor had worked out a *tentative* plan for getting the band members, as well as the band, back on track.

At times, both Wan Ju and Georgia wanted to apologize but each was a little *tentative* about the risk of her apology being rejected.

Quick Match 3

Match each word to its definition.

1. ____ deleterious	A.	to listen to or pay attention to
2. ____ tentative	B.	to resist something or a situation stubbornly
3. ____ catastrophic	C.	to put oneself in the middle of a situation
4. ____ egotism	D.	to cooperate in a work situation
5. ____ inundate	E.	to belittle; to criticize to make seem unworthy
6. ____ retrospect	F.	to gently correct someone's behavior verbally
7. ____ discordant	G.	able to put oneself in another's emotional place
8. ____ balk	H.	a look at things from the past
9. ____ defer	I.	to quote as an authority (as proof or evidence)
10. ____ intimate	J.	newly-born; just getting started
11. ____ empathetic	K.	a feeling of sadness and discouragement
12. ____ chasm	L.	to involve oneself in a bad situation to improve it
13. ____ doggedly	M.	knowing or understanding something thoroughly
14. ____ collaborate	N.	describes a first draft of a plan or idea
15. ____ nascent	O.	arranged in order by time
16. ____ cite	P.	to completely cover with water; overwhelm
17. ____ lyrics	Q.	a deep gorge in the earth
18. ____ intervene	R.	describes a harsh mixture of sounds
19. ____ dejection	S.	a strong, often negative, focus on oneself
20. ____ chide	T.	having a negative effect on someone
21. ____ interfere	U.	the words to a song
22. ____ cognizant	V.	describes a situation that resulted in sudden disaster
23. ____ heed	W.	with perseverance
24. ____ disparage	X.	to hint to someone; to tell indirectly
25. ____ chronological	Y.	to give in to someone else (not through force)

Sentence Completions 3

Choose the proper word or pair of words for each of the sentences below.

1. Radio stations and recording companies are regularly _____ with thousands of home recordings from would-be musical superstars.

    (a) intervened (b) cited (c) dejected (d) inundated (e) interfered

2. If your grandparents are old enough, they may remember the early, _____ stages of the birth of rock and roll in the 1950s.

    (a) chronological (b) catastrophic (c) nascent (d) retrospective
    (e) cognizant

3. Chuy finds it easier to work alone on a song than to _____ with someone else.

    (a) lyrics (b) collaborate (c) disparage (d) intimate (e) empathize

4. It is important to _____ good advice from experienced professional musicians and to _____ to their judgment when trying to get a start in the business.

    (a) cite . . . collaborate (b) disparage . . . empathize (c) heed . . . defer
    (d) balk . . . intervene (e) chide . . . interfere

5. While a young musician needs to be _____ determined to succeed in the music business to be able to get ahead, she must also be fully _____ of the fact that it is a very difficult business in which to do well.

    (a) doggedly . . . cognizant (b) tentatively . . . cited
    (c) empathetically . . . nascent (d) deleteriously . . . retrospect
    (e) egotistically . . . inundated

Chapter 4: Secrets

By the fifth week, Chuy was beginning to *juxtapose* unlikely rhythms and chord combinations in a *potpourri* of musical styles brought on by the band's research. True, mixing Motown and grunge at *whim* might make true music fans *wince*, but Chuy was having a great time creating odd *medleys*. So far, he had kept his experimentation to himself, not wanting to set Wan Ju off on some *tangent* about "purity" in music styles, but he was finding that he had a *predilection* for combining well-known elements in *unpredictable* ways. He had been content to let the others in the band *orchestrate* the types of music they would research each week, *eschewing* the opportunity to choose his favorite music himself. He had been greatly *intrigued* by Nick's suggestion and didn't want to *hinder* his own musical discovery *excursion* by focusing on the same music he was already enjoying.

Palpably excited, Chuy cornered Nick on Thursday of that week.

"Nick, you've got to hear this thing I've been working on!" Chuy *enthused*.

Nick was *stunned* by the change in his normally *laconic* friend. "Great," he answered, slightly *bewildered*. "As soon as possible?"

He and Chuy agreed to a *rendezvous* after classes that afternoon.

Meanwhile, Joaquin had been *scheming* with Georgia. He hated to be *devious*, but he knew that Nick had more than enough on his plate right now with trying to hold the band together while *fulfilling* the requirements of a complicated research project for history class. He hoped that Nick would realize he was trying to help rather than *meddle* in affairs that weren't strictly his business. Indeed, Georgia was very supportive and tried to *bolster* Joaquin's confidence by *asserting* that his involvement was welcome as far as she was concerned.

assert (uh-SURT) (verb) to state something positively and firmly.

> When Georgia had an opinion, she tended to *assert* it as fact, whereas Wan Ju made clear that she was stating an opinion.

> Sometimes Wan Ju just wanted to *assert* her authority as band leader but she realized that respect should be earned, not demanded.

bewilder (bi-WIL-dur) (verb) to confuse, particularly with unclear or contradictory information.

> The subtle differences among different types of popular music tended to *bewilder* Chuy's parents.

> Chuy was *bewildered* by all of the emotion flying around during rehearsals; he just wanted to play music.

bolster (BOWL-stur) (verb) to support.

> Joaquin tried to *bolster* Nick's attitude by talking with him about things other than the band and its problems.

Wan Ju tried to *bolster* support for the band by buying a small advertisement on their behalf in the school newspaper.

devious (DEE-vee-us) (adjective) sneaky, dishonest; not following the accepted way of doing things.

Nick felt a little guilty about being so *devious* in trying to make peace between the band members.

Chuy felt a little *devious* since he didn't immediately share his musical insights with anyone but Nick.

enthuse (en-THOOZ) (verb) to be very excited about something.

When asked about the band, Georgia tended to *enthuse* about Nick's singing, Wan Ju's creativity, and Chuy's guitar skills.

Fearing it might not work, Nick was hesitant to *enthuse* too much about his plan in front of Joaquin.

Usage Issues   *enthuse*

In most cases in English, a basic word form exists (for example, *predict*) and words are created from that basic word for other parts of speech (for example, *prediction* as a noun, or *unpredictable* as an adjective). Sometimes a word is a "back-formation" which means that a more complex form is made into a simpler form. *Enthuse* is actually a back-formation of *enthusiasm*, and is a verb created from that noun. Because this back-formation is fairly recent in this word's history, not all grammarians and word specialists approve of the use of *enthuse* as proper English. It is becoming more common in everyday use, however, and is likely to be more generally acceptable in the next few years.

---

eschew (eh-SHOO) (verb) to avoid or reject something.

In their anger, the girls might have *eschewed* Nick's musical exploration plan, but they were both too fair-minded to do something like that.

Chuy *eschewed* copying another's guitar work and preferred to work out his own riffs and combinations.

Word Play   *eschew*

Although a marvelous word, *eschew* is, nonetheless, not very commonly used in everyday conversation. It is, however, part of my favorite bumper sticker. Years ago I saw a puzzling bumper sticker that warned its readers to *Eschew obfuscation*! At the time, I knew neither word and hurried home to the dictionary to look them both up. *Eschew obfuscation*, I found, is a very confusing way to warn people to "Avoid confusion." I was charmed by the wry joke and have remembered both words ever since.

---

excursion (ik-SKUR-zhun) (noun) a short outing or trip. (plural: excursions)

> On the weekend, Wan Ju's family planned a nice *excursion* to the beach to help Wan Ju relax from her stressful week.

> One of the dreams of the band members was the possibility of taking little *excursions* to play at various school dances throughout the region.

fulfill (fu-FIL) (verb) to complete a job; to satisfy a need.

> As occupied as they all were with the band outside of school hours, each of the band members still had to *fulfill* two fine arts or music credits at school to qualify to graduate.

> Music was a necessary part of life to Wan Ju and she needed to work within music to *fulfill* her own identity.

hinder (HIN-dur) (verb) to get in the way of someone or something; to interfere negatively with someone's efforts.

> When two singers are singing in harmony, they have to listen to their own voices with great attention, since listening too carefully to the other person's part could *hinder* their own singing.

> A part-time job can *hinder* a musician's chance to rehearse often enough, but it also can provide needed cash for new equipment.

intrigued (in-TREEGD) (verb) to become interested in something.

> Nick was *intrigued* with Chuy's unusual guitar work.

> Joaquin was *intrigued* with the idea of joining a band, but he knew he didn't really have much to offer such a group.

juxtapose (JUK-stu-poze) (verb) to place side by side.

> Nick had tried to *juxtapose* the value of each girl's contribution to the band to see who should leave, but he found both musicians to be equally valuable to the group.

> When she *juxtaposed* rehearsal and music class, Wan Ju was sad to find that she was enjoying music class much more these days.

laconic (lu-KAH-nik) (adjective) describes someone who speaks little.

> Despite being *laconic* in his everyday dealings with the world, Chuy was an enthusiastic singer when the band was playing.

> Not the *laconic* type, Wan Ju had plenty to say to people if they even hinted that they were interested in hearing about her band.

meddle (MED-dl) (verb) to interfere in other people's business.

> One of Georgia's friends tried to *meddle* in her argument with Wan Ju by criticizing Wan Ju in front of Georgia.

> "No one *meddles* in my friendships," Georgia told her other friend. "Please stop saying mean things about my friend. We'll work out our own problems."

medley (MED-lee) (noun) a mixture, often of parts of songs strung together. (plural: medleys)

> Chuy's grandparents suggested he work on a *medley* of Henry Mancini songs, but they hardly recognized their favorite music when Chuy played it back for them in his own style.

> The band entertained themselves playing a *medley* of really weak songs and substituting silly lyrics for the real ones.

orchestrate (OR-ku-strayt) (verb) to plan and execute a plan; to organize something in such a way that the organizer is also in control.

> The band was hoping to play at the school's talent show and Nick was going to *orchestrate* all of the arrangements for the performance.

> Wan Ju *orchestrated* the establishment of the band but she, too, often followed Nick's lead in the day-to-day operations of the band.

palpable (PAL-pu-bl) (adjective) capable of being touched; tangible or real.

> The tension in the room was almost *palpable* before Nick suggested his music exploration project.

> The calluses on Chuy's fingertips were *palpable* evidence of how much he practiced on his guitar.

potpourri (poe-poo-REE) (noun) an unexpected or unusual variety of things grouped together. (plural: potpourris)

> In her bedroom, Georgia had a *potpourri* of toy musical instruments left over from her childhood.

> Although Wan Ju was well-known for being a country music fan, her musical tastes actually covered a *potpourri* of periods and styles.

predilection (pre-du-LEK-shun) (noun) a preference for something. (plural: This word is not usually used in the plural.)

> Wan Ju's *predilection* for "purity" in musical styles was greatly overstated by her friends; she enjoyed experimenting with music as much as anyone.

> Georgia had a *predilection* for direct speech and action and this sometimes made her seem bossy when she didn't mean to be.

rendezvous (RAHN-di-voo) (noun) a preplanned meeting at a particular time and place. (plural: rendezvous)

> Joaquin had planned a secret *rendezvous* with Georgia.

> When he played his guitar, Chuy sometimes felt as though he had a future *rendezvous* with fame when the playing went well.

scheme (SKEEM) (verb) to plot; to create secret or sneaky plans.

> Chuy was *scheming* to find a way for the band to play at the local college's on-campus pub even though they weren't old enough to do so.

> Wan Ju and Nick *schemed* to try to find a way to convince their parents to let them rehearse later into the night, despite the noise.

stunned (STUND) (adjective) overwhelmed or dazed.

> The band was *stunned* to find out that they would not be allowed to practice their own music in the school music room.

> The first time Nick's parents heard the band play one of Nick's songs, they were *stunned* by the developing talent they could see in their son.

tangent (TAN-junt) (noun) something that is a change of course; something slightly off-topic. (plural: tangents)

> While talking about the Beatles one time, Chuy went off on a *tangent* with his opinion of Paul McCartney's solo music.

> Wan Ju would closely follow her sheet music when playing, but Georgia would often go off on *tangents* "just to see what might develop."

unpredictable (un-pri-DIK-tu-bl) (adjective) describes something unexpected; difficult to foresee.

> The band's future was *unpredictable*. Unless they could work out their differences, they would have to break up.

Georgia's moods could really be *unpredictable,* and sometimes Nick and Chuy got as irritated with her as Wan Ju was.

whim (HWIM) (noun) a sudden idea; a wish for something. (plural: whims)

On a *whim*, Wan Ju bought everyone in the band a CD of a country music artist she thought might surprise them a bit.

It may only have been a *whim*, but Joaquin hoped he might be able to help the band relax and have fun again.

wince (WINTZ) (verb) to flinch in pain or fear (often used to define one's facial expression in such a situation).

When Georgia started up the argument all over again, Nick visibly *winced* and tried to change the subject.

Learning to play a twelve-string guitar, Georgia *winced* at the pain in her fingers when she practiced too much in a day.

Quick Match 4

Match each word to its definition.

1. ___	predilection	A.	to confuse with unclear information
2. ___	hinder	B.	capable of being touched; tangible, real
3. ___	assert	C.	to plot; to create secret or sneaky plans
4. ___	intrigued	D.	unexpected; difficult to foresee
5. ___	rendezvous	E.	to plan and execute that plan
6. ___	bewilder	F.	a sudden idea or wish for something
7. ___	juxtapose	G.	to state something positively and firmly
8. ___	scheme	H.	to avoid or reject something
9. ___	bolster	I.	to place side by side
10. ___	laconic	J.	a preplanned meeting
11. ___	stunned	K.	to interfere negatively with someone's efforts
12. ___	devious	L.	a change of course
13. ___	meddle	M.	a short outing or trip
14. ___	tangent	N.	a mixture, often of parts of songs strung together
15. ___	enthuse	O.	to become interested in something
16. ___	medley	P.	to flinch in pain or fear
17. ___	unpredictable	Q.	to complete a job; satisfy a need
18. ___	eschew	R.	overwhelmed or dazed
19. ___	orchestrate	S.	to support
20. ___	whim	T.	to interfere in other people's business
21. ___	excursion	U.	an unusual variety of things grouped together
22. ___	palpable	V.	describes someone who speaks little
23. ___	wince	W.	to be very excited about something
24. ___	fulfill	X.	a preference for something
25. ___	potpourri	Y.	sneaky; dishonest

Sentence Completions 4

Choose the proper word or pair of words for each of the sentences below.

1. Chuy planned a _____ with Nick at a local music store to introduce him to someone else who might like to join the band.

   (a) whim   (b) potpourri   (c) rendezvous   (d) medley   (e) tangent

2. The recording company wanted to _____ public interest in a band by asking the band members to take part in a walkathon to help the homeless.

   (a) bolster   (b) juxtapose   (c) meddle   (d) bewilder   (e) fulfill

3. An argument within a band can not only _____ the band's progress, but also, if not resolved, can cause the band to break up.

   (a) fulfill   (b) juxtapose   (c) meddle   (d) orchestrate   (e) hinder

4. The _____ chord change made Chuy _____ in surprise and pain when he heard its discordant combination.

   (a) devious . . . orchestrate   (b) palpable . . . eschew   (c) stunned . . . assert
   (d) laconic . . . enthuse   (e) unpredictable . . . wince

5. Because of a lack of talent, the band manager _____ playing an instrument herself, but she showed a fortunate _____ for promoting and managing a band well.

   (a) asserted . . . rendezvous   (b) eschewed . . . predilection
   (c) fulfilled . . . medley   (d) orchestrated . . . scheme
   (e) bolstered . . . excursion

Chapter 5: Starting Over?

Nick was late to rehearsal that week and was surprised to see that only Wan Ju was there ahead of him. *Disquieting* as it was that no one else was there, Wan Ju and Nick *nevertheless* fell into conversation about some of the music elements that had *piqued* their interest over the past five weeks of *auditory* research. Nick was tempted to *impart* to Wan Ju some of what was going on with Chuy, but he didn't *yield* to the urge; he wanted Chuy to be free to *disclose* these discoveries in his own way.

After what seemed an *interminable* amount of time, Chuy and Georgia showed up together, both grinning ear-to-ear. They tried to sound *contrite* for being late, but their obvious cheerfulness far *outweighed* their *repentance*. Wan Ju sensed their excitement.

"What's going on?" she *challenged*. "What are you two up to?"

Georgia giggled.

"Wan Ju, I've been such a pain. Could we start over?" Georgia *appealed*. Wan Ju *visibly thawed*.

"The fault has been mine," Wan Ju admitted quietly. "I have not been the leader I had hoped to be; Nick has shown me that these last few weeks."

This *sentimental* discussion was making Nick uncomfortable. Glancing at him, Chuy hurriedly interrupted,

"Wan Ju, Georgia put together a collection of *vintage* country-and-western songs that she thought you would like and had me burn them on a CD for you. What I didn't tell Georgia, though," Chuy added, "is that I *interspersed* some of my own experimentation among a few of the pieces."

"It was Joaquin's idea to help me figure out a way to help make peace." Georgia admitted, "We were late tonight because of getting the CD ready." She finished with a *suspicious* look at Chuy regarding his "experimentation" on the CD.

"Chuy has *outlined* some of his *brainstorming* with me already," Nick said. "Let's hear the CD."

The *troupe* sat down and listened to the CD together, starting and stopping it regularly to laugh, to comment, and sometimes to groan at Chuy's *unorthodox* treatment of some of the tunes. Despite her reputation as a music purist, Wan Ju both laughed the loudest at the mix of musical styles and was most careful to make note of the more *innovative* of Chuy's creations.

"I guess we're at a new beginning," she said. "Shall we start all over again with a new *repertoire* of songs at our next rehearsal?"

As a unit, they all shouted their agreement.

appeal (uh-PEEL) (verb) to ask for something urgently or sincerely.

> Wan Ju tried to *appeal* to the head of the arts department at school, but she was still told that their band could not practice after school hours on school property.

> After Nick's parents told him that practice had to stop by 9:00 P.M. each night, Nick *appealed* to their reasonable nature by asking for an extension until 9:30 P.M.

auditory (AW-du-tor-ee) (adjective) having to do with sound or hearing.

> Joaquin's *auditory* testing when he was a child showed that he had trouble hearing higher-pitched sounds.

> The real *auditory* organ is the ear, but sometimes Chuy felt that it was the rhythm of the guitar strings' vibration through his fingers that really helped him "hear" the music.

brainstorm (BRAYN-storm) (verb) to approach a problem individually or as a group by throwing out solutions or ideas spontaneously and without careful thought (reserving thoughtful discussion for later).

> Each week, the band gathered to *brainstorm* about a musical tradition to explore in the upcoming week.

> When Wan Ju decided to start the band, she had *brainstormed* the talents of all of the music students she could think of to help her decide whom to invite to join her.

challenge (CHAL-unj) (verb) to ask a question with defiance; to argue or dispute; to offer someone else or another team a chance to fight or compete with you.

> Wan Ju and Georgia had *challenged* each other's idea of how the song should be played.

> As they developed their new style, the band hoped to *challenge* other groups' ideas on how certain songs should be played.

contrite (KAHN-tryt) (adjective) feeling sorry for one's actions or words.

> Even when she was still upset with Wan Ju, Georgia was secretly *contrite* for some of the awful things she had said to her friend.

> Joaquin was *contrite* for interfering in Nick's band's business, but Nick was grateful for his help.

disclose (dis-KLOZE) (verb) to reveal; to uncover.

> Looking for advice, Nick had decided to *disclose* the band's problems to one of the school's counselors.

> The research into musical styles unexpectedly *disclosed* Chuy's talent for combining musical traditions in new ways.

disquieting (dis-KWY-ut-ing) (adjective) troubling; showing a lack of peace or restfulness.

> Both Wan Ju and Georgia had found it *disquieting* to think that their friendship might not survive this argument.

Nick found it *disquieting* to think that the band would have to break up if they all decided to go to different colleges after graduation.

Similar Sounds   *accept* and *except*

These two words aren't pronounced exactly the same but the pronunciation is similar enough to confuse people. *Accept* means "to agree to something or to receive something," whereas *except* means "to leave something out or to exclude something." So, if you haven't been put on a list of people for swimming lessons but that's fine with you, you might have "*accepted* that you have been *excepted* from the lessons."

---

impart (im-PART) (verb) to make known (as in, to reveal a secret); to give someone a share of something.

> Wan Ju's aunt used to be in the music business and she *imparted* all kinds of useful information to Wan Ju about the recording industry.

> When Georgia asked for some help, Chuy *imparted* a number of tips about playing a guitar creatively.

innovative (I-nu-vay-tiv) (adjective) describes something new and improved.

> Chuy's most *innovative* guitar work was usually done on songs that others had previously found old and overdone.

> Georgia continued to try *innovative* approaches to their music by introducing unexpected musical instruments into their rehearsals.

interminable (in-TURM-nu-bl) (adjective) taking so long that it is difficult to measure the actual amount of time; endless.

> On their after-school rehearsal days, the band members usually found their last-period classes to be *interminable*.

> Nick had felt that it was an *interminable* amount of time from the day he ordered his new snare drum until the day it was delivered, but it was really only two weeks.

intersperse (in-ter-SPURS) (verb) to spread something around and between other things.

> Georgia gradually learned to *intersperse* her more blunt suggestions with genuine praise for other people's work, softening the impact of some of her criticisms.

> Nick began to write a lot of songs for the band, *interspersing* his own and Joaquin's lyrics to see how they sounded.

nevertheless (ne-vur-thu-LES) (adverb) however; in spite of that.

> Joaquin couldn't sing or play an instrument; *nevertheless*, he became an important member of the group because of his skill with lyrics.

> Wan Ju and Georgia's argument had caused great problems with the band; *nevertheless*, once they made peace, the band had new energy.

outline (OWT-line) (verb) to give a general idea of something; to sketch out the main points of something.

> Before each rehearsal, Nick and Wan Ju liked to *outline* to everyone else what they were hoping to accomplish that day.

> For an assignment in speech class, Chuy *outlined* the value of music in society and why music should be considered as creative an art as painting or sculpture.

outweigh (owt-WAY) (verb) to be more important than (something else).

> Ultimately, the desire to be friends *outweighed* the girls' disagreement about the song.

> A true musician knows that raw talent is *outweighed* by long and steady practice.

pique (PEEK) (verb) to awaken or arouse (a reaction or emotion).

> Georgia's manner sometimes still *piqued* Wan Ju's anger, but she resisted attacking Georgia's tone and the moment usually passed harmlessly.

> Despite her past dislike of the style, Georgia's interest in country music was *piqued* by the interesting songs Wan Ju had had them listen to.

repentance (ri-PEN-tnts) (noun) the state of being sorry for one's past words or actions. (plural: This word is not usually used in the plural.)

> Georgia's *repentance* for the trouble between her and Wan Ju was complete, and she apologized sincerely.

> Nick had hoped for peace in the band but hadn't expected total *repentance* from both of the girls.

repertoire (RE-pu-twahr) (noun) the selection of performance pieces (such as songs or plays) that a group has prepared and is ready to perform. (plural: This word is not usually used in the plural.)

> Nick's *repertoire* of jokes often eased tensions when the band was overtired and a little touchy with one another.

Chuy added considerably to his *repertoire* of songs after spending weeks listening to other people's favorites.

International	*repertoire*

One of the elements that has made English so popular around the world in the past century is its flexibility. If English doesn't have a word for something, it often freely borrows from another language and incorporates that word. *Repertoire* is a French word that has been adopted into English along with others such as *rendezvous* and *gauge*.

Of course, with many French words in English, the reason they have come to us is historical: in 1066 the Normans, whose first language was French, conquered Britain and introduced French as the language of government. The two languages have been intricately interwoven ever since.

---

sentimental (sen-tu-MEN-tl) (adjective) overly emotional in a sweet or romantic way.

> No one in the band really enjoyed playing the more *sentimental* ballads, but they had to admit that their audience often asked for these songs.

> Disappointed that a girl he was interested in didn't really like him, Nick wrote the most *sentimental* song he had ever put on paper.

suspicious (su-SPI-shus) (adjective) distrustful or doubtful of someone or something.

> As the band improved, they became *suspicious* that members of other bands might be trying to imitate their sound.

> The history teacher was *suspicious* that Nick was writing music in class instead of taking history notes.

thaw (THAW) (verb) to bring from a frozen state to room temperature (can be used to describe intense emotions that may soften over time).

> The ice *thawed* in Chuy's forgotten iced tea as he labored on a chord change that didn't sound quite right.

> Angry over the damage to her flute, Georgia's manner didn't *thaw* until the young man offered to pay for the damage he had done.

troupe (TROOP) (noun) a group of people, often touring performers. (plural: troupes)

> The school brought in a *troupe* of actors to perform during an assembly.

> Chuy's parents belonged to a *troupe* of amateur performers who liked to juggle and perform magic tricks in children's hospitals.

unorthodox (un-OR-thu-dahks) (adjective) describes someone or something that does not follow the usual or expected pattern; non-traditional.

> Chuy developed a reputation for playing *unorthodox* but interesting guitar riffs.

Nick's approach to leadership may have been *unorthodox*, but he did a nice job of helping the band to heal.

vintage (VIN-tij) (adjective) describes something that holds classic or traditional appeal.

Georgia liked to wear *vintage* clothing and regularly wore old clothes that her mother had worn when she was in school.

Not all of the *vintage* music that the band had listened to seemed out-of-date; some was amazingly modern in sound and attitude.

visibly (VI-zu-blee) (adverb) obviously; clearly seen.

Although he said little, Chuy was *visibly* relieved when Georgia and Wan Ju apologized to each other.

If the band was *visibly* exhausted, Wan Ju would interrupt the rehearsal and suggest that they stop for the night.

yield (YEELD) (verb) to give in to an impulse, to pressure, or to another's point of view.

Nick was happy to *yield* his leadership role back to Wan Ju.

Ultimately, Wan Ju *yielded* to Georgia's opinion on the song that caused them all that grief and let Chuy do something more interesting with it.

Quick Match 5

Match each word to its definition.

1. ___	impart	A.	to ask for something urgently or sincerely
2. ___	yield	B.	endless
3. ___	repertoire	C.	the state of being sorry for one's past actions
4. ___	challenge	D.	a group of people, usually touring performers
5. ___	visibly	E.	having to do with sound or hearing
6. ___	repentance	F.	to spread something between other things
7. ___	disquieting	G.	non-traditional
8. ___	vintage	H.	to awaken or arouse a reaction or emotion
9. ___	pique	I.	to throw out ideas or solutions spontaneously
10. ___	disclose	J.	to bring from a frozen state to room temperature
11. ___	unorthodox	K.	describes feeling sorry for one's actions or words
12. ___	outweigh	L.	however; in spite of that
13. ___	contrite	M.	distrustful or doubtful
14. ___	troupe	N.	to reveal; to uncover
15. ___	nevertheless	O.	with classic or traditional appeal
16. ___	brainstorm	P.	something new and improved
17. ___	thaw	Q.	a selection of performance pieces
18. ___	intersperse	R.	overly emotional in a sweet or romantic way
19. ___	auditory	S.	to give the general idea of something
20. ___	suspicious	T.	showing a lack of peace or restfulness
21. ___	interminable	U.	to give in to an impulse or pressure
22. ___	appeal	V.	to be more important (than something else)
23. ___	outline	W.	to make known, to reveal a secret
24. ___	innovative	X.	clearly; obviously
25. ___	sentimental	Y.	to ask a question with defiance; argue, dispute

Sentence Completions 5

Choose the proper word or pair of words for each of the sentences below.

1. Any _____ of performers is likely to have arguments from time to time.

    (a) unorthodox   (b) repentance   (c) yield   (d) vintage   (e) troupe

2. When Wan Ju first asked people to join her band, she quickly _____ her ideas, but if they showed interest, she explained her plans in much more detail.

    (a) appealed   (b) interspersed   (c) outlined   (d) brainstormed   (e) piqued

3. When the musician was found guilty of copying another's work, he was very _____ as he apologized and promised sincerely never to do it again.

    (a) auditory   (b) suspicious   (c) disquieting   (d) contrite   (e) sentimental

4. The advertisement for a Battle of the Bands contest _____ their interest and _____ them to come up with some new songs to use in the competition.

    (a) imparted . . . outweighed   (b) appealed . . . interspersed
    (c) disclosed . . . yielded   (d) piqued . . . challenged
    (e) brainstormed . . . thawed

5. As their _____ of songs grew, the band's _____ playing of those songs helped them develop a reputation for being on the cutting edge of new music.

    (a) brainstorm . . . interminable   (b) repertoire . . . innovative
    (c) outline . . . disquieting   (d) troupe . . . unorthodox   (e) pique . . . vintage

WRITING ACTIVITY

Love Hurts!

On the human emotional roller coaster, love can be happy or sad. One can rise to the heavens on an updraft of soaring love or be plunged into the depths of despair when a fickle heart turns against what was thought to be a true, eternal love relationship.

Hmmmmmm.

I know I didn't write THAT paragraph well, but do you know who does write the best lines about broken hearts? Country-and-western singers do! The "he/she-done-me-wrong" song is legendary in American music.

Using as many of this section's vocabulary words as is possible (a minimum of twelve), compose the lyrics of an unhappy country-and-western love song. Your song must contain at least two verses plus a chorus. (Note that the *words* must be sad but the *intent* may be humorous!)

You may set your words to a particular well-known tune. For the true musical/rhythmical artists in the crowd, though, the ideal would be to compose your own original tune as well. Be brave! Have fun!

SECTION 2: TOUCH AND TALENT

Learning Style: The Bodily/Kinesthetic Learner

If you find it tough to sit still for long periods of time without moving some part of your body in some way, one of your primary intelligences is likely that of the **bodily/kinesthetic learner**.

Are you someone who is very aware of your body—how it feels, when it's hungry or thirsty, what stretches feel best? Do you learn best by doing things physically rather than having them explained to you? Are you the first in line to take part in sports or any physical activity? Do you have a tendency to tap, rap, or pitter-pat if you are confined to a seated position for a long time?

If you have answered "yes" to several of the above, this is one of your stronger intelligences.

Possible Approaches

- **VoCubes.** Yes, I'm going to send you off to make flashcards as many others have done, but I promise we will do something interesting with these. Take three-by-five-inch index cards, write a vocabulary word on one side and the corresponding part of speech and definition on the other side. Make six of these. Next, take a cardboard box that is a six- or seven-inch cube and adhere a clear plastic pocket on each face (that's six pockets). Each pocket should have three sealed edges and one open edge so that flashcards can be slipped into them. Basically, you have created dice with words on each side instead of dots—we call these VoCubes, and you can use these in word games to help you learn vocabulary.

  You can even vary the cubes by color-coding your cards by parts of speech to give yourself an edge in remembering these word functions. For example, use red index cards for verbs, yellow for adverbs, blue for nouns, and green for adjectives. Index cards are available in all of these colors, or simply use white cards with a variety of ink colors.

- Game 1: Fill one VoCube with nouns and fill another VoCube with verbs. Roll the two "dice" and make a clear sentence out of the two words that end face up. Check the definitions to make sure your sentence makes sense. This game can be played individually or in groups. When playing alone, you could be given a time limit to come up with a strong sentence after the dice stop rolling. In groups, the player who comes up with the best sentence in the shortest amount of time could be declared the winner. Make up your own group or individual variations, timed or not. You may use a combination of noun/verb dice, noun/adjective dice, or verb/adverb dice.

- Game 2: Fill a VoCube with any combination of vocabulary words, create a circle of students, and play catch. The student who catches the VoCube must, as quickly as possible, make up a reasonable and clear sentence using the vocabulary word that shows on the top of the cube. (Some groups prefer to declare the face on which your right thumb lands to be the vocabulary word that must be used in the sentence; you may do whichever your group prefers.) Instead of creating sentences, your group may want to give definitions of the words when they catch the VoCube. Putting a spin on the VoCube when you throw it to the next person helps keep new words turning up. The key is to keep the game moving quickly; it's more fun and you cover more words in less time.

- **Sandwriting.** Fill a one- to two-inch-deep tray with a layer of sand. (I like to use a large, rectangular foil baking pan with a bag of fine, colored decorative sand from a craft store.) Physically spell out the vocabulary word in the sand with your finger, while either listening to a friend read the definition or repeating the definition yourself. Clear the word out of the sand writing, and redraw the word while using it in a sentence. You have a physical memory and this will help that word attach itself to your finger. For some of the longer vocabulary words which might not quite fit in your tray, write them out by individual syllables.

- **Charades.** In two groups, play charades with vocabulary words. This is often easiest if you work with the words in syllables. The person who guesses the word correctly must then use the word properly in a sentence for the team to earn the point.

- **Bouncing Ball.** Bounce a ball as you review your vocabulary words. Have a partner handy to read the words and definitions to you so that you can repeat them as your body is moving and bouncing the ball.

- **Listen and Move.** Try recording your vocabulary words on CD-RW and playing it while you do housework (tidying your room, dusting, vacuuming, washing dishes). Leave pauses between words on the CD to give you time to repeat the word and the definition and to come up with a sentence using that word. Of course, you could also play this CD while doing something fun, like bouncing a hacky-sack (a small, knitted kick ball) from one foot to the other.

Chapter 6: Life Is a Kick

Some days it just seemed like too much work. Priyanka wiped the *perspiration* from her forehead and returned to her ready *stance*. Kelsey stuck her head in the gym looking for Maura and spotted her friend.

"Pree, what are you up to?" she *queried* from the door.

"Doing forms," Priyanka puffed. "You know, karate." She noticed Kelsey's *mystification*.

"Forms or 'katas' are sets of *choreographed* moves," she responded patiently. "I know about twenty forms already. I'm practicing for a competition next weekend."

"Okay," *rejoined* Kelsey *vaguely*. "Tell Maura I'm looking for her." She vanished.

Priyanka sighed. She was used to her friends' total *indifference* to karate but now and then it would be nice to have some encouragement. She sighed again, and *steeled* herself to get back to work since she only had another fifteen minutes left in her study hall period. Because she competed at the national level (and remained pretty *conscientious* about her school work at the same time), her study hall teacher allowed her to practice if most of her homework was finished for the day.

Just *prior* to karate class that night, Pree and her brother Sanjay were in the ring running through a couple of forms just for practice. Where Pree was *painstaking* in her work, Sanjay was only *competent*. He enjoyed karate hugely but he didn't have his sister's *cutthroat* competitiveness. They both realized this truth and were *unruffled* by it. Indeed, Pree thought *ruefully*, sometimes Sanjay seemed to enjoy class more because he wasn't so concerned with perfection. It was fun, though, to work together on the forms and have a *sibling* who could *critique* your work knowledgeably.

What Sanjay admired about his sister was her natural feel for karate. He tried explaining it to his friend once as her "body knowing what it needed to know before it knew it knew it." His friend was *stymied* by the comment but Sanjay was satisfied that his *convoluted* observation was the most accurate *assessment* he had managed so far to describe his sister's *prowess*. When they were younger, Sanjay had occasionally felt a *twinge* of jealousy when he watched his sister's easy, *unforced* power but now he was more often *envious* of the strength of her will to succeed than he was of her natural skill.

assessment (uh-SES-munt) (noun) the act of grading something or someone or measuring their progress. (plural: assessments)

> The higher the level Pree competed at in karate, the tougher the *assessments* became.

> Pree's self-*assessment* of her skill at karate was often lower than that of the judges who graded her work and thought it was very good.

choreographed (KOR-ee-uh-grafd) 1. (adjective) described as planned physical moves, as in dance; 2. (verb) choreograph: the action of putting together a set of moves to create a dance. (In this case, because the katas have set moves in a set order, they are similar to a formally choreographed dance.)

> One of Sanjay's projects for phys ed class was to *choreograph* his own dance to the music of his choice. No matter how he worked at it, he was amused that his dances always looked like katas.

> For her next belt level in karate, Pree *choreographed* and performed her own kata.

competent (KOM-pu-tunt) (adjective) showing a capable level of skill at a particular task.

> Sanjay looked very skilled at karate until one saw his sister. After that, one could see he was *competent* but not particularly talented.

> Pree was having trouble making her latest form look even *competent*. Right now she was doing it really sloppily.

conscientious (kahnt-shee-ENT-shus) (adjective) working from a principled position; describes one who is careful and thorough about one's work.

> Pree was more *conscientious* about her karate practice, while Sanjay was more *conscientious* about his homework.

> Their being *conscientious* about any of their work was a fairly new development for them. They felt getting their work done helped them avoid unpleasant situations and they both liked that.

convoluted (KAHN-vu-LOO-ted) (adjective) complicated; intricate.

> When her homework wasn't done and she wanted to be released from study hall to practice, Pree could come up with some rather *convoluted* logic to try to convince the teacher.

> When done quickly, some of the katas looked really *convoluted*. To learn them, though, one simplified them by breaking them into smaller, clearer parts.

critique (kri-TEEK) (noun) a formal review of a performance in which strong points as well as weak points are discussed. (plural: critiques)

> When Pree's instructor gave a *critique* of her work, she always focused on Pree's weak points; Sanjay's *critiques* always focused on Pree's strengths.

> Pree was skilled enough to give a balanced and reasonable *critique* of her own instructor's work as well.

cutthroat (KUT-throat) (adjective) without mercy; relentless in competition.

> Pree was *cutthroat* even in practice and only the best in the dojo (karate studio) were willing to work with her.

> Sanjay was hardly lazy. He was competitive without the *cutthroat* need to win at all costs all the time.

Easy Errors   ***desert, desert,* and *dessert***

Sometimes words will have the same spelling but different pronunciations when they are different parts of speech. The noun *desert*, which means "a dry landscape with little rain," is pronounced DE-zert, with the emphasis on the first syllable. The verb *desert*, which means "to leave someone or something without permission or without planning to return" has the emphasis on the second syllable (di-ZERT), which is the same pronunciation and emphasis as the word *dessert*, which means "something sweet to eat, usually at the end of a meal." In this last case, the spelling and meaning differ, but the pronunciation remains the same. Confused? Just remember that you wouldn't be willing to *desert* (di-ZERT) a tent in the *desert* (DE-zert) if your hosts were offering sweet dates and figs for *dessert* (di-ZERT).

---

envious (EN-vee-us) (adjective) a feeling of jealousy or an unhappy desire for something someone else has.

> Pree was occasionally *envious* of the skill of a rival competitor, but she knew she had the ability to be that good if she just worked at it.

> Her friends didn't really understand Pree's attachment to karate, but they were sometimes a little *envious* of the amount of traveling she did to compete nationally.

indifference (in-DI-frunts) (noun) a total lack of interest in a particular subject; a state of being unbiased. (plural: This word is not usually used in the plural.)

> Pree's friends' *indifference* to her karate was both a sore point and a source of amusement for Pree. How could they like her so much while ignoring something that was so much a part of her?

> Years before, Sanjay had been taking karate for several weeks when Pree stopped in to watch his class. On that day, her *indifference* turned to intense interest.

mystification (mis-tu-fu-KAY-shun) (noun) the state of being bewildered. (plural: mystifications)

> One of Pree's incentives to become good at karate was to remove her *mystification* as to how they could jump so high doing flying kicks.

> Neither of their parents had had any interest in martial arts at all, so to have two children heavily involved in karate was a source of *mystification* for them.

painstaking (PAYN-stay-king) (adjective) very careful; going to a great deal of trouble to do something well.

> Pree didn't like her math homework much because of the *painstaking* detail necessary to do consistently well at it.

> In computer class, Sanjay really enjoyed the *painstaking* aspect of installing new cards in a computer cleanly and properly.

perspiration (pur-spu-RAY-shun) (noun) sweat. (plural: This word is not usually used in the plural.)

> Pree's goal in doing forms was never to let the judges see any *perspiration*; she felt the katas should look powerful but effortless.

> Twice a week, the students sparred in karate class. Wearing protective gear and fighting always bathed them all in *perspiration* in no time.

prior (PRYR) (adjective) something that comes before something else in the order of things.

> *Prior* to her interest in karate, Pree was active in soccer and basketball at school.

> Preferring individual to team sports, Sanjay's *prior* interest was swim team.

prowess (PROW-us) (noun) high-level ability or skill. (plural: This word is not usually used in the plural.)

> Pree's *prowess* on the soccer field had been unmatched and her teammates were sorry to see her leave soccer for karate.

> While not the only chess star on campus, Sanjay had a fair amount of *prowess* in that area, too.

query (KWIR-ee) 1. (noun) a question. (plural: queries); 2. (verb) to question.

> Before a tournament, it wasn't unusual for Pree to *query* every little hand movement and body angle in the form she was going to compete with.

> Sometimes she *queried* her instructor in such detail, the instructor became impatient and made Pree do push-ups to calm herself.

rejoin (ri-JOIN) (verb) to reply to someone; often, to reply to someone's reply sharply.

> Pree was very patient with younger students and was happy to *rejoin* to their concerns.

> Usually, Sanjay was in a good mood but if he *rejoined* sharply to something Pree said, she knew enough to leave him alone for awhile.

ruefully (ROO-ful-ee) (adverb) reacting to something with regret or sorrow.

> Pree wanted to be perfect at karate right away and she reflected *ruefully* on her years of soccer, knowing now that she could have been perfecting her karate years earlier.

> Whatever their levels, Sanjay and Pree were careful not to compete against each another. There had once been an unpleasant competition on which they now both looked back *ruefully*.

Pieces and Parts   *-ly*

A suffix is something added to the end of a word to change the meaning or part of speech. The suffix *-ly* is most often used to change a word into an adverb form. Thus, *happy* is the adjective and *happily* is the adverb; *vague* is the adjective and *vaguely* is the adverb.

In very few cases (such as *likely* and *unlikely*), an *-ly* ending goes on an adjective, so if you are trying to determine a word's part of speech in a sentence, look carefully at the sentence's structure. Remember that an adjective can only tell you more about (or "modify") a noun—but an adverb is a very useful kind of word that can modify another adverb (*very* happily), an adjective (*amazingly* beautiful), or a verb (drive *quickly*).

---

sibling (SI-bling) (noun) a brother or a sister. (plural: siblings)

> There were plenty of *siblings* taking karate together at Pree and Sanjay's dojo. Their motto was "the family that kicks together, sticks together."

> Although Sanjay didn't know it, Pree admired her *sibling's* easy-going and relaxed approach to life.

stance (STANTS) (noun) physical or mental posture; often, a starting standing position for a particular sport. (plural: stances)

> There were several *stances* or ways to stand in karate, including a front *stance* (with one's weight evenly distributed to both feet) and a back *stance* (with one's weight mostly on the back foot).

> Some people criticized Pree's parents for letting her focus so much on karate, but their *stance* was that if the young woman was passionate about something worthwhile, she should pursue that passion.

steel (STEEL) (verb) to strengthen oneself to do something difficult or unpleasant.

> Not as strong a fan of sparring as his sister, Sanjay sometimes had to *steel* himself to participate.

> After her poor showing on her geometry test, Pree *steeled* herself for her parents' disapproval.

stymied (STY-meed) (verb) to be puzzled or confused; blocked from doing what one wants or needs to do; to be thwarted.

> Sanjay was *stymied* one time in competition when he absolutely could not remember the first move of his kata.

> Pree was *stymied* by certain proofs in geometry and felt she would never figure them out.

twinge (TWINJ) (noun) a small, sharp, sudden pain or emotion. (plural: twinges)

> Sanjay occasionally felt a *twinge* of guilt that math came so much more easily for him than it did for his sister.

> Pree felt a *twinge* in her right ankle that night before class so she wrapped it before working out.

unforced (un-FORSD) (adjective) when something comes easily; not strained; not produced by effort.

> Sanjay's natural good humor was *unforced* and it made him an easy friend to make and keep.

> Sanjay may have looked upon his sister's skill at karate as *unforced*, but she felt she put a terrific amount of effort into it.

unruffled (un-RUF-fuld) (adjective) calm; not easily upset.

> Sanjay remained *unruffled* by most things in life, whereas Pree felt things very deeply.

> Pree was very good, though, at looking totally *unruffled* if she made a mistake doing a kata. That control and presence of mind earned her many points.

vaguely (VAYG-lee) (adverb) in an indistinct and undirected way; without focus.

> Not having finished her homework, Pree answered the literature question *vaguely*, hoping she was close enough to satisfy the teacher.

> Catching up on her reading and not paying attention to her brother, Pree answered his question *vaguely* in hopes he would leave her alone.

Quick Match 6

Match each word to its definition.

1. ____ mystification	A.	something that comes before another
2. ____ sibling	B.	to plan physical moves, as in a dance
3. ____ assessment	C.	to question
4. ____ rejoin	D.	sweat
5. ____ stymied	E.	high-level ability or skill
6. ____ critique	F.	a small, sharp, sudden pain or emotion
7. ____ ruefully	G.	jealous
8. ____ choreograph	H.	not strained; not produced by effort
9. ____ painstaking	I.	a brother or sister
10. ____ twinge	J.	careful and thorough about one's work
11. ____ steel	K.	physical or mental posture
12. ____ prior	L.	without focus; in an indistinct way
13. ____ unforced	M.	act of grading or measuring progress
14. ____ convoluted	N.	calm; not easily upset
15. ____ perspiration	O.	to reply to someone
16. ____ vaguely	P.	unbiased; a lack of interest in something
17. ____ cutthroat	Q.	to strengthen oneself for something difficult
18. ____ stance	R.	complicated; intricate
19. ____ unruffled	S.	a formal review of a performance
20. ____ conscientious	T.	going to a lot of trouble to do something well
21. ____ prowess	U.	relentless in competition; without mercy
22. ____ envious	V.	to be puzzled or confused; thwarted
23. ____ query	W.	a capable level of skill at a particular task
24. ____ indifference	X.	reacting with regret or sorrow
25. ____ competent	Y.	the state of being bewildered

Sentence Completions 6

Choose the proper word or pair of words for each of the sentences below.

1. After each competition, their instructor pulled the competitors aside to _____ their work in detail as a way to help them get better.

    (a) query   (b) twinge   (c) critique   (d) painstaking   (e) stymie

2. She was more likely to _____ her work severely than were the others who worked with her.

    (a) assess   (b) stymie   (c) steel   (d) rejoin   (e) envy

3. At first, he was puzzled by the pattern to the exercise they were doing and he simply followed along in _____.

    (a) prowess   (b) competence   (c) indifference   (d) envy   (e) perspiration

4. The athlete's _____ and natural ability were more obvious to his _____ and others than they were to himself.

    (a) assessment . . . stymie   (b) prowess . . . sibling
    (c) competence . . . critique   (d) envied . . . indifferent
    (e) choreography . . . query

5. Working with _____ grace, she effortlessly executed the _____ kata.

    (a) cutthroat . . . competent   (b) painstaking . . . indifferent
    (c) conscientious . . . assessment   (d) unforced . . . convoluted
    (e) unruffled . . . rejoined

Chapter 7: Tinkering

Sanjay muttered to himself as he *tinkered* with the engine *components*. A *haphazard* question in science class the week before—"If there's such a thing as an <u>internal</u> *combustion* engine in a car, is there such a thing as an <u>external</u> combustion engine?"— had *elicited* a positive response from the teacher, who suggested the class do a little personal research on the matter. Sanjay found out from a book in the library that the steam engine was a type of external combustion engine, but he didn't find that as *enthralling* as the *physics* behind how a car engine works. He found the book's *explication* of how the engine worked *incomprehensible*, though, and was frustrated in his attempts to get a *lucid* understanding from other people's explanations.

Sensitive to his son's skills, Sanjay's father somehow *wheedled* an old car motor out of the owner of a local junkyard and brought it home for Sanjay to work with. *Energized*, Sanjay threw on some old clothes and, in minutes flat, was happily *engrossed* in his explorations.

Sanjay's touch was *deft*, his fingers skillful, and in just a few days he had the motor totally disassembled. The trick now, of course, was to put it back together and figure out how it worked in the process! While not truly *ambidextrous*, Sanjay was *proficient* enough with either hand to be able to *manipulate* small parts *adroitly*. As he began to *piece* the big V-8 back together again, he consulted the *unintelligible* book that had first sent him on this *quest* and, amazingly, it became more and more *explicit* and helpful as he *delved* deeper into the project. It did take him *substantially* longer to reassemble the motor than it did to take it apart, but once he had finished rebuilding it, he understood internal combustion engines in a way that no book could have *clarified* for him.

adroitly (uh-DROIT-lee) (adverb) with dexterity; skillfully.

> Sanjay took the engine apart carefully and *adroitly* in record time.

> Whenever someone in the family had a knot in a shoelace, Sanjay was always the one to *adroitly* straighten it out.

ambidextrous (am-bi-DEK-strus) (adjective) not specifically right-handed or left-handed; able to use either hand interchangeably.

> While he preferred to use his left hand, Sanjay was *ambidextrous* enough to do fine work with his right hand, too.

> Sanjay could *ambidextrously* remove a screw with each hand at the same time.

clarify (KLA-ru-fy) (verb) to make easier to understand; to remove confusion.

> To *clarify* how the engine worked, Sanjay picked up an old owner's manual at a used book store.

He tried to explain why he was spending so much time with the engine, but it was a little difficult to *clarify* his reasons to others.

combustion (kum-BUS-chun) (noun) the process of burning. (plural: This word is not usually used in the plural.)

The *combustion* that provides energy to the engine really is a small, controlled fire inside the engine.

Concerned about the danger of fire from the grease on the old engine, Sanjay kept it away from the house to minimize the possibility of *combustion*.

component (kum-PO-nunt) (noun) a small part of a larger machine or system. (plural: components)

Sanjay and Pree both broke down their katas into *component* parts to learn them more thoroughly.

Sanjay had been interested in radios for a while, and he still had some *components* he had been using to build one.

deft (DEFT) (adjective) describes someone who is skilled with his or her hands and can work quickly; adroit.

Sanjay came from a family of weavers and needleworkers and he felt he was so *deft* because he had inherited the skill.

Pree's skill seemed to be in larger movements because she was not as *deft* as Sanjay in detail work.

delve (DELV) (verb) to dig into something; to search at length and in detail.

As part of her next level in karate, Pree was expected to *delve* into the history and language of karate.

If something caught Sanjay's interest, he was not content until he had *delved* into it in quite a bit of detail.

elicit (i-LI-sut) (verb) to call out from someone or something; to draw out.

Sanjay tried to *elicit* information about engines from a number of sources, but he really was much better at working things out himself.

Pree's advice to her friends to try karate had, so far, *elicited* no responses.

Similar Sounds   *elicit* **and** *illicit*

If *elicit* is a verb that means "to draw something out of someone," and *illicit* is an adjective that describes something that is "unacceptable or illegal," a police officer may try to *elicit* from a witness a description of the person who committed an *illicit* act.

---

energized (EH-nur-jyzd) (adjective) invigorated; full of activity or energy.

> Once Sanjay and Pree finished their stretches and warm-ups at the beginning of class, they were *energized* and ready to learn karate.

> Sanjay could get so *energized* and involved in a new project that he would not take time out to eat.

engrossed (en-GROSD) (adjective) to be deeply involved in something; to be absorbed in something.

> *Engrossed* in his engine manual, Sanjay had to be reminded to get his homework done.

> Pree was so *engrossed* in working through a new form that she didn't realize that a number of others had stopped to watch her.

enthralling (en-THROL-ing) (adjective) totally captivating or enchanting.

> Sanjay was finding his new project *enthralling* and it was tough for him to pay attention to anything else.

> When Pree first saw karate being done, she found it *enthralling* and had to be a part of it herself.

explication (EK-splu-KAY-shun) (noun) explanation. (plural: explications)

> The teacher's *explication* of the internal combustion engine was thorough, but Sanjay couldn't entirely figure it out.

> Sanjay's *explication* to his literature teacher about why his homework wasn't finished did not satisfy him.

explicit (ik-SPLI-sut) (adjective) very clear, with no areas undefined or implied.

> The manual was *explicit* in most areas but was frustratingly vague in others.

> Sanjay was given *explicit* instructions to finish his literature homework tonight or no engine for three days.

Easy Errors   *explicit* vs. *implicit*

These two words both have to do with understanding something. If a piece of information is made *explicit*, the information is "made very clear, with no areas undefined or implied." If the piece of information is made *implicit*, it is assumed to be understood but "is not directly expressed." So someone may assume you know *implicitly* that you shouldn't cheat on your homework but may not make it *explicit* whether doing your homework together with another student is actually cheating or not.

---

haphazard (hap-HA-zurd) (adjective) without an order or a plan; by chance.

> At first, Sanjay's method of taking the engine apart was *haphazard*, but after a while he worked out a system for keeping related parts close together.

> In earlier years, Pree's approach to getting her homework done had been *haphazard*, but her organizational skills had improved enormously in the past two years.

incomprehensible (in-kom-pri-HEN-su-bl) (adjective) cannot be understood.

> It was almost *incomprehensible* to Pree how people could be indifferent to the grace, power, and beauty of karate.

> The shop manual Sanjay got from the library was nearly *incomprehensible* to him until he began working with the engine's parts themselves.

lucid (LOO-sud) (adjective) very clear; well-explained; easy to understand.

> After the engine was completely rebuilt (and thoroughly cleaned), Sanjay found the shop manual *lucid* and studied it carefully.

> Their instructor *lucidly* explained the proper way to perform a flying kick.

manipulate (mu-NI-pyu-layt) (verb) to control by skilled use of one's hands; to deviously twist (a situation) to one's own purposes.

> Pree was also good at working with weapons in karate and she could *manipulate* the bo (a straight, long stick) with ease and grace.

> When Sanjay fell behind in his science homework, he tried to convince the teacher the engine was a science project. Although supportive, the teacher would not be *manipulated* and insisted on Sanjay finishing the homework assigned.

piece (PEES) (verb) to put together, one part at a time; to join or unite separate parts together into a whole.

> Just as Sanjay's aunt liked to *piece* together quilt squares, Sanjay liked to *piece* together engines.

After learning the parts of a form, Sanjay and Pree *pieced* it back together to run through it completely.

physics (FI-ziks) (noun) the science of the interaction of matter and energy; the processes that obey those laws of interaction. (plural: This word, defined in this way, is always used in the plural.)

Sanjay found *physics* satisfying and wished that all of the science classes focused on that area.

It was the *physics* of the engine that fascinated him: why and how it did what it did.

proficient (pru-FI-shunt) (adjective) to be skilled at a task at an advanced level.

Sanjay's science teacher was also *proficient* with engines and encouraged Sanjay in his explorations.

As Pree became *proficient* in her more advanced forms, she had to remember to practice her earlier forms to stay sharp with them too.

sensitive (SEN-su-tiv) (adjective) aware of the skills, attitudes, or personalities of others.

Sensitive to their children's physical gifts, Sanjay and Pree's parents still pressed them to improve their academics.

Sanjay and Pree were *sensitive* to each other's moods and tried to be understanding—most of the time.

substantially (sub-STAN-shul-lee) (adverb) doing something in a larger amount or with a more important factor; significantly.

It had taken Pree *substantially* longer to learn a new form when she was a beginner.

Pree had to work *substantially* harder at math to succeed than her brother did.

tinker (TING-kur) (verb) to work with an apparatus with a purpose but without a specific plan; to experiment with something with one's hands; to fiddle.

The newer electronic and computerized engines were impossible to *tinker* with, so Sanjay was grateful for his old V-8.

Sanjay's father had *tinkered* with building radios when he was younger.

unintelligible (un-in-TEL-ij-ibl) (adjective) difficult or impossible to understand.

Pree was so tired after class one night that she was *unintelligible*. She went to bed without dinner and fell asleep immediately.

Sanjay could always tell when he was daydreaming too much in class because the teacher's words would become *unintelligible*.

wheedle (HWEE-dl) (verb) to try to get something from someone by flattering or tricking them with words.

Pree's father had doubted her interest in karate at first and she had had to *wheedle* him into letting her take lessons.

Pree had tried to *wheedle* her math teacher into letting her skip her homework once, but it didn't work.

Quick Match 7

Match each word to its definition.

1. ___	elicit	A.	to be absorbed in something
2. ___	haphazard	B.	very clear; easy to understand
3. ___	ambidextrous	C.	to experiment with something by hand
4. ___	deft	D.	to dig into something at length
5. ___	physics	E.	totally captivating
6. ___	explicit	F.	significantly; larger amount or importance
7. ___	substantial	G.	able to use either hand interchangeably
8. ___	adroitly	H.	to deviously twist to one's own purposes
9. ___	delve	I.	cannot be understood
10. ___	component	J.	to get something by flattery or trickery
11. ___	tinker	K.	to draw out from someone or something
12. ___	engrossed	L.	difficult or impossible to understand
13. ___	piece	M.	dextrous; skilled with one's hands
14. ___	sensitive	N.	with dexterity; skillfully
15. ___	energized	O.	without an order or plan; by chance
16. ___	unintelligible	P.	made clear, with no undefined areas
17. ___	incomprehensible	Q.	small part of a larger machine or system
18. ___	combustion	R.	skilled at a task at an advanced level
19. ___	lucid	S.	full of activity or energy; invigorated
20. ___	explication	T.	to put together one part at a time
21. ___	wheedle	U.	the process of burning
22. ___	manipulate	V.	explanation
23. ___	clarify	W.	aware of the skills, attitudes of others
24. ___	proficient	X.	to make easier to understand
25. ___	enthralling	Y.	science of interaction of matter and energy

Sentence Completions 7

Choose the proper word or pair of words for each of the sentences below.

1. Sanjay tried to _____ his teacher into accepting his engine project as extra credit in science class.

     (a) piece   (b) clarify   (c) engross   (d) delve   (e) manipulate

2. Sanjay noticed that babies were often more _____ than adults and he wondered why people weren't encouraged to use both hands for all tasks.

     (a) ambidextrous   (b) deft   (c) energized   (d) sensitive
     (e) adroit

3. The amount of homework that night was _____ and he knew he wouldn't be able to work on his engine after school.

     (a) clarified   (b) unintelligible   (c) substantial   (d) enthralling   (e) lucid

4. Although not normally _____ , he found that he could _____ fit the nuts onto the proper bolts.

     (a) sensitive . . . proficiently   (b) deft . . . adroitly
     (c) lucid . . . ambidextrously   (d) energized . . . explicitly
     (e) enthralling . . . substantially

5. Once the teacher's _____ explanation cleared things up for him, he no longer found the process _____ .

     (a) component . . . haphazard   (b) energized . . . engrossed
     (c) proficient . . . sensitive   (d) incomprehensible . . . deft
     (e) lucid . . . unintelligible

Chapter 8: Discovering Oneself

Mr. Carrothers sat patiently while Sanjay *wrestled* with the computer hardware problem he was trying to *dissect*. This quiet *persistence* was part of Mr. Carrothers' charm as a teacher but also the main focus of some students' *aggravation* with him.

"Why can't he just <u>tell</u> us?" some would groan under their breath. "It's not like I think of computer programming as my *vocation*. I just want to get through this class."

Sanjay felt as much frustration sometimes in the *process*, but the *elation* he felt when he finally solved a *complex* problem usually made up for the delayed *gratification*. That's not to say that Sanjay didn't occasionally join in with the grumpy students and *broadcast* his own irritation, but, for the most part, he *grudgingly* understood Mr. Carrothers' emphasis on their solving their own problems. Sanjay saw Mr. Carrothers as the *quintessential* teacher, the type who let his students find their own ways, and he admired this about him.

What amused Mr. Carrothers was that he had come to teaching *unwittingly*, truly accidentally, and his students did not *recognize* this at all. At sixteen, he hadn't been able to *linger* one single moment longer than he had to before he dropped out of school and went to work in construction. Dean had loved construction work: the *precision*, the team work, the *tactile* experience of working with different materials. A chance *encounter* with a *discarded* computer was his *impetus* into a new hobby. After a year of *fiddling* with hardware and software, Dean was *dissatisfied* with his level of knowledge, so he *enrolled* in a technical school to *solidify* his practical understanding of computers. In time, this led him into community college and, later, a university degree program in computer science. He found his need for information and experience was *insatiable*, and he also felt a growing hunger to share his knowledge. Teaching had become a new passion.

aggravation (a-gru-VAY-shun) (noun) a feeling of irritation or of increasing irritation. (plural: aggravations)

> Dean liked to tinker with things but his *aggravation* with his limited knowledge of computers led him to take the next step.

> It's odd the way *aggravation* can turn into satisfaction almost instantly if one finally figures out a problem.

broadcast (BRAWD-kast) (verb) to make known to a lot of people or over a wide area.

> While many of the students had a tendency to *broadcast* their complaints, they were often less vocal with their compliments to a teacher.

> Dean didn't like to *broadcast* his past. He preferred to keep his private life private.

complex (KOM-pleks) (adjective) intricate; complicated; with many interconnected parts.

>Many problems that seemed *complex* when presented to him were really simple once Sanjay figured them out.

>Pree actually preferred *complex* geometry problems to simple ones because they made her slow down and work step-by-step.

discarded (dis-KARD-ed) 1. (adjective) thrown away, often in the garbage or trash. 2. (verb) to reject or to throw away.

>Sanjay liked to use *discarded* food jars to store his small car parts while working on the engine.

>When solving computer problems, Sanjay often *discarded* almost as many potential solutions as he came up with.

dissatisfied (dis-SA-tus-fyd) (verb) to disappoint or not fulfill someone's expectations of something.

>It was ironic that as *dissatisfied* as Dean had been with high school, he spent years in post-secondary education working with computers.

>Pree might be *dissatisfied* with some of her performances but, deep down, she did take pride in her work.

dissect (dy-SEKT) (verb) to take apart into small pieces to examine closely.

>After Dean had *dissected* his own computer to the best of his ability, he went on to formal study of computers.

>Sanjay had done a *dissection* of a frog in biology class once, but he preferred to *dissect* engines and math problems.

Pieces and Parts   *dis-*

A prefix is something added to the beginning of a word to change the meaning. The prefix *dis-* is used to mean "opposite of," "lack of," "apart," or "away." Thus, *dissect* is *dis* (apart) + *secare* (to cut) and means "to take apart into small pieces." *Discard* is *dis* (away) + *card* (playing cards) and refers to the custom of throwing away unneeded cards during a card game.

---

elation (i-LAY-shun) (noun) a feeling of great joy and pride; jubilance. (plural: This word is not usually used in the plural.)

>Pree's *elation* when she won a competition knew no bounds.

>Sanjay felt both a jubilant *elation* and a quiet pride when he had completely rebuilt his engine.

encounter (in-KOWN-tur) 1. (verb) to come into contact with; to meet, often unexpectedly. 2. (noun) a meeting, often a short or chance meeting. (plural: encounters)

> Once at a tournament, Pree *encountered* an old friend from elementary school whom she hadn't seen in years.

> Each *encounter* with a new aspect of computers seemed to fascinate Dean even more.

enroll (en-ROL) (verb) to enter one's name on a list or to register to become a participant (usually used for a new person at a club or a school).

> Although Sanjay was the first to *enroll* in karate, Pree soon passed him by in passion and skill.

> Sanjay was thinking about *enrolling* in a nuclear physics program for college but he needed to know more about it first.

fiddle (FI-dl) (verb) to tinker with something; to work on something with one's hands without a clear idea of a goal.

> Dean didn't want to just *fiddle* with computers; he wanted to really understand them.

> At first, Sanjay felt as though he were merely *fiddling* with the engine, but as he got into it, he developed a plan for the work.

gratification (gra-tu-fu-KAY-shun) (noun) a feeling of satisfaction. (plural: gratifications)

> It was with extreme *gratification* that Pree accepted her first trophy.

> The delayed *gratification* of solving a particularly difficult problem was often more satisfying than getting a correct answer right off.

grudgingly (GRUJ-ing-lee) (adverb) given or allowed with reluctance or negative feeling.

> Pree's parents were firm about her getting enough sleep at night, but they *grudgingly* gave permission now and then for an extra-late night of homework.

> When the students had worked hard and still couldn't find a solution to one of his problems, Dean gave the answer almost *grudgingly*.

impetus (IM-pu-tus) (noun) the driving force behind something; a stimulus. (plural: impetuses)

> Pree's *impetus* was a desire to be the best.

> Sanjay's *impetus* was a deep desire to know.

insatiable (in-SAY-shu-bl) (adjective) cannot be satisfied.

>After a tournament, Pree's thirst was nearly *insatiable* and she always went through several bottles of water.

>Mr. Carrothers' curiosity about computers was almost *insatiable*.

linger (LIN-gur) (verb) to be unwilling or slow to leave a place; to tarry.

>Sanjay would often *linger* in the upper hallway, hoping to get a chance to chat with his science teacher about his engine.

>Mr. Carrothers *lingered* at the end of the school day in case students needed to come into the computer lab to finish work.

persistence (pur-SIS-tunts) (noun) firmly sticking with something despite obstacles; tenacity. (plural: This word is not usually used in the plural.)

>Earlier in his life, Mr. Carrothers didn't see *persistence* as one of his personal qualities. Now he does.

>Pree had both *persistence* and skill; neither quality alone could have gotten her as far as she had gone already.

precision (pri-SI-zhun) (noun) the state of being exact or correct. (plural: This word is not usually used in the plural.)

>Dean had enjoyed the *precision* and art of construction work. "A sloppy job of drywall work," he used to say, "might as well have your signature on it. It's yours forever."

>Sanjay's *precision* in rebuilding his engine impressed his father.

process (PRAH-ses) (noun) a series of steps or operations needed to bring about an end result. (plural: processes)

>Teaching students to follow a logical thought *process* was the toughest part of teaching computer, as far as Dean was concerned.

>No one had ever really explained to Sanjay how to follow a logical *process*; he understood it without being told.

quintessential (kwin-tu-SEN-shul) (adjective) describes the ideal of its kind; the most representative member of a group; most purely typical.

>Neither Pree nor Sanjay was the *quintessential* student, but they both did well in school.

>Some automobile fans think of the V-8 as the *quintessential* engine: heavy, rugged, and easy to work on.

Usage Issues   *vocation, evocation,* **and** *invocation*

It is easy to mix up these three words since they all come from the same root: *voc-*. This root corresponds to the word *voice* from *vocare*, which means "to call." A *vocation* is "an occupation for which one feels a calling," an *evocation* is "the calling up of a spirit or ghost," and *invocation* is "a prayer or a call for help." So if you are a priest, in your *vocation* you might offer *invocations* to prevent *evocations* of evil spirits.

---

recognize (RE-kig-nize) (verb) to know something or someone again from past experience.

> Pree didn't *recognize* her old friend at the tournament until she heard her name called.

> Sanjay wished universities would *recognize* only his technical talent and not worry about his literature grades.

solidify (su-LID-i-fy) (verb) to make firm or hard; to unite.

> To do well overall in the tournament, Pree knew she had to perform well in forms and *solidify* her lead in weapons.

> Mr. Carrothers liked to have his students work together on projects so, by the end of the term, each class usually had *solidified* into a team.

tactile (TAK-tl) (adjective) something that can be touched; tangible.

> Mr. Carrothers had enjoyed building with stone, brick, and wood because each material had its own *tactile* feel and nature.

> Most forms were done alone, moving through the air. Sanjay preferred the *tactile* sensation of working with a weapon.

unwittingly (un-WI-ting-lee) (adverb) without intention; without awareness.

> In one tournament, Sanjay announced to the judges which form he was going to do and then, *unwittingly*, performed a different one.

> On Pree's day to make lunch, she *unwittingly* put mustard on Sanjay's sandwich and had to listen to him complain for the entire week.

vocation (vo-KAY-shun) (noun) an occupation for which one is particularly well-suited. (plural: vocations)

> Mr. Carrothers had truly taken his computer hobby and made it a *vocation*.

> Pree didn't really know what her *vocation* might be, although she was pretty sure she didn't want to teach karate.

wrestle (RE-sul) (verb) to struggle with someone by grabbing, holding, and trying to bring them down to the floor; to struggle with oneself, as with one's conscience or something that is difficult to do.

> In some types of martial arts, students are taught to *wrestle* or to use other close contact techniques.

> When he first caught the computer bug, Dean *wrestled* with himself about whether or not to go back to school.

Quick Match 8

Match each word to its definition.

1. ____	complex	A.	to make known to a lot of people
2. ____	recognize	B.	to be unwilling to leave a place
3. ____	vocation	C.	to register as a participant
4. ____	dissect	D.	a feeling of irritation or increasing irritation
5. ____	broadcast	E.	something that can be touched; tangible
6. ____	gratification	F.	to tinker with something without a goal
7. ____	linger	G.	sticking with something despite obstacles
8. ____	quintessential	H.	intricate; complicated; interconnected parts
9. ____	elation	I.	to make firm or hard; unite
10. ____	solidify	J.	to come into contact with
11. ____	persistence	K.	a well-suited occupation
12. ____	aggravation	L.	cannot be satisfied
13. ____	unwittingly	M.	rejected; thrown away in the trash
14. ____	fiddle	N.	to know something from past experience
15. ____	dissatisfied	O.	given or allowed with reluctance
16. ____	impetus	P.	to struggle with something or someone
17. ____	process	Q.	a feeling of great joy and pride; jubilance
18. ____	grudgingly	R.	the state of being exact or correct
19. ____	enroll	S.	without intention; without awareness
20. ____	wrestle	T.	to take apart into small pieces to examine
21. ____	discarded	U.	the ideal of its kind; most purely typical
22. ____	tactile	V.	to not fulfill someone's expectations
23. ____	precision	W.	driving force behind something; stimulus
24. ____	insatiable	X.	a feeling of satisfaction
25. ____	encounter	Y.	series of steps needed for an end result

Sentence Completions 8

Choose the proper word or pair of words for each of the sentences below.

1. The newest computer programs have an endless, _____ need for memory.

    (a) tactile   (b) unwitting   (c) complex   (d) insatiable
    (e) grudging

2. Sticking with something is critical to success. One needs to combine practice with _____ to reach one's goals.

    (a) gratification   (b) impetus   (c) elation   (d) vocation
    (e) persistence

3. We are all _____ with our lives at some time or another, but rather than it being a cause for sadness, it should be an encouragement to change things.

    (a) recognized   (b) elated   (c) dissatisfied   (d) solidified
    (e) fiddled

4. It is ironic that the _____ to change Mr. Carrothers's life came from something _____ in the trash.

    (a) impetus . . . discarded   (b) gratification . . . dissatisfied
    (c) persistence . . . fiddled   (d) aggravation . . . broadcast
    (e) precision . . . unwittingly

5. The _____ professionals were the ones who so closely fit their _____ that one couldn't imagine their doing anything else with their lives.

    (a) complex . . . impetus   (b) quintessential . . . vocations
    (c) insatiable . . . processes   (d) tactile . . . encounters
    (e) recognized . . . persistences

Chapter 9: The Favor

What Sanjay did not know was that Mr. Carrothers saw a bit of himself in the boy and his sister. Both Pree and Sanjay were active, *hands-on* learners, as Mr. Carrothers was himself, and he wanted to *hearten* and support these two students as he had not felt supported himself. He *intentionally* gave Pree assignments in computer class that *necessitated* a search through both hardware and software *options* to find a solution. With Sanjay, he *nurtured* his *role* as a *mentor* to keep the boy *engaged* in school. Because of the teacher's *professionalism*, the two never *suspected* that he had *singled* them *out* in his own mind. That was just fine to Mr. Carrothers. He was seeking to *generate* independent learners in his classroom, not a *following* of students who admired him personally.

Pree *materialized* so suddenly in Mr. Carrothers' room Tuesday that it *startled* him. She had a *boon* to beg of him, she said. Mr. Carrothers grinned at her language, knowing it *signaled* that she was going to ask for a *sizable* favor. She, Sanjay, and a few others needed a ride to a local karate competition this Saturday because their usual ride had had to *rescind* his offer due to car trouble. Since Mr. Carrothers had a van that would fit all of them plus their sparring equipment, she had come to *entreat* him to be their ride. Dean was happy to say yes, but he warned Pree that his van was old and *temperamental*. *Jubilant* at having a ride, Pree *acknowledged* the *assent* and forgot all about the *caveat*.

acknowledge (ik-NAH-lij) (verb) to admit or recognize something as true or real.

> Mr. Carrothers enjoyed it when the students seemed to *acknowledge* him as a support in more than just computer class.

> Dean *acknowledged* that he could have found a shorter path to his current profession, and he hoped to save Sanjay from the same sort of trouble.

assent (uh-SENT) 1. (noun) an agreement to something. (plural: This word is not usually used in the plural.); 2. (verb) to agree to something; consent.

> After his *assent*, Dean got a little nervous about his old van and went home to check it thoroughly before Saturday.

> After Mr. Carrothers *assented* to take them on Saturday, Pree was excited that he would finally have a chance to see her and Sanjay do their karate.

boon (BOON) (noun) a favor. [This word isn't used much in daily speech anymore.] (plural: boons)

> As a special *boon* to his late morning class, Mr. Carrothers let them go to lunch a little early one day.

After she related her chat with Mr. Carrothers to her friends, they teased Pree and asked the *boon* of borrowing her notes that night.

caveat (KA-vee-at) (noun) a caution or warning. (plural: caveats)

The karate instructor's daily *caveat* was for the students to carefully protect any sore muscles or joints from further injury.

Pree's mother agreed to let her go to the tournament on Saturday with the *caveat* that Sunday would be taken up with a large school project that Pree had due.

Similar Sounds   *assent* vs. *ascent*

Assent as a verb means "to agree to something," and *ascent* as a noun is the "action of going up or climbing." So, even if you were an experienced mountain climber, you might think twice before you *assent* to an *ascent* of Mount Everest!

---

engaged (en-GAYJD) (adjective) involved or interested in something or someone.

When doing katas, Pree was totally *engaged* in what she was doing and seldom noticed what others around her were up to.

Sanjay was involved and *engaged* in most of his classes, but he still had a little trouble getting excited about literature.

entreat (en-TREET) (verb) to beg for something; to ask for something sincerely.

After someone missed a day of school, he or she would *entreat* Pree for her notes. Everyone knew Pree took great notes in class.

Pree *entreated* Sanjay to help her with a science project.

following (FAH-lu-wing) (noun) a group of people who admire or want to be like another; adherents to a specific cause. (plural: This word is not usually used in the plural.)

Each spring when students registered for fall classes, there was quite a *following* of students who didn't want to take computer science unless it was with Mr. Carrothers.

Karate had a larger *following* at the school than Pree realized. It was just that her friends were particularly uninterested in it.

generate (JE-nu-rayt) (verb) to start or initiate; to begin to produce.

Pree kept trying to *generate* interest in karate with her friends, but Sanjay kept telling her to forget about it.

Sanjay was interested in *generating* all kinds of power, not just power from internal combustion engines.

hands-on (HANDZ-on) (adjective) describes an activity that requires participation.

Of course they looked at the theory of how a computer worked, but Mr. Carrothers preferred *hands-on* activities in which the students replaced hardware in the computers.

Sanjay particularly liked labs in science class because he preferred the *hands-on* application of what he had learned.

hearten (HAR-tn) (verb) to encourage; to build confidence in someone; to support.

Whenever his students got discouraged in class, Mr. Carrothers would try to *hearten* them by emphasizing their successes so far.

Sanjay was amazed that Pree seldom got discouraged in karate. He periodically needed to be *heartened* by his instructor.

intentionally (in-TENCH-unuh-lee) (adverb) on purpose; done deliberately.

Mr. Carrothers would *intentionally* mix easy problems in with the difficult ones to keep his students encouraged.

In competition, Pree *intentionally* chose the most difficult kata she knew because she thought it would earn her more points.

jubilant (JOO-bu-lunt) (adjective) extremely excited and happy about something; joyful.

Sanjay was *jubilant* when he finally finished rebuilding his engine.

The entire household was *jubilant* the first time Pree qualified for a national competition.

materialize (mu-TIR-ee-uh-lize) (verb) to appear suddenly in physical form.

During the chemistry lab, Sanjay saw the desired gas *materialize* before his delighted eyes.

Pree used to worry a lot about serious injuries, but she was careful about small ones and, so far, nothing serious had *materialized*.

mentor (MEN-tor) (noun) an older person or an expert who helps one progress in one's field; a trusted counselor. (plural: mentors)

Pree liked to act as *mentor* to some of the younger girls at her dojo.

Sanjay was beginning to appreciate Mr. Carrothers as a *mentor* even though he wasn't the young man's official school advisor.

necessitate (ni-SE-suh-tayt) (verb) to require; to make unavoidable.

> The driver's car trouble *necessitated* finding another ride.

> Doing well in Mr. Carrothers' class *necessitated* being ready to work—and think—hard.

nurture (NUR-chur) (verb) to gently help to grow and develop; to sustain and nourish.

> Pree had a love of literature and tried to *nurture* it in Sanjay, but she felt that might be a lost cause.

> The best teachers were said to "*nurture* one's love of learning." Sanjay figured the best teachers were the ones that made him do the work.

option (AHP-shun) (noun) an alternative; one choice out of several. (plural: options)

> Pree had the *option* of going to the tournament on Saturday or getting some schoolwork done.

> Sanjay had, for once, finished his weekend work by Friday night so his *options* were the tournament, hanging with friends, or sleeping.

professionalism (pru-FESH-nu-li-zum) (noun) the state of showing one's proper training and development in a particular field through one's actions, knowledge, or standards. (plural: This word is not usually used in the plural.)

> *Professionalism* was just as important to Pree in karate as it was to Mr. Carrothers in teaching.

> The instructor's *professionalism* prevented her from praising Pree too highly, but she was very impressed with the girl's work.

rescind (ri-SIND) (verb) to take back permission that has already been given; to annul.

> The parent hated to *rescind* the offer to drive the students to the tournament but it was uncertain if the vehicle would be repaired in time.

> Pree's mother once had to *rescind* permission for Pree to go to a tournament because her homework had not been completed in time.

Similar Sounds   *rescind* vs. *resend*

If the verb *rescind* means "to take back permission that has already been given" and *resend* as a verb means "to send something again," their meanings are roughly opposite one another despite their similarity in sound. To keep them straight, remember that someone may *rescind* permission to *resend* credit card information a second time over the Internet if she thinks the website concerned may be insecure.

role (ROL) (noun) an unofficial job or position; a part one plays. (plural: roles)

> Although Mr. Carrothers was not Sanjay's official advisor, he did perform that *role* for other students at the school.

> Pree enjoyed her *role* as teacher and helper to the younger girls.

signal (SIG-nl) (verb) to indicate to someone by using gestures or signs.

> When Sanjay was outside working on his engine, Pree just knocked on the window to *signal* to him to come in for supper.

> When Mr. Carrothers looked at his watch in class, the students knew he was *signaling* to them to hurry up.

single (out) (SIN-gul) (verb) to mark someone as special in some way; to show someone as distinct or different from others.

> If Sanjay were to *single out* his least favorite class at school, it would have to be English.

> Pree was embarrassed at school when others *singled* her *out* as someone dangerous because of her karate skills.

sizable (SY-zu-bl) (adjective) a large size or a large amount; big. (Also spelled *sizeable*.)

> By the time everyone on the team packed their sparring gear, there was a *sizable* amount of stuff to go into the van.

> Pree thought it was a *sizable* favor to ask Mr. Carrothers to drive them on the weekend, but he was flattered to be asked to do it.

suspect (sus-PEKT) (verb) to imagine or think that something might be true.

> His students never *suspected* that Mr. Carrothers was a high school dropout.

> While he didn't intentionally hide his past, Mr. Carrothers *suspected* the school administration would be happier if he didn't admit to his students that he himself had hated high school.

temperamental (tem-pru-MEN-tl) (adjective) prone to sudden emotional changes, moody; likely to be unpredictable.

> Everyone gets a little *temperamental* in their teen years, although Sanjay tried hard to cover his bad moods with good attitudes.

> Pree was having a terrible time in class one day with a *temperamental* computer that got caught in a loop and would not shut down properly.

Quick Match 9

Match each word to its definition.

1. ____ boon
2. ____ hands-on
3. ____ jubilant
4. ____ assent
5. ____ nurture
6. ____ professionalism
7. ____ generate
8. ____ rescind
9. ____ single (out)
10. ____ acknowledge
11. ____ sizable
12. ____ temperamental
13. ____ caveat
14. ____ mentor
15. ____ role
16. ____ necessitate
17. ____ materialize
18. ____ following
19. ____ intentionally
20. ____ suspect
21. ____ entreat
22. ____ signal
23. ____ option
24. ____ hearten
25. ____ engage

A. to agree to something; consent
B. showing proper training in a field
C. to start or initiate; to begin to produce
D. on purpose; done deliberately
E. big; a large amount
F. a caution or warning
G. an alternative; one choice of several
H. to imagine something may be true
I. to require; to make unavoidable
J. a favor (archaic)
K. to sustain and nourish
L. a group of people who admire someone
M. to show someone as distinct from others
N. to encourage, to build confidence
O. a trusted counselor
P. to admit or recognize something as true
Q. extremely excited and happy; joyful
R. an unofficial job or position; a part one plays
S. involved or interested in something
T. to take back permission already granted
U. to indicate to someone by gesture or sign
V. describes an activity that requires participation
W. moody; likely to be unpredictable
X. to beg or ask for something sincerely
Y. to appear suddenly in physical form

Sentence Completions 9

Choose the proper word or pair of words for each of the sentences below.

1. Every karate student had to sign a contract that contained the _____ that injuries were likely to happen in this sport.

    (a) option   (b) boon   (c) intention   (d) caveat   (e) signal

2. Pree tried not to act too _____ when she won because she didn't want to make others feel bad. She saved her joy for the drive home.

    (a) engaged   (b) heartened   (c) professional   (d) temperamental   (e) jubilant

3. On next year's schedule, taking Mr. Carrothers' class _____ dropping drama class because of a schedule conflict.

    (a) heartened   (b) rescinded   (c) engaged   (d) necessitated   (e) nurtured

4. For Sanjay, _____ activities _____ more learning than reading and discussion did.

    (a) intentional . . . materialized   (b) sizable . . . suspected
    (c) hands-on . . . generated   (d) jubilant . . . nurtured
    (e) mentored . . . entreated

5. She did not have to _____ him for long before he happily gave his _____.

    (a) entreat . . . assent   (b) nurture . . . boon   (c) suspect . . . following
    (d) acknowledge . . . caveat   (e) hearten . . . option

Chapter 10: Its Result

Early on Saturday morning, Mr. Carrothers phoned Pree with his own favor to ask.

"I know I promised to drive you today," he said, "but one of the teachers' hard drives crashed and I have to get over there and *salvage* what I can. Don't worry, though, my brother will act as *chauffeur* and take care of everything, if that's okay."

Disappointed that Mr. Carrothers wouldn't be along, Pree was, nevertheless, relieved that they could still use the van and greeted his brother *cordially* when she met him at the school. After greeting him as "Mr. Carrothers," the brother shook her hand and *amended*, "The name is Whittaker—half-brothers, you know."

This was the first bit of personal information the group had ever *unearthed* about Mr. Carrothers but it was to be their last, for Mr. Whittaker, as *affable* as he was, was as *taciturn* as they come and no other information was *forthcoming*. He helped them load their gear in the van, made sure everyone was wearing a seatbelt, and drove to the tournament with fewer than ten words said.

This tournament had not been a part of Pree's national competition, so she had been able to *slacken* her nervousness and *revel* in the sport a bit. Totally *spent* at the end of the day, they all piled into the van, tired, sweaty, and *ravenous*. When Mr. Whittaker turned the key, the engine *cranked* and cranked but would not start.

There was a *collective* groan from the *martial* artists *onboard*. Mr. Whittaker was calm but *perplexed*. He ran a *checklist* in his head—plenty of gas, checked the oil—and couldn't *fathom* what he might have missed in preparing for the trip. Not in the least *feckless*, Mr. Carrothers had trusted his brother because he was so thorough. *Forlorn*, Mr. Whittaker opened the hood of the van to gaze *despondently* at an engine he knew nothing about.

He felt someone come and stand beside him.

"Maybe the distributor cap is loose," *conjectured* this voice to his right as a hand reached across the engine and adjusted some *thingamajig* Mr. Whittaker didn't recognize.

"Try it now," called Sanjay to another student in the van.

As the key was turned, the beautiful sound of an engine starting *reverberated* across the parking lot.

affable (A-fu-bl) (adjective) pleasant; easy to get along with.

> Both brothers were *affable* in their own ways, although it was easier to have a real conversation with Mr. Carrothers.

> The team liked the *affable* Mr. Whittaker, but they were disappointed in their attempts to learn more about Mr. Carrothers.

amend (uh-MEND) (verb) to correct; to change for the better.

> After Pree turned in her literature essay, she remembered a paragraph she had meant to *amend* but hadn't.

> After Sanjay managed to find the problem in the engine, Mr. Whittaker *amended* his mood from desperation to relief.

chauffeur (sho-fur) 1. (verb) to drive others in a vehicle. 2. (noun) a driver hired to drive others in a vehicle. (plural: chauffeurs)

> With little confidence because she drove so little, Pree preferred being *chauffeured* to driving herself.

> Sanjay had heard that limousine *chauffeurs* made pretty good money and he thought that might be a good part-time job in college.

checklist (CHEK-list) (noun) a list of items to be remembered or marked off in certain situations. (plural: checklists)

> Mr. Carrothers had run a safety *checklist* on his old van before he gave it to his brother to drive.

> Before every tournament, Pree ran a *checklist* of everything she needed to take so that she had all her gear ready.

Usage Issues   *compound words*

Checklist is an example of a compound noun, a single noun made up of two distinct words that already have meaning. If you have a *list* of items, you may need to be sure everything is there so you may *check* off items on that list to be thorough; a *checklist* is a compound noun that expresses both of these thoughts in a thrifty way. Look for other compound words such as *cutthroat, broadcast,* and *hands-on.*

---

collective (ku-LEK-tiv) (adjective) describes one thing done by a group as a whole.

> Although no one else on the team matched Pree's karate skills, their *collective* talents in art, music, and team sports were pretty impressive.

> It was in everyone's best interest to do well because there were also trophies for a team's *collective* scores at this tournament.

conjecture (kun-JEK-chur) 1. (verb) to reach a conclusion or evaluation on little evidence; to guess. 2. (noun) a guess; a judgment based on slim evidence. (plural: conjectures)

> Sanjay *conjectured* that the problem might be a loose distributor cap because the engine did turn over, it just wouldn't start.

> The team was thrilled with Sanjay's *conjecture*, as well as Sanjay's success.

cordially (KOR-ju-lee) (adverb) warmly and sincerely; politely.

> Mr. Whittaker greeted the students *cordially*, having heard a lot about them from Mr. Carrothers.

Pree did poorly in the sparring that day and *cordially* congratulated the first-place winner.

crank (KRANK) (verb) to start or operate, usually by turning a handle; the action of an engine turning over and starting.

> The term "*crank*" for starting a car engine is probably left over from the early days when one did, indeed, repeatedly turn a handle to start an engine.

> To celebrate, Mr. Carrothers had invited them all over for hand-*cranked*, homemade ice cream after the tournament.

despondently (di-SPAHN-dunt-lee) (adverb) with deep sadness; dejectedly.

> Pree had enjoyed a relaxed tournament for a change and did not react *despondently* at her second-place in sparring.

> When Mr. Whittaker looked so *despondently* at that engine it was mixed with hopelessness, since he had no idea what to do.

fathom (FA-thum) (verb) to understand. (Most often used in the negative.)

> Mr. Whittaker could not *fathom* how a young man like Sanjay could understand an old van like Mr. Carrothers'.

> It was difficult to *fathom* what could be more fun than spending an afternoon at karate with friends and finishing up with homemade ice cream.

feckless (FEK-lus) (adjective) undependable; irresponsible and careless.

> The team had learned that some of the parents were *feckless* in making transportation promises; they couldn't be depended on to keep their word.

> Pree kept a close eye on some of the younger team members who could be *feckless* crossing a parking lot.

forlorn (fur-LORN) (adjective) sad; abandoned and lonely.

> Pree couldn't be too *forlorn* about her second-place finish because she had had such a good time.

> Mr. Carrothers was a little *forlorn* at missing the tournament because he had wanted to watch the competition.

forthcoming (forth-KU-ming) (adjective) coming soon; approaching.

> After a long day of competition, the *forthcoming* ice cream was beginning to seem more important than any trophy.

With a national tournament *forthcoming* in a couple of weeks, it was nice for Pree to be able to relax and practice at the same time.

martial (MAR-shul) (adjective) having to do with war or warriors. [*Martial arts* refer to arts of defense that are also sports, such as karate, aikido, or tae kwon do].

> There were quite a few families who practiced *martial* arts together at Pree and Sanjay's dojo.

> Pree didn't see the sense of having some kind of *martial* computer game when you could really fight (under controlled conditions, of course) during sparring class.

onboard (AHN-BORD) 1. (adjective) describes passengers or cargo in a vehicle; describes being in agreement with someone. 2. (adverb) the state of being in the vehicle or in agreement.

> Pree was nervous to fly to one competition, but once she was *onboard* the airplane, she was fine.

> Mr. Carrothers assigned a large project at the end of the term, but he wasn't sure all of the students were *onboard* with it.

perplexed (pur-PLEKST) (adjective) totally confused or puzzled.

> Pree was *perplexed* when she couldn't find her mouthguard, but then she realized she was looking in someone else's sparring bag.

> Once when Sanjay was totally *perplexed* as he worked on his engine, he took a break to sort out his ideas a bit.

Usage Issues   ***thingamajig* and others**

There is a proud history in English of using created nouns to fill in when we can't remember the name of something—*thingamajig* is just one example of this great tradition! Other words that fill in nicely when the precise noun is lacking are *doohickey, thingamabob,* and *whatchamacallit.* These words often vary according to the part of the country or the world that one lives in. I challenge you to come up with two or three others!

---

ravenous (RA-vu-nus) (adjective) extremely hungry.

> It was foolish to offer to buy enough pizza for a *ravenous* karate team after a tournament—you could go broke!

> Until he was called to dinner, Sanjay didn't always notice how *ravenous* he was when he was deeply involved in a project.

revel (RE-vul) (verb) to enjoy hugely; to take great pleasure in something.

> It had been good for Pree to have a relaxing tournament and *revel* in the pleasure of the activity instead of being anxious about its outcome.

> Sanjay *reveled* in the praise heaped on him by the team on the drive home with Mr. Whittaker.

reverberate (ri-VUR-bu-rayt) (verb) to be repeatedly echoed, as are sound waves.

> The legend of Sanjay's rescue of the team *reverberated* in the culture of the dojo for years to come.

> Sometimes the sound of a car's engine *reverberating* is just noise but, in other cases, it can be music.

salvage (SAL-vij) (verb) to save what can be saved from loss or destruction or from its wreckage.

> After she finished her project on Sunday, Pree managed to *salvage* a little time to talk on the phone with her friends.

> Mr. Carrothers *salvaged* quite a bit of the teacher's lost data but gave the teacher a good-natured lecture about the value of backing up data regularly.

slacken (SLA-kun) (verb) to lessen in intensity; to relax standards a bit; to slow down.

> Pree had learned a pretty good lesson that day: occasionally, it's fine to *slacken* things a bit.

> Sanjay was interested in *slackening* his pace on his literature a bit, but his parents were not as interested in that as he was!

spent (SPENT) (adjective) exhausted.

> Their energy *spent*, the competitors were looking forward to a nice dinner.

> While not completely *spent*, Pree was as ready as the others to go home after the tournament.

taciturn (TA-su-turn) (adjective) describes someone who has little to say; habitually wordless.

> A chatty person doesn't usually know what to say to a *taciturn* person, but generally, saying little is the key to harmony.

> Sanjay's uncle had always been *taciturn*, and the two of them played long, quiet, happy card games together.

thingamajig (THING-uh-muh-jig) (noun) a term used for a thing whose name is unknown or forgotten. [Informal English]

> Mr. Whittaker had heard of a distributor cap but he had no idea what such a *thingamajig* would look like.

> Until he looked them up in the manual, Sanjay didn't know the name of several *thingamajigs* that he had removed from the engine.

unearth (un-URTH) (verb) to dig up or to discover; to uncover something hidden.

> Rather than *unearth* information about Mr. Carrothers, his brother just made him seem even more mysterious.

> During his engine rebuilding, Sanjay found he had *unearthed* a race fanatic in himself as he became more interested in NASCAR.

Quick Match 10

Match each word to its definition.

1. ___	affable	A.	extremely hungry
2. ___	reverberate	B.	to save from loss or destruction
3. ___	martial	C.	warmly and sincerely; politely
4. ___	amend	D.	to lessen in intensity; to slow down
5. ___	spent	E.	with deep sadness; dejectedly
6. ___	chauffeur	F.	pleasant; easy to get along with
7. ___	taciturn	G.	guess; judgment based on slim evidence
8. ___	forthcoming	H.	describes passengers or cargo in a vehicle
9. ___	revel	I.	to understand
10. ___	checklist	J.	to enjoy hugely; to take great pleasure
11. ___	onboard	K.	totally confused or puzzled
12. ___	forlorn	L.	to correct; to change for the better
13. ___	salvage	M.	to be repeatedly echoed
14. ___	collective	N.	to start or operate
15. ___	feckless	O.	exhausted
16. ___	ravenous	P.	to drive others in a vehicle
17. ___	conjecture	Q.	with little to say; habitually wordless
18. ___	unearth	R.	irresponsible and careless
19. ___	despondently	S.	a term for an unknown or forgotten name
20. ___	thingamajig	T.	describes one thing done by a group as a whole
21. ___	cordially	U.	to dig up or discover; to uncover
22. ___	slacken	V.	coming soon; approaching
23. ___	fathom	W.	sad; abandoned and lonely
24. ___	perplexed	X.	a list to be remembered or checked off
25. ___	crank	Y.	having to do with war or warriors

Sentence Completions 10

Choose the proper word or pair of words for each of the sentences below.

1. It was pure _____ on her part, but Pree theorized that she would do better in national tournaments if she relaxed a little more in local ones.

    (a) martial   (b) conjecture   (c) affability   (d) despondence   (e) perplexity

2. There had been times when Sanjay had been really _____ about his losses during karate tournaments, but now he was happy if he felt he had performed well by his own standards.

    (a) despondent   (b) affable   (c) ravenous   (d) cordial   (e) perplexed

3. Her friends teased Pree about her second-place "loss" on Monday, and she had to work hard to _____ her reputation as a martial artist.

    (a) crank   (b) revel   (c) salvage   (d) fathom   (e) slacken

4. Most of the people at the tournament were friendly and _____ so the team found it easy to be _____ with their rivals.

    (a) forlorn . . . collective   (b) affable . . . cordial
    (c) forthcoming . . . reverberate   (d) despondent . . . slacken
    (e) taciturn . . . perplexed

5. The team members who had thought Mr. Whittaker irresponsible and _____ when the van wouldn't start were anxious to _____ their opinions when they found there was a legitimate problem.

    (a) despondent . . . revel   (b) spent . . . unearth   (c) feckless . . . amend
    (d) forlorn . . . fathom   (e) perplexed . . . crank

WRITING ACTIVITY

Machinery Magic

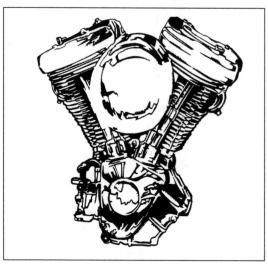

Yes, indeed, this does appear to be an internal combustion engine. All you technophiles out there, I'm sure, recognized it immediately.

Well, this exercise is for YOU. This is for you poor language-phobes who patiently put up with literature and composition classes every day. This is for the scientifically-aware who find the technical world an unusually welcoming and friendly place to be. This, indeed, is the time for all of you mechanically-unchallenged to strut your stuff on the printed page.

The assignment? Create an imaginary, hopefully useful, machine. Using at least ten of this section's words, either explain what this amazing contraption does or how it works. (You may, if you like, describe both.) Indeed, you are also challenged to add a carefully-crafted drawing or three-dimensional model of this marvelous machine to make its description complete.

Ladies and Gentlemen, start your engines!

SECTION 3: AT THE MALL

Learning Style: The Interpersonal Learner

If your motto is "the more, the merrier," one of your primary intelligences is likely that of the **interpersonal learner**.

Are you someone who enjoys spending time with buddies and groups? Are you the one everyone comes to for advice? Are you often the life of the party or the organizer of clubs and committees? Do you learn best by sharing ideas and working on projects in pairs or in groups? Do you seem to have a natural talent for understanding other people and their relationships?

If you have answered "yes" to several of the above, this is one of your stronger intelligences.

Possible Approaches

Your most obvious strength is socializing, so let's put that to work to your advantage. You and a group (this works equally well with partners) should make one set of flashcards using cards of your choice—most students use three-by-five-inch index cards. Write a vocabulary word on one side, and pass the card on to the next member in the group. That person writes your word's part of speech and definition on the other side. Everyone in the group should take part at this stage, doing several words apiece. With four or five in your group, you will all finish this step in just a few minutes. Divide the completed cards evenly among the members of the group. One member at a time should flash a word and read its part of speech and definition. Move on to the next person, who does the same. After the group has reviewed all of the vocabulary cards aloud three times, it is time to drill.

- **Drill 1.** One person flashes a card and says the word aloud. The first group member to correctly give the part of speech and definition of that word goes next. The object of the game is to be the first to use up your own cards. That doesn't put you out of the game or end the game (we are reviewing after all!) but I know it will be a confidence-builder for you.

- **Drill 2.** If you have an even number of people, divide the group into pairs. Do Drill 1 in pairs until you are sure of your cards and then switch cards with another pair. This drill gives you greater repetition in a shorter time than Drill 1. For a final group experience, end the day's review with a round of Drill 1.

- **Variation.** Try color-coding your cards to give yourself an edge in remembering parts of speech. For example, use red index cards for verbs, yellow for adverbs, blue for nouns, and green for adjectives. (Index cards are available in all of these colors.) Alternatively, color-code the words themselves by using different pen or marker colors for different parts of speech on regular white index cards.

- **Around the World.** In this large group or whole-class game, each player is trying to beat every other player on an individual basis. One person at the front of the room holds all the flashcards. The first two players stand and they are flashed a card. The first player to state the correct definition moves to stand beside the next participant; the loser in that first round sits down. Once again, a card is flashed and the first one to state the correct definition moves on to stand beside the next participant. The loser of the round sits down again. If any one participant manages to beat everyone in the group without sitting, he or she is said to have gone "Around the World."

- **Story Building.** In this game, the group as a whole composes a story out loud, with each group member building on the previous member's efforts. One person starts the story and may use several sentences to create a setting or build a mood. Somewhere in their text, they must use a given vocabulary word properly. At a critical point, that student stops the story and passes it on to the next person. This person must continue the story in a logical way (although it can go off in a different direction) and also must use a given vocabulary word properly. At a point of great interest in the story, that student passes the turn on to the next group member. The game ends either when the vocabulary words have all been used, or when each person in the group has had a turn. (Decide ahead of time on the ending point so that the last person can actually tie up the loose ends and finish the story.) The object of the game is to become stronger at using the vocabulary words in an understandable context—and to have fun with the group while learning vocabulary.

Chapter 11: A First Step

Jenna had *misgivings* about interviewing for the job at Corner Candles but she really wanted to earn some of her own money. She didn't know if her *apprehension* came from *consigning* herself to the *workforce* in the first place or from the fact that she would be confined to a *minuscule* shop at an *obscure* end of the mall for hours at a time if she did get the job.

Ms. Torelli was *brisk* and efficient in the interview, *cataloging* the days and hours Jenna would be expected to be at work, the *initial* pay, and her *discount* on store *stock*. Jenna *stammered* her answers to questions about her favorite subjects at school, her *extracurricular* activities, and her work experience (in *actuality*, her lack of work experience). Ms. Torelli stopped and looked at Jenna for a moment, as though *gauging* her *veracity* and her *potential* value as an employee.

"Can you start tomorrow?" Ms. Torelli asked.

"Uh, well," Jenna *stumbled* over her words nervously. "Do I, uh, have the job?"

"If you want it," responded Ms. Torelli *good-naturedly*. "What do you think?"

"I'll be here at ten," *declared* Jenna in a firmer voice.

"Be here at nine," Ms. Torelli instructed. "We open at ten."

That night Jenna could barely sleep, and in the morning she *agonized* over what to wear. She decided on her *trendiest* jeans and a *modest* sweater. She caught an earlier bus than she needed to (just in case) and was waiting *expectantly* outside the store when Ms. Torelli arrived at 8:30 A.M.

Ms. Torelli looked at her approvingly. "An *auspicious* beginning," she grinned at Jenna.

actuality (ak-chu-WA-lu-tee) (noun) the true situation; reality. (plural: actualities)

> Because of her nervousness it seemed like a long time, but in *actuality* it took less than an hour.

> Working in a store might seem boring, but in *actuality* there are plenty of things to do even when customers aren't in the store.

agonize (A-gu-nize) (verb) to worry about something intensely; to suffer great physical or emotional pain.

> Jenna didn't know if she had *agonized* more over the thought of the interview or the reality of going to work.

> It is an exaggeration to say that Jenna actually "*agonized*" over her job but it's not a great exaggeration; she was extremely emotional about it.

apprehension (a-pri-HEN-shun) (noun) a feeling of approaching problems; a feeling of dread or fear of the future. (plural: apprehensions)

> Ms. Torelli had always run her store by herself so she had some *apprehension* about taking on a new employee.

Jenna wasn't nervous about meeting new people in the store because she liked that. Her *apprehension* was that she would not do well operating the cash register.

auspicious (aw-SPI-shus) (adjective) describes good timing for something lucky to happen.

It was *auspicious* that Jenna even heard about the job at Corner Candles. She overheard a friend of her mother's talking about it.

Ms. Torelli had reluctantly decided to hire someone she hadn't particularly liked for the job until Jenna walked in: an *auspicious* moment for Ms. Torelli!

brisk (BRISK) (adjective) energetic and efficient.

Some people found Ms. Torelli's *brisk*, efficient tone of voice a bit rude.

Afraid to be late on her first day, Jenna had walked *briskly* from the bus stop to the store, only to find she was extremely early.

catalog (KA-tu-lahg) [also spelled *catalogue*] 1. (verb) to list, usually in order; 2. (noun) a book or pamphlet that shows a list or collection of things, often for sale. (plural: catalogs, catalogues)

Jenna had *cataloged* a number of good reasons to have a job, but the main reason for her was just to make some money.

Ms. Torelli ordered most of her candles for the store from *catalogs,* but she occasionally went to a day-long candle show for new stock.

consign (kun-SINE) (verb) to give (something or someone) to the permanent care of another or of another institution.

As Jenna was to find out, she could not *consign* her training as a store clerk to a better teacher than Ms. Torelli.

The store kept her so busy that sometimes Ms. Torelli felt she had *consigned* her entire life to its welfare.

declare (di-KLAYR) (verb) to say aloud with great energy or commitment; to say emphatically or with authority.

"I got a job!" Jenna *declared* when she got home that night.

When Ms. Torelli told her friend about Jenna being early the first day, the friend *declared* that Jenna would surely be a great help in the store.

discount (DIS-kount) 1. (noun) an amount of money taken off the price of an item, often for a purchaser buying in large amounts or for an employee. (plural: discounts) 2. (verb) the action of reducing the price of an item.

> Because she was so nervous during the interview, Jenna couldn't remember later what her employee *discount* would be.

> Ms. Torelli occasionally *discounted* items for her friends to buy, but with a small store, she really couldn't afford to do that very often.

expectantly (ik-SPEK-tunt-lee) (adverb) looking ahead to something with pleasure; with anticipation.

> Ms. Torelli looked at Jenna *expectantly* as she nervously tripped over her answers to the interview questions.

> Jenna's mom looked up from her book *expectantly* when Jenna came home, knowing she had had her first job interview.

Usage Issues   *comparatives* **and** *superlatives*

Trendy is an adjective that describes something that is "currently fashionable or stylish." To describe something that is even more stylish right now, one could use the adjective *trendier*, which is referred to as a *comparative* adjective because it compares the trendy item to one that is more trendy. To describe the most fashionable item, though, one would use a *superlative* adjective and call that item the *trendiest* item of the group.

Most adjectives of one or two syllables in English can have the *-ier* ending added to make them comparatives or the *-iest* endings added to make them superlatives, whereas longer adjectives (such as *beautiful*) use *more* and *most* to make comparatives and superlatives. (*More beautiful* is the comparative and *most beautiful* is the superlative.)

---

extracurricular (EK-stru-ku-RI-kyu-lur) (adjective) describes activities outside of classes (usually school-sponsored activities).

> Jenna was very active in the Spanish Club at school, but that *extracurricular* commitment would not interfere with her job.

> When Ms. Torelli was in school, her favorite *extracurricular* activity had been drama.

gauge (GAYJ) (verb) to assess, judge, or evaluate; to measure accurately.

> One of the tricks to running a successful store was trying to *gauge* accurately which candles would sell and which ones would not.

> Ms. Torelli had strong interpersonal skills and she *gauged* a person's character quite accurately after only a short conversation.

good-naturedly (good-NAY-churd-lee) (adverb) in a pleasant, comfortable, cheerful way.

> Jenna got on the wrong bus at first that morning and the bus driver *good-naturedly* let her get off the bus without paying her fare.

> Being so naturally pleasant and cheerful herself, Ms. Torelli was always surprised when someone didn't behave *good-naturedly*.

initial (i-NI-shul) (adjective) first; at the beginning.

> Jenna's *initial* reaction at being hired was disbelief.

> Ms. Torelli's *initial* feeling about Jenna was positive and that only deepened as she spoke to the young woman.

minuscule (MI-nus-kyool) [also spelled *miniscule*] (adjective) very, very small.

> Because her mom insisted on Jenna saving some money, she decided to set aside a *minuscule* amount from each paycheck for that purpose.

> Some people work very hard at finding a first job; Jenna luckily had used only a *minuscule* amount of energy finding hers.

misgivings (mis-GI-vings) (noun) feelings of hesitation; doubts about a course of action. (This word is normally used in the plural.)

> Jenna's mom had some *misgivings* about Jenna taking a job, but she knew her daughter was ready for more responsibility.

> Ms. Torelli had had *misgivings* about the person she interviewed earlier, so she was relieved when Jenna came in.

modest (MAH-dust) (adjective) not flashy or showy; quiet and conventional in manner or dress.

> Ms. Torelli could see that Jenna wasn't one to brag and was *modest* about her grades and personal skills. She liked that.

> Jenna chose that particular *modest* sweater to wear to work because it did not show any bare tummy and it was not too low-cut or tight.

obscure (ab-SKYOOR) (adjective) not easily seen or understood; indistinct.

> Corner Candles was in an *obscure* part of the mall, away from the major department stores and food court.

> While it was very clear to Ms. Torelli, it was *obscure* to Jenna why she had been hired for this job.

potential (pu-TEN-shul) (noun) a value in a person or situation that isn't completed or fulfilled yet. (plural: This word is not usually used in the plural.)

> Ms. Torelli could already see great *potential* in Jenna as an employee.

> The store wasn't doing much business yet, but Ms. Torelli knew that if she could open several small stores, she had the *potential* to do very well.

stammer (STA-mur) (verb) to speak with unplanned pauses or repeated syllables.

> Jenna didn't usually *stammer* but she was very nervous during her interview.

> One of the reasons Ms. Torelli had loved drama so much was that thinking carefully about her lines as an actress had helped her overcome her tendency to *stammer* a bit.

Pieces and Parts   *ver-* and endings

Veracity comes from the Latin *verus* (true) + *–ity* (a suffix in English that makes a word into a noun). Looking at suffixes or word endings is a great way to figure out a word's part of speech in a sentence. For instance, *veracious* is an adjective from the same root word that means "truthful" and we know it is an adjective by its *-ious* ending.

---

stock (STAHK) 1. (noun) a supply of goods, often for a store. (plural: For this meaning, the word is not used in the plural.); 2. (verb) the action of putting those goods on shelves for future sales.

> Since there wasn't room for everything on the shelves, Ms. Torelli had a small room in the back of the store where she kept her excess *stock*.

> After a big mall-wide sale, Ms. Torelli had to stay at the store two hours after closing to *stock* the shelves again. That was when she decided she needed an assistant.

stumble (STUM-bl) (verb) to trip over something and almost fall down; to make a mistake.

> It was important to keep the back room tidy because if one were to *stumble* and fall, one would likely damage some candles.

> When Ms. Torelli first opened her store, she *stumbled* when she made her prices too low and she wasn't making enough money to pay her bills.

trendiest (TREN-dee-est) (adjective) most up-to-date and fashionable. [This is the superlative form of the adjective *trendy*. The comparative form is *trendier*.]

> Jenna knew that there was a brand of jeans that was the *trendiest* by far but she couldn't afford to buy them.

Jenna sometimes had trouble keeping up with which brand of jeans was *trendier* than the other.

veracity (vu-RA-su-tee) (noun) truthfulness. (plural: This word is not usually used in the plural.)

Ms. Torelli had doubted the *veracity* of her previous job applicant, although she could not say exactly why she had had doubts.

It was easy to tease Jenna because she just assumed the *veracity* of everything she was told unless it was proven otherwise.

workforce (WURK-fors) (noun) the collection of all the people in a society (or a particular group) who have paying jobs. (plural: This word is not used in the plural.)

As nervous as she was about joining the *workforce*, Jenna was also very excited about it.

Her mom had joined the *workforce* at fifteen, and has had at least a part-time job ever since.

Quick Match 11

Match each word to its definition.

1. ___ obscure	A.	to suffer great physical or emotional pain
2. ___ discount	B.	to say emphatically or with authority
3. ___ actuality	C.	first, or at the beginning
4. ___ potential	D.	to list, usually in order
5. ___ expectantly	E.	most up-to-date and fashionable
6. ___ agonize	F.	very, very small
7. ___ stammer	G.	a true situation; reality
8. ___ extracurricular	H.	a value that isn't completed or fulfilled yet
9. ___ apprehension	I.	not easily seen or understood; indistinct
10. ___ stock	J.	to give to the permanent care of another
11. ___ gauge	K.	an amount of money taken off a price
12. ___ auspicious	L.	with anticipation
13. ___ stumble	M.	truthfulness
14. ___ good-naturedly	N.	to assess, judge, or evaluate
15. ___ brisk	O.	to trip over something and almost fall down
16. ___ trendiest	P.	quiet and conventional in manner or dress
17. ___ initial	Q.	the people in a group who have paying jobs
18. ___ catalog	R.	in a pleasant, cheerful way
19. ___ veracity	S.	a feeling of dread or fear of the future
20. ___ minuscule	T.	to speak with unplanned pauses
21. ___ consign	U.	energetic and efficient
22. ___ workforce	V.	doubts about a course of action
23. ___ misgivings	W.	a supply of goods, often for a store
24. ___ declare	X.	describes activities outside of class
25. ___ modest	Y.	good timing for something lucky to happen

Sentence Completions 11

Choose the proper word or pair of words for each of the sentences below.

1. Once one _____ oneself to the world of work, one develops a new outlook on different aspects of life, such as taxes and benefits.

    (a) obscures   (b) gauges   (c) agonizes   (d) consigns   (e) discounts

2. Employees are often offered a ten or twenty percent _____ on the price of items sold in the store they work for.

    (a) potential   (b) catalog   (c) discount   (d) modest   (e) stock

3. Sometimes judging the _____ of what someone tells you can be difficult. It is wise to check the facts yourself.

    (a) apprehension   (b) discount   (c) workforce   (d) initial   (e) veracity

4. Jenna felt great _____ about her _____ job in retail.

    (a) potential . . . trendiest   (b) apprehension . . . initial
    (c) misgivings . . . stammer   (d) veracity . . . modest   (e) discount . . . brisk

5. She feared that she might not be doing a good job. In _____ , she was showing great _____ as an employee.

    (a) catalog . . . apprehension   (b) initial . . . obscure
    (c) auspicious . . . modesty   (d) veracity . . . discount
    (e) actuality . . . potential

Chapter 12: In Training

"Today your job is to *survey* the store and *eavesdrop* on my conversations with customers," instructed Ms. Torelli. "I will teach you how to operate the cash register on another day. First you must be able to *maneuver* your way through the stock and our *clientele*."

"Boy, an easy day," Jenna thought *smugly*. "My new boss is really *lax*."

By the end of her first morning, Jenna *regretted* that *innocent* thought. In this tiny shop, it seemed an *eternity* from one hour to the next once she had *scanned* the shelves in a *cursory* way in the morning. Ms. Torelli was busy with all kinds of *random* tasks but Jenna felt she had nothing to do at all. Late in the morning, Ms. Torelli *furnished* Jenna with a feather duster and *directed* her to dust the stock on the shelves. Initially *appreciative* of something to do, Jenna was horribly bored after only ten minutes of moving each *individual* candle out of the way, dusting the shelf, and *restoring* the candles to their previous positions. As she worked her way down the shelves, her movements slowed until they were positively *sluggish*. On the fourth *aisle*, she noticed a little *cast* candle in the shape of a whelk, her favorite seashell. Instantly, it all became clear to her. She wasn't really cleaning these already-spotless shelves; this was Ms. Torelli's way to help her *impress* the stock in the store on her memory.

From then on, Jenna was much more *mindful* of which candles were where as she dusted. When she had finally finished all of the shelves, she went back to *peruse* them in much more detail one more time. Jenna saw now that the candles were divided into *categories* by color on the shelves. She *ascertained* that she was going to need to pay a lot more attention to this kind of detail if she were going to do well at this job.

aisle (I-uhl) (noun) a passageway for people to walk through indoors. In a store, it usually has shelves on either side with items for sale on those shelves. (plural: aisles)

> While Jenna was dusting the shelves in one *aisle*, Ms. Torelli was rearranging the candles in another.

> Corner Candles had six narrow *aisles* with twelve shelves of candles and related items for sale.

appreciative (uh-PREE-shu-tiv) (adjective) showing thanks or gratitude.

> After dusting the store shelves, Jenna was more *appreciative* of the effort it took to keep larger stores clean and tidy.

> Ms. Torelli was *appreciative* of Jenna's careful work in putting candles right back where she got them after dusting.

ascertain (A-sur-TAYN) (verb) to make sure of something, often through looking for evidence.

> Without Jenna's knowledge, Jenna's mother had made quiet inquiries through friends to *ascertain* Ms. Torelli's character.

Watching Jenna on her first day, Ms. Torelli *ascertained* that she would need to keep this young woman busy to keep her happy.

cast (KAST) 1. (adjective) formed by pouring a liquid into a mold and letting it cool and harden into a particular shape. 2. (verb) the action of forming an item from a mold.

Ms. Torelli had all kinds of *cast* candles but Jenna liked the seashell-shaped ones the best.

As a teenager, Ms. Torelli had *cast* her own candles in wet, packed sand.

category (KA-tu-gor-ee) (noun) a grouping of items based on similar characteristics. (plural: categories)

Ms. Torelli kept track of her expenses by different accounts in her book-keeping. Now that she had her first employee, she would have to open a new *category* under "payroll."

Jenna could see that one could arrange the store in different ways: by subject (nature or scents); by color; or by one of several other possible *categories*.

clientele (kly-un-TEL) (noun) the group of people a particular business or service serves. (plural: This word is not used in the plural.)

Ms. Torelli tried to stock candles that her *clientele* would like, not necessarily that she alone would like.

Jenna found in her first few weeks that Ms. Torelli already had a loyal *clientele* who came to the store on a regular basis.

cursory (KUR-su-ree) (adjective) not careful; done quickly and without attention to detail.

Jenna didn't understand at first that a *cursory* look around the store was not enough for her to know the stock well.

Some customers came in, gave a *cursory* glance at the store, and left. Jenna's goal was to try to get some of those people to stay and shop.

direct (di-REKT) (verb) to give orders to someone; to guide in specific ways.

After closing, Ms. Torelli *directed* Jenna to mop the floor before they left.

Ms. Torelli's goal in training Jenna was to guide her in subtle ways so that she didn't have to *direct* her in all things.

eavesdrop (EEVZ-drahp) (verb) to deliberately listen to someone else's private conversation.

> Although it is normally rude to *eavesdrop*, Ms. Torelli encouraged Jenna to secretly listen to her conversations with customers to learn how to deal with them properly.

> One time, Jenna found she was accidentally *eavesdropping* on a private conversation between Ms. Torelli and a friend of hers, so she moved away from them.

Similar Sounds   *aisle*, *I'll* and *isle*

An *aisle*, as we know, is a space for walking and, as well, it is used in the idiom *walk down the aisle* to mean "get married." *I'll* is a contraction of *I will* (*I + will – wi = I'll*). *Isle* is, of course, another word for "island." So if you and the love of your life decide to get married in Tahiti, you could say "*I'll* walk down the *aisle* on a tropical *isle!*"

---

eternity (i-TUR-ni-tee) (noun) a length of time so long that it cannot be measured; a length of time with no beginning and no end. (plural: eternities)

> That first morning seemed like an *eternity* to Jenna but it was only three hours.

> After her third work day, Jenna felt it would take her an *eternity* to learn everything she needed to know to do a good job.

furnish (FUR-nish) (verb) to supply all that is needed (often refers to providing furniture).

> To be hired by Ms. Torelli, Jenna had to *furnish* her with her Social Security number.

> It took Jenna a while to realize that Ms. Torelli was *furnishing* her not only with a feather duster but with a chance to learn about the store's stock.

impress (im-PRES) (verb) to create or produce a clear vision or image of something; to create strong, favorable feelings about someone or something.

> The first time Jenna went to lunch from work, it took her a long time to find the food court. She needed to *impress* that routing in her mind more clearly so that she wouldn't be late getting back to work.

> Jenna was anxious to *impress* Ms. Torelli with her work habits, but she wasn't really sure how to do that yet.

individual (in-du-VIJ-wul) (adjective) separate; apart from others; its own kind.

> Jenna was learning that not only did each candle have its own look, it also had its own *individual* scent.

> Jenna was a little nervous of customers in general, but she usually liked each one on an *individual* basis.

innocent (I-nu-sunt) (adjective) without meanness, evil, or guilt; inexperienced, candid, or honest.

> When she got her first paycheck, Jenna was surprised at the amount of money taken out for the government. Until then, she had been *innocent* of the idea of Social Security taxes.

> One day, Jenna gave a lady too much change and the cash receipts didn't balance at the end of the day. Ms. Torelli forgave her because she knew Jenna was *innocent* of any intentional error.

lax (LAKS) (adjective) without firm standards; not very strict.

> Jenna soon realized that Ms. Torelli was not *lax* at all, but quite strict about doing things properly.

> Jenna found that she had to be careful about not getting *lax* with her homework now that she had a job commitment as well.

maneuver (mu-NOO-ver) (verb) to move strategically in a particular environment, operation, or military action.

> At first, Jenna didn't think it would take much skill to wait on people in a store. After watching Ms. Torelli, she could see how one could kindly and honestly *maneuver* another into buying something.

> It was so tight in the back room, it was tough for two people to *maneuver* back there.

mindful (MYND-ful) (adjective) keeping something in mind; attentive.

> Jenna was *mindful* of Ms. Torelli's example and always tried to speak pleasantly to the customers.

> Ms. Torelli was *mindful* of Jenna's inexperience and tried not to give her too much responsibility too fast.

peruse (pu-ROOS) (verb) to read or look over carefully or with great attention.

> Corner Candles also sold canned heat, used to heat dishes at a buffet table. These had to be handled carefully so Jenna knew she had to *peruse* the instructions before selling any.

One day, Ms. Torelli let Jenna check a shipment and was gratefully amused at how carefully Jenna *perused* the order form and compared it to the candles received.

random (RAN-dum) (adjective) without particular order or pattern; unrelated; not systematic.

Some customers seemed to drop in at *random*, with no interest in candles whatsoever. Jenna found this odd.

At first glance, Jenna felt the candles in the store were *randomly* placed and not in any special order.

Easy Errors   **dropping the final *-e* with *-ing***

Many people have trouble with spelling different forms of familiar words. For instance, the verb *peruse* ends with an *-e*, so if we need to add *-ing*, we must remember to drop that final *-e* and spell the new word *perusing*. This is also true of the words *confuse/confusing*. So when *perusing* your essays for spelling errors, don't *confuse* the final *-e* rule for *-ing*!

---

regret (ri-GRET) (verb) to feel sadness or disappointment for something done (or not done) in the past.

Jenna worked hard because she didn't want to make Ms. Torelli *regret* hiring her.

After two months of work, Jenna saw a pair of shoes she really liked and she *regretted* putting aside so little money in savings from her paychecks so far.

restore (ri-STOR) (verb) to put back into place or to return something to where it belongs; to put something back into its original condition.

At the end of each work day, one of Jenna's jobs was to find candles that customers had moved around and *restore* them to their proper places.

One Saturday morning, Ms. Torelli came to work tired and in a bad mood. In just one hour, though, Jenna's cheerfulness *restored* her own.

scan (SKAN) (verb) to look over quickly for one specific factor, deliberately excluding other details.

Once she knew the stock in the store, Jenna could quickly *scan* for a particular candle that a customer might want.

Jenna found that *scanning* the shelves quickly on her first day didn't particularly help her learn the stock in the store.

sluggish (SLU-gish) (adjective) slow to move; showing little activity or movement.

> Jenna was normally *sluggish* getting out of bed, but she leapt out of bed with great energy her first three weeks on the job.

> Candle sales were *sluggish* in the spring and Ms. Torelli had been a little nervous about adding an employee at that time.

smugly (SMUG-lee) (adverb) doing something in a way that shows one is very satisfied with oneself (sometimes to the point of being insulting); complacently.

> Once when Jenna made a mistake, a customer looked at her and *smugly* said, "See? I knew I was right!"

> At times, Ms. Torelli watched Jenna almost *smugly* because she was so satisfied with her choice of employee.

survey (sur-VAY) (verb) to look over an area and note its special characteristics; to look at carefully; to systematically ask people their opinions and keep data that organizes the information given.

> Jenna didn't realize it that first day, but Ms. Torelli was careful to *survey* and evaluate everything she did.

> Ms. Torelli *surveyed* the stock in the store and realized she needed to order more scented candles.

Quick Match 12

Match each word to its definition.

1. ____	innocent	A.	to make sure of something (with evidence)
2. ____	appreciative	B.	to give orders to someone; to guide
3. ____	smugly	C.	keeping something in mind; attentive
4. ____	direct	D.	showing little activity or movement
5. ____	eternity	E.	to listen to someone's private conversation
6. ____	survey	F.	separate; apart from others; its own kind
7. ____	aisle	G.	the action of forming something from a mold
8. ____	lax	H.	to look over quickly for one particular factor
9. ____	sluggish	I.	to create a clear image of something
10. ____	cast	J.	to look at something and note what's special
11. ____	individual	K.	showing thanks or gratitude
12. ____	mindful	L.	to move strategically
13. ____	scan	M.	to put back in original position or condition
14. ____	eavesdrop	N.	a length of time without beginning or end
15. ____	category	O.	to read or look over with great attention
16. ____	restore	P.	without evil or guilt; inexperienced, candid
17. ____	peruse	Q.	a group of people served by a business
18. ____	ascertain	R.	without particular order or pattern; unrelated
19. ____	regret	S.	to supply all that is needed
20. ____	furnish	T.	an indoor passageway for people
21. ____	cursory	U.	in a self-satisfied (and often insulting) way
22. ____	maneuver	V.	without firm standards; not very strict
23. ____	random	W.	feeling of sadness for something in the past
24. ____	impress	X.	quickly and without attention to detail
25. ____	clientele	Y.	a grouping of items with similarities

Sentence Completions 12

Choose the proper word or pair of words for each of the sentences below.

1. Ms. Torelli was _____ that even pleasant customers could also be shoplifters.

    (a) ascertained   (b) mindful   (c) smug   (d) cursory   (e) individual

2. Sometimes, one might feel manipulated and _____ into buying something one doesn't really want or need.

    (a) regretted   (b) furnished   (c) maneuvered   (d) perused   (e) restored

3. After _____ customers in the mall, researchers found that four out of five customers preferred sales clerks who were very knowledgeable about the stock in their stores.

    (a) surveying   (b) furnishing   (c) restoring   (d) maneuvering
    (e) scanning

4. The _____ in the store covered many different ages and interests so Ms. Torelli had to be careful to _____ the store with a wide variety of candles.

    (a) eternity . . . eavesdrop   (b) individual . . . peruse
    (c) category . . . direct   (d) clientele . . . furnish
    (e) appreciative . . . maneuver

5. Rather than glance at the store's stock in a _____ way, Jenna vowed to _____ it carefully and thoroughly.

    (a) lax . . . maneuver   (b) cursory . . . peruse
    (c) random . . . cast   (d) appreciative . . . furnish   (e) sluggish . . . . direct

Chapter 13: Watching Your Words

By her second week, Jenna was feeling much more *self-assured* and *confident* about her duties. She and Ms. Torelli had *conferred* regarding Jenna's clothes. ("While you do look very *well-groomed*, I need you to look more businesslike. I would like you to wear khakis and loafers instead of jeans and running shoes with your nice sweater and buttoned shirts to work here. Many of my customers are older and feel that jeans—even ones as nice as yours—are unprofessional.") They had also had *numerous* conversations about dealing with customers. Ms. Torelli had praised Jenna's natural *congeniality* and had helped her learn how to steer her more *garrulous* customers away from *aimless* chatter and toward a sale: "Don't *pressure* them, of course, but do try to keep them on track."

Today, Jenna had made a bet with herself to try to sell some less-popular candles. One lady was looking *appraisingly* at a rather ugly red, white, and blue candle that Jenna knew was left over from last summer.

"That is one of our most popular candles," Jenna *avowed*. "We have trouble keeping enough of them in the store for our customers!"

The lady looked around the store some more and *eventually* bought the *patriotic* candle before she left. There was an *abundance* of customers at the time but later, when no one else was in the store, Ms. Torelli asked Jenna to speak with her *discreetly* in the stock room. She asked Jenna about the sale of the red, white, and blue candle.

"Jenna, were you aware that that candle was year-old stock?" Ms. Torelli *posed*. "You told her it was a very popular candle."

"I know," said Jenna proudly. "Because of that she bought the candle."

Ms. Torelli looked *stricken* but spoke in a *measured* voice.

"Jenna, you have a gift for *banter* with people but you must be careful not to let your natural ability fall into *glibness* and *insincerity*. It is never right to lie to a customer, however *innocuous* it may seem at the time. She may very well have bought that candle anyway, but to have the sale *tainted* by a *prevarication* makes me very uncomfortable. I would rather not have a sale at all than to have a dishonest one."

Surprised at first, Jenna thought through the wisdom of what Ms. Torelli was saying. *Chastened*, she promised to stick to the truth from now on.

abundance (a-BUN-dunts) (noun) a large number, plentiful; more than needed. (plural: This word is not usually used in the plural.)

> The store had such an *abundance* of small, white candles that Ms. Torelli put them on sale for half price.

> On Saturday afternoons, they often had an *abundance* of customers and had trouble waiting on everyone fairly.

aimless (AYM-lus) (adjective) without a goal, purpose, or direction.

> With a few minutes left at the end of her lunch break, sometimes Jenna became one of the *aimless* ones, wandering in and out of shops on her way back to work.

> Some of the little old ladies who came into the store lived alone and came to the mall for company. Jenna realized that was why some of them just wanted to chat *aimlessly*.

appraisingly (uh-PRAYZ-ing-lee) (adverb) in a way that calculates the value of something; in a judgmental way.

> Ms. Torelli had looked at Jenna *appraisingly* while trying to decide whether or not to hire her.

> The more Jenna looked around the mall, the more she began to shop *appraisingly*, looking for quality and value in the items she bought.

avow (uh-VOW) (verb) to say with absolute sincerity as true; confess.

> After the sale of the red, white, and blue candle, Jenna *avowed* to herself that she would never again twist the facts to make a sale.

> Later, Jenna *avowed* her guilt in the incident to her mother, who praised Ms. Torelli's delicate handling of the situation.

banter (BAN-tur) 1. (noun) cheerful, good-natured conversation; playful conversation that may include gentle teasing and wit. (plural: This word is not used in the plural.); 2. (verb) the action of playful conversation.

> Jenna gradually became less impatient to make a sale and became more comfortable with the *banter* that came before it with many of the customers.

> One morning, Ms. Torelli and Jenna started *bantering* back and forth about something silly, and they both got the giggles.

Easy Errors   *appraise* vs. *apprise*

As a verb, *appraise* means "to estimate the monetary value of an item." *Apprise*, on the other hand, means "to give someone some information or to let them know something." So, if you took your grandfather's gold pocket watch to a jeweler, that person might *appraise* that watch for you and then *apprise* you of its value.

---

chastened (CHAY-snd) (adjective) knowingly corrected of a wrong, either through language or action.

> *Chastened* by Ms. Torelli's correction of her action, Jenna was a little shy about coming to work the next day.

Ms. Torelli could understand Jenna's discomfort since she remembered feeling *chastened* for something she had done on her first job.

confer (kun-FER) (verb) to talk with one another to compare attitudes or views or to make decisions together; to consult together.

Jenna was late to work one afternoon because she had had to *confer* with her advisor about the next year's courses at school.

After a few weeks of work, Ms. Torelli was *conferring* with Jenna about which new candles she thought should be ordered.

confident (KAHN-fu-dent) (adjective) showing faith in someone or some situation; certain of success in a situation.

Despite their small setback, Ms. Torelli was *confident* of Jenna's ability to succeed in sales.

A little less *confident* after her talk with Ms. Torelli, Jenna was a little more careful in her conversations and a lot more honest.

congeniality (kun-JEE-nee-al-i-tee) (noun) a state of being friendly, pleasant, and easy to get along with. (plural: This word is not usually used in the plural.)

Retail sales seemed a perfect fit for Jenna's natural *congeniality* with others.

After much thought, Ms. Torelli decided that the reason she hadn't liked the earlier candidate for the job was that her *congeniality* had seemed fake, not natural.

discreetly (di-SKREET-lee) (adverb) in a quiet way that doesn't call undue attention to itself; in a restrained fashion; prudently.

Ms. Torelli didn't want to risk embarrassing Jenna in front of a customer, so she talked to her *discreetly* in the back room.

Once, when Jenna thought a customer was going to walk out of the store without paying for a candle, she *discreetly* asked Ms. Torelli how she ought to handle it.

eventually (i-VENT-shwa-lee) (adverb) at an unspecific time in the future.

Eventually, Ms. Torelli hoped to open several candle stores.

Jenna *eventually* came to see her "patriotic candle incident" as a learning experience and gently joked with Ms. Torelli about it.

garrulous (GER-uh-lus) (adjective) describes someone who talks endlessly and excessively, often of trivial matters.

> Jenna soon got pretty good at pulling clues out of some customers' *garrulous* speech and directing them to the right candles.

> One of Jenna's more *garrulous* teachers came into the store one day and started a long conversation with Ms. Torelli about how nice Jenna was.

glibness (GLIB-nus) (noun) the quality of speaking easily and comfortably, sometimes associated with insincerity or deceit. (plural: This word is not used in the plural.)

> Ms. Torelli always thought of "banter" as a positive trait and "*glibness*" as a negative trait, but not everyone agreed with her.

> Some salespeople have a *glibness* that consists mostly of mindless comments they have made up in the past and keep repeating.

innocuous (i-NAH-kyu-wus) (adjective) harmless.

> Some people feel that one "little, white lie" is *innocuous,* but Ms. Torelli looks upon it as the beginning of a dangerous habit.

> For most people, a candle shop is an *innocuous* place. For others with severe allergies, the smells can be very irritating.

insincerity (in-sin-SER-uh-tee) (noun) a state of not being straightforward or totally honest.

> Jenna had taken for granted the *insincerity* of some salespeople, but now she began to see that one didn't have to do business that way to succeed.

> There was not a note of *insincerity* in Jenna's apology, and Ms. Torelli forgave her freely and immediately.

measured (ME-zhurd) (adjective) balanced and unemotional; careful and restrained.

> When the customer began to yell at Jenna for a simple mistake, Ms. Torelli came over and, in *measured* tones, asked the customer to leave.

> Rather than lose her temper with the little boy who had knocked over the display, Jenna asked him in a *measured* way if he would help her put things back.

numerous (NOOM-rus) (adjective) many.

> As they became more comfortable together, there were *numerous* opportunities after the store was locked up for the night for the two to giggle about silly situations that had happened that day.

> Because she was taller than Ms. Torelli, Jenna was asked to reach something on upper shelves so many times that were too *numerous* to mention.

patriotic (PAY-tree-AH-tik) (adjective) marked by pride in, or love of, one's country.

> For national holidays, Ms. Torelli liked to do a window display in *patriotic* colors.

> Jenna had friends at school from other countries who were just as *patriotic* about their own nations as she was about the United States. Their pride in their countries made her want to travel and see these places for herself.

Similar Sounds   *confident* and *confidant*

When you confide your secrets to someone, you have made that person your *confidant* (or *confidante*, if it is a female friend). This is different from "being certain of success" which is a meaning of *confident*. It is true, of course, that you must be *confident* of your friend's good will and ability to keep a secret to make him a *confidant*.

---

pose (POZ) (verb) to offer for consideration.

> Ms. Torelli tried to *pose* the question carefully, not wanting to upset Jenna.

> The more Jenna learned about the retail business, the more questions she *posed* to help her understand everything.

pressure (PRESH-ur) (verb) to try to force or push someone into doing something.

> It used to bother Jenna when a salesperson *pressured* her to buy something, but now she was interested in observing this behavior and learning how to improve her own sales technique.

> Some of her customers disliked being *pressured* into making a decision, but others seemed to like Jenna to lead them gently to a final purchase.

prevarication (pri-ver-uh-KAY-shun) (noun) a lie; something stated that is not truthful. (plural: prevarications)

> Jenna became more careful about little white lies at home, too, preferring not to say anything rather than to give a *prevarication*.

> Any *prevarication* was unacceptable to Ms. Torelli.

self-assured (self-uh-SHURD) (adjective) confident and poised.

> As weeks went past, Jenna became more *self-assured* in the store and Ms. Torelli felt free to take an occasional lunch break in the food court instead of bringing her lunch every day.

> Knowing how to talk to people and run the cash register made Jenna feel more professional and *self-assured* at work.

stricken (STRI-kun) (adjective) overwhelmed by something physically or emotionally unpleasant.

> After telling her mother about Ms. Torelli's disapproval of her, Jenna was *stricken* with remorse and had a good cry about it.

> One of Jenna's favorite customers was a woman who was *stricken* with arthritis. She moved very slowly and feebly but she had a delightful twinkle in her eye and a great sense of humor.

taint (TAYNT) (verb) to make something less pure or less wholesome.

> In Ms. Torelli's opinion, the mall water was *tainted* with too much chlorine so she brought her own bottled water to the store to drink.

> When unpacking new candles one day, Jenna noticed a yellow candle *tainted* with an ugly swirl of red wax so they returned that one to the manufacturer.

well-groomed (wel-GROOMD) (adjective) describes someone who is tidy and clean personally and in dress.

> Most of their customers were *well-groomed*, but one woman always came into the store in sloppy clothes with her hair uncombed.

> One day, a *well-groomed* man came into the store to ask directions and ended up buying three candles from Jenna. She was proud of that sale.

Quick Match 13

Match each word to its definition.

1. ___	numerous	A.	knowingly corrected of a wrong
2. ___	well-groomed	B.	speaking easily and, perhaps, insincerely
3. ___	measured	C.	to make decisions together; to consult
4. ___	aimless	D.	to offer for consideration
5. ___	insincerity	E.	describes someone who talks excessively
6. ___	avow	F.	tidy and clean personally and in dress
7. ___	innocuous	G.	a large number; plentiful; more than needed
8. ___	self-assured	H.	marked by pride in one's country
9. ___	glibness	I.	to make something less pure or wholesome
10. ___	prevarication	J.	harmless
11. ___	garrulous	K.	without a goal, purpose, or direction
12. ___	chastened	L.	being certain of success in a situation
13. ___	eventually	M.	playful, good-natured conversation
14. ___	pose	N.	many
15. ___	discreetly	O.	at an unspecific time in the future
16. ___	patriotic	P.	confident and poised
17. ___	abundance	Q.	to push someone to do something
18. ___	stricken	R.	state of not being totally honest
19. ___	congeniality	S.	as if calculating the value of something
20. ___	confer	T.	overwhelmed by something unpleasant
21. ___	banter	U.	a lie; something untruthful
22. ___	taint	V.	a state of being easy to get along with
23. ___	appraisingly	W.	careful and restrained; balanced
24. ___	pressure	X.	in a restrained fashion; prudently
25. ___	confident	Y.	to say with sincerity as true; confess

Sentence Completions 13

Choose the proper word or pair of words for each of the sentences below.

1. When it was quiet in the store, Ms. Torelli would sometimes _____ various made-up situations to Jenna and ask her what she would do in those cases.

    (a) avow   (b) pressure   (c) taint   (d) confer   (e) pose

2. In some stores, salespeople don't have time for their more _____ customers and cut them off as they are chatting and telling their stories.

    (a) garrulous   (b) chastened   (c) measured   (d) self-assured
    (e) numerous

3. Although it took all day, Ms. Torelli _____ had a chance to show Jenna how to operate the cash register.

    (a) appraisingly   (b) eventually   (c) innocuously   (d) glibly
    (e) avowedly

4. There are _____ occasions in retail for a pleasant clerk to show his or her

    _____.

    (a) abundance . . . glibness   (b) measured . . . pressure
    (c) aimless . . . banter   (d) numerous . . . congeniality
    (e) chastened . . . glibness

5. Because Jenna wanted to be honest with her customers, she did not respect a salesclerk she met whose _____ bordered on _____.

    (a) banter . . . abundance   (b) pressure . . . taint
    (c) glibness . . . insincerity   (d) congeniality . . . confident
    (e) taint . . . innocuous

Chapter 14: Complications

Laughing, the friends sipped their drinks and *savored* their lunch together.

A number of Jenna's friends worked at the mall on the same days she did, but they almost never saw one another because of their *disparate* schedules. By *coincidence*, they all had been given their lunch breaks *concurrently* today.

Two of the girls were talking about an *incident* that had happened with a customer that morning.

"When she came out of the changing room," one of them *chortled*, "she heard us *jabbering* about how *appalling* her taste in clothes was. I guess our comments were pretty *snide* and she just dropped the clothes and dashed out of the store. It was *hilarious*."

The girl saw Jenna's *aghast* expression and added *defensively*, "We didn't mean for her to hear us. We couldn't help it."

Just then, Kwesi came up to the table.

"Hi, guys. Hey, listen," he said to T.J., *indicating* his watch, "aren't you due back at the store now?"

"Yeah, yeah," said T.J. "If I take an extra ten minutes, it's no big deal. We all *vouch* for one another if we're late. You know that."

Kwesi *obstinately* stood by the table looking at T.J. until the *latter* stood up in disgust and *stamped* back to work. Kwesi followed him at a distance.

"What was that all about?" Marissa asked.

"It's pretty *awkward*," explained Shaniece *sotto voce*. "Kwesi got T.J. a job where he is assistant manager. T.J. is *continually* late and sometimes is rude to the customers and their boss. The boss told Kwesi that he is personally *accountable* for T.J. and if T.J. doesn't improve soon, Kwesi will have to fire T.J."

"But they're on the team together!" Jenna said in *dismay*.

"I know," said Shaniece. "I don't know what Kwesi will do."

As she worked around the candles for the rest of the afternoon, Jenna was *preoccupied* with her lunch conversation. Ms. Torelli noticed how *absentminded* she was but didn't say anything to Jenna about it. Ms. Torelli decided that whatever was bothering Jenna would *surface* soon enough if it were any of her business.

absentminded (ab-snt-MYN-dud) (adjective) not paying attention to one's immediate surroundings; distracted by what one is thinking.

> When Jenna was lost in thought, she became *absentminded* and had a tendency to perform the same task over and over again.

> Once, Ms. Torelli *absentmindedly* put her lunch on the display shelf and the candle she was holding in the refrigerator in the back room.

accountable (uh-KOWN-tu-bl) (adjective) responsible.

> Jenna had an individual code on the cash register and she knew she was *accountable* for the accuracy of every sale rung up on her code.

Kwesi knew T.J. wasn't doing a good job and he did, indeed, feel responsible for it. He was worried about their friendship, though, if being *accountable* meant he had to fire his teammate.

aghast (uh-GAST) (adjective) horrified; amazed in a shocked way.

Jenna was *aghast* that her friends might find their own rudeness funny rather than embarrassing.

Ms. Torelli was *aghast* at a parent who decided to change a baby's diaper on an empty shelf of the store. Ms. Torelli offered the customer the restroom at the back of the store for that task.

appalling (uh-PAWL-ing) (adjective) terrible; causing dismay.

The girls might have felt their customer's taste was *appalling*, but Jenna felt it was their behavior that should be described that way.

After several weeks on the job, Jenna found it *appalling* how much stock they lost each week to shoplifters.

awkward (AW-kwurd) (adjective) clumsy; unskillful; difficult to manage.

What the girls hadn't mentioned to Jenna was the *awkward* moment of silence when their customer had come out of the changing room and heard them. They covered their embarrassment with laughter.

Because the stock in the back room was stacked by tiny Ms. Torelli, sometimes Jenna felt *awkward* trying to move around back there.

chortle (CHOR-tl) (verb) to laugh in a way that is sort of a chuckle and a snort together.

Once Jenna thought a customer had made a joke and she was ready to *chortle* out loud when she realized that he was serious.

Ms. Torelli's laughter began with little feminine giggles, but if a situation were really funny, she often *chortled* very noisily.

coincidence (ko-IN-su-dents) (noun) two or more events or circumstances that occur at the same time unexpectedly. (plural: coincidences.)

At first Jenna thought it was just a *coincidence* that she needed a job when Ms. Torelli needed an employee, but she later decided to see it as fate leading her to the perfect first job.

One customer thought it was a great *coincidence* that Jenna went to the same school as her son, but Jenna didn't think so since it was the closest school to the mall.

concurrently (kun-KUR-unt-lee) (adverb) when two or more events happen during the same period of time.

> Some of the students at Jenna's school were taking both high school courses and community college courses *concurrently*.

> Jenna wanted to take her little sister to see a movie at the mall, but the movie was showing *concurrently* with Jenna's working hours.

continually (kun-TIN-yoo-ul-lee) (adverb) over and over again; repeatedly.

> Jenna was so *continually* startled by the mall's public address system that it was becoming a joke between her and Ms. Torelli.

> Jenna was constantly forgetting the sales tax rate on some items in the store and Ms. Torelli had to remind her *continually*.

Easy Errors   ***continually* vs. *continuously***

Continually describes an action that happens over and over again whereas *continuously* describes an action that goes on and on and doesn't stop. So a student may *continually* make low grades if he or she *continuously* misunderstands what the teacher is saying.

---

defensively (di-FEN-siv-lee) (adverb) in a self-protective way; in a manner that excuses oneself from blame.

> The girls reacted *defensively* to Jenna because they knew she was right.

> When some customers were rude to Jenna, she had to resist a tendency to react *defensively*.

dismay (dis-MAY) 1. (noun) a feeling of disappointment or disillusionment; a loss of faith in someone or something. (plural: This word is not used in the plural.); 2. (verb) to become disillusioned or lose enthusiasm.

> Jenna was filled with *dismay* the first time she found that her cash receipts didn't balance at the end of the day.

> Jenna was *dismayed* to find her friends could behave badly and then brag about it.

disparate (di-SPER-ut) (adjective) separate and distinct.

> She hadn't expected them to have such *disparate* points of view about customer service.

> Although they all worked at retail stores, their jobs could be quite *disparate*: some of them worked with customers; others stocked shelves; and still others had management positions.

hilarious (hi-LAYR-ee-us) (adjective) very, very funny.

> Jenna and the customers thought it was *hilarious* when Ms. Torelli laughed so hard that she snorted.

> While it wasn't so *hilarious* to her, Ms. Torelli had to admit that her snorting laugh was pretty funny.

incident (IN-su-dunt) (noun) a minor event or occasion; a happening; an action leading to serious consequences. (plural: incidents)

> While not a huge event, the delivery of her first paycheck was a significant *incident* to Jenna.

> On her way back from lunch one day, Jenna had an *incident* in which someone tried to take her purse from her.

indicate (IN-duh-kayt) (verb) to gesture in a way to show someone something; to point something out to someone.

> Although the husband was still chatting with Ms. Torelli, his wife tried to *indicate* pleasantly that it really was time to go.

> When Jenna said she really liked her job, two of the girls looked at each other and rolled their eyes, *indicating* that they wouldn't feel the same way about selling candles.

jabber (JA-bur) (verb) to talk rapidly about light, unimportant things.

> Some of her customers just *jabbered* on while they paid their bill and Jenna learned to smile and agree without paying much attention to what was said.

> Ms. Torelli and Jenna were careful not to *jabber* to each other while customers were in the store, in case they needed help.

latter (LA-tur) (noun) the last of two people or things. [The first of two people or things is referred to as "the former."] (plural: This word is not used in the plural.)

> Given the choice of chicken or a hamburger for lunch, Ms. Torelli always chose the former and Jenna always chose the *latter*.

> Balancing the cash register and mopping the floor were two jobs that had to be done at the end of each day. Jenna always did the *latter*.

obstinately (AHB-stu-nut-lee) (adverb) stubbornly.

> It wasn't in Kwesi's nature to behave *obstinately*, but he had to push T.J. to do the right thing for his own sake.

One customer *obstinately* refused to believe Jenna when she said they were sold out of an item he wanted and would not leave until Ms. Torelli assured him of the same thing.

preoccupied (pree-AH-kyoo-pyd) (adjective) lost in thought.

Jenna became *preoccupied* with trying to figure out the differences between her friends' school personalities and work personalities.

She was so *preoccupied* with her thoughts, she didn't realize that it was already closing time.

savor (SAY-vur) (verb) to enjoy slowly to prolong the pleasure; to appreciate completely.

Sometimes with work, homework, and school, there was little time to be with friends. Because of that, they really *savored* their chances to sit and talk together.

Ms. Torelli really *savored* the chicken at the Chinese restaurant in the food court and she ordered it whenever she could.

snide (SNYD) (adjective) expressed in a way that looks down on someone else as inferior; mean or malicious.

Sometimes Jenna couldn't help making a *snide* comment about a particularly difficult customer, but she always did it under her breath after the customer had left the store.

The customer the girls had criticized was so humiliated by their *snide* comments that she never shopped in their store again.

Similar Sounds   *incidents* vs. *incidence*

If an *incident* is "a small event or occurrence" then *incidents* (plural) is two or more "small events or occurrences." *Incidence* is very close in meaning but refers to a specific occurrence or frequency of occurrence. All of these words are nouns. So one might say "the *incidence* of negative *incidents* taking place during class is declining" to mean "the rate of small problems in class is lessening."

---

sotto voce (SAH-to VO-chee) (adjective) in a soft, very quiet voice. This is an Italian phrase that we have adopted into English.

Sometimes when making change, it helped Jenna to count it out loud *sotto voce* before she counted it out to the customer.

When Jenna was doing something wrong, Ms. Torelli was quick to correct her kindly, either *sotto voce* or in private in the back room.

stamp (STAMP) (verb) to walk heavily, bringing the feet down with force, usually showing anger.

> The small child began to *stamp* her foot when her babysitter told her not to eat the candy-shaped candle.

> The customer *stamped* out of the store when Jenna said they were out of the requested candle.

surface (SUR-fus) (verb) to come out of hiding; to become obvious to all.

> On days when she was particularly tired from lots of homework the night before, Jenna's emotions would *surface* unexpectedly and Ms. Torelli had to give her longer breaks.

> Ms. Torelli always figured that any problem between two people would eventually *surface* and could be taken care of when it did.

vouch (VOWCH) (verb) to assert; to give support to another's position with personal guarantees.

> Although Jenna couldn't *vouch* for it for sure, she was convinced she lost weight running around on the days when the store was really busy.

> Jenna didn't have any business references when she applied for the job at Corner Candles but she did supply Ms. Torelli with names of several responsible adults who would *vouch* for her.

Quick Match 14

Match each word to its definition.

1. ___	concurrently	A.	responsible
2. ___	obstinately	B.	separate and distinct
3. ___	vouch	C.	to talk quickly of unimportant things
4. ___	chortle	D.	to appreciate completely
5. ___	latter	E.	not paying attention; distracted by thinking
6. ___	surface	F.	events happen in the same period of time
7. ___	awkward	G.	horrified; amazed in a shocked way
8. ___	jabber	H.	in a soft, very quiet voice
9. ___	stamp	I.	the last of two people or things
10. ___	appalling	J.	events happen together unexpectedly
11. ___	indicate	K.	mean or malicious
12. ___	sotto voce	L.	a loss of faith in someone or something
13. ___	aghast	M.	to bring the feet down with force
14. ___	disparate	N.	excusing oneself from blame
15. ___	incident	O.	lost in thought
16. ___	snide	P.	very, very funny
17. ___	absentminded	Q.	terrible; causing dismay
18. ___	coincidence	R.	to support with personal guarantees
19. ___	hilarious	S.	minor event
20. ___	savor	T.	stubbornly
21. ___	dismay	U.	over and over again; repeatedly
22. ___	accountable	V.	to become obvious to all; emerge
23. ___	defensively	W.	a laugh that combines a chuckle and snort
24. ___	preoccupied	X.	to point something out to someone
25. ___	continually	Y.	clumsy; unskillful; difficult to manage

Sentence Completions 14

Choose the proper word or pair of words for each of the sentences below.

1. When asking someone to be a job reference for you, be sure it is someone who will _____ for you in a positive, not a negative, way!

    (a) stamp   (b) indicate   (c) vouch   (d) jabber   (e) savor

2. Sales people are _____ restoring stock to its proper place since customers regularly move stock around as they shop. It is a constant job.

    (a) obstinately   (b) snidely   (c) defensively   (d) awkwardly
    (e) continually

3. Winter season was a time during which lots of people decorated their houses with candles. It was no _____ that Corner Candles did very well during that time of the year.

    (a) incident   (b) dismay   (c) coincidence   (d) sotto voce   (e) aghast

4. Confused and upset, Jenna was both _____ and _____ by her friends' rudeness to customers.

    (a) snide . . . accountable   (b) appalled . . . dismayed
    (c) obstinate . . . aghast   (d) chortled . . . hilarious
    (e) preoccupied . . . awkward

5. Lost in thought, Jenna _____ put someone else's candles in one lady's bag by mistake and was put in the _____ position of having to run out of the store and ask the second lady for the candles back.

    (a) absentmindedly . . . awkward   (b) concurrently . . . disparate
    (c) obstinately . . . snide   (d) continually . . . preoccupied
    (e) defensively . . . appalling

Chapter 15: Some Answers

Jenna swept the hair back from her forehead wearily. After ringing up *myriad* sales today, she was beginning to wear out. Being busy was much more fun than the *tedium* of waiting for customers to come into the store, but she could use a *respite*. She and Ms. Torelli had *collided* twice near the floating candles, and she had *sideswiped* her boss another time trying to get to the cash register through a crowd. After Ms. Torelli had *secured* the door at the end of the day, they both *collapsed* in the back room.

Jenna's *fatigue* made her less *guarded* with her boss, and she began to tell her about some of the things her friends had been saying about working and customers.

"My friends are nice people, Ms. Torelli, really they are," Jenna *affirmed*. "But some of the things they do and say at work are just awful. And, they all say that I could make at least a dollar more per hour if I were working at the department store instead of here, and I just don't know about that. . ." Jenna *trailed* off, afraid she had gone too far.

Ms. Torelli listened *wordlessly* until Jenna had *exhausted* her concerns.

"About your first concern—your friends," began Ms. Torelli. "Many times the *primary* problem is that new employees are not properly trained in how to deal with customers. You and I have spent a lot of time talking about customer service, though, haven't we?"

Jenna nodded.

"Some of your friends work for companies that think they are too busy to train their people *adequately*. The big companies sometimes think it is easier to fire someone who isn't working out and hire someone new than it is to *cultivate* an employee properly. This is, I think, a false *assumption*. I'm sure your friends <u>are</u> nice people—although if I were you I would be careful of the two who *gossiped* so rudely in public about a customer. That seems quite *malicious* to me."

"As to your second concern," Ms. Torelli smiled, "This has been on my mind as well. Last night I went over my sales figures for the last four months since you have been here. There has been a jump in sales in the past two months and I believe some of that increase is due to your *infectious* smile and *spirited* assistance here in the store. Customers like you and want to come back to do business with you. And that is very good for me."

Jenna relaxed the *tension* in her shoulders and nodded slightly.

"I believe a raise should be based *solely* on the work being done, not on what other people make or how long you have been working somewhere. Based on our sales figures and your progress, you do deserve a raise. We are small though, Jenna, and I cannot afford to give you another dollar an hour."

Jenna's smile faded and she began to look *downcast*.

"Don't *despair*!" laughed Ms. Torelli. "There are other possibilities. In exchange for your staying here, I will teach you more about how to run a small business: banking concerns, taxes, ordering products. That way, when you finally do have to leave here, you will be even more valuable to your next employer. As well, I will offer you a three percent *commission* on every sale you make to *augment* your hourly rate. What do you say?"

Jenna *beamed* and stuck out her hand to shake on the deal.

affirm (uh-FURM) (verb) to say something positively or with conviction; to declare to be true.

> Ms. Torelli *affirmed* what Jenna had suspected: she was a very valuable employee.

> Later that week Shaniece *affirmed* to Jenna that T.J. had quit his job.

assumption (uh-SUMP-shun) (noun) a conclusion reached without proof. (plural: assumptions)

> Jenna's *assumption* had been that the only way to be paid was by an hourly rate; she hadn't considered Ms. Torelli's suggestions before.

> Ms. Torelli hadn't realized that Jenna had been talking with her friends about pay. Her *assumption* was that she would surprise Jenna with her offer.

augment (AWG-munt) (verb) to add to something that already exists; to increase in size or quantity.

> To *augment* the candle sales, Ms. Torelli began to stock interesting candle holders to see if that would be profitable.

> To try to *augment* her clientele, Ms. Torelli occasionally donated sets of interesting candles to local school fundraising events.

beam (BEEM) (verb) to smile broadly.

> Jenna knew her mother would *beam* when she explained her new arrangement with Ms. Torelli.

> The customer *beamed* when Jenna found just the right candle for her in the back room.

collapse (ku-LAPS) (verb) to fall in on itself; to cave in; to break down through exhaustion or bad health and be unable to continue.

> The boxes in the back room were stacked in a dangerous way and Jenna decided to rearrange them before they could *collapse*.

> A customer *collapsed* in their store one day. While Jenna called 911, Ms. Torelli used her first aid skills to help the man.

collide (kuh-LYD) (verb) to bump into, usually with force; to have opposite sides come into violent contact.

> Over lunch, Jenna's friends' attitudes toward work tended to *collide* with her own.

Jenna absentmindedly *collided* with a small child as she was walking back to work and she apologized sincerely to both the child and his mother.

commission (kuh-MI-shun) (noun) a bonus added on to one's pay; benefits for work done. (plural: commissions)

Teasingly, Jenna asked her mother for a *commission* for her doing a good job of washing the dishes.

Jenna's mother offered her a hug as *commission* for the successful completion of each dishwashing job at home.

cultivate (KUL-tu-vayt) (verb) to take care of in such a way as to encourage growth; nurture.

Wanting to *cultivate* her friends' skills in sales, Jenna began to offer them bits of Ms. Torelli's advice.

With Jenna doing such a good job in the store, Ms. Torelli now had a little spare time in which to *cultivate* her hobby of watercolor painting.

Easy Errors   ***alright* vs. *all right***

All right is a way of expressing that things are acceptable or just fine. *Alright* is a misspelling and isn't actually an acceptable word in English. So, it isn't *all right* to use *alright* in your writing!

---

despair (di-SPAYR) (noun) a feeling of deep disappointment and hopelessness. (plural: This word is not used in the plural.)

Before she met Jenna, Ms. Torelli did *despair* over finding an employee worth training.

At first, Jenna *despaired* of ever being good at her job.

downcast (DOWN-kast) (adjective) depressed; to look down, often in discouragement.

Kwesi was *downcast* about his problem with T.J.

Ms. Torelli was *downcast* when she first heard the pride in Jenna's voice about the sale of the red, white, and blue candle.

exhaust (ig-ZOST) (verb) to completely use up or wear out; to finish or run out of something.

On Saturdays, Jenna would *exhaust* a lot of her energy just trying to dodge around customers to get to what she needed.

One day Jenna cleaned so thoroughly that she *exhausted* the store's supply of glass cleaner.

fatigue (fu-TEEG) (noun) a state of being extremely weary or tired, either mentally or physically. (plural: This word, defined in this way, is not used in the plural.)

> Ms. Torelli gave Jenna a few days off during exams because Jenna's mental *fatigue* after an exam made her useless in the store.

> Jenna didn't dare sit long in the back room after a busy day at work because once *fatigue* set in, it was tough to drag herself out of the mall to the bus stop.

guarded (GAR-ded) (adjective) careful, restrained.

> Jenna was normally very *guarded* in what she said to adults.

> She was less *guarded* when she was tired, though, and had a tendency to reveal secrets then.

infectious (in-FEK-shus) (adjective) contagious or "catching;" something easily passed on from one person to the next, such as a disease or a smile.

> Ms. Torelli found yawning as *infectious* as smiling and couldn't stop doing either if a customer was yawning or smiling.

> Jenna's good humor was often quiet but was so *infectious* that customers almost couldn't help being in a good mood around her.

malicious (mu-LI-shus) (adjective) with evil or mean intent; with the intention of harming another.

> Jenna loved to gossip with her friends but when the comments began to get *malicious* about someone, she felt uneasy.

> Some customers had a *malicious* desire to upset younger salespeople in stores. When one came to Corner Candles, Ms. Torelli smoothly took over the sale to protect Jenna.

myriad (MEER-ee-ud) (adjective) a large number and/or variety.

> When window shopping in the mall, Jenna was sometimes dazzled by the *myriad* items for sale from around the world.

> Jenna's mother had *myriad* reasons to be thankful for Ms. Torelli's guidance of Jenna.

respite (RES-pit) (noun) a short break from activity or exertion. (plural: respites)

> Her lunch break was meant to be a *respite* from effort, but sometimes waiting in line for food and finding a table to eat at was more work than work itself.

> Ms. Torelli seemed able to get back to work with great energy after only a five-minute *respite*.

secure (si-KYOOR) (verb) to lock; to fasten firmly.

> Ms. Torelli was careful to *secure* the store's doors before she left each night.

> She taught Jenna how to *secure* the roll-down gate at the front of the store, which could be a little tricky to lock.

sideswipe (SYD-swyp) (verb) to bump into someone or something from the side.

> During the Christmas shopping season, Jenna was *sideswiped* so often by hurried shoppers that she began to bring her lunch and eat in the quiet of the back room.

> Ms. Torelli's van was *sideswiped* by a car at high speed on the way to work one day and she was shaken about it for hours.

Word Play   **heteronyms**

Heteronyms are two or more words that are spelled the same but mean different things and are pronounced differently. For example, *minute* (MI-nut) meaning "a specific period of time consisting of sixty seconds" and *minute* (my-NOOT) meaning "very, very small," are heteronyms, as are *bass* (BASS), "a kind of fish," and *bass* (BASE), "a stringed musical instrument." Time yourself and see how many other pairs you can come up with in five minutes. (They are surprisingly addictive once you get started!)

---

solely (SOL-lee) (adverb) only; by oneself or by itself.

> Jenna was *solely* responsible for certain daily duties and she took her responsibility very seriously.

> T.J. wanted to blame Kwesi for his having to leave his job, but he knew the responsibility was *solely* his own.

spirited (SPEER-uh-tud) (adjective) energetic, enthusiastic.

> One evening in the food court, the friends gathered after work to share *spirited* stories about their jobs and fellow workers.

> The customers enjoyed Jenna's *spirited* and upbeat personality.

tedium (TEE-dee-um) (noun) boredom; boredom by reason of length of time or dullness of activity during that time. (plural: This word is not usually used in the plural.)

> On their really slow days, the *tedium* drove both Ms. Torelli and Jenna just about crazy.

> Carefully checking a shipment from a manufacturer had a fair amount of *tedium* to it, but it was very important to be accurate.

tension (TEN-shun) (noun) a state of being stretched tight, as in nerves or muscles; a condition of physical, mental, or emotional strain. (plural: tensions)

> *Tension* once ran high in the store when a customer loudly accused Jenna of giving her less change than she was due.

> There was very little *tension* between Jenna and Ms. Torelli and both women were grateful for that.

trail (off) (TRAYL) (verb) to become quieter and less confident; to gradually dwindle in intensity.

> The chatty customer's story began to *trail off* as she realized she had told it to Jenna and Ms. Torelli before.

> Jenna's words *trailed off* as she realized her mother had fallen asleep in the chair listening to Jenna's work stories.

wordlessly (WURD-lus-lee) (adverb) without comment or verbal reaction; silent.

> After her mother fell asleep, Jenna *wordlessly* covered her with a blanket and went to bed herself.

> Jenna listened *wordlessly*, troubled about how her friends talked about their jobs.

Quick Match 15

Match each word to its definition.

1. ___ commission	A.	to increase in size or quantity; to add to
2. ___ affirm	B.	a feeling of deep hopelessness
3. ___ solely	C.	a conclusion reached without proof
4. ___ cultivate	D.	to bump into from the side
5. ___ assumption	E.	to completely use up or wear out
6. ___ myriad	F.	only; by oneself or by itself
7. ___ spirited	G.	to declare to be true
8. ___ despair	H.	with evil or mean intent
9. ___ augment	I.	to lock or fasten firmly
10. ___ sideswipe	J.	to take care of; to encourage growth
11. ___ downcast	K.	to gradually dwindle in intensity
12. ___ tedium	L.	a short break from activity or exertion
13. ___ exhaust	M.	easily passed on among people
14. ___ beam	N.	depressed; to look down
15. ___ tension	O.	a bonus added to one's pay at work
16. ___ fatigue	P.	energetic, enthusiastic
17. ___ infectious	Q.	to bump into, usually with force
18. ___ wordlessly	R.	careful, restrained
19. ___ malicious	S.	a large number and/or variety
20. ___ collapse	T.	a state of being stretched tight; strain
21. ___ guarded	U.	to smile broadly
22. ___ trail (off)	V.	silent; without comment or verbal reaction
23. ___ respite	W.	a state of being extremely tired or weary
24. ___ collide	X.	boredom by reason of time or dullness
25. ___ secure	Y.	to cave in; to break down with exhaustion

Sentence Completions 15

Choose the proper word or pair of words for each of the sentences below.

1. Ms. Torelli was really nervous about her business at first, but her rising sales and her success with her employee have released a lot of the _____ she was feeling at the beginning.

    (a) commission   (b) tedium   (c) fatigue   (d) tension   (e) respite

2. Ms. Torelli needs to be careful not to _____ her small profit margin by paying Jenna more than she can afford to pay her.

    (a) secure   (b) exhaust   (c) sideswipe   (d) collapse   (e) affirm

3. To _____ her allowance, Jenna had originally intended to tutor other students part-time to make money.

    (a) cultivate   (b) augment   (c) secure   (d) respite   (e) myriad

4. Many salespeople work _____ for _____ and don't actually make any money on an hourly or salary basis at all. This makes their pay quite variable from week to week.

    (a) securely . . . malice   (b) guardedly . . . tension   (c) wordlessly . . . despair
    (d) solely . . . commission   (e) spiritedly . . . respite

5. When _____ hits someone hard it isn't unusual for that person also to feel sad and _____ in their weariness.

    (a) fatigue . . . downcast   (b) despair . . . infectious   (c) tedium . . . spirited
    (d) tension . . . affirmed   (e) respite . . . malicious

WRITING ACTIVITY

The Put-Down Poem

"Why, you %#@# &%&##%!"

Vulgar language. Sigh. What an inelegant way to make your distaste for someone (or that someone's behavior) clear to all within earshot. While some attest that what is lacking in today's North American social order is common courtesy, I contend that what is truly missing is uncommonly-personal (and creative) *discourtesy*!

While I do not intend to encourage anyone to be rude, sometimes a nice, creative put-down on someone else's bad behavior is just the ticket for recovering one's own good humor.

That brings us to the Put-Down Poem, a kind of rant and chant, repetitive poem that tells someone—in creative and specific ways—just how loathsome they are to you. Of course, if you are truly angry with someone, sometimes the Muse won't come to you. But perhaps a little friendly teasing . . .

Here are the ground rules:
- Use no names or clear identifiers that relate to real people.
- Use at least twelve of this section's vocabulary words.
- Your text must make sense.
- It must be clear from the context that you understand the meanings of the words that you use.
- No boring and uncreative profanity or near profanity allowed!

> *Self-assured* of your wit and *congeniality*;
>
> *Aimless* and *insincere* in *actuality*.
>
> I have *misgivings* of your *potential*—
>
> You seem quite inconsequential!

Now, after a bit of deliberation, you should follow your inspiration!

SECTION 4: INTERIORS

Learning Style: The Intrapersonal Learner

If you find that you are very comfortable in your own company, pursuing your own private thoughts, one of your primary intelligences is likely that of the Intrapersonal learner.

Do you find it easier than others to pinpoint or analyze your exact emotions in a particular setting? Do you find it more productive to work on projects by yourself, making your own choices about what direction those projects should take? Are you interested in the well-being of others in your community and the world? Are you willing to explore and work towards solutions to major social problems such as homelessness or injustice? Are you confident in your sense of personal morality? Can you set appropriate goals for yourself and work toward them independently? Are you usually quite confident in your abilities and skills?

If you have answered "yes" to several of the above, this is one of your stronger intelligences.

Possible Approaches

- **Basic Flashcards.** Remember all of those flashcards your teachers have been asking you to make for years for studying vocabulary? You may be one of the few for whom this approach actually works! Take cards of your choice—most students use three-by-five-inch index cards—and write your vocabulary word on one side and its part of speech and definition on the other side (see Variations 1 and 2 below for additional ideas on this stage). Drill yourself on these cards for five to ten minutes each day.

- Variation 1: Try color-coding your cards by part of speech to give yourself an edge in remembering parts of speech. For example, use red index cards for verbs, yellow for adverbs, blue for nouns, and green for adjectives. (Index cards are available in all of these colors.)

- Variation 2: Instead of color-coding your cards, color-code the words themselves. Use different pen or marker colors for different parts of speech on regular white index cards. Be consistent in your color choices from week to week; if red is for verbs the first week, it should be the color for verbs for all of your flashcards from then on.

  - **Bulk Method Drill.** Gather all of your flashcards in a pile for your first and second study sessions. Read the words and guess the definitions on each card and check yourself. When you have finished with all of the cards, shuffle them and read the definitions and guess the words for each card and then check yourself. Remove those cards that you knew well on both runs. For each succeeding study session, run the words both ways and eliminate the words you know well. This will ensure that you spend more time on the words that are harder for you and less time boring yourself with words you already know.

- **Select Method Drill.** Divide the flashcards as evenly as possible into the number of days you have to study them. For instance, if you have twenty-five vocabulary words per week to work on, divide them into five groups of five to study Monday through Friday. Carry that day's vocabulary words with you throughout the day and review them and drill yourself on those words at least five times that day. Go out of your way in conversation, writing, or class discussions to try to use your day's words correctly. By the end of the week, you will be much more familiar with your words than you would have been in one, or even two, hour-long study sessions.

- **Write with Your Words.** Write down stories of deeply personal experiences from your life using vocabulary words. Choose episodes from your life that touch on strong emotions—fear, anger, happiness—for the best retention of the words and their use. (Remember that if you are writing down stories to turn in to your teacher or for your classmates to help you with, don't write about anything so personal that you don't want others to know about it!)

Chapter 16: The Dreaded Group Project

Ms. Mbede once again, with her usual *exuberant zest*, announced a group project for the class to work on. Cynthia's heart sank. The last group project had involved all of the students in the room and *coordinating* everyone's part in it had been, to Cynthia's mind, a *quagmire* of *tangled logistics* and missed opportunities. This current *mission* was at least manageable; they would be working in pairs or *trios* instead of as one large *assembly*. This assignment wouldn't *entail* that much work, Cynthia *reasoned*. She and one lone *accomplice* could take care of it.

She *scouted* the room, looking for some harmless, *inoffensive* partner who wouldn't *impede* her plans for the project. She spotted Mariel, whose eyes were also desperately *roaming* the room. Cynthia wasn't well *acquainted* with Mariel. They had been at the same schools for years but had had few classes together. Suddenly, she felt certain. Cynthia *gesticulated covertly* to Mariel with both an eyebrow and her hand. Mariel seemed to *deliberate* for a moment and nodded gratefully just before Ms. Mbede asked Cynthia whom she might like to work with. With a *sidelong* glance at Mariel checking for *acquiescence*, Cynthia gave Mariel's name. Both girls seemed satisfied.

Ms. Mbede was somewhat *caught off-guard*. She had long thought that Cynthia and Mariel's personalities were well *suited* and had been *confounded* as to why the two girls had not yet formed a friendship. She was encouraged that they would be working together on this project.

accomplice (uh-KAHM-plus) (noun) someone who helps another commit a crime. (The word is now often used more casually to mean someone who helps another commit a particular act.) (plural: accomplices)

> Ms. Mbede was happy to be an *accomplice* in trying to get Mariel and Cynthia to know each other better.

> Cynthia was hoping to find an *accomplice* who would be happy to let her work independently within the group project.

acquainted (uh-KWAYNT-ed) (adjective) familiar with someone or something else.

> The girls were well *acquainted* with what was expected of them in this project.

> Mariel and Cynthia were *acquainted* with each other's best friends, but they just hadn't really had a chance to get to know each other well.

acquiescence (a-kwee-EH-sns) (noun) agreeing with someone passively; agreeing by going along with someone. (plural: This word is not usually used in the plural.)

> Mariel's immediate *acquiescence* showed her relief at finding a suitable partner for the project.

> Cynthia was relieved by Mariel's *acquiescence* since she didn't really want Ms. Mbede to assign her to a large group.

assembly (uh-SEM-blee) (noun) a group of people gathered together for a specific purpose (often for governmental, religious, or educational reasons). (plural: assemblies)

> At the previous all-school *assembly*, Ms. Mbede announced the formation of a new debate team in the school.

> In their hometown, the city government is referred to as the "Municipal *Assembly*," and the mayor is in charge of the group.

catch off-guard (KACH off-GARD) (idiomatic expression) to surprise or startle someone, particularly if that person was prepared for one decision or result and a different one was made.

> Occasionally Ms. Mbede would announce a graded in-class project for that day. This wasn't designed to *catch* students *off-guard*, but to see how well they could think on their feet.

> Mariel was *caught off-guard* that Cynthia wanted to work with her.

confounded (kun-FOWN-dud) (adjective) confused or puzzled.

> Cynthia was usually very strong in math, but she had had a problem in last night's homework that absolutely *confounded* her.

> Generally Cynthia was determined to complete anything she started, and it *confounded* her even more that she actually grew willing to give up on a particular math problem.

coordinate (ko-OR-di-nayt) (verb) to work efficiently and in harmony of effort with others toward a common goal.

> The two girls would need to *coordinate* their efforts to produce a strong report together.

> Mariel liked to *coordinate* her outfits carefully, and her clothes always went together well.

Easy Errors   *discreet* vs. *discrete*

Discreet is an adjective that describes a person who behaves modestly, prudently, and with restraint. *Discrete* is another adjective but it describes something that is separate and distinct from other things. So, the *discreet* babysitter put each *discrete* item back where it belonged before the child's parents came home and found the child had made a mess.

---

covertly (ko-VERT-lee) (adverb) secretly; describes doing something secretly and discreetly, so as not to be discovered by others.

> Some of the students passed notes to one another *covertly* in class as they tried to line up partners.

When Mariel had finished her work in class, she often *covertly* read a novel while pretending to still be looking at her textbook.

deliberate (di-LI-bu-rayt) (verb) to think about a decision deeply and thoroughly before finalizing that decision.

Cynthia liked to *deliberate* carefully about a writing assignment before finally sitting down to key in her first draft.

Ms. Mbede *deliberated* seriously on whether or not she should assign students to groups herself instead of giving them a choice of partners.

entail (in-TAYL) (verb) to have or require as a necessary part or result.

It would *entail* a fair amount of planning to finish this project successfully.

Getting to one's locker and then to the next class in only five minutes *entailed* careful planning and quick feet.

exuberant (ex-OO-ber-unt) (adjective) showing extreme joy or enthusiasm.

Most of the students left Ms. Mbede's class in an *exuberant* mood each day because her own enthusiasm rubbed off on them.

Mariel couldn't figure out how Ms. Mbede could manage to look *exuberant* even on days when the class knew her allergy problems were really bothering her.

gesticulate (je-STI-kyu-layt) (verb) to motion to someone else while speaking, usually with one's hand; to communicate with gestures.

Ms. Mbede would often *gesticulate* wildly in the middle of a class discussion. If she were walking between desks, it was a prudent student who watched out and ducked as her hands enthusiastically waved dangerously close.

Cynthia *gesticulated* to Mariel that she needed to borrow a pen by pretending to write in the air.

impede (im-PEED) (verb) to slow the progress of, or interfere with, someone or some project.

Mariel realized that the homework she had in other classes tonight might *impede* her getting started on this project until tomorrow night.

A partner in a project often *impeded* Cynthia's work since her partner seldom had the same commitment to doing a good job that Cynthia did.

inoffensive (in-uh-FEN-siv) (adjective) harmless; unable to cause insult.

> Cynthia preferred a partner who was *inoffensive* and a little shy and, therefore, easily told what to do. Cynthia wasn't really bossy; she was just precise about things.

> Some students liked to do reports on *inoffensive* topics, but Mariel liked to take a controversial position in an essay and do the research to support it well.

logistics (lu-JIS-tiks) (noun) the details of taking care of or managing an operation or project. (plural: This word is usually used in the plural.)

> It was much easier to manage the *logistics*—meeting times, division of work, personal research—working in pairs than in a large group.

> What the students didn't realize is that Ms. Mbede assigned the original project not for the sake of the finished product but to see exactly how well this group of students could manage the *logistics* of a large, awkward project thoughtfully and creatively.

mission (MI-shun) (noun) a special assignment. [This word usually carries the feeling that there is something important or meaningful about the assignment.] (plural: missions)

> Ms. Mbede made it her *mission* to help her students learn to think for themselves as much as possible.

> Mariel had some strong ideas about this latest project and she decided it was her *mission* to persuade Cynthia to agree with her.

Usage Issues   **number words**

There are a number of words in English to describe numbers of things. For instance, nouns for *two* include *pair, brace, duo, twosome,* or *dyad,* depending on usage; nouns for *three* include *trio, threesome, triad,* and *trilogy.* For the *second* of a list, we can use *secondary* or *secondarily;* for *third,* we can use *tertiary.* It is worth checking a thesaurus to get to know some of the unfamiliar terms for very familiar numbers.

---

quagmire (KWAG-myr) (noun) a bog or swamp; a difficult situation. (plural: quagmires)

> Cynthia had thought of the large project as a *quagmire* because the people in the group seemed so overwhelmed with the idea of the whole thing that they became bogged down in trying to work out the details.

> When she had too much homework to complete in one night, Mariel sometimes felt that she was trapped in a *quagmire* by the weight of the work she was carrying.

reason (REE-zn) (verb) to figure out a problem by using the mind to organize available facts; the action of working out a logical solution to an issue or problem.

> Cynthia hadn't been able to *reason* out that math problem in her homework, but when the teacher put it on the board in class the next day, it made perfect sense to her.

> Mariel *reasoned* that she could finish her part of the project in about five hours' time, including research, if she had Cynthia's full cooperation.

roam (ROM) (verb) to wander without apparent purpose or plan.

> Unlike those of some students, Cynthia's mind did not tend to *roam* while in class but stayed firmly fixed on most of what was going on in the room.

> During study time in class, Ms. Mbede's eyes *roamed* the classroom looking for students who were passing notes instead of studying.

scout (SKOWT) (verb) to search; to look around an area to understand its layout.

> When playing basketball, Cynthia would *scout* the gym quickly to find the best teammate to receive a pass from her.

> Before school had started this year, Mariel had *scouted* the halls for her locker so that she wouldn't be confused on the first day.

sidelong (SYD-long) (adjective) describes looking at someone or something out of the corner of one's eye; sideways.

> With a *sidelong* glance, Ms. Mbede noticed a note moving from the first row of seats to the second.

> One of Cynthia's skills on the basketball court was a quick, *sidelong* look at the person guarding her while still being aware of the location of the ball.

suit (SOOT) (verb) to be an ideal fit for a particular purpose.

> It didn't usually *suit* Cynthia to have a partner but she was hoping things might work out well with Mariel.

> Schoolwork *suited* Mariel and she usually received good grades as a result.

tangle (TANG-gul) (verb) to twist things together in such a way that they become a mess and are difficult to sort out.

> Cynthia's hair used to *tangle* when she was playing basketball so she started to wear it in a shorter cut for convenience.

Some people get *tangled* up with competing homework assignments but Cynthia and Mariel had no trouble keeping all of those things straight.

trio (TREE-oh) (noun) a group of three. (plural: trios)

Mariel played in a chamber music *trio* that she and two friends had put together during music class the year before.

Both Mariel and Cynthia were happier working as a duo than a *trio* despite the fact that it meant a little more work for each of them.

zest (ZEST) (noun) spirited enthusiasm. (plural: This word, defined in this way, is not used in the plural.)

Ms. Mbede had a *zest* for life and for teaching that entertained her students.

Mariel enjoyed it when a student presented an oral report with energy and *zest*, but she herself was always more low-key in front of a crowd.

Quick Match 16

Match each word to its definition.

1. ___ accomplice	A.	confused or puzzled
2. ___ entail	B.	to figure out a problem with logic
3. ___ scout	C.	to think about a decision deeply before deciding
4. ___ acquainted	D.	familiar with someone or something else
5. ___ covertly	E.	a group of three
6. ___ sidelong	F.	a bog or swamp; a difficult situation
7. ___ roam	G.	to work in harmony of effort with others
8. ___ acquiescence	H.	to twist items together, making a mess
9. ___ deliberate	I.	to slow the progress of someone or something
10. ___ reason	J.	someone who helps another commit a crime
11. ___ exuberant	K.	spirited enthusiasm
12. ___ suit	L.	harmless; unable to cause insult
13. ___ assembly	M.	secretly and discreetly
14. ___ impede	N.	to wander without apparent purpose or plan
15. ___ quagmire	O.	to motion to someone while speaking
16. ___ coordinate	P.	a special assignment
17. ___ tangle	Q.	a group of people gathered for a specific purpose
18. ___ inoffensive	R.	showing extreme joy or enthusiasm
19. ___ catch off-guard	S.	the details of managing an operation or project
20. ___ mission	T.	looking at someone from the corner of one's eye
21. ___ trio	U.	agreeing with someone passively
22. ___ gesticulate	V.	to be an ideal fit for a particular purpose
23. ___ logistics	W.	to search; to look around an area
24. ___ zest	X.	to have as a necessary part or result
25. ___ confounded	Y.	to surprise or startle someone with a new result

Sentence Completions 16

Choose the proper word or pair of words for each of the sentences below.

1. In business, when a project is set up and ready to go, all one needs is the supervisor's _____ to set things in motion.

    (a) mission   (b) quagmire   (c) entail   (d) zest   (e) acquiescence

2. Mariel and Cynthia will need to get together to _____ the project and arrange duties and timetables.

    (a) deliberate   (b) suit   (c) coordinate   (d) logistics   (e) impede

3. It was too noisy in the cafeteria to be heard, so instead of calling out, she _____ wildly to get her friend's attention.

    (a) tangled   (b) caught off-guard   (c) acquainted   (d) gesticulated
    (e) reasoned

4. Her eyes _____ the room, looking for a likely _____ to help her in the project.

    (a) scouted . . . mission   (b) roamed . . . accomplice
    (c) confounded . . . entail   (d) suited . . . logistics   (e) impeded . . . assembly

5. Being careful not to look directly at his neighbor, the young man looked _____ at him, _____ checking to see if they were working on the same chapter.

    (a) sidelong . . . covertly   (b) inoffensive . . . exuberantly
    (c) entail . . . assembly   (d) accomplice . . . coordinately
    (e) acquainted . . . acquiescently

Chapter 17: Coming Together

After the bell and before they dashed off to their next classes, the girls *hurriedly* agreed to meet for lunch to *allocate* jobs for the project. From what little she had seen of Cynthia's school work, Mariel *credited* her with standards on *par* with her own, as far as *academics* were concerned. She *fretted* a bit that Cynthia might want to have a lot of meetings to work through various parts of the project. Mariel *favored* taking on a task and working through it independently, without outside help. During some down time in the class before lunch she worked out a *preliminary* plan for a sharp *delineation* of the project's work into two *distinct* sections. She hoped somehow to *persuade* Cynthia to *undertake* one of those parts and leave the other to her.

Mariel was unpacking her lunch as Cynthia set down her tray. They were both a little *discomfited*, not ever really having had a true conversation before. At first they chatted *haltingly*, but as lunch progressed, they felt more and more at ease. Mariel was trying to figure out how to *broach* the subject of how she wanted to divide up the project, when Cynthia, *averting* her eyes in embarrassment, began.

"Mariel, about the project. I sort of, well, usually work alone and I, uh, don't really like having a partner—I don't mean you, I mean ANY partner, if you know what I mean . . ." Cynthia *faltered*, unsure of whether or not she had hurt her new friend's feelings.

What Cynthia hadn't seen was Mariel's delighted nodding in agreement, which became more *vigorous* as Cynthia continued.

"I'm just the same! I hate having a partner!" Mariel said *breathlessly*.

Their eyes *locked*. They both began to *snicker*, and then broke into full laughter.

"I was so worried about hurting your feelings!"

"No, I was worried about hurting yours!"

Once they had *sobered*, Cynthia continued. "However we feel, Ms. Mbede wants us to work together. I guess we need to *apportion* the work in some way that we share the project evenly."

Mariel *triumphantly* pulled out the work plan she had already started; Cynthia looked at her in delight. The two of them spent the last few minutes of lunch sorting out their *respective* jobs for this now-welcome project.

academics (a-kuh-DEM-iks) (noun) a general term that refers to subjects studied in school. (plural: This word is usually used in the plural.)

> Although success in *academics* is of primary importance for college admissions, many colleges want someone who has also participated heavily in sports and school clubs.

> Mariel wasn't worried about her *academics*, but she did have a tendency to skip sports and she knew she should be participating much more.

allocate (A-luh-kayt) (verb) to assign certain tasks according to a plan; to set something aside for a special purpose.

> Although Cynthia *allocated* her own tasks slightly differently from Mariel's initial plan, the work was still evenly divided.

> To give the students a head start on their projects, Ms. Mbede decided to *allocate* a certain amount of class time for them to consult at school.

apportion (uh-POR-shun) (verb) to split tasks or the amount of work that needs to be done among a number of people according to a plan.

> For the earlier large project, Ms. Mbede gave the students the responsibility to *apportion* the work equally among themselves.

> It is tougher to *apportion* work fairly within a group when some people work substantially faster than others. Should one divide the work based on time spent working or on the amount produced?

avert (uh-VERT) (verb) to turn away; to avoid (something).

> Cynthia hoped to *avert* hurting Mariel's feelings.

> Mariel was anxious to *avert* any possibility of a misunderstanding.

breathlessly (BRETH-lus-lee) (adverb) describes feeling so much anticipation or anxiety that one (figuratively) forgets to breathe; unable to take in air properly, gasping.

> When Cynthia tried out for the basketball team, she had waited *breathlessly* to find out if she had made the cut.

> When running late, Mariel sometimes arrived somewhat *breathlessly* since she still had occasional problems with asthma.

broach (BROCH) (verb) to introduce an idea or topic for consideration or discussion.

> Ms. Mbede had wanted to *broach* the subject of Mariel and Cynthia becoming better acquainted with each other.

> Cynthia nervously *broached* the subject of working independently within the project rather than working together.

Similar Sounds   *broach* vs. *brooch*

These two words are pronounced the same way but mean different things. *Broach* is a verb that means "to introduce an idea or topic for consideration or discussion." A *brooch*, however, is "a decorative pin used to fasten layers of clothing together or to act as decoration on clothing." So, a man might *broach* to his family the subject of giving his grandmother's antique *brooch* to his new wife.

credit (KRE-dit) (verb) to acknowledge someone's responsibility for doing something; to trust; to see certain positive character traits in someone.

> Cynthia *credited* Mariel with good sense for the plan she had already written up for them.

> Since the girls worked hard in school, Ms. Mbede *credited* them both with strong work ethics.

delineation (di-li-nee-AY-shun) (noun) the act of showing something in words, pictures, or gestures. (plural: delineations)

> As the girls looked over Mariel's *delineation* of duties for the project, they found a few places to make changes.

> For the display board they wanted to prepare for the project, Cynthia sketched a *delineation* of the layout of the pictures and information.

discomfit (dis-KUM-fut) (verb) to be uncomfortable in a situation; to embarrass.

> The reason Ms. Mbede never approached the girls about forming a friendship was that she did not want to *discomfit* the girls or make them feel self-conscious.

> Even as Cynthia was embarrassed to tell Mariel her feelings, Mariel was trying not to *discomfit* Cynthia for the same reason.

distinct (di-STINKT) (adjective) 1. separate in some way; different from others. 2. clearly seen.

> The girls worked out several *distinct* areas in which they could both work and contribute to the project.

> There was a *distinct* change in both girls' attitudes once Cynthia had made her confession.

falter (FAWL-tur) (verb) to slow down performing an activity through fatigue or doubt; to be unsteady in speech or action.

> Mariel went right to work on the project as soon as she finished her daily homework and only *faltered* when she got too tired to focus her eyes and had to go to bed.

> When Cynthia's stepfather asked her how her day went, she had so much to say that she *faltered*, tripped over her words, and had to start again.

favor (FAY-vur) (verb) 1. to prefer. 2. to support.

> Mariel *favored* using a variety of research tools (including books, articles, and the Internet) because she felt it made for a stronger report.

> After twisting her knee painfully in basketball practice, Cynthia tended to *favor* it for the rest of the week and wore a knee support to protect it.

fret (FRET) (verb) to show one's worry in an agitated way; to be uneasy.

> Mariel didn't *fret* about Cynthia's work habits anymore after they had had lunch together and talked things over.

> Both girls *fretted* a bit about the project even though they were confident they would do well on it.

haltingly (HAWL-ting-lee) (adverb) to do something in fits and starts with moments of hesitation and wavering.

> Mariel's sister asked her about her project, and Mariel explained it to her *haltingly* since she wasn't far enough along to have it all thought out yet.

> When she had to do an oral report in class, Cynthia usually went to the front of the room reluctantly and *haltingly*.

hurriedly (HUR-ud-lee) (adverb) describes doing something in a great rush.

> With the library closing, Cynthia *hurriedly* checked out the books she needed.

> Mariel *hurriedly* gave Cynthia a call from the office supply store to say that she would be glad to pick up the poster board for the project.

lock (LAHK) (verb) to hold something in place; to fasten or secure.

> By the end of their lunch discussion, the girls had *locked* their project jobs in place.

> To think without distraction, Mariel *locked* her eyes on a spot on the table in front of her and didn't speak for a minute.

par (PAHR) (noun) at the same level; equal. (plural: This word is not usually used in the plural.)

> Some people felt their school gave too much homework, but Mariel felt it was on *par* with the other schools in the area.

> Cynthia's excitement was on *par* with Mariel's when Mariel found just the book they needed on a shelf in the school library.

persuade (pur-SWAYD) (verb) to try to convince someone, using a reasonable or an emotional argument, to agree to a new point of view or course of action.

> Cynthia had thought that she was going to have to *persuade* Mariel to work separately on the project.

In the past, Mariel had worked hard to *persuade* Ms. Mbede to give up group projects, but it never worked.

preliminary (pri-LI-muh-NER-ee) (adjective) describes something that happens in the early stages of a process to prepare for the main part of the process; introductory.

With the *preliminary* research done, the girls went home to write up their first drafts of their sections.

The final plan to split the work did not vary too much from the *preliminary* plan that Mariel had presented to Cynthia.

Usage Issues　　　　　　　　　　*disregardless, irregardless* vs. *regardless*

This one is easy because only *regardless* is a proper word in English! *Regardless* means "in spite of," so one might say, "*Regardless* of what was said, I know that job was done well and on time." To add *dis-* or *ir-* as prefixes to this word would make it repetitive and wouldn't be useful.

---

respective (ri-SPEK-tiv) (adjective) describes relating two or more people or skills on an individual basis to other qualities.

Cynthia and Mariel felt that their *respective* skills were writing and researching. (Mariel saw herself as the researcher.)

They felt they could get their *respective* parts finished within about three days, well before the actual due date of the project.

snicker (SNI-kur) (verb) to laugh quietly, often slightly muffled in sound.

Most of the students tried very hard not to *snicker* when someone made an obvious mistake in class.

The first week of school, plenty of students *snickered* at Ms. Mbede's manner; by the second week, they were in love with her energy.

sober (SO-bur) (adjective) quiet, serious, and responsible.

Even though she was very excited about the project, Mariel tried to explain it in a *sober* manner so that her sister understood its importance.

The girls laughed at a typographical error in one of their sources but became *sober* almost immediately when the librarian rushed over.

triumphantly (try-UM-funt-lee) (adverb) in a manner that is openly victorious; rejoicing in being the winner.

When Cynthia announced *triumphantly* to her family that she had made the basketball team, she knew she had a great opportunity ahead of her.

When the school library didn't have a book they needed, Mariel *triumphantly* produced it from the county library.

undertake (un-dur-TAYK) (verb) to take on a particular task oneself.

The introduction to any project is tough to write, but Mariel volunteered to *undertake* that challenge.

Cynthia was unwilling to *undertake* the project until she had thoroughly studied for her history quiz.

vigorous (VI-guh-rus) (adjective) with great strength, force, and/or energy.

With her point of view well supported by research, Mariel launched a *vigorous* argument in favor of change in one part of the project.

Looking at Ms. Mbede's energy today, it was difficult to realize that she had not always been a *vigorous* adult because of serious illness.

Quick Match 17

Match each word to its definition.

1. ___ sober	A.	acknowledge another's responsibility for action
2. ___ apportion	B.	introductory; an early stage of a process
3. ___ triumphantly	C.	subjects studied in school
4. ___ snicker	D.	to show worry in an agitated way; to be uneasy
5. ___ favor	E.	to convince someone of another point of view
6. ___ avert	F.	the act of showing something in words, pictures, or gestures
7. ___ persuade	G.	to laugh quietly, often slightly muffled in sound
8. ___ respective	H.	to set something aside for a special purpose
9. ___ falter	I.	describes relating two or more skills individually to others
10. ___ breathlessly	J.	to prefer; to support
11. ___ hurriedly	K.	to introduce a topic or idea for consideration
12. ___ preliminary	L.	to split tasks among a number of people
13. ___ distinct	M.	quiet, serious, and responsible
14. ___ lock	N.	to be unsteady in speech or action
15. ___ broach	O.	at the same level; equal
16. ___ discomfit	P.	describes doing something with points of hesitation
17. ___ fret	Q.	in an openly-victorious manner
18. ___ undertake	R.	feeling intense anticipation; in a gasping way
19. ___ delineation	S.	to take on a particular task oneself
20. ___ par	T.	describes doing something in a great rush
21. ___ vigorous	U.	to be uncomfortable in a situation; embarrass
22. ___ academics	V.	with great strength, force, and/or energy
23. ___ haltingly	W.	to turn away; to avoid (something)
24. ___ credit	X.	to hold something in place; to fasten or secure
25. ___ allocate	Y.	separate in some way; clearly seen

Sentence Completions 17

Choose the proper word or pair of words for each of the sentences below.

1. Cynthia was hoping to _____ any hurt feelings by expressing herself as carefully as possible.

    (a) allocate   (b) snicker   (c) discomfit   (d) persuade   (e) avert

2. One of the requirements of the project was that the students _____ the work evenly so that each had an equal chance of doing well.

    (a) apportion   (b) breathlessly   (c) fret   (d) favor   (e) avert

3. Their _____ planning meeting went very well and they were certain that their second meeting would go just as well.

    (a) delineation   (b) vigorous   (c) preliminary   (d) respective   (e) sober

4. Although she _____ working independently, she would _____ a group project if it were required.

    (a) favored . . . undertake   (b) allocated . . . falter   (c) fretted . . . apportion
    (d) persuaded . . . lock   (e) averted . . sober

5. Unwilling to _____ her with an embarrassing comment, Cynthia was uncertain how to _____ the subject tactfully.

    (a) persuade . . . falter   (b) favor . . . snicker   (c) discomfit . . . broach
    (d) credit . . . avert   (e) lock . . . undertake

Chapter 18: Three's a Crowd

Only two days into the project, the girls were already *staunch* friends. Not only that, but the work was progressing *expeditiously*; Cynthia had almost finished the "background" section of the report while Mariel was *finalizing* the section on "*opposing* views." They looked to be on target to finish the project almost a week in *anticipation* of the assigned due date. While that may have seemed like *overkill* to some of their friends, both girls liked to keep the *penultimate* week of the term as open as possible for last-minute assignments since the final week was generally reserved for in-class term tests. Neither liked to be rushed or surprised by new projects late in the term.

They were ten minutes into Ms. Mbede's class when Landry walked in, *tardy*, with a note. Ms. Mbede motioned for him to be seated and then turned to Cynthia and Mariel, who were now sitting in *adjacent* seats.

"Cynthia, Mariel, since Landry was absent when the project assignments were made, I would like him to work with you on your project." Expecting no *dispute* from these two particular students, Ms. Mbede slid almost *seamlessly* went back into her lesson.

Mariel was *crestfallen* but Cynthia was *indignant*. It was so unfair! At the end of class she nearly *bounded* to Ms. Mbede's desk while Mariel *inched* forward almost *apologetically*.

"Ms. Mbede, it is so unfair of you to assign Landry to us!" Cynthia exploded.

Ms. Mbede raised an eyebrow and looked steadily at Cynthia. Cynthia *wilted* and began again.

"I'm sorry Ms. Mbede, but it really does seem *unjust*. Mariel and I," Cynthia motioned to the girl finally sliding up behind her, "have almost finished the project already. We have nothing for him to do."

Mariel nodded in agreement. Ms. Mbede was quiet at this *juncture*, thinking. She *sighed* and answered the girls.

"I'm disappointed that you are so *obdurate* about this, Cynthia. Landry is a nice young man and should be very *amenable* to any of your suggestions of what you might like him to do. Everyone else in the class except for you two is working in groups of three; I'm afraid that I cannot *equitably* place him with any one of those groups. Since you are so concerned with fairness yourself, I know you must understand my reasons."

Cynthia did not miss the *undercurrent* of criticism in Ms. Mbede's comment; she knew when she was beaten. *Meekly* agreeing to their new partner, the two girls left the room and walked sadly to their next classes.

adjacent (uh-JAY-snt) (adjective) beside or close to.

> Since Ms. Mbede didn't assign seats in her class, the girls were free to sit next to each other in *adjacent* seats if they wanted to do so.

> The school was *adjacent* to a supermarket so there were always problems with people parking at the supermarket when no spaces were available on campus.

amenable (uh-MEE-nuh-bl) (adjective) willing to take advice; cooperative.

> Ms. Mbede wanted to be *amenable* with the girls but she could see no clear reason why Landry shouldn't work with them.

> Cynthia was usually *amenable* to reasonable change, so even Mariel was surprised at her outburst.

anticipation (an-ti-suh-PAY-shun) (noun) foreseeing something to come; the feeling of expecting or looking forward to something. (plural: This word is not usually used in the plural.)

> The girls were in *anticipation* of finishing the project and moving on to something else when Landry's participation in the group changed everything.

> Landry looked forward in *anticipation* to working with Mariel and Cynthia because he knew they were bright.

apologetically (uh-pah-luh-JE-ti-klee) (adverb) in a manner that accepts blame or guilt; in a manner that shows one is sorry for a wrong one has done.

> Cynthia *apologetically* told the coach that she thought she shouldn't play in this week's game because her knee was still injured from practice.

> When Landry realized that the girls were uncomfortable with a third person in the group, he nodded *apologetically* to them as he left class that day.

bound (BOWND) (verb) to move quickly and cover a lot of ground at once; to leap.

> Although quieter at school, Mariel would *bound* from one topic to another at the dinner table at home.

> As the rest of the team *bounded* up the court during the game, Cynthia watched in disappointment from the bench.

crestfallen (KREST-fahl-lun) (adjective) to be discouraged or disappointed; dejected.

> Cynthia was *crestfallen* as she watched her team lose the game.

> Mariel was *crestfallen* over Landry's participation at first, but as the day went on, she regained her natural good humor.

dispute (di-SPYOOT) (verb) to argue over something; to disagree or debate.

> Although disappointed, the girls could not *dispute* Ms. Mbede's logic in assigning Landry to their group.

> Ms. Mbede was unwilling to *dispute* the matter with Cynthia.

equitably (EH-kwu-tuh-blee) (adverb) equally; done in fairness and without bias.

> With the work already divided *equitably* between them, the girls were unsure of what Landry could do for the project.

> Disappointed in the game's outcome, Cynthia couldn't fault the referee since she had dealt *equitably* with both teams during the game.

expeditiously (ek-spuh-DI-shus-lee) (adverb) done both quickly and efficiently.

> The best solution seemed to be to help Landry know what to do for the project as *expeditiously* as possible.

> Mariel tried to deal with disappointment *expeditiously*, but it usually took Cynthia a little longer to adapt to change.

Pieces and Parts   ex-

Expeditiously has several interesting parts beginning with *ex-* (out of). Next comes *ped* (feet) because the root of this word comes from the idea that feet that are released from restraint or fetters (thus, the *ex-* prefix) are free and quick and speedy. Finally added on are *-ious* (adjective suffix) and *-ly* (adverb suffix). Whew! We end up with an adverb that means "done both quickly and efficiently."

---

finalize (FY-nuh-lyz) (verb) to complete; to put in finished form.

> It seemed important to *finalize* Landry's role in the project as soon as possible.

> Mariel had been about to *finalize* the conclusion of their paper when Ms. Mbede added the new member to the group.

inch (INCH) (verb) to move forward very slowly and/or in small steps.

> Unwilling to be a part of a conflict, Mariel *inched* reluctantly toward Ms. Mbede and Cynthia.

> Until they were sure of each other, Cynthia and Mariel had each *inched* her way toward telling the other about her discomfort with group projects.

indignant (in-DIG-nunt) (adjective) describes a feeling of anger because of something that is not fair or not worthwhile.

> Cynthia became *indignant* immediately, without considering Ms. Mbede's point of view first.

> Occasionally Mariel would become *indignant* over a homework assignment that seemed unnecessary or a waste of her time.

juncture (JUNK-chur) (noun) a point where two or more things are joined together; a particular point in time, especially a particularly important point in time. (plural: junctures)

> The way the girls had the project planned, the *juncture* of their two reports would be difficult to spot.

> At this *juncture*, the girls had almost finished the project.

meekly (MEEK-lee) (adverb) with humility and cooperation.

> Replying to Ms. Mbede *meekly* was Cynthia's way of showing that she hadn't meant to be disrespectful.

> Mariel had nodded *meekly* and silently at Ms. Mbede's words.

obdurate (AHB-duh-rut) (adjective) willfully stubborn and unwilling to change one's mind; stubbornly unrepentant for wrongs one has committed.

> Although usually flexible, Cynthia could be *obdurate* if someone crossed her.

> Mariel needed time to cool off after an argument with her sister, so if her mother intervened too early, Mariel would be *obdurate* and unapologetic.

opposing (uh-POZ-ing) (adjective) describes something that is opposite to another thing or in contrast to it.

> Both girls were firm in their opinions but open-minded enough to listen to *opposing* points of view.

> For the project, Cynthia was in charge of writing about one point of view on the issue, and Mariel was to explain both *opposing* arguments.

overkill (O-vur-kil) (noun) effort or results that are much greater than required; excessive.

> Mariel had a tendency to spend too much time on minor elements of homework and her parents occasionally warned her about the dangers of *overkill* and the stress that can result.

> The girls didn't really consider it *overkill* to be finished with the project early since other projects were also due soon.

penultimate (pi-NUL-tuh-mut) (adjective) second from the last on a list.

> Cynthia had been the *penultimate* person chosen for the team, but she worked hard to make up for any weaknesses she had as a player.

Growing tired of her constant grading, Ms. Mbede was relieved that grading the projects would be the *penultimate* grade she would need for each student for the term.

seamlessly (SEEM-lus-lee) (adverb) describes moving from one activity to the next without a noticeable change; uninterrupted.

Ms. Mbede always had at least two different activities planned for every class, and she glided expertly and *seamlessly* from one to the next.

The girls had decided that if each of them wrote several separate sections of the report, instead of blending in each section, that the report itself would flow more *seamlessly* from section to section.

sigh (SY) (verb) to exhale slowly and deeply in a way that shows deep thought or feeling.

Cynthia watched the first hour of one of her favorite movies, *sighed*, and then shut if off because she knew she had work to finish that night.

Looking at college information, Mariel *sighed*, wondering how one could really know how to choose the right college.

Similar Sounds   *sighs* **and** *size*

When one *sighs*, one exhales slowly and deeply. *Sigh* is also a noun form of this action and *sighs* is its plural. Be careful of spelling with this verb and noun because another noun, *size*, sounds the same as the plural. *Size* is the "physical area or dimensions of an item." So, the *size* of one's *sighs* lets others determine one's mood.

---

staunch (STAWNCH) (adjective) loyal; steadfast.

Mariel had been hesitant about confronting Ms. Mbede but, as a *staunch* ally of Cynthia's, she had to support her friend's position.

It is said that only one's dog is *staunch* and steadfast, but Cynthia noticed how hard it was for Mariel to back her up with Ms. Mbede, and she respected Mariel's loyalty all the more for doing so.

tardy (TAR-dee) (adjective) after the accepted or scheduled time; late.

According to the school office, Landry wasn't really *tardy* since he had a note from his family doctor explaining his absence.

Mariel had a horror of turning in *tardy* work because it would upset her entire homework schedule for the week if she did so.

undercurrent (UN-dur-kur-unt) (noun) an emotion or message that runs underneath (and possibly different from) the direct message being given to someone. (plural: undercurrents)

> Cynthia and Mariel were both very aware of the *undercurrent* of disapproval in Ms. Mbede's voice.

> Skilled as she was at understanding people's emotions, Cynthia found it odd when her brother missed the *undercurrents* in other people's words.

unjust (un-JUST) (adjective) not fair; unequal; biased.

> With a strong sense of fairness, Mariel resented it deeply when she felt that someone was being *unjust*.

> The whole situation was *unjust*, Cynthia decided, but there wasn't much any one of them could do about it.

wilt (WILT) (verb) to droop; to show exhaustion, fatigue, or weakness.

> Ms. Mbede was famous for her "look" when she was displeased, and these two girls were not the first to *wilt* under it.

> If she hadn't had enough water to drink in the twenty-four hours before a game, Cynthia *wilted* when she stumbled off the court at the end.

Quick Match 18

Match each word to its definition.

1. ____ tardy	A.	second from the last on a list
2. ____ finalize	B.	to show exhaustion, fatigue, or weakness
3. ____ juncture	C.	beside or close to
4. ____ seamlessly	D.	to argue over something; to disagree, debate
5. ____ wilt	E.	with humility and cooperation
6. ____ penultimate	F.	a message running underneath another
7. ____ dispute	G.	equally; done in fairness and without bias
8. ____ adjacent	H.	uninterrupted; without noticeable change
9. ____ unjust	I.	to be discouraged or disappointed; dejected
10. ____ expeditiously	J.	a joining point; a particular point in time
11. ____ overkill	K.	willfully stubborn; not repentant
12. ____ amenable	L.	done both quickly and efficiently
13. ____ undercurrent	M.	willing to take advice; cooperative
14. ____ inch	N.	not fair; unequal; biased
15. ____ bound	O.	exhale deeply showing strong feeling
16. ____ obdurate	P.	foreseeing something to come; expectation
17. ____ indignant	Q.	to put into finished form; to complete
18. ____ crestfallen	R.	something opposite or in contrast to another
19. ____ anticipation	S.	in a manner that accepts guilt and is sorry
20. ____ sigh	T.	excessive effort or results
21. ____ opposing	U.	to leap; to move quickly over a lot of ground
22. ____ apologetically	V.	loyal; steadfast
23. ____ meekly	W.	to move very slowly or in small steps
24. ____ equitably	X.	becoming angry over unfairness or unworthiness
25. ____ staunch	Y.	arriving after the scheduled time; late

Sentence Completions 18

Choose the proper word or pair of words for each of the sentences below.

1. Although discouraged and _____ by the change of events, they didn't stop to think about how the third person felt about the situation.

    (a) opposing   (b) apologetic   (c) staunch   (d) crestfallen   (e) seamless

2. Sitting in her _____ class of the day, Cynthia couldn't help wishing that it were the final period and she could be packing up to leave in a few minutes.

    (a) juncture   (b) penultimate   (c) anticipation   (d) adjacent   (e) finalize

3. Being content to work in pairs is not the same as being _____ to working in larger groups.

    (a) crestfallen   (b) indignant   (c) amenable   (d) adjacent   (e) unjust

4. While a decision may seem _____, being inflexible or _____ will not help make it fairer.

    (a) overkill . . . amenable   (b) disputed . . . staunch
    (c) finalized . . . opposing   (d) adjacent . . . tardy   (e) unjust . . . obdurate

5. Once the teacher made a final decision on the matter, Cynthia and Mariel behaved _____ and spoke _____ for challenging the teacher.

    (a) crestfallen . . . indignantly   (b) meekly . . . apologetically
    (c) expeditiously . . . unjustly   (d) obdurate . . . staunchly
    (e) tardy . . . equitably

Chapter 19: Disconnections

Lunch that day was a *gloomy* affair, with Cynthia *fuming* and Mariel looking *woebegone*. Landry tried to join them after they had all eaten, but the girls spoke to him so *icily* that he *retreated* to his original table to finish his drink and chat with his friends.

It wasn't until the end of the school day that the two of them felt *remorseful* about their *callous* treatment of Landry.

"It may be unfair for him to be thrust upon us, but I guess we shouldn't have been that rude." Cynthia admitted *reluctantly*.

"Yes, yes," Mariel agreed *wholeheartedly*, "I have felt bad about it all day. I had been thinking about calling him tonight to discuss the project but I wanted to make sure that was fine with you before I did."

With everything now out in the open, the girls *reconsidered* their project and found a few gaps in their work where they felt Landry could *contribute* without upsetting their *overall* plan. Mariel was sure that she could *settle* everything that night.

By morning, Mariel was sure she could never settle anything with Landry—ever!

"He was impossible!" she *sputtered* to Cynthia, who was amazed to see Mariel's temper for the first time. "No matter what I said, he disagreed with me or *contradicted* me!"

This *contentious characterization* did not seem to fit with Cynthia's knowledge of Landry as a pleasant, easy-going person.

"Look," she *soothed*, "he and I have a study hall together. I'll tell Ms. Jenkins that we need to consult on a project. I'll have a talk with him."

"Good luck!" said Mariel *testily*. "It's not as easy as you think."

After study hall, Cynthia truly *identified* with Mariel's frustration.

"It's not so much that he is *recalcitrant*," complained Cynthia, "but that he never listens. He wanted to *alter* every topic we set aside for him and go off in all kinds of directions that wouldn't fit our project at all! Besides that, he wants to work in *conjunction* with me on my part and I don't want him messing it up. I don't see how we can make this work at all!"

Unbeknownst to the two girls, the object of their anger was just around the corner at his own locker. After hearing their joint *tirade*, he quietly slipped out the side door of the hall.

alter (AWL-ter) (verb) to change.

> It would be very difficult to *alter* the direction of the project at this late date.

> Landry *altered* some of their ideas to fit his own.

callous (KA-lus) (adjective) tactless or unfeeling in behavior or speech toward another or others.

> With their strong sense of justice, the girls regretted their *callous* attitude toward Landry.

It wasn't Ms. Mbede's intention to be *callous*, but she hadn't appreciated the girls' objection to having another partner.

characterization (ker-ik-tuh-ruh-ZAY-shun) (noun) the description of a person's personality or behavior. (plural: characterizations)

Cynthia's *characterization* of Landry as pleasant and easy-going was absolutely accurate.

When Mariel gave herself an honest *characterization*, she had to admit that she could be a little impatient with other people at times.

conjunction (kun-JUNK-shun) (noun) a joining of two items; "in conjunction" refers to doing something together as a joint effort. (plural: conjunctions)

The *conjunction* of Mariel's sections with Cynthia's sections of the project on the due date would have been very smooth.

Landry liked bouncing ideas off a partner when working on a project, so he thought that working in *conjunction* with Cynthia on a section would not only be fun but also more productive.

contentious (kun-TEN-shus) (adjective) quarrelsome; argumentative.

Neither of the girls was naturally *contentious* and preferred to find a calm solution to most problems.

Ironically, Landry was far from *contentious* himself but enjoyed brainstorming multiple ideas before settling on an approach to a project.

Similar Sounds   *alter* vs. *altar*

Alter is a verb that means "to change" and *altar* is a noun that means "a structure upon which or in front of which religious ceremonies are held." Therefore, it would be correct to say "to *alter* the *altar* would interfere greatly with any religious ceremony."

---

contradict (kahn-truh-DIKT) (verb) to argue against another's point of view or argument.

Cynthia didn't want to *contradict* her new friend, but she could not imagine that Landry had been as difficult as Mariel said.

Landry hadn't *contradicted* Mariel but had just been offering other suggestions for the project.

contribute (kun-TRI-byoot) (verb) to put effort or resources toward a joint endeavor or project.

> Landry was eager to *contribute* to the project.

> Cynthia and Mariel had already *contributed* so much to the project that it looked like a lot of unnecessary work to make major changes now.

fume (FYOOM) (verb) to feel or show anger or frustration. (Often, "to fume" is to feel more anger than is being shown on the surface.)

> Mariel continued to *fume* all through the rest of her homework that night after having spoken to Landry on the phone.

> Despite his upbeat nature, Landry *fumed* a bit that night, too, frustrated with what he saw as Mariel's inflexibility.

gloomy (GLOO-mee) (adjective) dark, dreary, sad, depressed.

> Cynthia's mood was *gloomy* as she thought over the changes she might have to make in her work.

> Mariel's *gloomy* mood affected everyone in her family, so they all decided to go to bed early to escape her negative attitude.

icily (EYE-si-lee) (adverb) without warmth; chillingly.

> When Mariel's sister asked for help with her math homework that night, Mariel *icily* replied that she had her own work to do.

> It was unusual for Cynthia to behave *icily* to someone since she was usually much more direct in expressing her feelings.

identify (eye-DEN-tuh-fy) (verb) to feel a strong connection or empathy with another person or character and his or her experiences.

> Landry could *identify* with all those male characters in movies who never seem to know exactly why women are upset with them.

> After trying to understand Landry's work style herself, Cynthia could *identify* with Mariel's irritation.

overall (O-vur-awl) (adjective) describes something as a whole, including all of its major characteristics and/or factors.

> If the girls had looked at the *overall* situation, they might have realized that they were making too much of a relatively small problem.

> Landry was frustrated with the project *overall* because he wasn't sure how he was supposed to work with reluctant partners.

recalcitrant (ri-KAL-suh-trunt) (adjective) stubborn; unwilling to cooperate with authority or unwilling to accept advice.

> If Landry were to describe himself, he would never have seen himself as stubborn or *recalcitrant*.

> Cynthia's outburst to Ms. Mbede was the teacher's first clue that Cynthia could be *recalcitrant* if challenged.

reconsider (ree-kun-SI-dur) (verb) to think about an issue or question again because the possibility exists that one might change one's mind.

> Ms. Mbede was hoping the girls would *reconsider* their resistance to Landry's participation.

> Landry *reconsidered* his own position in the project and came up with a plan for himself.

reluctantly (ri-LUK-tunt-lee) (adverb) unwillingly; without enthusiasm; with a resistant attitude.

> Landry *reluctantly* told his folks about his problems with the project when they asked him about it.

> When Cynthia awoke in the night and thought about the situation, she had to admit to herself, *reluctantly*, that she and Mariel were being a bit unreasonable.

remorseful (ri-MORS-ful) (adjective) with great regret for one's previous actions.

> As *remorseful* as Mariel felt about her fit of temper, she justified it by remembering Landry's lack of cooperation.

> In the light of day, Cynthia was less *remorseful* than she had been in the middle of the night.

retreat (ri-TREET) (verb) to leave, particularly to pull back from a dangerous or unpleasant situation.

> Rather than confront the girls at their lockers, Landry decided to *retreat* silently to think things over.

> When Ms. Mbede answered Cynthia's challenge, Cynthia *retreated*.

settle (SE-tl) (verb) to solve a problem in a way in which both parties agree to the solution.

> It was becoming increasingly difficult to *settle* the situation.

> Because the two girls worked in similar ways, it had not been difficult for them to *settle* how to do the project together.

soothe (SOOTH) (verb) to calm; to ease pain or bring relief.

> Mariel's mother helped *soothe* her daughter by chatting with her while they did the dishes together.

> Ms. Mbede would have been happy to help *soothe* the situation if anyone had let her know what was going on.

Easy Errors   *callus* vs. *callous*

Callus is a noun that names the tough, hard skin that develops, often on one's hands or feet, because of repeated use of the same spot; it is a kind of protection that the body builds to toughen the overused skin. *Callous*, however, is an adjective that describes "tactless or unfeeling behavior or speech toward another." *Callous* can also describe the condition of having calluses on the body, but it is an adjective, not a noun. So, if people are rude and *callous* toward you, your heart may form a hardened *callus* to protect you from further emotional pain.

---

sputter (SPU-tur) (verb) to spit out words, usually in excitement, anger, or frustration.

> When Mariel's mother wondered aloud if the girls were being a bit unreasonable, Mariel *sputtered* with indignation.

> While he hardly *sputtered* with excitement, Landry had been very pleased at first at being assigned to two intelligent and hardworking partners for this project.

testily (TES-tuh-lee) (adverb) with irritation or impatience.

> When his parents pressed him for details, Landry replied *testily* that he could handle it himself.

> Mariel was sorry for answering her sister so *testily* and later went to her and asked about the math problem.

tirade (TY-rayd) (noun) a long, angry speech. (plural: tirades)

> If the girls had realized that Landry—or anyone—could hear them, they would have calmed their *tirade* to a heated, but private, discussion.

> Although articulate, picking a fight in answer to a *tirade* was not really Landry's style.

unbeknownst (un-bi-NONST) (adjective) unknown; happening without the knowledge (of someone).

> *Unbeknownst* to the class, Ms. Mbede was planning a pop quiz for the next class.

> *Unbeknownst* to the rest of the faculty, Ms. Mbede was a very active volunteer in her community.

wholeheartedly (hol-HAR-tud-lee) (adverb) with no hesitation or regret; enthusiastically.

> *Wholeheartedly* in favor of group projects, Ms. Mbede felt they were an excellent way for students to learn how to adapt to group situations before they went to work full-time.

> Mariel had become *wholeheartedly* in favor of including Landry graciously in their project until she tried to talk with him on the phone.

woebegone (WO-bi-gahn) (adjective) describes someone or something that suffers from deep sorrow and/or neglect.

> As Mariel went around the house with a *woebegone* expression for several days, her parents just sighed and gave her time to figure things out for herself.

> Cynthia felt *woebegone* and isolated from the team at being left out of the game because of her injury.

Quick Match 19

Match each word to its definition

1. ___	reconsider	A.	dark, dreary, sad, depressed
2. ___	fume	B.	describes something as a whole
3. ___	contribute	C.	without enthusiasm; with resistance
4. ___	woebegone	D.	with irritation or impatience
5. ___	reluctantly	E.	to feel or show anger or frustration
6. ___	gloomy	F.	suffering from deep sorrow or neglect
7. ___	contradict	G.	a long, angry speech
8. ___	wholeheartedly	H.	without warmth; chillingly
9. ___	remorseful	I.	the description of a person's personality
10. ___	icily	J.	happening without the knowledge (of someone)
11. ___	contentious	K.	to feel a strong connection with another
12. ___	unbeknownst	L.	to pull back from an unpleasant situation
13. ___	retreat	M.	a joining of two items
14. ___	identify	N.	with regret for one's previous actions
15. ___	conjunction	O.	stubborn; unwilling to cooperate
16. ___	tirade	P.	to calm; to ease pain or bring relief
17. ___	settle	Q.	to change
18. ___	overall	R.	with no hesitation or regret
19. ___	characterization	S.	to argue against another's point of view
20. ___	testily	T.	to spit out words, usually in excitement
21. ___	soothe	U.	tactless or unfeeling in behavior or speech
22. ___	callous	V.	to solve a conflict or problem
23. ___	recalcitrant	W	to put effort toward a joint endeavor
24. ___	sputter	X.	to think about an issue or question again
25. ___	alter	Y.	quarrelsome; argumentative

Sentence Completions 19

Choose the proper word or pair of words for each of the sentences below.

1. His _____ of the girls included his understanding of their intelligence and strong work ethic, along with a sensitivity to their level of frustration.

   (a) conjunction   (b) retreat   (c) tirade   (d) characterization
   (e) woebegone

2. He enjoyed working with other people and liked to _____ his own ideas in a variety of areas.

   (a) contribute   (b) contradict   (c) sputter   (d) retreat   (e) soothe

3. Group projects can be difficult and _____ even for people who usually work together in harmony.

   (a) remorseful   (b) contentious   (c) recalcitrant   (d) callous
   (e) conjunction

4. He could understand the girls' resistance and even _____ with their frustration, so he _____ went over to talk to them at lunch.

   (a) alter . . . testily   (b) contribute . . . wholeheartedly
   (c) woebegone . . . unbeknown   (d) fume . . . remorsefully
   (e) identify . . . reluctantly

5. Unwilling to _____ the project or make changes, she set off on an unreasonable _____ that made it difficult to talk until she calmed down.

   (a) contradict . . . fume   (b) alter . . . contentious   (c) reconsider . . . tirade
   (d) contribute . . . sputter   (e) settle . . . retreat

Chapter 20: Honoring Differences

Landry no longer *proffered* his suggestions or comments on the project. Cynthia and Mariel were *baffled* by this change but delighted with what they assumed was his *compliance*. When they had completely printed up their *impeccable* sections of the project, they gave copies to Landry. Asking him for his section so that they could turn in the whole project early, he *courteously* replied that it would be ready on the due date but not before. Unhappy as they were, the girls had to be satisfied with that.

They didn't admit their nervousness aloud until two days before the due date when Mariel heard some *ominous* gossip and rushed to Cynthia to repeat it.

"Sanjay told Walker that Landry told him that we had really *offended* him and he would not in any way work with us on this project. He said if we couldn't give any *credence* to his suggestions and ideas then he couldn't really *rely* on us either. What do you suppose it means, Cynthia? Do you think he will *renege* on the deal and not do his part at all?"

The *gravity* of the matter could not be *exaggerated*. Ms. Mbede would take their lack of cooperation into consideration for their grade but also in her personal opinion of them both. While Cynthia didn't seek the *universal approbation* of all of her teachers, she was fond of Ms. Mbede's class and was unwilling to disappoint her. When Landry politely but firmly refused to discuss the matter with them, they were even more worried.

On the due date in class, Ms. Mbede decided *impulsively* that each group should give a *synopsis* of its project as an oral report. Mariel and Cynthia *blanched*. They both hated giving oral reports and, in absolute trust, neither had read the other's report. Of course, neither of them had read Landry's portion either. The girls were in a *quandary* and trying to figure out a solution to this new problem when Landry volunteered their group to go first! Cynthia was *seething* with anger and Mariel's emotions were in *turmoil* as they all rose from their seats to go to the front of the room.

"Oh, no, no, no," sang out Ms. Mbede in her *mellifluous* voice, "we don't need a whole chorus up here. Just talk together and decide who will give the report."

Landry came up to the girls and they had a quick conference.

"I asked to go first in case we have problems," he whispered, "It won't be so obvious if some other group hasn't already done a terrific job at their report."

Much calmer, the girls nodded.

"I'm sorry now," he admitted, "but I am the only one who has read all three of our reports. If you two trust me to do this, I can make it work. I'm really the only one who can," he added *urgently* when he saw their *dubious* expressions. The girls had no choice but to trust him.

After thirty seconds of tension, the girls relaxed. Landry was funny, *perceptive*, and in full control of all of the information in the three sections of the report. He knew *intuitively* which parts to include and which to omit to delight the audience and please the teacher. It was not a long oral report, but it was a winner. Cynthia and Mariel clapped the loudest at the end of what had truly been a skilled performance.

"I guess sometimes we might need to be able to mix our style with others," said Mariel over the applause.

"I guess we have some apologizing to do," answered Cynthia.

approbation (a-pruh-BAY-shun) (noun) warm praise or approval. (plural: This word is not usually used in the plural.)

> Landry really appreciated the *approbation* of the class during his oral report.

> Ms. Mbede showered *approbation* on the entire team for a job well done.

baffled (BA-fld) (adjective) puzzled; greatly confused.

> The girls were *baffled* at first by Landry's offer for their group to go first.

> Mariel and Cynthia were *baffled* (not to mention very nervous) about Landry's unwillingness to discuss the tension in the group.

blanch (BLANCH) (verb) to go pale, usually in fear.

> Mariel didn't know which was more embarrassing: her tendency to blush in embarrassment or her tendency to *blanch* in apprehension.

> While perfectly willing to give oral reports if they had time to prepare, the girls *blanched* when something like that was assigned at the last minute.

compliance (kum-PLY-uns) (noun) the state of going along with someone or something; cooperation and obedience. (plural: This word is not usually used in the plural.)

> Ms. Mbede expected *compliance* from Mariel and Cynthia and had been very surprised when they objected to her decision about Landry.

> Despite his *compliance* with the main outlines of every assignment, Landry liked to stretch assignments creatively in unexpected directions.

courteously (KUR-tee-us-lee) (adverb) politely; graciously.

> Landry may have spoken to the girls *courteously*, but they could read the hurt and anger in his eyes.

> To make up for her bad temper the week before, Mariel tried to treat her family particularly *courteously* after the project was turned in.

credence (KREE-dns) (noun) the belief that something is true or trustworthy. (plural: This word is not usually used in the plural.)

> Landry, Mariel, and Cynthia all put great *credence* in the idea that people are basically nice.

> A great believer in rehabilitation, Mariel didn't put any *credence* in the idea that people couldn't change their characters if they really wanted to.

Pieces and Parts   *cred-*

Credence is from *credere* (believe or trust) + *-ence* (quality of). So *credence* is "the quality of belief or trust in something." We have many more words in English from this root having to do with belief: *credible, credulous, credentials, incredible,* and *incredulous* to name a few.

---

dubious (DOO-bee-us) (adjective) doubtful or uncertain; describes something or someone of unreliable, possibly bad, character.

> Despite their knowledge of his ease in front of a class, the girls were still *dubious* of Landry's ability to speak on all of their work.

> When a student turned in a report of *dubious* scholarship, Ms. Mbede had to speak with him quietly about plagiarism.

exaggerate (ig-ZA-juh-rayt) (verb) to overstate an argument or point of view; to make something seem bigger or greater than it actually is.

> Mariel's mother felt that Mariel *exaggerated* the girls' problem with Landry.

> In his oral report, Landry slightly *exaggerated* certain elements of the girls' research to make a clearer point.

gravity (GRA-vu-tee) (noun) the seriousness or importance of a situation. (plural: This word is not usually used in the plural.)

> Since their report was on a serious topic, Landry's humor and easy manner were in welcome contrast to the *gravity* of the material he discussed.

> Ms. Mbede remained unaware of the *gravity* of the problems this trio had experienced.

impeccable (im-PEK-uh-bl) (adjective) without blemish or flaw; clean and perfect.

> Landry had to admire the clean, *impeccable* presentation of the girls' sections of the report.

> Landry had always had *impeccable* manners and, ironically, he had managed to use those flawless manners to make the girls uncomfortable.

impulsively (im-PUL-siv-lee) (adverb) describes something quickly without thinking it through first.

> After class, Cynthia *impulsively* asked Landry to join them for lunch that day.

> Ms. Mbede had *impulsively* added the oral report to each project to raise the scores of the students who were strong speakers but weaker writers.

intuitively (in-TOO-uh-tiv-lee) (adverb) describes understanding something quickly and perceptively from an internal knowledge that doesn't depend on formal training.

> Mariel *intuitively* understood her own feelings and motivations and used this understanding to read the emotions of people around her.

> Cynthia knew *intuitively* that a quick apology would not do; she and Mariel needed to offer Landry the courtesy of a full explanation.

mellifluous (me-LI-flu-wus) (adjective) smooth and sweet.

> Part of the *mellifluous* quality of Ms. Mbede's voice came from her years of experience in radio before she became a teacher.

> As well, Ms. Mbede's parents had both been *mellifluous* and powerful speakers in their own rights.

offend (uh-FEND) (verb) to say or do something that angers another in a personal way; to hurt another's feelings through an (intentional or unintentional) insult.

> Mariel didn't want to *offend* Landry even further by not apologizing properly.

> Cynthia and Mariel had *offended* Landry deeply and they both knew it.

ominous (AH-muh-nus) (adjective) threatening.

> With an *ominous* rain cloud looming, the girls decided to eat indoors today instead of at their regular table in the courtyard.

> Although nervous about their upcoming apology, the girls certainly did not expect any kind of an *ominous* situation to develop over lunch.

perceptive (pur-SEP-tiv) (adjective) describes someone who is able to read the emotions and reactions of other people well and to respond appropriately.

> Landry was *perceptive* enough to see the girls' honest repentance.

> While the group was talking before their oral report, Ms. Mbede was *perceptive* and read the tension of each member.

proffer (PRAH-fer) (verb) to submit or offer to someone for their acceptance.

> At lunch that day, Cynthia and Mariel decided to *proffer* their sincerest apologies to Landry for their bad behavior.

> Landry then *proffered* that he had overheard their locker talk and apologized for not dealing with that—and them—more directly.

quandary (KWAHN-dree) (noun) a feeling of uncertainty. (plural: quandaries)

> The girls were in a *quandary* over whether or not to ask for copies of Landry's part of the report at this stage.

> In a *quandary* over whether or not to be totally candid, Landry decided not to confess the full measure of his hurt feelings over this matter.

Easy Errors   ***its*** **and** ***it's***

It's is the contraction of *it is* (*it* + *is* − *i* = *it's*). *Its* is a possessive form of *it*; in other words, *it* owns something. If your cat owned a toy, you might say "*It's its* toy" to mean "It is the toy that belongs to it (the cat)."

---

rely (ri-LY) (verb) to depend on someone or something for support or help.

> Cynthia preferred not to *rely* on anyone else in school work but she had to depend on others on the basketball court.

> From then on, Mariel *relied* on Cynthia as one of her very best friends.

renege (ri-NEG) (verb) to pull out of a deal already agreed upon; to fail to fulfill a promise already made.

> The more Mariel knew about Landry, the more she knew he would never *renege* on a deal, no matter how upset he might be.

> Because of her injury, Cynthia had had to *renege* on her promise to participate in every game for the entire season.

seething (SEETH-ing) (adjective) to be under the effect of strong emotion, usually anger.

> Cynthia hadn't realized how tense she was until she experienced how quickly she was *seething* with anger when Landry volunteered for the oral report.

> The students never saw Ms. Mbede *seething* with anger, but they had witnessed a bit of her temper.

synopsis (suh-NAHP-sus) (noun) a brief outline or overview of a project. (plural: synopses)

> Many teachers asked for a *synopsis* of a project a few days before it was due as a gentle reminder to their students to get it finished in time.

> Ms. Mbede summarized several of the students' *synopses* during lunch in the faculty room that day because she was impressed with their work.

turmoil (TUR-moyl) (noun) a state of extreme emotion or tumult. (plural: This word is not used in the plural.)

> All *turmoil* put aside, the three of them had a very pleasant lunch together.

> Mariel and Cynthia were beginning to wonder why they had let their anxieties create so much *turmoil* for them all.

universal (yoo-nuh-VUR-sul) (adjective) describes something that applies to everyone.

> The *universal* consensus after lunch was that they would all be willing to work together (really work <u>together</u>) on a project again.

> Despite the almost-*universal* student resistance to group projects, Ms. Mbede was convinced of their value in the children's education.

urgently (UR-junt-lee) (adverb) in a very important or insistent manner.

> The nice part of always spacing out and planning her homework schedule was that Mariel never had to call anyone *urgently* the night before a project was due to check on its requirements.

> Mariel did, however, call Cynthia *urgently* that night with some news.

Quick Match 20

Match each word to its definition.

1. ____	quandary	A.	without blemish or flaw; clean and perfect
2. ____	proffer	B.	a brief outline or overview of a project
3. ____	approbation	C.	puzzled; greatly confused
4. ____	rely	D.	a state or feeling of uncertainty
5. ____	perceptive	E.	a state of extreme emotion or tumult
6. ____	baffled	F.	to go pale, usually in fear
7. ____	renege	G.	able to read the emotions of other people well
8. ____	ominous	H.	understanding something quickly from inside
9. ____	blanch	I.	to fail to fulfill a promise already made
10. ____	seething	J.	warm praise or approval
11. ____	offend	K.	to submit to someone for their acceptance
12. ____	compliance	L.	under the effect of strong emotion, usually anger
13. ____	synopsis	M.	doubtful or uncertain
14. ____	mellifluous	N.	threatening
15. ____	courteously	O.	describes doing something without thinking it through
16. ____	turmoil	P.	to overstate an argument or point of view
17. ____	intuitively	Q.	the belief that something is true or trustworthy
18. ____	credence	R.	describes something that applies to everyone
19. ____	universal	S.	cooperation and obedience
20. ____	impulsively	T.	to hurt another's feelings through insult
21. ____	dubious	U.	in a very important or insistent manner
22. ____	urgently	V.	the seriousness or importance of a situation
23. ____	impeccable	W.	to depend on someone for support or help
24. ____	exaggerate	X.	smooth and sweet
25. ____	gravity	Y.	politely; graciously

Sentence Completions 20

Choose the proper word or pair of words for each of the sentences below.

1. While not really worried about their grades, the entire team was hoping for _____ from the teacher for the effort they had put into the project.

   (a) compliance   (b) approbation   (c) turmoil   (d) gravity   (e) universal

2. He didn't _____ an explanation when asked for one.

   (a) blanch   (b) exaggerate   (c) renege   (d) proffer   (e) rely

3. Although confused by his behavior, they didn't find it _____ until they heard the negative rumors.

   (a) impeccable   (b) perceptive   (c) ominous   (d) universal   (e) mellifluous

4. In a(n) _____ over what to do, she couldn't decide if his answering politely and _____ was a good or bad sign.

   (a) compliance . . . intuitively   (b) synopsis . . . impulsively
   (c) approbation . . . urgently   (d) quandary . . . courteously
   (e) credence . . . impeccably

5. When emotions run high and one is _____ with anger, it is difficult not to _____ someone else with a thoughtless comment.

   (a) blanching . . . urgently   (b) seething . . . offend   (c) ominous . . . turmoil
   (d) dubious . . . proffer   (e) perceptive . . . renege

WRITING ACTIVITY

Video Dating Advertisement

Before the Internet made face-to-face dating services in real offices obsolete, people could join these services, which offered them a chance to really be themselves (or whomever they liked)—on videotape! One paid a fee, filled out an information form, and had a few minutes one-on-one with a video camera to "sell" oneself and look for the partner of one's dreams.

If *you* were given four to six minutes, how would you describe yourself? How would you describe your dream date? Using as many section words as possible, create a dating profile of yourself. (Videotaping is optional.)

Hmmm. Is that too personal for an intrapersonal learner?

Okay, then, let's go for creativity. If you prefer, create a character as outrageous as you like, male or female, shy or outgoing, friendly or combative, and play that person for your four-to-six, vocabulary-rich minutes.

Ground rules? Only that you be kind to yourself, your character, and those around you and steer away from any questionable comments or profanity that might make someone skip your video. Remember, this "person" wants to be presented at his or her best!

Ladies and gentlemen, let's go retro!

SECTION 5: WORDS, WORDS, WORDS!

Learning Style: The Verbal/Linguistic Learner

If words and language hold the magic of the world for you, one of your primary intelligences is likely that of the Verbal/Linguistic learner.

Are you a reader? A storyteller? A memorizer? Is word play (Scrabble, rhymed jokes, double-meanings, crossword puzzles) your favorite play? Are you the grammarian in your family, the best speller in the neighborhood? Do people see your wit as sharper than a kitchen knife? Do you always read the instructions—first?

If you have answered "yes" to several of the above, this is one of your stronger intelligences.

Possible Approaches

- **Flashcards.** We'll start with flashcards—something that I am sure you have been asked to do before—and move on from that basic strategy. Take cards of your choice (most students use three-by-five-inch index cards) and write your vocabulary word on one side and its part of speech and definition on the other side. Choose a friend or family member to help drill you on these cards for ten minutes each week night. By the end of the week—Bingo!—you will know your vocabulary words cold in time for the quiz.

  - Variation 1: Try color-coding your cards by parts of speech to give yourself an edge in remembering these word functions. For example, use red index cards for verbs, yellow for adverbs, blue for nouns, and green for adjectives. (Index cards are available in all of these colors.)

  - Variation 2: Instead of color-coding your cards, color-code the words themselves by using different pen or marker colors on regular white index cards.

- **Fortune cookies.** For each of your vocabulary words, write a profound (or silly) fortune cookie message to help you remember the word. The sillier the saying, the easier the word will be to remember.

- **Riddles.** Try writing riddles with your vocabulary words. The riddles should include word definitions or sentences that show the vocabulary word used in context. These can be jokes or they can be traditional riddles in which one gives clues (often in rhymed verse) to help people identify a secret or hidden object, person, or place.

- **Proverbs.** In his *Poor Richard's Almanac*, Benjamin Franklin took wise sayings and made them easy to remember. "Early to bed and early to rise / Makes a man healthy, wealthy, and wise" was his clever way of reminding people to take care of themselves and work hard for success. Pretend you are Benjamin Franklin and, using vocabulary words wisely and well, write some proverbs or axioms that would be excellent advice for your readers.

- **Words in Context.** A great way to learn a word is to put it into context; here are some ways of contextualizing your vocabulary lists:

  - **Try the Internet:**
    Key an unusual word into a general search engine (or into the search engine of a national newspaper such as *The Washington Post* or *The New York Times*) and browse through what turns up. Pay special attention to precisely how a word is used. Ask yourself: What is the word's position in the sentence? What words are often found next to it? What sorts of things does it describe or act on? What consistent patterns of usage turn up? For instance, although "iota" and "miniscule" both refer to something small, one would never use them interchangeably. Know *how* to use your words.

  - **Consult a thesaurus:**
    Look up a given vocabulary word in a thesaurus and choose three synonyms for that word. Then look those three words up in a dictionary. What range of meanings does your word have? How are the "synonyms" different from your vocabulary word? In what context might you choose one of these words and not another?

  - Alternatively, perform the same activity as above with your vocabulary word but work through the antonyms this time.

  - **Try reading:**
    Encountering a word in a print advertisement, a novel, a non-fiction book, a magazine article, or in an on-line magazine is the best way to see how people are using your word. Read widely and often as your strongest vocabulary-building technique!

Chapter 21: Sowing

"My brain is fried. Can I drop here for a minute, Gabe?"

Gabe looked up from his book at Zerah who looked absolutely worn out. It was a beautiful day and Gabe had been enjoying his *solitary* read in the *singularly*-deserted school courtyard, but he couldn't be rude to one of his best friends.

"Sure. No problem," Gabe *fibbed*, "but I thought you were busy choosing pieces to put into the *annual literary* magazine."

"I am. I was. It's *grueling*, Gabe. There are so many great drawings and poems we have to *cull* because the school can't afford a magazine any longer than 56 pages. The *limitation* is driving me nuts."

Gabe nodded at her sympathetically. "It's too bad we can't *expand* it," he said, "because only a few of us get work accepted by the magazine each year and I think a greater number of *voices* should be heard and recognized."

"You are so right!" *boomed* a voice from behind them, making them both jump. It was Julian. They should have known; he had a *preternatural* talent for sneaking up on people.

"We need another *forum* for our writing and art," he *averred*.

At this latest *intrusion*, Gabe sighed and, *noting* his page, closed his book. The courtyard's unusual period of solitude was over. He looked at Julian *indifferently*, but Zerah looked more *speculatively*. She had a *glimmering* of an idea.

"What about an extra-credit performance of work in class?" she suggested.

"What about something more public? A live reading here in the courtyard during lunch?" Julian added.

"What about a live performance in the *auditorium*? You know, sell tickets, like for a school play?" Gabe said.

They continued to *bounce* ideas back and forth, getting more and more excited. Finally, they all liked Gabe's idea of a public performance the best. They decided that if this really were to be a *viable* alternative, they needed to get a *faculty sponsor*. That began another round of brainstorming in which they decided which teacher was the most likely candidate to say "yes."

annual (AN-yul) (adjective) describes something that happens on a yearly basis.

> The school holds an *annual* auction to raise money for the band and chorus each fall.

> The *annual* prom is an event that the seniors look forward to for the entire year.

auditorium (aw-duh-TOR-ee-um) (noun) a large building or room in which a group can hear a public speech or performance. (plural: auditoriums; less common, auditoria)

> The school *auditorium* is just large enough to seat all of the students and teachers at one time.

> For school events involving students and their parents, the school sometimes rents the civic *auditorium* in town because it is bigger than their own.

aver (uh-VUR) (verb) to swear to be true; to state positively; to assert.

> Zerah *averred* that there was so much writing talent at the school that it was tough for her to edit the school magazine.

> The school administration *averred* that they didn't have enough money in the budget to expand the size of the magazine this year.

boom (BOOM) (verb) to make a deep, loud sound.

> The band teacher's voice would always *boom* across the room, making it easy for the students to hear what he had to say.

> Julian could speak quietly but usually he *boomed* anything he had to say in a deep, rich voice.

candidate (KAN-duh-dayt) (noun) a person who is running for public office; a person who is likely to fulfill a particular role. (plural: candidates)

> Ms. Ruhakana, the drama teacher, was a possible *candidate* as a teacher who would be willing to help them.

> Zerah and Gabe are both able student leaders and likely *candidates* to lead this project.

Word Play   **adding to *annual***

Annual comes from the root *annus* (year), so that is straightforward. Some of the words we create from *annual*, though, can be a little confusing. *Biannual*, for instance, means *semi-annual* or "twice a year" whereas *biennial* (note the spelling change) means "every two years" or refers to an event that lasts for two years. To save confusion, *semi-annual* is usually used in place of *biannual*. *Triennial* is used for an event that happens every three years or lasts for three years.

---

cull (KUL) (verb) to cut out or eliminate the weak or sickly from a group; to select.

> Some of the teachers would *cull* the weaker writing before it reached Zerah's desk.

While sitting on the bench and talking, Zerah absentmindedly *culled* the dead leaves from the patch of garden next to them and threw them in the trash can.

expand (ik-SPAND) (verb) to enlarge, increase in number, or make bigger.

A few years earlier, the magazine had decided to *expand* to its current size.

The submissions to the magazine had not *expanded* in the past few years because many students knew they had little chance of their work being chosen for publication.

faculty (FA-kul-tee) (noun) a group of teachers or professors at a school. (plural: faculties)

The *faculty* at this school was generally very open to helping students with new projects.

Although a bit shy about approaching the *faculty* for help, Gabe knew that it was a worthwhile project.

fib (FIB) 1. (verb) to state a small or childish untruth. 2. (noun) a little lie; a "small, white lie." (plural: fibs)

Gabe didn't usually *fib* to anyone, but Zerah looked as though she needed to talk.

Julian told a *fib* about needing a drink of water. Really, he just wanted to step outside for a moment to clear his head before returning to class.

forum (FOR-um) (noun) any public area (a place or a print source) that provides a place for open discussion of issues. (plural: forums; less often, fora)

The student council was the main *forum* for students to present new ideas and requests for change.

On Tuesdays, the International Policy Club was a *forum* for students who wanted to discuss world politics.

glimmering (GLI-mur-ing) (noun) a small, unfinished idea whose details flicker in and out of one's mind; a dim, flickering light. (plural: glimmerings)

Gabe and Zerah really had no more than a *glimmering* of an idea of how to approach this project.

Julian had a *glimmering* of a hope that he could get a few uninvolved friends of his to submit some of their writing to this project.

grueling (GROO-uh-ling) (adjective) extremely arduous or difficult; describing something mentally or physically difficult or exhausting.

> It wasn't the physical effort of the work that Zerah found so *grueling*, but the intellectual effort of making all those choices.

> Gabe's academic schedule was pretty *grueling* this year, so a few quiet minutes in the courtyard were precious to him.

indifferently (in-DI-frunt-lee) (adverb) describes something done without interest or bias.

> Gabe had heard Julian's initial idea *indifferently*, but as they all talked about it, he became more involved.

> Some of the students who had reacted *indifferently* to other projects might be very interested in this one.

intrusion (in-TROO-zhun) (noun) an uninvited interruption; the act of forcing oneself into a private situation without permission. (plural: intrusions)

> Although Zerah's visit was a bit of an *intrusion*, Gabe reacted sympathetically to her situation.

> Some might have considered Julian's *intrusion* into a private conversation to be rude, but Zerah and Gabe knew he didn't mean any harm.

limitation (li-muh-TAY-shun) (noun) a restriction; something that reduces someone's ability to do something. (plural: limitations)

> The only *limitation* facing Gabe was the amount of time he could spend on this project.

> Julian's main *limitation* in taking part in extracurricular activities was that he had to take the bus home in the afternoons.

Pieces and Parts   *aud-*

This root is from the Latin *audire* (to hear) and is the base of many words in English, such as *auditorium* (a room in which to hear), *audio* (sound from an electronic device such as a radio), and *audience* (a group who hears a performance).

---

literary (li-tuh-RAYR-ee) (adjective) having to do with books, written text, and/or authors.

> Zerah's *literary* achievements not only involved editing the magazine but also writing for the neighborhood newsletter.

A *literary* critic for the school newspaper, Julian spent a lot of his spare time reading the latest science fiction novels that came out.

note (NOTE) (verb) to make a record of something; to observe.

> When Zerah reviewed work for the literary magazine, she would *note* each student's grade level as well as his or her name on each strong piece of work.

> Julian *noted* Gabe's growing excitement and got more interested in the project himself.

preternatural (pree-tur-NA-chu-rul) (adjective) beyond what is considered natural; greater than the normal.

> Julian's unconscious but *preternatural* skill at moving silently made some people nervous.

> Zerah noticed one ninth-grader's work that had a *preternatural* grasp of human emotions, and she wondered if the student had copied that work or if he really were that talented.

singularly (SING-gyu-lur-lee) (adverb) describes something done in a manner that is unusual and unique.

> Julian was *singularly* proud of his little sister's musical talent.

> Zerah was *singularly* aware of her responsibility to make the magazine as representative of the entire, diverse student body as she could manage.

solitary (SAH-luh-ter-ee) (adjective) describes someone or something that is alone.

> The students couldn't see a single, *solitary* reason why this show wouldn't be successful.

> After several days of editing the magazine alone, Zerah began to feel that she was in *solitary* confinement in the classroom after school.

sow (SO) (verb) to plant or scatter seeds in soil so that they can grow.

> Although he didn't actually *sow* any of the seeds himself, Gabe had helped the class prepare the garden for the planting.

> That year, the junior class had taken over a plot of land on campus and *sown* vegetable seeds as a local service project to help feed the poor.

speculatively (SPE-kyu-luh-tiv-lee) (adverb) describes reasoning out a conclusion without sufficient evidence; by way of guessing or conjecture.

> When Zerah saw Mr. Carrothers walking across the courtyard, she wondered *speculatively* if he might be willing to help with their new project.

When Gabe asked a first-year English teacher to help, she looked at him *speculatively* as though to see if he were really capable of making such a project work.

sponsor (SPAHN-sur) (noun) a wealthy or authoritative person who helps a project succeed by assuming certain responsibilities on behalf of others. (plural: sponsors)

While the students would have welcomed a *sponsor* to contribute money to help the project, their primary need was for a faculty member who would speak for them.

Although intrigued with the project, Ms. Ruhakana was too busy to be the *sponsor* for it.

viable (VY-uh-bl) (adjective) possible and practical; able to be successful.

The three realized that the project would only be *viable* if they could manage to get a larger group of students together to run it.

It would only be *viable*, too, if they could reserve the school auditorium for a suitable performance date.

voice (VOYS) (noun) the individual style or expression of a particular author. (plural: voices)

Julian's writing had a very distinctive *voice*, and Zerah always knew when she was reading his pieces even if she hadn't looked at the name on the work.

Julian felt that a number of students' opinions and *voices* were unheard because the literary magazine was too short to adequately express the full diversity at the school.

Quick Match 21

Match each word to its definition.

1. ___	literary	A.	to swear to be true; to state positively
2. ___	expand	B.	a dim, flickering light; unfinished idea
3. ___	note	C.	in an unusual and unique manner
4. ___	limitation	D.	extremely arduous or difficult
5. ___	cull	E.	happening on a yearly basis
6. ___	preternatural	F.	by way of guessing or conjecture
7. ___	intrusion	G.	to make a deep, loud sound
8. ___	voice	H.	done without interest or bias
9. ___	singularly	I.	to give a small or childish untruth; a little lie
10. ___	indifferently	J.	large room for a group to hear a public speech
11. ___	candidate	K.	beyond what is considered natural
12. ___	solitary	L.	individual style of a particular author
13. ___	grueling	M.	to cut out or eliminate; to select
14. ___	boom	N.	an uninvited interruption
15. ___	sow	O.	any public area for open discussion of issues
16. ___	glimmering	P.	to plant or scatter seeds in soil to grow
17. ___	aver	Q.	person likely to fill a particular role
18. ___	speculatively	R.	group of teachers or professors at a school
19. ___	forum	S.	a wealthy person who helps a project succeed
20. ___	annual	T.	to enlarge, increase in number, or make bigger
21. ___	sponsor	U.	possible and practical; able to be successful
22. ___	fib	V.	having to do with books, written texts, or authors
23. ___	auditorium	W.	alone
24. ___	viable	X.	a restriction
25. ___	faculty	Y.	to make a record of something; to observe

Sentence Completions 21

Choose the proper word or pair of words for each of the sentences below.

1. Zerah had a(n) _____ skill for seeing the possibilities in an author's writing and skillfully helping that author become even better.

   (a) glimmering   (b) solitary   (c) preternatural   (d) indifferent
   (e) grueling

2. The three students _____ in a three-way promise that they would make this show happen.

   (a) expanded   (b) boomed   (c) fibbed   (d) sowed   (e) averred

3. Because Zerah was so involved in student life on campus, she was a natural _____ for coming up with new projects for the students.

   (a) candidate   (b) faculty   (c) limitation   (d) boom   (e) intrusion

4. While the magazine was a good public _____ for student writing, Julian felt the school needed a(n) _____ alternative to reach more students and a greater audience.

   (a) auditorium . . . candidate   (b) sponsor . . . grueling
   (c) intrusion . . . annual   (d) forum . . . viable   (e) glimmering . . . expanded

5. It takes an experienced reader like Zerah to recognize true _____ talent in work and to _____ the weaker writing.

   (a) annual . . . fib   (b) literary . . . cull   (c) preternatural . . . sow
   (d) viable . . . note   (e) grueling . . . expand

Chapter 22: Germination

After several *abortive* attempts with a number of teachers, Zerah, Gabe, and Julian finally found a sponsor in Mr. Garcia, one of the English teachers. They had *frankly* been surprised at being turned down by four other teachers in *succession*; the students were convinced their idea was a *certified* hit. While they all liked Mr. Garcia and were grateful for his support, not one of them had been in any of his classes so they were all a little *wary* of his *involvement*.

If Mr. Garcia *sensed* their *discomfort*, he never let on. He wrote an *entry* for the daily *announcements* of an *organizational* meeting for the next day, and the trio was *gratified* to see another seven students show up for that. That *core* of ten put together a plan to write an article asking for *submissions* for the next issue of the on-line newspaper (Nisa and Dylan); to create folders to give to each English teacher for submissions (Julian and Rosario); and to contact the music and drama teachers for *input* (Zerah and Hakim). Mr. Garcia agreed to *promote* the idea to the other teachers in the teachers' *lounge*, and Gabe just said *cryptically* he had something he was going to work on *independently*.

Both the drama and music teachers were *keen* to be involved *peripherally* in the project, despite not having time to be full-time sponsors. Although they hoped that most students would choose to perform their own *manuscripts* on stage, Hakim and Zerah arranged for *auditions* for certain drama students who might be interested in *interpreting* other students' writing for them. The next step seemed to be to pick a performance date.

abortive (uh-BOR-tiv) (adjective) unsuccessful in producing an intended result.

> The students' first four attempts to get a faculty sponsor were *abortive* and they were beginning to think they wouldn't be able to do the show after all.

> After their third *abortive* attempt, they went to see the assistant principal for advice and suggestions.

announcement (uh-NOWN-smunt) (noun) a public notice of news or information. (plural: announcements)

> After the all-school *announcement*, a number of students came up to Gabe to ask him about the project.

> Zerah also asked Gabe and Julian to make *announcements* in their English and drama classes about the upcoming show.

audition (aw-DI-shun) (noun) a try-out by an actor or musician for a role in a show. (plural: auditions)

> Several students asked Zerah when and where the *auditions* would be even before the first meeting had been held.

An *audition* made Julian nervous although he was comfortable performing in front of a group.

certified (SUR-ti-fyd) (adjective) true, verified as accurate.

> For safety reasons, the school required that at least one adult in each section of the building be a *certified* CPR practitioner.

> Now that Gabe was a *certified*, licensed driver he could run errands for the show if he needed to do so.

core (KOR) (noun) the center; the important or essential part of something. (plural: cores)

> While Gabe, Julian, and Zerah understood the *core* purpose of the show, others joined just to have fun.

> One of the reasons Mr. Garcia was happy to help with the show was that it fulfilled one of the *core* values of the school: "to go beyond the ordinary."

cryptically (KRIP-tik-lee) (adverb) mysteriously; in a way that implies a hidden meaning.

> To raise interest among the faculty, Mr. Garcia spoke *cryptically* of a "new, grassroots movement" before he explained the student show to them.

> As *cryptically* as Gabe spoke, most of the others were too busy with their own jobs to wonder about his secret.

discomfort (dis-KUM-furt) (noun) a feeling of mental uneasiness; a feeling of slight physical pain or awkwardness. (plural: This word is not usually used in the plural.)

> Ms. Ruhakana had felt some *discomfort* at refusing to sponsor the group, fearing that the students would not be able to do the show without her support.

> Because Gabe didn't really know Mr. Garcia, he had felt *discomfort* speaking to the teacher about being their sponsor.

entry (EN-tree) (noun) an insertion in a printed or spoken text; the opening through which one comes into an area, contest, or group. (plural: entries)

> The *entry* Mr. Garcia put into the day's announcements was fun and interesting and drew a lot of attention to the show.

> Julian, Zerah, and Gabe were a little nervous about their *entry* into management roles for this show.

frankly (FRANK-lee) (adverb) candidly; using honesty that is direct but not deliberately cruel.

> When she didn't accept someone's work for the magazine, Zerah tried to give the writer a reason without speaking too *frankly* about the flaws in their writing.

> Julian was *frankly* amazed that support was growing so quickly for the show.

germination (jur-muh-NAY-shun) (noun) the time at which something (usually a seed) begins to sprout and grow. (plural: This word is not usually used in the plural.)

> Gabe was just as excited about the *germination* of his idea as he had been about the *germination* of the seeds in the vegetable garden!

> Mr. Garcia was happy to see an organized group participating in the *germination* of this project.

Similar Sounds   *lightening* vs. *lightning*

If someone is in the process of making something less heavy or less intense, that person is *lightening* a load. If one sees flashing light in the sky that is associated with a thunderstorm, one sees *lightning*. So, if one notices the *lightning lightening* during a thunderstorm, then the storm must be moving away.

---

gratified (GRA-tu-fyd) (adjective) extremely pleased and satisfied.

> The assistant principal was *gratified* that her advice had been helpful to the students.

> Although he knew he hadn't been the students' first choice as sponsor, Mr. Garcia was, nevertheless, *gratified* to have been asked to help.

independently (in-duh-PEN-dunt-lee) (adverb) without assistance or control of others; describes something done by one's own choice.

> Although eager to work *independently* on the project, the students were grateful for Mr. Garcia's helpful advice.

> Most of the works being submitted for consideration for the show had been written *independently*, although a few were the product of collaboration between two writers.

input (IN-put) (noun) information given to someone (or something, as in the case of a computer) to help formulate a decision. (plural: This word is not usually used in the plural.)

> In organizing the magazine, Zerah had to track down some of the *input* she needed on each of the contributors because it hadn't been included with their submissions.

> The *input* Mr. Garcia offered about texts suitable for performance was invaluable to them.

interpret (in-TUR-prut) (verb) 1. to orally present text to illustrate its full meaning. 2. to analyze data to help come to an explanation.

> Two of the actors who came to the audition asked if they could also *interpret* their own work for the show.

> Gabe was pleased that another seven people had come to help, but he wasn't certain whether to *interpret* that many as evidence of support for, or indifference to, the show.

involvement (in-VAHLV-munt) (noun) the participation of individual people or groups in a common cause or goal. (plural: This word is not usually used in the plural.)

> The *involvement* of the drama and music teachers was a big help.

> Mr. Garcia was hoping to encourage the *involvement* of a number of musicians in the show as well.

keen (KEEN) (adjective) 1. very eager, enthusiastic. 2. very smart, intellectually clever.

> The assistant principal was *keen* to get the local newspaper to cover the event since the students were taking the lead organizing the show.

> The core group was full of *keen*, energetic students who were willing to work overtime to make the show happen.

lounge (LOWNJ) (noun) a public room in which to relax (or wait, as in a train station). (plural: lounges)

> Mr. Garcia always grinned to himself at the name "Teachers' *Lounge*" because he seldom saw teachers relaxing there without having something to work on for class with them.

> The student council was hoping for permission to make an unused classroom into a student *lounge* for seniors who had study hall.

manuscript (MAN-yoo-skript) (noun) a handwritten or typed text intended for publication that has not yet been published. (plural: manuscripts)

> Zerah—and her eyes—greatly preferred typed *manuscripts* to handwritten ones since she sometimes had to strain to understand the handwriting.

Ms. Ruhakana had been working on the *manuscript* of an original play for the last two years, and she felt it was almost ready to send to a publisher.

organizational (or-gu-nu-ZAY-shnul) (adjective) for creating order and structure; describes the systematic gathering of resources for a particular purpose.

The *organizational* structure of the core group was focused on pairs of people getting various jobs done together.

Gabe felt there were likely to be some *organizational* problems as they got closer to rehearsals and performance dates since no one person was really in charge.

peripherally (puh-RI-fru-lee) (adverb) describes doing something on the outside edges; in a not very important way.

Mr. Garcia tried to operate *peripherally* unless the students asked him for specific advice or help.

Most of the drama students were already involved in an upcoming play, so they could only be involved *peripherally* in this production.

promote (pruh-MOTE) (verb) to enthusiastically endorse something; to encourage others to become involved in a project or to accept a product.

Julian spoke positively of the show to *promote* attendance at the performance.

With their teachers' blessings, Gabe and Zerah personally *promoted* the show in each of their classes to encourage written submissions.

Easy Errors   **errors in comparatives**

Some adjectives are what we call *absolutes* and that means that they cannot be more or less of themselves. For example, if something is *unique*, "one of a kind," it cannot be more or less *unique* than anything else; it is already in its nature to be one of a kind and that cannot be changed. For that reason, it is always incorrect to use "*more unique*," "*less unique*," or "*uniquer than*." The same is true of other absolutes such as *round* or *square*: something round or square either is or is not round or square; it cannot be more or less round or square than something else.

---

sense (SENS) (verb) to get a feeling for or about something, based on intuition or physical stimuli (such as taste, touch, hearing, seeing, smelling).

Although it hadn't been done before, Mr. Garcia *sensed* that this show could be very successful.

The students *sensed* Mr. Garcia's enthusiasm and found his positive attitude infectious.

submission (sub-MI-shun) (noun) an item offered for approval (such as a printed text for publication) or for a contest (such as an entry form for a drawing). (plural: submissions)

> Julian and Rosario hoped the brightly-colored envelopes would encourage multiple *submissions* of work from each class.

> Rosario felt odd about offering her own work as a *submission* when she was also a reader and judge; Julian agreed to read hers.

succession (suk-SE-shun) (noun) the act of following an orderly list (often of people, particularly for the orderly rise of royalty to power). (plural: successions)

> The *succession* of classes that day were a blur to Gabe since he was busy thinking about the show and not his school work.

> Zerah was trying to work out the *succession* of steps they would have to go through to be sure everything was prepared in time.

wary (WER-ee) (adjective) somewhat suspicious of someone or something; cautious.

> Gabe was grateful for the new students' help; he was a little *wary* that taking on so much work himself would make him fall behind in his school work.

> Until the students had a faculty sponsor, the assistant principal was *wary* of giving them too much encouragement.

Quick Match 22

Match each word to its definition.

1. ____ wary
2. ____ gratified
3. ____ lounge
4. ____ succession
5. ____ germination
6. ____ core
7. ____ keen
8. ____ submission
9. ____ frankly
10. ____ certified
11. ____ involvement
12. ____ sense
13. ____ entry
14. ____ audition
15. ____ interpret
16. ____ promote
17. ____ discomfort
18. ____ announcement
19. ____ input
20. ____ peripherally
21. ____ abortive
22. ____ cryptically
23. ____ independently
24. ____ organizational
25. ____ manuscript

A.   for creating order and structure
B.   a feeling of mental uneasiness or physical pain
C.   participation in a group for a common cause
D.   a try-out by a performer for a role in a show
E.   to orally present a text; to analyze data
F.   to enthusiastically endorse something
G.   public notice of news or information
H.   information given to help formulate a decision
I.   a handwritten or typed text for publication
J.   to get a feeling about something from intuition
K.   a public room in which to relax or wait
L.   unsuccessful in producing an intended result
M.   in a not very important manner
N.   mysteriously; with a hidden meaning
O.   very eager; enthusiastic
P.   an insertion in printed or spoken text
Q.   the act of following an orderly list
R.   the time a seed begins to sprout and grow
S.   by one's own choice; without assistance
T.   true; verified as accurate
U.   extremely pleased and satisfied
V.   an item offered for approval or for a contest
W.   the essential part of something; the center
X.   candidly; with direct honesty
Y.   feeling a little suspicious; cautious

Sentence Completions 22

Choose the proper word or pair of words for each of the sentences below.

1. Unable to take a central role in the production because of other commitments, the music teacher was only involved _____ in the show.

    (a) independently   (b) peripherally   (c) frankly   (d) keenly   (e) abortively

2. One would think that a writer would be the best one to _____ his or her own work but performance is actually a very different skill from writing.

    (a) audition   (b) promote   (c) discomfort   (d) interpret   (e) certify

3. Several of the submitted _____ didn't have student names on them and it took Rosario some time to track down the authors of those pieces.

    (a) input   (b) successions   (c) cores   (d) manuscripts   (e) lounges

4. One must be cautious of someone who speaks _____ since it is wise to be _____ of someone whose words can be interpreted different ways.

    (a) cryptically . . . wary   (b) frankly . . . gratified
    (c) peripherally . . . discomfort   (d) independently . . . keen
    (e) abortively . . . interpret

5. The _____ meeting was held to plan the _____ of any people interested in helping out in the production.

    (a) germination . . . submission   (b) lounge . . . audition
    (c) organizational . . . involvement   (d) announcement . . . succession
    (e) certified . . . entry

Chapter 23: Sprouting

Julian and Rosario were getting *bleary-eyed* reading all the work that had been submitted. The show was *alarmingly* close; they had only had twenty-seven days from the moment the *notion* was *conceived* until the performance date because of the limited *availability* of the auditorium. For the first week after the announcement, only a few pieces of writing had *trickled* in. When the increasingly *distraught* editors appealed to Mr. Garcia, he *mobilized* the teachers into a *campaign* of creative writing across the *curriculum* and now Julian and Rosario were *awash* in prose and poetry. They had tried to *recruit* Zerah to help them read but, knowing what she did already about how difficult such a job could be, she *declined*. Besides, she still had the literary magazine to finish.

Just last night, an exciting new *factor* had come into play. Bursting into Mr. Garcia's room where the whole crew was at work, Gabe had excitedly told them about a second *phase* he had been working on for the show.

"We have been disappointed not to have student artwork in the show as well as written work," he explained to *enlighten* those not a part of earlier conversations. "But now we don't have to be. The art department will lend us all the *paraphernalia* for posting art they can get their hands on so that we can have an art show in the *foyer* before the live performance. Also, the mom of one of the art students and her company (they do *marketing*) are willing to *subsidize* our having tickets printed for the *conjoint* show! We can sell them around the area the week *preceding* the show. Real, professional tickets with the show title and date and time and everything on them!"

Gabe looked at Zerah, whose eyes were also shining with excitement.

"And any *proceeds*, Zerah, will be *funneled* right to the literary magazine!" Gabe said *resolutely*.

alarmingly (uh-LAR-ming-lee) (adverb) in a manner that gives a warning or creates upset and fear.

> With the show date so close, *alarmingly* few submissions would mean that the whole show would have to be canceled.

> "We may not be able to do the show, Mr. Garcia!" Rosario had blurted out *alarmingly*.

availability (uh-vay-lu-BIL-uh-tee) (noun). The state of being ready to be used; accessibility. (plural: This word is not usually used in the plural.)

> The *availability* of display boards for art work would add a whole new visual dimension to the show.

> Mr. Garcia also sent Nisa and Dylan to check on the *availability* of a maintenance person to be on hand during the performance in case of problems.

awash (uh-WAHSH) (adjective) flooded.

> *Awash* with manuscripts good and bad, Rosario and Julian had to read and consult quickly on each entry before going on to the next.

> Dylan wrote multiple drafts of anything he was going to submit to the school newspaper. When Nisa found him that day, he was *awash* in piles of crumpled up paper that showed how frustrating this writing session had been.

bleary-eyed (BLEE-ree-YD) (adjective) describes eyes that are filmy and/or have clouded vision as a result of overuse or exhaustion.

> Mr. Garcia was *bleary-eyed* in class on Friday since he had been losing sleep over helping to plan the show.

> The tiny print on some of the submissions made Rosario even more *bleary-eyed* than the quantity of her reading.

campaign (kam-PAYN) (noun) an organized plan involving a group of people to achieve a strategic goal, often used to describe a series of military operations. (plural: campaigns)

> In her *campaign* to get students' work published, Zerah had been discouraged by the short, maximum length of her finished magazine.

> Even science and math teachers joined Mr. Garcia's *campaign* of writing in all subject areas; Rosario and Julian received a number of poems about photosynthesis and triangles!

conceive (kun-SEEV) (verb) 1. to create or develop (an idea) in the mind. 2. to understand.

> Gabe, Zerah, and Julian had each *conceived* of the final show a little differently, and the energies of another seven students were adjusting those expectations daily as well.

> At times, Gabe couldn't *conceive* of how everything could be accomplished in time.

conjoint (kun-JOINT) (adjective) combined, joint, united.

> The show was moving from a *conjoint* project of the English and art departments to one involving the music and drama departments as well.

> Mr. Garcia decided to hold a *conjoint* meeting of all the teachers involved so that the departments were clear on what their responsibilities might be.

curriculum (cu-RI-kyu-lum) (noun) the plan of study for a particular academic course or program of courses. (plural: curricula, curriculums)

> Ms. Ruhakana was working out a way to include work on this project as part of the *curriculum* for her Technical Theater course.

> The English department's *curriculum* involved encouraging students to submit work for publication, so submitting work for performance was a natural extension of that.

decline (di-KLYN) (verb) 1. to turn (someone) down politely; to say no politely. 2. to drop in vigor or quality gradually.

> The teachers who had politely *declined* the opportunity to sponsor the show were still happy to help as they were able.

> The quality of Julian's completed homework was *declining* as he spent more time on the show and less on his school work.

Similar Sounds   ***where* and *wear***

Where refers to a physical place but *wear* refers to something you place on your body, such as clothing or make-up. So if you bought a new outfit for a party, your friends might ask you, "*Where* will you *wear* that great new dress?"

---

distraught (di-STRAHT) (adjective) extremely upset and agitated emotionally.

> One evening when Julian was planning the show, his computer malfunctioned and, thinking he had lost all of his work, he became *distraught*.

> Though not *distraught* over it, Zerah was extremely disappointed that the literary magazine could not be longer.

enlighten (in-LY-tn) (verb) to make something clearer or more understandable to someone; to inform.

> An interesting side effect of the show was that cast and crew members were *enlightened* by some of the excellent writing that they were working with.

> Gabe and Zerah *enlightened* them all about the importance of the show's success for expanding the literary magazine.

factor (FAK-ter) (noun) one element among several that make up a whole. (plural: factors)

> One *factor* of the show that had been missed so far was costuming and Hakim and Nisa took it upon themselves to work on that.

Other *factors* that they remembered but still hadn't had a chance to finalize were onstage lighting and sound.

foyer (FOY-r) (noun) the entryway in a building or house; a lobby in a public building. (plural: foyers)

The *foyer* of the school was a large, open area that was perfect for an art exhibit.

A concession stand selling snacks and drinks would be set up in the *foyer* during the first act of the show to make a little more money during intermission.

funnel (FU-nl) (verb) to direct a flow of something (such as liquid or money) in the direction that one wants it to go.

Mr. Garcia found himself *funneling* all of his spare time into helping the students pull the show together.

The assistant principal was pleased that the school did not have to *funnel* much money into supporting this show.

marketing (MAR-kuh-ting) (noun) the business of the trade of goods between a manufacturer or distributor and a buyer; the business of promoting a product, service, or group. (plural: This word is not usually used in the plural.)

The *marketing* of this show was of utmost importance, Nisa thought, because she didn't want people to think it would just be like reading one's work aloud in English class.

The art student's mom helped with the *marketing* by donating some money for printing the student-produced posters that were going to be all over town.

mobilize (MO-buh-lyz) (verb) to activate; to make ready to move; to prepare.

Ms. Ruhakana *mobilized* the drama department to clean out the backstage areas in preparation for the show.

One day when everyone was discouraged and worn out from overwork, Rosario managed to *mobilize* the whole crew by moving part of the rehearsal to the stage itself.

notion (NO-shun) (noun) a frivolous idea or whim; an opinion or idea. (plural: notions)

At the beginning, Gabe had had a *notion* that he would be able to run everything in the show, but the growing complexity of the job made him glad to have lots of help.

Secretly, Mr. Garcia had a *notion* that if the show was successful this year, it might make a terrific annual event.

paraphernalia (per-uh-fu-NAYL-yu) (noun) accessories or equipment needed for (or associated with) a particular activity. (plural: This noun is used with either a plural or a singular verb.)

Nisa went backstage and was bewildered by all the lighting and sound *paraphernalia* piled up ready for use.

There wouldn't be an elaborate set onstage for this show, so most of the *paraphernalia* needed for building sets was put out of the way in storage.

phase (FAYZ) (noun) 1. a particular stage in a process. 2. a temporary condition, usually related to one's behavior or development. (plural: phases)

The planning *phase* of the show was almost finished and everyone was ready for the next stage: rehearsals.

Dylan had been going through a *phase* of being really bored at school, so this show was a real energizer for him.

preceding (pri-SEE-ding) (adjective) coming before (something else) in time or position.

Rosario had spent the *preceding* weekend finishing her reading and editing so that she would be ready for a final script consultation with Julian on Monday.

There had been an art exhibit earlier in the year that had not been well attended, and Gabe was hoping this show would have more visitors than the *preceding* one.

Easy Errors   ***preceding* and *proceeding***

Preceding is an adjective that describes "something coming before something else in time or position" and *proceeding* is a noun that means "a course of action" or is used in the plural, *proceedings*, to mean "a series of events taking place in a particular location." So, one might say, "*Preceding* the student council *proceedings*, the officers had lunch together."

---

proceeds (PRO-seedz) (noun) the profits from sales or fundraising. (plural: This word, defined in this way, is always used in the plural.)

The assistant principal was happy to have the *proceeds* from the show go to expand the literary magazine.

The art department did not make any extra claim on the show's *proceeds* because the literary magazine contained both text and art.

recruit (ri-KROOT) (verb) to persuade someone to join a certain group, often the military.

> Mr. Garcia managed to *recruit* a couple of teachers to help him supervise everything the night of the show.

> Dylan *recruited* a couple of friends to help him unravel all of the cables and wires backstage.

resolutely (re-zuh-LOOT-lee) (adverb) describes doing something with firm resolve; in a determined manner.

> Behind in math, Julian *resolutely* sat down to get that done during study hall so that he wouldn't miss rehearsal time later.

> Gabe had *resolutely* vowed that this show would be the best that they could all put together.

subsidize (SUB-suh-dyz) (verb) to help others by contributing towards the cost of something on their behalf (often, the government giving money to individuals or groups to support certain government programs or priorities).

> The parent's marketing firm decided to *subsidize* both the tickets and some of the advertising posters.

> The school *subsidized* the show by paying the maintenance person overtime to be available to help and to lock up the school afterwards.

trickle (TRI-kul) (verb) to dribble; to flow very lightly.

> Two weeks away from the show, new volunteers continued to *trickle* in to rehearsals, offering to help in some way.

> Money began *trickling* in as tickets went on sale.

Quick Match 23

Match each word to its definition.

1. ___ enlighten   A. to activate; to make ready to move; to prepare
2. ___ paraphernalia B. describes eyes that are filmy or have clouded vision
3. ___ alarmingly   C. business of promoting a product, service, group
4. ___ campaign   D. to say "no" politely; to drop in vigor or quality
5. ___ factor   E. in a manner that gives warning, or that creates upset and fear
6. ___ availability   F. in a determined manner
7. ___ conceive   G. a frivolous idea or whim; an opinion or idea
8. ___ conjoint   H. to direct a flow of something
9. ___ awash   I. particular stage in a process; temporary condition
10. ___ marketing   J. to persuade someone to join a group
11. ___ funnel   K. an organized plan to achieve a strategic goal
12. ___ subsidize   L. the entryway in a building or house; lobby
13. ___ trickle   M. the profits from sales or fundraising
14. ___ foyer   N. extremely upset and agitated emotionally
15. ___ preceding   O. one element among several that make up a whole
16. ___ curriculum   P. accessories or equipment for a particular activity
17. ___ mobilize   Q. flooded
18. ___ bleary-eyed   R. the flow of a small amount of liquid; dribble
19. ___ decline   S. being ready to be used; accessibility
20. ___ phase   T. plan of study for a particular academic course
21. ___ resolutely   U. coming before in time or position
22. ___ distraught   V. to inform; to make clearer, more understandable
23. ___ recruit   W. combined, joint, united
24. ___ notion   X. to help by contributing to the cost of something
25. ___ proceeds   Y. to understand; to create or develop in the mind

Sentence Completions 23

Choose the proper word or pair of words for each of the sentences below.

1. _____ in strong musicians, writers, and artists, there was a lot more creative talent in the school than many people in the community realized.

    (a) Bleary-eyed   (b) Distraught   (c) Awash   (d) Preceding   (e) Resolutely

2. A number of teachers had regretfully _____ the offer to sponsor this program.

    (a) trickled   (b) declined   (c) conceived   (d) enlightened   (e) subsidized

3. The students at the school raised money in a variety of ways with the _____ going to various extracurricular programs on campus.

    (a) curriculum   (b) preceding   (c) notion   (d) proceeds   (e) factor

4. To produce the _____ production, the students needed to _____ assistance from both the drama and art departments.

    (a) conjoint . . . mobilize   (b) curriculum . . . enlighten
    (c) foyer . . . subsidize   (d) availability . . . funnel   (e) factor . . . decline

5. The team continued to _____ helpers in their _____ to attract the best writers and performers in the school to participate.

    (a) conceive . . . availability   (b) enlighten . . . proceeds
    (c) decline . . . trickle   (d) funnel . . . phase   (e) recruit . . . campaign

Chapter 24: Burgeoning

What had started out as a light *fancy* was quickly becoming a show that needed *punctilious* attention. Gabe was busy *shepherding* shy artists. Julian and Rosario had almost concluded their work of *winnowing* out unsuitable pieces but still had to *contend* with writers who wanted to edit their work "just one last time." Nisa continued to *publicize* the show by producing an article a week for the school newspaper, and she had *subsequently* become deeply involved in the *staging* of the pieces along with Julian and Rosario.

These three *self-appointed* directors had tried several different organizing *principles* for planning the *format* of the show. At first, they organized the pieces by length, which made the show *choppy* at the beginning with shorter pieces and *plodding* at the end with the longer ones. The next system they tried was by grade level, *theorizing* that it might be unfair to *showcase* the work of older, more *sophisticated* student writers to the *disadvantage* of younger, less experienced ones. That didn't really work since talent and skill didn't seem to be as directly related to age as they had expected. They finally reorganized everything roughly by topic, with short and long pieces *intermingled*, and that seemed to work the best.

Small rehearsals were taking place all over the *grounds*. Two flutists, a guitarist, and three percussionists from the music program had volunteered to provide music for some of the pieces. Someone *sauntering* by Mr. Garcia's room after school might hear any number of musical and *vocal* combinations *wafting* through the door as the writers and musicians *improvised* together. Nisa and Julian ran back and forth from the main rehearsals in the auditorium to the experimental work going on in Mr. Garcia's room to listen, approve, or disapprove, and make recommendations. It was a *hectic* pace as they counted down the final days to the performance!

burgeoning (BUR-jun-ing) (adjective) sprouting; putting out new leaves or growth; beginning to flourish and grow.

> The *burgeoning* cast and crew sometimes made it difficult to keep order during rehearsals.

> Mr. Garcia was impressed with the *burgeoning* talent of many of the first-time performers.

choppy (CHAH-pee) (adjective) short, jerky sections with many transitions.

> Julian was doing one of his own pieces, a deliberately *choppy* poem with lots of sharp sounds to echo the sound of a machine.

> Nisa and Rosario struggled with placing two strong but short pieces in the program because they wanted to avoid a *choppy* feeling.

contend (kun-TEND) (verb) to struggle or compete with; to deal with.

> Julian's patience was being tested by having to *contend* with a variety of artistic personalities.

> Rosario happily *contended* with different personalities because she liked the challenge of helping disparate people get along with one another.

disadvantage (dis-ud-VAN-tij) (noun) a factor that makes a situation more prone to failure or loss; a negative trait. (plural: disadvantages)

> The main *disadvantage* of the timing of the show was trying to get rehearsal time onstage around the drama department's already-scheduled rehearsals.

> As a leader, Julian had a bit of a *disadvantage* since he wasn't as skilled as some at dealing with people.

fancy (FAN-see) (noun) a whim; imagination. (plural: fancies)

> Sometimes reading others' work inspired a *fancy* in Zerah to sit down and do some writing herself.

> In the *fancies* of her mind, Zerah could imagine all kinds of situations and images.

format (FOR-mat) (noun) the structure or plan for a performance or a printed page. (plural: formats)

> With the *format* of the show worked out, Julian and Rosario immediately began working on the staging of the show.

> The *format* of the advertising posters was very attractive, with student artwork and bold-faced text.

Easy Errors   *their, there,* and *they're*

When a group of people have something, it is *their* something; *their* shows possession of an item or items by a group. *There* is a word that shows location. *They're* is a contraction of *they* and *are*: they + are – a = they're. So if you want to explain where your fellow campers are on a camping trip, you might say, "*They're* in *their* tent over *there* by the campfire."

---

grounds (GROWNZ) (noun) the property around a specific building or set of buildings. (plural: This word, defined in this way, is always used in the plural.)

> The *grounds* of the school were particularly attractive and at one point, Gabe had considered doing the show outside.

> There were several buildings on the school *grounds* that were off-limits to students.

hectic (HEK-tik) (adjective) confusing and busy at the same time.

> Mr. Garcia's day had become extremely *hectic*, between preparing for his classes, teaching, and helping with the show.

> The students weren't sure how they would manage many more of these *hectic* days.

improvise (IM-pruh-vyz) (verb) 1. to write, recite, or perform without prior preparation or rehearsal. 2. to try to solve a problem or fix something with only what is available at the time (i.e., not necessarily with the proper tools or supplies).

> Nisa advised performers to be ready to *improvise* onstage if they forgot their lines.

> Julian *improvised* many of his instructions as a director since he hadn't had any previous experience at it.

intermingled (in-tur-MING-gld) (adjective) mixed together (in such a way that the combined elements are still distinguishable, such as a mixture of different colored golf balls).

> The *intermingled* music and text was promising to make a very entertaining show.

> The *intermingled* grade levels in the show encouraged friendships that normally would not have developed.

plodding (PLAHD-ing) (adjective) describes a slow, heavy movement; trudging.

> The *plodding* developmental stage of each individual act was hard on Nisa who liked to move quickly on things.

> The *plodding* pace of the early rehearsals, with constant starts and stops, was hard on everyone.

principle (PRIN-suh-pul) (noun) an ideal in which one believes and tries to follow; a basic truth. (plural: principles)

> Some of the writing in the show dealt with basic *principles* of life such as the value of love and truth.

> Mr. Garcia followed the *principle* of the students learning as much as possible by doing as much as possible.

Similar Sounds   ***principle** and **principal***

Principle is a noun that means "an ideal in which one believes and tries to follow." A *principal* is either "the most important person involved in a situation" or "the leader who presides over a group, particularly a leader of a school." So you might say, "The *principal's* main *principle* for running the school is to treat all people fairly."

---

publicize (PU-bluh-syz) (verb) to spread information to the general population, often to promote an event or product.

> Nisa had also written some short pieces for the local newspaper to *publicize* the event.

> Julian had *publicized* the show by going on a local cable radio station to talk about it for a few minutes.

punctilious (punk-TI-lee-us) (adjective) very precise; strictly meticulous in all details.

> Extremely *punctilious* about the show's sound, Dylan rearranged the sound elements repeatedly to get them just right.

> Unlike Zerah, the directors enjoyed the freedom of not having to be *punctilious* about spelling and punctuation since their text was being presented orally.

saunter (SAWN-tur) (verb) to stroll; to walk slowly and leisurely.

> The assistant principal *sauntered* past the rehearsals as often as she had time to do so because she enjoyed the buzz of activity.

> Early to rehearsal one day, Julian had a rare chance to *saunter* through the courtyard and get a little fresh air.

self-appointed (self-uh-POYN-tud) (adjective) describes taking responsibility upon oneself without formal outside approval.

> The directors may have been *self-appointed*, but the cast had few complaints about the work they were doing.

> Gabe made himself the *self-appointed* financial officer and handled all of the money coming and going for the project.

shepherd (SHEP-urd) (verb) to guide and protect a group.

> Gabe tried to encourage and *shepherd* the artists so that they felt appreciated.

> Rosario *shepherded* most of the drama and English students while Nisa and Julian focused a bit more on the musical component.

showcase (SHO-KAYS) (verb) to display someone or something in a way that makes it look its best.

> This show would really *showcase* students who normally had no way to shine publicly at the school.

> The yearbook staff would be *showcasing* the show by having a page in the yearbook devoted to the production.

sophisticated (suh-FIS-tu-kay-ted) (adjective) 1. stylish. 2. having gained practical knowledge of the world that replaces one's naïveté or simple innocence.

> Hakim was planning some *sophisticated* costumes for a couple of the pieces.

> Some of the students were really experienced and *sophisticated* writers, even as young as they were.

stage (STAYJ) (verb) to set up or direct a performance.

> The directors tried to *stage* the show as simply as possible.

> Parts of the show were *staged* with several speakers on the stage at once, highlighted in turn by spotlights.

subsequently (SUB-si-kwent-lee) (adverb) later; describes an action that follows another in time or sequence.

> After ordering snacks to sell at intermission, the students *subsequently* found out they could have ordered them cheaper from a different source.

> The show started with a few, quiet individual pieces and *subsequently* moved faster and became livelier with more people on stage.

theorize (THEE-uh-ryz) (verb) to think through or create an idea or explanation often based on limited information); to guess or speculate in an educated and informed way.

> Gabe *theorized* that the reason the show was working out was that most people involved were actually having fun with it.

> Julian *theorized* that more people would attend the show if the actual details of the performance were not revealed ahead of time.

vocal (VO-kul) (adjective) 1. relating to one's voice; able to produce sound. 2. outspoken.

> Some students' *vocal* output was too quiet for the auditorium and they had to be trained to project their voices better.

> Zerah was *vocal* about Gabe's decision to use some pieces submitted to the literary magazine as part of the show.

waft (WAHFT) (verb) to float gently on air, usually said of a gentle sound, a light breeze, or a pleasant scent.

> The thin, slight music of a lone flute *wafted* over the air from the rehearsal in Mr. Garcia's room and people stopped in the hall to listen to its magic.

> Hungry after hours of rehearsal, students gathered in the auditorium once the welcome smell of pizza (courtesy of Mr. Garcia) *wafted* through the backstage area.

winnow (WIN-o) (verb) to separate the wheat from the chaff (so, also refers to separating the unwanted or unneeded parts from the desired parts of something).

> As readers, the directors had had to *winnow* out some weak writing, but they couldn't do the same with weak readers of strong writing; they just had to work with the performers until they improved.

> Some of the written works were too wordy and had to be *winnowed* down for clarity and effect.

Quick Match 24

Match each word to its definition.

1. ___	grounds	A.	to struggle or compete with; to deal with
2. ___	shepherd	B.	to speculate in an educated or informed way
3. ___	waft	C.	to write, recite, perform without rehearsal
4. ___	choppy	D.	to stroll; to walk slowly and leisurely
5. ___	self-appointed	E.	sprouting; putting out new growth
6. ___	vocal	F.	to guide and protect a group
7. ___	theorize	G.	mixed together
8. ___	winnow	H.	to set up or direct a performance
9. ___	plodding	I.	describes short, jerky sections with many transitions
10. ___	contend	J.	to separate the unwanted from the desirable
11. ___	saunter	K.	a whim; imagination
12. ___	subsequently	L.	relating to one's voice; outspoken
13. ___	disadvantage	M.	slow, heavy movement; trudging
14. ___	publicize	N.	very precise; strictly meticulous in all details
15. ___	stage	O.	describes taking responsibility upon oneself
16. ___	punctilious	P.	a negative trait
17. ___	principle	Q.	describes an action that follows another in sequence
18. ___	sophisticated	R.	property around a set of buildings
19. ___	fancy	S.	to display something at its best
20. ___	intermingled	T.	an ideal or basic truth one tries to follow
21. ___	burgeoning	U.	stylish; describing a lack of innocence or naïveté
22. ___	format	V.	confusing and busy at the same time
23. ___	improvise	W.	to float gently on air
24. ___	showcase	X.	to spread information to the general population
25. ___	hectic	Y.	a structure or plan for page or performance

Sentence Completions 24

Choose the proper word or pair of words for each of the sentences below.

1. Some of the language the students used in their written work was surprisingly mature and _____ for writers so young.

    (a) burgeoning (b) sophisticated (c) plodding (d) choppy
    (e) intermingled

2. The show was very carefully planned but the performers had to be ready to _____ to cover up a problem if something were to go wrong.

    (a) publicize (b) shepherd (c) waft (d) winnow (e) improvise

3. Along the way to the completion of this show, the students had to _____ with small rehearsal spaces, missing people, and late submissions among other problems.

    (a) contend (b) publicize (c) stage (d) shepherd (e) waft

4. This production was a perfect _____ for highlighting the _____ talent in the art, English, music, and drama departments at the school.

    (a) format . . . hectic (b) principle . . . sophisticated
    (c) showcase . . . burgeoning (d) grounds . . . self-appointed
    (e) fancy . . . publicized

5. If Mr. Garcia were to _____ about the reasons for the show's success, he would likely say that the meticulous and _____ attention to detail by the students was the main reason.

    (a) improvise . . . self-appointed (b) contend . . . burgeoning
    (c) publicize . . . vocal (d) theorize . . . punctilious (e) saunter . . . hectic

Chapter 25: Fruition

Opening-night *jitters* wasn't a *term* that even came close to describing her emotions, Cinnamon *determined*. She had three poems to do in the show and putting on her make-up and *attire* for her first poem, she knew with *certainty* that she would never be able to *recollect* a word of any of them. Pree was sympathetic but *distracted*. She had submitted a short story that Julian had divided into five sections *slated* to come into the show at different points. She was not only worried about her lines but also about remembering all of her *cues* properly.

In the lobby, Gabe was *patrolling* the displays, smiling and making sure no one touched the art. He had *solicited* a few of the artists to be there to talk about their work, and some of the audience members were genuinely interested in what the students had to say. Others were happy to *cruise* around the pieces and look at them *perfunctorily* as they waited for the auditorium doors to be opened.

Nisa and Zerah were putting the last-minute touches on the snacks they would be selling from the *concession* stand during the *entr'acte*. The group had sold fully half of all their preprinted tickets before the show date so they all knew there would be a decent *house* for that night's performance.

The auditorium doors were opened ten minutes before the show, announced with a *flourish* by one of the drummers. The audience was eager to enter and get settled, which helped the show start on time. Largely *ignorant* of *blunders* in the show that seemed *glaring* and obvious to the cast, the audience laughed *uproariously* and *applauded* appropriately. The final piece, a touching poem of loss and *redemption* by Cinnamon, had the crowd almost in tears just moments before they were clapping enthusiastically for the entire cast.

Exhausted but pleased with how the show had gone, Gabe and Julian looked at each other as the crowd *filed* out. The two of them had one other secret to share with Zerah: there was now enough money for another three pages to be added to the literary magazine this year! A *decided* success.

applaud (uh-PLAWD) (verb) to show approval for something, usually by clapping one's hands together repeatedly after a public performance.

> The audience would *applaud* approvingly after almost every piece.

> Before the show, the assistant principal *applauded* the cast and crew for their creative commitment to the production.

attire (uh-TYR) (noun) clothing, especially fancy or elaborate clothing. (plural: This word is used for both singular and plural.)

> Most of the students wore everyday *attire* as their costumes.

> Cinnamon had particularly elaborate *attire* for her last piece.

blunder (BLUN-dur) (noun) a serious mistake that happens through clumsiness, lack of knowledge or confusion. (plural: blunders)

> Dylan was frustrated by a lighting *blunder* at the end of the first act.

> One actor almost made the *blunder* of going onstage at the wrong time, but Pree managed to stop him in time.

certainty (SUR-tn-tee) (noun) a sure knowledge of something. (plural: certainties)

> The *certainty* of a job well-done helped everyone sleep well that night.

> After the success of this show, Mr. Garcia felt it was a *certainty* that this would become an annual event.

cruise (KROOZ) (verb) to move along, in a vehicle or on foot, in a leisurely manner looking casually around oneself or for something.

> Gabe enjoyed being able to slow down and *cruise* around the artwork for a few minutes before the show.

> Some of the audience members just *cruised* past the concession table to see what was there, but most of them stopped for something to eat or drink during the intermission.

cue (KYOO) (noun) a signal given to indicate that it is time to start a task.

> The drummer's flourish was a *cue* to the audience to enter the auditorium.

> Dylan was proud not to have missed a single sound *cue* for the entire show.

decided (di-SYD-ed) (adjective) definite; without any argument or doubt.

> The teachers all considered the evening a *decided* victory for those who felt that students should be given more responsibility for on-campus events.

> The assistant principal wanted everyone to write down the steps they had taken to produce the show so that there would be a *decided* plan for the next year's production.

determine (di-TUR-mun) (verb) to figure out something or decide on it for certain.

> Adding up the ticket and concession sales, Gabe and Julian tried to *determine* whether the show had actually made a profit.

> Zerah had *determined* that she was going to enjoy the show and just not worry about whether or not it made a profit for the magazine.

distracted (di-STRAKT-ed) (adjective) describes having one's focus pulled away by an unrelated sound, sight, or other stimulus; unsettled emotionally.

> After the light cue mistake, the *distracted* audience had to pull their attention back to the important action onstage.

> In the second act, a *distracted* Cinnamon was running all around backstage trying to find her other shoe.

entr'acte (AHN-trakt) (noun) an intermission or break between sections of a performance. (plural: entr'actes)

> The *entr'acte* came a little late in the show, making the second act shorter than the first.

> Watching the show from the back of the auditorium, Nisa had to rush out to tend the concession table when the *entr'acte* began.

file (FYL) (verb) to walk in a line.

> When the cast all *filed* out at the end of the show for the curtain call, they were all happy at the sound of the applause.

> In preparation for a possible fire, the cast and crew had *filed* out of the auditorium for three practice fire drills a week before the performance.

flourish (FLUR-ish) (noun) a fanfare; elaborate movements or music that draw attention to something or someone. (plural: flourishes)

> For one funny piece, the musicians had prepared a long and elaborate *flourish* of music only to have the speaker recite a quick limerick and leave the stage.

> Gabe would have liked to begin the show with a *flourish* of trumpets but none of the trumpet players had decided to become involved in the show.

Easy Errors   *flammable*, *inflammable*, **and** *nonflammable*

Two of these words mean the same thing: *flammable* and *inflammable* both refer to something that burns very easily (such as paper or wood). *Nonflammable* refers to items that do not burn (such as water and concrete).

---

fruition (froo-I-shun) (noun) the state of bearing fruit; the final achievement of a desired accomplishment. (plural: This word is not usually used in the plural.)

> There was a great satisfaction in Gabe, Julian, and Zerah to see their little, tiny idea come to *fruition* so dramatically.

Because of timing, the *fruition* of the art show had had to come even faster than that of the live production.

glaring (GLAYR-ing) (adjective) very obvious; shining uncomfortably brightly.

Dylan felt that that one failed light cue was a *glaring* mistake, but others seemed to have missed it.

The *glaring* lights above the stage made it difficult for the performers to see individual people in the audience.

house (HOWS) (noun) the seating area of a performance space such as a theater; the audience that is seated in such a space. (plural: houses)

With the *house* more than half full, Gabe knew there would be at least a small profit from the show.

The *house* was made up mostly of friends and family of those working in the show so it was a very friendly and forgiving audience.

ignorant (IG-nr-unt) (adjective) uneducated or unknowing; showing a lack of knowledge, understanding, or education.

Initially *ignorant* of anything to do with lighting, one crew member followed Dylan around to learn everything he could.

When Ms. Ruhakana saw how *ignorant* some of the performers were about the technical side of stage work, she resolved to promote her Technical Theater course more actively.

jitters (JI-turs) (noun) nervous energy that shows itself to others by shaky movements. (plural: This word is usually used in the plural.)

Although Cinnamon had a bad case of the *jitters*, she looked absolutely calm and professional on stage.

Pree seldom got the *jitters* too seriously before a karate tournament, but she had been terribly nervous about tonight's performance.

patrol (puh-TROL) (verb) to move around an area, on foot or by vehicle, especially for security or observation.

The supervising teachers found it difficult to pull themselves away from the show to *patrol* the halls during the production.

Mr. Garcia was *patrolling* the backstage area more out of nervousness than need.

perfunctorily (pur-FUNK-truh-lee) (adverb) done with little interest; done routinely and with indifference.

> Busy thinking about other things, Zerah *perfunctorily* accepted tickets from audience members as she made sure that she hadn't forgotten anything important.

> One of the teachers came across a student at his locker and *perfunctorily* reminded the student to return to the auditorium.

recollect (re-kuh-LEKT) (verb) to remember something; to recall to one's mind.

> Mr. Garcia could not *recollect* being personally involved in a more successful production.

> Having had to perform one poem barefooted, Cinnamon *recollected* where she had put her other shoe in time for the curtain call at the end.

redemption (ri-DEM-shun) (noun) rescue; the act of saving someone from sinfulness; the restoration of one's character or reputation after a loss. (plural: redemptions)

> The *redemption* of a lost soul was the theme of Cinnamon's last poem.

> Julian had had a reputation with the teachers of being a bit lazy, so his hard work on this show was a *redemption* of his character in their eyes.

Similar Sounds   *stationary* and *stationery*

Stationary is an adjective that describes "someone or something that is not moving and is remaining in one place." *Stationery*, however, is a noun describing writing paper and envelopes. So a young woman might "remain *stationary* in her chair as she used her violet-colored *stationery* to write a letter to her aunt."

---

slate (SLAYT) (verb) to schedule.

> The cast and crew had to empty the stage of their belongings right after the show because the auditorium was *slated* for a community political meeting the next day.

> Hakim had been *slated* to have a study hall in his schedule the next year, but he was so interested in this work that he decided to take drama instead.

solicit (suh-LI-sit) (verb) to ask for something (such as donations or votes) by persuasion or by organized effort.

> Nisa and Zerah had a clean, gallon jar on the concession table to *solicit* additional donations for the literary magazine.

> The team sent a nice thank you letter to the marketing company in case they might need to *solicit* help from them again in the future.

term (TURM) (noun) specific language used to identify a particular idea or action. (plural: terms)

> By the end of this show, Nisa knew the proper *term* for each piece of backstage equipment that she had earlier found so confusing.

> Mr. Garcia had struggled to find just the right *term* to define this show and decided he would refer to it as an "oral anthology."

uproariously (up-ROR-ee-us-lee) (adverb) loudly, hilariously, and without restraint.

> After the show, everyone was so excited by the success that they were giddy and laughed *uproariously* at any small thing.

> Zerah laughed *uproariously* when she found she had absentmindedly put the money in the refrigerator and the leftover snacks in the lockbox while talking with Gabe after the show.

Quick Match 25

Match each word to its definition.

1. ____ uproariously
2. ____ applaud
3. ____ term
4. ____ attire
5. ____ solicit
6. ____ blunder
7. ____ slate
8. ____ certainty
9. ____ redemption
10. ____ cruise
11. ____ recollect
12. ____ cue
13. ____ perfunctorily
14. ____ decided
15. ____ patrol
16. ____ determine
17. ____ jitters
18. ____ distracted
19. ____ ignorant
20. ____ file
21. ____ house
22. ____ flourish
23. ____ glaring
24. ____ fruition
25. ____ entr'acte

A. to schedule
B. a signal to start a task
C. to remember something; to recall to mind
D. to walk in a line
E. seating area of a performance space; audience
F. to move leisurely while casually looking around
G. done routinely and with indifference
H. to ask for something by persuasion
I. fancy or elaborate clothing
J. final achievement of a desired accomplishment
K. showing a lack of knowledge, education
L. a sure knowledge of something
M. very obvious; shining brightly
N. loudly, hilariously, without restraint
O. a serious mistake through clumsiness, confusion
P. restoration of one's character or reputation
Q. to show approval, usually by clapping
R. elaborate movements or music to draw attention
S. to figure out something for certain
T. nervous energy
U. an intermission
V. specific language to identify an idea or action
W. definite; without any argument or doubt
X. to be unsettled emotionally
Y. move around an area for security or observation

Sentence Completions 25

Choose the proper word or pair of words for each of the sentences below.

1. Another way the group could have raised money would have been to _____ advertisements from local businesses to print in the program that evening.

    (a) cruise   (b) determine   (c) solicit   (d) file   (e) slate

2. There is usually someone backstage following the script to be sure that no performer misses his or her _____ to go onstage or offstage at the right time.

    (a) entr'acte   (b) cue   (c) flourish   (d) jitters   (e) attire

3. With a(n) _____ born of experience, Ms. Ruhakana knew without a doubt after watching the first full rehearsal that this show would be successful.

    (a) ignorance   (b) fruition   (c) redemption   (d) attire   (e) certainty

4. Cinnamon was confused and _____ by the bright, _____ lights when she first stepped out on stage during dress rehearsals.

    (a) decided . . . term   (b) distracted . . . glaring   (c) determined . . . house
    (d) filed . . . entr'acte   (e) solicited . . . blunder

5. Rather than clap _____ just to be polite, the audience _____ enthusiastically because they really enjoyed the show.

    (a) perfunctorily . . . applauded   (b) uproariously . . . cruised
    (c) ignorantly . . . patrolled   (d) decidedly . . . recollected
    (e) certainty . . . slated

WRITING ACTIVITY

Vocabulaire Extraordinaire

Life exists to be a significant challenge, pressing us to perform greater and greater feats of skill and daring.

Pushing on,

ever striving,

ever competing with ourselves,

hurling ourselves into a frenzy of anticipation

and accomplishment!

But, fortunately, not in THIS particular writing activity. (Whew!)

Your simple—albeit creative—task this time is to write no more than ten logical sentences. Simple, right? The challenge (of course there *must* be a challenge) is to use *every single one* of a chapter's vocabulary words, in a logical fashion, in those sentences.

The Rules:

1. You must use every single vocabulary word in a given chapter.
2. You may change the form of the word to make it fit your sentence. (For example, a singular noun may become a plural, a verb form may change to a noun form, an adverb form to an adjective form.)
3. Your sentences must make logical sense.
4. For an even greater challenge, try to use all of a chapter's vocabulary words logically in fewer than ten sentences.

Sharpen your pencils! Be impressive!

SECTION 6: THE RHYTHM OF THE EARTH

Learning Style: The Naturalist Learner

The Way
Go out into Earth.
Roll in moss, lick a pebble,
dance a circle round a tree, catch
a falling feather on your palm,
watch a turtle head thumb up
from pond to measure you—
smile greeting,
for this going out is going in,
in to your root nature,
for you are Earth, and if you are
to know yourself, you must know
the rest of Earth, and know too
that each atom of your flesh has been
since Earth has been,
and always has been shared
with all alive, and know as well
how in each live cell the spirals dance,
as spiraled stardust coalesced
into the sun and Earth
and eventually you,
for going out is going in.
　　　　　　　　　　—*John Caddy*

If you find yourself much more relaxed and alert when you are outside breathing the fresh air, one of your primary intelligences is likely that of the Naturalist learner.

　　Are you someone who is acutely aware of the differences in the feel and smell of the air from one season to the next? Are you fascinated by the creepy-crawlies in the lawn that others find disgusting? Are you a collector: minerals, types of leaves, butterflies? Are animals closer to your heart than most humans? Are you surprised when others find it difficult to see the difference between an ash tree and an elm tree? Do you spend free time trying to work out solutions to ecological issues such as pollution and acid rain? Is it as necessary for you to feel the texture of the earth beneath your toes as it is for you to breathe?

If you have answered "yes" to several of the above, this is one of your stronger intelligences.

Possible Approaches

- *Categorizing.* One of your strengths is being able to group items into categories. Use this to your advantage and study your words by part of speech (noun, verb, adjective, and adverb) or by negative and positive definitions (for example, negative: badger, perfidious, underhanded; positive: blithe, embolden, melodious).

- *Flashcards.* Making flashcards for studying vocabulary may not have been a great technique for you in the past, but how about trying it with scented markers? You could divide your vocabulary words into parts of speech and assign a scent to each. (For example, nouns: banana; verbs: roses; adjectives: raspberry; adverbs: licorice.) Perhaps it would be easier for you to group words by meaning: for example, words that have to do with "smart"—such as "clever" and "sly"—should get their own scented marker. You also might consider giving particularly difficult words their own, individual marker scent. Don't underestimate your nose's connection to your intellect!

  - **Variation.** Instead of using regular three-by-five-inch index cards, cut flashcards from colored construction paper in the shapes of different leaves, flowers, and animals. Write the word on one side of your flashcard and the meaning on the other. Use these cards for review.

  - **Draw a Plant.** If you like to draw, create a simple line drawing of one of your favorite plants. Using those lines as a guide, outline your plant in vocabulary words to help you build both a physical and visual memory of how the words are spelled.

  - **Animals in Action.** When you are learning verbs, imagine native wild animals (squirrels, bears, deer) or exotic zoo animals (pandas, koalas, elephants) performing those actions. Those are images that will stay with you!

  - **Review vocabulary while you tend your pets.** Scratch your cat behind the ears and review several words aloud. Review a vocabulary word for every time that you throw a ball for your dog while you play fetch together. Connecting each word to a pleasurable activity involving a live creature will help you remember the words you review.

  - **Go outside to study!** This is your natural environment. Relate the vocabulary words to your observations of nature each day.

Chapter 26: Wild Child

Although an *astute* student of nature, Isabelle was not your typical tree-hugger *traipsing* through the forest. Yes, she liked to *indulge* in long nature walks. Yes, she enjoyed keeping records of her *meticulous* observations of plant and animal life: she had an *affinity* for oddities and looked around for unusual or *subtle* changes in her forest—always *alert*, she once spotted an *indolent* garter snake sunning itself on a fallen tree.

Unlike the usual student of the natural world, however, Isabelle wasn't a *cautious*, silent figure slinking through the woods. Ever *boisterous*, she sort of exploded into the woods, sending birds shrieking into the skies and small, furry creatures diving into their burrows. Not for her the *melodious* songs of the meadowlark on the edge of the field or the brooding *melancholy* of a catbird's song from a *thicket* of bushes—she was lucky to catch a glimpse of a *befuddled* squirrel scrambling for a safe hideaway. She loved her woods anyway, from the beauty of the clear blue skies to the *noisome* smells of *malodorous* skunk cabbage in the spring and the occasional *fetid* old bear droppings she found on some of her more *clamorous* encounters with hanging vines and overgrown paths.

Some of her *cronies* at school *badgered* her for her *solo* wanderings, but rather than discourage Isabelle, their *criticisms* merely *emboldened* her to offer her friends, with a twinkle in her eye, a bite of an *edible* plant and a chance to *escort* her to the woods the next day to try it out for themselves.

affinity (uh-FI-nu-tee) (noun) a close attraction or connection between items or people. (plural: affinities)

> Lucy had an *affinity* for cats, even the shy ones, who seemed to trust her right away.

> Showing his *affinity* for surfing, Kwesi spent every minute he could at the shore either surfing or studying other expert surfers.

alert (uh-LURT) 1. (adjective) to be ready, wide-awake, watchful. 2. (noun) a warning of a specific danger. (plural: alerts)

> I am wide-awake and ready to go birding in the mornings, but I cannot stay *alert* in the afternoons; I get very drowsy then.

> When the squirrel saw the students entering the woods, it chattered an *alert* to warn the other squirrels of the possible danger.

astute (uh-STOOT) (adjective) wise, clever (in a good way).

> "It was very *astute* of you to ask that question," the park ranger praised. "Many people would not have seen the connection you make between those two ideas."

Orlando was too *astute* to accept the first explanation he was offered. He did his own research to confirm his observations on deer behavior.

badger (BA-jur) (verb) to pick on someone repeatedly; to hassle or pester someone. (This verb is named for a northern digging mammal because of its aggressive temper.)

You must quit nagging and *badgering* her about getting that work done! She is spending time arguing with you instead of doing the work.

Isabelle *badgered* her parents repeatedly until they finally allowed her to canoe by herself.

befuddled (bi-FU-dld) (adjective) confused. (Usually used of someone who is a little disorganized in the mind and easily muddled.)

Trying to hear the difference among the different bird calls left him so *befuddled* that he had to stop for the day.

The bat house came in a kit and all of the parts needed to be assembled at home. The instructions were so *befuddling* that I decided to take a break and go back to it later to see if they made more sense.

boisterous (BOY-stur-us) (adjective) happily noisy; exuberant and active. Also rough or violent (as in a *boisterous* game like dodge ball).

The bullfrogs sounded *boisterous* at night, keeping the campers awake with their constant, happy chugging.

After an early, quiet canoe on the lake, we were all ready to play a *boisterous* game like soccer and run off some energy.

cautious (KAW-shus) (adjective) very careful in words and actions.

A *cautious* boy, Tamir gently touched the odd beetle with a stick before nudging it off the walking trail for its own safety.

Isabelle was *cautious* not to tell where she found the rarest plants in the woods so that they might remain protected.

clamorous (KLA-mur-us) (adjective) noisy, loud. (Often used for a lot of people talking loudly all at once.)

The rest of the forest was so quiet that her thrashing through the woods and getting caught in the brambles sounded almost *clamorous*.

The school group was excitedly *clamorous* when they spotted the bald eagle flying overhead.

criticism (KRI-tu-si-zum) (noun) a judgment made on someone's actions, thoughts, or performance. A "criticism" doesn't have to be a negative or bad comment but in many cases it is. (plural: criticisms)

> The naturalist wrote a *criticism* of the scientist's theory in which she agreed with certain ideas and disagreed with others.

> Isabelle was used to *criticism* on her noisy behavior in the woods but it was impossible for her to walk as quietly as others did.

crony (KRO-nee) (noun) someone who hangs around with someone else; a good friend or buddy. (plural: cronies)

> He joined the Environmental Club so that he could have some *cronies* who enjoyed the outdoors as much as he did.

> She and her favorite *crony* would go rock climbing several times a month.

edible (EH-du-bl) (adjective) describes something that a person can safely eat.

> Science might consider some mushrooms *edible*, but they all taste like poison to me.

> Just because something is *edible* doesn't mean it can't be bad for you. Isabelle found she was allergic to those wonderful wild strawberries she used to pick in the woods in the spring.

Easy Errors   *ei* vs. *ie*

A big spelling problem for many people is whether to use *-ei* or *-ie* in certain words. The old verse repeated in grammar schools for years is of great help here:

"I" before "e"   (ex. belief)
Except after "c"   (ex. receive)
Or when sounded like "a"
In "neighbor" and "weigh."

There are, naturally, a few exceptions to this rule, but this is a great starting point for getting your spelling on track.

---

embolden (im-BOL-dun) (verb) to give courage to someone else; to encourage bravery in someone else.

> Isabelle remained still, hoping to *embolden* the young doe to come closer to her.

> Some of Isabelle's friends were *emboldened* to try one of the edible plants she offered them.

escort (ES-kort) (verb) to go along with someone on a walk, a trip, or a date either to protect the other or to enjoy his or her company.

> Isabelle's friends would occasionally *escort* her into the woods just to see what new, interesting discoveries she had made recently.

> When Isabelle was little, her older brother had *escorted* her to the woods and inspired in her a great love of the outdoors.

fetid (FE-tid) (adjective) describes something that smells really bad; stinky (synonym of *malodorous*).

> The *fetid* remains of old, rotting leaves filled the swamp.

> Wild animals and cars are a bad combination. Not only is wildlife being killed on our highways daily, but the *fetid* odor of dead animals fills the air in the immediate area.

indolent (IN-du-lunt) (adjective) lazy; inactive.

> Isabelle didn't always get her homework done but it wasn't because she was *indolent*. She was so busy with her wildlife observations, she just forgot about her schoolwork sometimes.

> When the weather cools, cold-blooded animals become sluggish and *indolent* because they don't have enough body heat to stay active.

indulge (in-DULJ) (verb) to give in to your own desires; to give yourself a treat.

> Whereas some of her friends really enjoy a trip to the mall, Isabelle likes to *indulge* herself by going bird watching.

> Blake is on a pretty tight budget but once a week he *indulges* himself by renting a wildlife video as a special treat.

malodorous (mal-O-du-rus) (adjective) describes something that smells really bad; stinky (synonym of *fetid*).

> There are all kinds of smells at the beach. I enjoy the smell of the salt air but I don't care for the *malodorous* dead fish rotting on the sand.

> Lilies are lovely flowers when they are fresh, but when they begin to wilt they start producing a strong *malodorous* scent and have to be thrown out.

melancholy (MEL-un-kah-lee) (adjective) sad.

> The haunting call of a Northern Loon always makes Jess a little *melancholy*.

> It was a *melancholy* situation: cold rain, leaky tent, and no ride home for three more days.

melodious (mu-LO-dee-us) (adjective) describes a sweet, pleasant voice or song.

> A cardinal only chirps randomly, but a mockingbird is a most *melodious* singer.

> When Nguyen first met her, he never even noticed her voice. He knew he was falling in love, though, when every word Isabelle said began to sound sweet and *melodious* to him.

meticulous (mu-TI-kyoo-lus) (adjective) showing great attention to small details; very careful in one's work.

> A mapmaker or cartographer needs to be extremely *meticulous* in his or her measurements to make sure a map is as accurate as possible.

> Evan was so *meticulous* in recording details of the woodpeckers' nesting habits that he was admired in local birding groups.

noisome (NOY-sum) (adjective) generally, bad for one's health. (Specifically, used to describe something that smells really bad.)

> The exhaust from all of the construction trucks made the air in the nearby woods *noisome* and nasty during the workday.

> The *noisome* herbal tea was difficult to swallow but she was determined to try the old Native American headache remedies.

Pieces and Parts   *mal-*

Mal- is from the Latin *malus* (bad) and works as a very active prefix in English: *malcontent* (someone who is always dissatisfied), *malevolent* (wishing ill on others), *maladroit* (someone whose fingers are clumsy) are just a few of the words from this list.

---

solo (SO-lo) (adjective) alone.

> Jenna made her first *solo* day-long canoe trip at the age of fourteen. She was nervous about being in the wilderness alone but it went very well.

> I have read about *solo* sailors who have sailed around the world on private sailboats. That is an awesome achievement, but I think the loneliness would kill me if the ocean didn't.

subtle (SU-tl) (adjective) 1. not obviously seen or heard. 2. complicated or difficult to solve in an intellectual way (when describing a problem).

> Nguyen's reaction to the chipmunk's arrival was very *subtle*, but the animal still ran off quickly at the young man's first move.

> Weather prediction is a *subtle* problem, not easily solved, with many variables (such as wind direction and humidity) to consider.

thicket (THI-kut) (noun) a thick growth of bushes and small trees, usually in a limited area. (plural: thickets)

> Despite their size, deer can hide in small *thickets* in the medians between lanes on major highways. A driver has to be careful to watch out for them.

> The fox chased the rabbit into a *thicket* of bushes and brambles that had openings small enough for the rabbit to escape through but not large enough for the fox to follow.

traipse (TRAYPS) (verb) to walk about without carefulness or great purpose.

> The unhappy students were forced to *traipse* about on the field trip in the pouring rain, trying hard to find all of the items on their scavenger hunt lists.

> Without a care in the world, they *traipsed* along the river, enjoying the sound of the water and the great company.

Quick Match 26

Match each word to its definition.

1. ___	solo	A.	to go along with someone on a walk
2. ___	meticulous	B.	exuberant and active
3. ___	traipse	C.	very careful in words and actions
4. ___	melodious	D.	loud, noisy (particularly when describing a crowd)
5. ___	accompany	E.	a judgment of someone's actions or words
6. ___	thicket	F.	a good friend or buddy
7. ___	subtle	G.	something one can safely eat
8. ___	melancholy	H.	sad
9. ___	cautious	I.	describes a sweet, pleasant voice or song
10. ___	crony	J.	showing great attention to small details
11. ___	embolden	K.	bad for one's health; stinks
12. ___	indulge	L.	confused; easily muddled in the head
13. ___	fetid	M.	alone
14. ___	befuddled	N.	to encourage bravery in someone else
15. ___	noisome	O.	describes something that smells really bad
16. ___	malodorous	P.	lazy; inactive
17. ___	affinity	Q.	to give yourself a treat
18. ___	criticism	R.	foul smelling
19. ___	alert	S.	not obviously seen or heard
20. ___	badger	T.	a thick growth of bushes and trees
21. ___	astute	U.	to walk about without great purpose
22. ___	boisterous	V.	a close attraction or connection
23. ___	indolent	W.	to be ready, wide-awake, watchful
24. ___	edible	X.	wise, clever (in a good way)
25. ___	clamorous	Y.	to pick on someone repeatedly; to pester

Sentence Completions 26

Choose the proper word or pair of words for each of the sentences below.

1. We were all surprised at how _____ Isabelle was at keeping her naturalist research notes; we assumed she would be as untidy with them as she was with her daily schoolwork.

    (a) astute   (b) indulgent   (c) meticulous   (d) indolent   (e) cautious

2. One must be very careful when picking mushrooms in the wild. Some, like morels and puffballs, are safely _____ but others are deadly if eaten.

    (a) fetid   (b) alert   (c) cautious   (d) indulgent   (e) edible

3. He was so closely connected to the natural world that he was _____ on rainy days and upbeat and happy on sunny days.

    (a) indolent   (b) cautious   (c) befuddled   (d) melancholy   (e) boisterous

4. The _____ sound of the birds in the trees that afternoon was sharply interrupted by the _____ cacophony of quarreling squirrels.

    (a) astute . . . badgering   (b) noisome . . . melancholy
    (c) melodious . . . . clamorous   (d) boisterous . . . alert   (e) subtle . . . solo

5. Normally extremely _____ the badger was _____ by the smell of the hiker's lunch and bravely came out of his burrow to investigate.

    (a) malodorous . . . indulged   (b) cautious . . . emboldened
    (c) alert . . . befuddled   (d) boisterous . . . made indolent
    (e) subtle . . . astute

Chapter 27: An Unhappy Plan

On one of her *meandering* walks with a *callow* youth from a lower grade, Isabelle *articulated* her desire to take a canoe out on a small pond to observe *aquatic* life. The poor young man, desperately in love with this *amateur* naturalist, foolishly agreed. *Blithely* unaware of Nguyen's *amorous* intentions towards her, Isabelle talked him into letting her handle the canoe.

When she started to paddle with her usual *aggressive* energy, Nguyen feared they would *capsize* in no time. At first pale with *trepidation*, Nguyen began to see the *advantage* of his situation. If they did, indeed, tip over, this *calamity* could be a blessing for him. In case of a *disastrous* dumping into the water, he would *jettison* his usual quiet and shy manner and take charge; he would seize the *unwieldy* canoe, flip it over, and *wrangle* them both back into its safety! He began to *ponder* the possibilities. He would become her equal instead of being some *lowly* kid she took along on her nature walks! She would have to give him the *mandatory* kiss for saving her life! *Slyly*, Nguyen decided to pull an *underhanded* trick on Isabelle and tip the canoe over himself.

Several minutes later, only hip-deep in water in the middle of the pond, Nguyen realized his mistake; since they could walk to shore, a dramatic rescue was hardly necessary. *Naively* unaware of Nguyen's spoiled plan, Isabelle laughed *amiably* at their dripping wet clothes and stringy hair as they gathered up all their floating belongings. Heartbroken that his *deception* had failed him, Nguyen *resolved* to find another way to earn Isabelle's love and admiration.

advantage (ud-VAN-tij) (noun) a positive opportunity; a characteristic that gives you a greater chance of success. (plural: advantages)

> You should take *advantage* of the extra time the teacher offered to complete this project and interview that famous scientist you know.

> Because I am tall, I have an *advantage* when climbing trees.

aggressive (uh-GRE-siv) (adjective) 1. very active. 2. usually tending to start fights or arguments; showing a tendency to attack.

> That poison ivy rash she got was very *aggressive* and spread rapidly before she could get it treated by the doctor.

> One needs to be careful around bears. They seem very gentle but can become *aggressive* and dangerous if hungry or threatened.

amateur (A-mu-tur) (noun) one who does something as a hobby, out of love, but not as a professional (sometimes used to express someone's weak or unskillful efforts on a project). (plural: amateurs)

> John may be an *amateur* wood-carver but two of his pieces look nicer than any professional work I have seen in the same field.

I tried to carve an opossum out of wood but my finished product was disappointingly that of an *amateur*, and sloppy.

amiable (AY-mee-uh-bl) (adjective) describes someone who is easy to get along with and very friendly in a comfortable way.

Don't be shy about kayaking with Laura for the first time. She is so *amiable* that she gets along with everyone right away.

Some animals just seem more *amiable* than others. Chickadees, for instance, always seem friendly to me, but alligators always seem to be in a bad mood!

amorous (A-muh-rus) (adjective) describes a feeling of romantic love.

The little lizards on the garden wall get *amorous* in the spring and chase one another around trying to find mates.

Lovebirds are not really more *amorous* than any other kind of birds; they just enjoy having company.

aquatic (uh-KWA-tik) (adjective) having to do with water (usually related to an activity or life-form that is associated with a natural body of water, like a pond, lake, or ocean).

Maura loves all *aquatic* creatures but is most interested in African cichlids, a large family of fish.

If you are interested in spiders, there are some amazing *aquatic* arachnids in the ponds of this area.

articulate (ar-TI-kyoo-layt) (verb) to express a thought clearly in speech.

Unless you *articulate* your kayaking instructions carefully, I am afraid that people may not be safe on the water.

Winston *articulates* our ideas so clearly that our study group always gets him to present our conclusions on our water quality study to the whole class.

blithely (BLYTH-lee) (adverb) in a happy, cheerful, joyous way.

"Hello, everyone," she called out *blithely* to the singing birds. "Isn't it a beautiful day?"

As tired as he was, he couldn't help looking at the rising sun *blithely* and with thanks.

calamity (ku-LA-muh-tee) (noun) an event that causes misery; a disaster. (plural: calamities)

> It would be terrible if there were a forest fire in our area. With so many homes in the woods, it could be a *calamity*.

> Worried about the environmental *calamity* caused by the oil spill, Isabelle raised money in her school to help pay for the cleanup.

Easy Errors   ***comprehensive* and *comprehensible***

Comprehend is a verb that means "to understand" so *comprehensible* is, logically, an adjective that means "easy to understand." Oddly enough, *comprehensive* is used slightly differently. It is usually used to mean "extensive in content" as in *comprehensive* exams (that cover an entire year's work, for instance). So, if you find chemistry *comprehensible* from week to week, you shouldn't have any trouble on the *comprehensive* exam at the end of the year."

---

callow (KA-lo) (adjective) inexperienced, immature.

> Because he was physically so small, people expected him to be much more *callow* than he was.

> The *callow* young man felt insecure sitting with the older crowd at the planning meeting for the new conservation area. He didn't know what to say to the people sitting around him.

capsize (KAP-syz) (verb) to turn upside down (usually a boat).

> It's not a problem if a kayak *capsizes* because they are very easy to flip back over again. Of course, the paddler still gets very wet!

> When the ferry boat *capsized* in the storm, many lives were lost in the cold water.

deception (di-SEP-shun) (noun) a trick designed to cheat or mislead someone. (plural: deceptions)

> Lewis pretended he had done his biology homework and his *deception* worked—the teacher never noticed. There was a problem, however, when he tried to pass the quiz on that material.

> Some insects are disguised. Walking Stick insects, for example, look like twigs and this *deception* protects them from predators.

disastrous (di-ZAS-trus) (adjective) unlucky (in a big way!), terrible, causing calamity

> Trying to backpack on the Appalachian Trail without some careful preparation can be *disastrous*.

The power of the tornado was *disastrous*. Seventeen houses were destroyed on one street alone. Fortunately, no one was killed.

jettison (JE-tu-sun) (verb) to throw away or cast off something that is useless.

"Why don't you just *jettison* that CD player so that your backpack is lighter?" he said to his best friend before they began their hike.

The rowboat was sinking quickly in the pond. To keep from getting wet, they *jettisoned* everything unnecessary from the boat but it still kept sinking.

lowly (LO-lee) (adjective) in a position below someone else; of humble status or origins.

I may only be a *lowly* student right now, but I have plans to be a great environmental engineer some day.

The small zooplankton in the ocean may seem like *lowly* life forms but without them many whales would starve.

mandatory (MAN-du-tor-ee) (adjective) describes something that must be done or is required.

It is *mandatory* that no visitor touch a native animal or plant in the Galapagos Islands in Ecuador.

To protect manatees in the channels in Florida, it is *mandatory* for boats to travel very slowly.

meander (mee-AN-dur) (verb) to wander around without particular purpose.

That little stream *meanders* all over the county, providing drinking water for cattle on many different farms.

As tourists, we decided to *meander* around the national park and let ourselves be surprised by all of its beautiful sights.

naïve (ny-eev) (adjective) overly innocent of the ways of the world; unsophisticated.

It was *naïve* for Isabelle to think that everyone was as concerned with environmental issues as she was.

More experienced with nature trails than fancy parties, Isabelle felt *naïve* and awkward at the reception for the world-famous naturalist.

ponder (PAHN-dur) (verb) to think long and hard on an issue or problem.

You're going to need to *ponder* carefully the correct sorting of your recyclable items from your trash.

As I *pondered* the differences between alligators and crocodiles, I realized that I needed more information about both.

resolve (ri-ZAHLV) (verb) to make a promise or vow to oneself; to make a similar vow or promise to oneself again.

> I will *resolve* to redouble my efforts to improve at rock climbing.

> After his bad experience, Nguyen *resolved* never again to go canoeing with Isabelle.

Easy Errors   *flotsam* **and** *jetsam*

You may come across these terms in your reading sometime so it is worth knowing the difference between them. *Jetsam* is items that are thrown out of a boat (i.e., jettisoned) to make the boat lighter in case of emergency. *Flotsam*, however, is broken pieces of a ship or cargo left floating after a ship has sunk. So, *jetsam* may help a ship survive an emergency, but *flotsam* shows that attempts to save a ship failed.

---

slyly (SLY-lee) (adverb) describes something done in a way that is both sneaky and clever.

> When Nguyen *slyly* offered to help her with the paddling, she didn't know she was about to get wet.

> Isabelle found that the best way to attract a shy cat was to *slyly* pretend to ignore the creature.

trepidation (tre-pu-DAY-shun) (noun) a feeling of fear or dread. (plural: This word is not usually used in the plural.)

> The *trepidation* I feel before I go caving is almost worse than the feeling I get actually squeezing through a narrow space.

> It was with great *trepidation* that I handed in my nature project. I didn't feel confident that I had done well on it.

underhanded (un-der-HAN-ded) (adjective) dishonest; sneaky.

> It was *underhanded* of you to steal Mkame's idea for the Science Fair project.

> She made a big deal out of how good exercise was for us all but, in an *underhanded* way, she took the shortcut on the hike without telling the rest of us about it.

unwieldy (un-WEEL-dee) (adjective) awkward or difficult to carry because of size or weight; clumsy.

> The beached porpoise was *unwieldy* as the group tried to lift it enough to get it back into the water.

My telescope, being both large and heavy, was *unwieldy* as I tried to get it up the stairs and into my dorm room at the university.

wrangle (RANG-gul) (verb) to round up (usually a herd of livestock); to capture and confine to a specific area (like a corral for livestock).

When cattle graze freely on hundreds of acres of land, cowboys periodically must *wrangle* them for a head count.

Cowboys may find it a lot of work to *wrangle* cattle, but when I was in middle school, I think my teacher found us tougher to round up and control.

Quick Match 27

Match each word to its definition.

1. ___	sly	A.	easy to get along with; friendly
2. ___	meander	B.	smart or clever in a sneaky way
3. ___	capsize	C.	happy, cheerful, joyous
4. ___	amiable	D.	to express a thought clearly
5. ___	naïve	E.	a feeling of dread or fear
6. ___	amorous	F.	awkward due to weight or size; clumsy
7. ___	trepidation	G.	to round up (usually said of livestock)
8. ___	blithe	H.	describes a feeling of romantic love
9. ___	disastrous	I.	unsophisticated; overly innocent of the world
10. ___	resolve	J.	a trick designed to cheat or mislead someone
11. ___	jettison	K.	unlucky (in a big way!)
12. ___	aggressive	L.	to think long and hard on an issue or problem
13. ___	unwieldy	M.	in a position below someone else; humble
14. ___	calamity	N.	to make a promise or vow to oneself
15. ___	lowly	O.	inexperienced, immature
16. ___	articulate	P.	a positive opportunity
17. ___	mandatory	Q.	having to do with water
18. ___	wrangle	R.	very active; showing a tendency to attack
19. ___	deception	S.	describes something that must be done
20. ___	advantage	T.	to turn upside down (usually a boat)
21. ___	aquatic	U.	one who loves something as a hobby not a job
22. ___	callow	V.	a disaster; an event that causes misery
23. ___	ponder	W.	untrustworthy; traitorous
24. ___	underhanded	X.	to wander without particular purpose
25. ___	amateur	Y.	to throw away or cast off something useless

Sentence Completions 27

Choose the proper word or pair of words for each of the sentences below.

1. Rather than follow the clearly marked trails, they got lost in the national park as they _____ from one area of interest to another.

   (a) pondered   (b) articulated   (c) meandered   (d) wrangled   (e) capsized

2. They did not realize that staying on the groomed trails was _____; the parks imposed a fine on people who went off the trails into the woods.

   (a) mandatory   (b) amiable   (c) blithe   (d) disastrous   (e) underhanded

3. Because the canoe was in danger of _____ in the swift current, Bill was forced to _____ some of his extra supplies to lighten the load in the canoe.

   (a) meandering . . . articulate   (b) capsizing . . . jettison
   (c) wrangling . . . unwieldy   (b) deceiving . . . advantage
   (e) pondering . . . wrangle

4. Her underhanded _____ was all the more believable to her friend because, although that friend was very smart in a lot of ways, he was much too honest to suspect such a(n) _____ and sneaky trick.

   (a) calamity . . . amateur   (b) trepidation . . . aggressive
   (c) advantage . . . lowly   (d) deception . . . sly   (e) resolve . . . amiable

5. Young in both knowledge and experience, the _____ youth was so _____ about life in the woods that he slept with his backpack full of food as a pillow so that he could protect it at night.

   (a) amiable . . . blithe   (b) sly . . . aggressive   (c) callow . . . naïve
   (d) aquatic . . . underhanded   (e) articulate . . . amorous

Chapter 28: Some Things Fishy

Isabelle's best friend was Maura, an *effervescent* redhead with a *penchant* for breeding aquarium fish. Because she was so fond of her fishy friends, she *abstained* from eating all seafood, thinking it was almost *churlish* to treasure some of them but consume others. Maura felt *scorn* for those hobbyists who were satisfied with mere guppies; she bred several species of cichlids (pronounced "sick-lids"), African fish from Lake Malawi and its neighboring *rift* lake, Lake Tanganyika. Over the years, Maura had *accumulated* twelve fish tanks, ranging from several ten-gallon tanks to a seventy-five-gallon tank. She was *captivated* by the complex behavior of her fish and was careful to keep the more *pacific* and gentle species away from the more *antagonistic* and aggressive fish.

Maura had a *knack* for keeping her tanks in top condition. To encourage her fish to breed, she was *assiduous* about monitoring the water conditions in her tanks. To *mitigate* the problems of chlorine and other additives in her tap water, Maura would fill buckets of water a day before she needed them and leave them in the open air to let the worst chemicals evaporate. She would then *judiciously* adjust the pH (the alkalinity or acidity of the water) and, when it was a perfect match for her tank's water, she would add it carefully. As careful as she was, the practice always made her fish a little nervous; she could read their emotions because her cichlids became *pallid* with fear when major changes happened in the tank. About fifteen minutes after a water change, though, the fish would be *mollified* by the quiet in their tank and their colors would become brighter and their markings clearer as they relaxed. Maura loved being able to relate to her fish emotionally like this.

What *jeopardized* the calm in a tank the most was, of course, whenever she introduced a new fish to an established tank. The *hostility* shown by the established males to a new male in the tank could be life-threatening to the newcomer. To *inhibit* their *bellicose* tendencies, Maura would sometimes rearrange the plants and rocks in the tank so that the older males' territories would be unfamiliar to them. The most *implacable* male could often be confused and calmed by this action. Once the territory problems were *alleviated*, the fish lived quite *amicably* together and Maura delighted in their *mock brawls* and amorous adventures.

abstain (ab-STAYN) (verb) to hold back from doing something by your own choice.

> Although the vote was close, Isabelle chose to *abstain* from voting because she couldn't decide which group was right.

> Some animal rights supporters feel that killing any animal is wrong, while others feel that *abstaining* from legal hunting practices isn't necessary.

accumulate (uh-KYOO-myu-layt) (verb) to gather together or to pile up; to increase.

> As Maura *accumulated* different species of fish, she found she had to increase the number of tanks she had to buy to keep them all well.

Maura's weekend jobs began to *accumulate* as she had to tend all of those extra tanks.

alleviate (uh-LEE-vee-ayt) (verb) to lessen the pain or difficulty of something.

To *alleviate* the amount of work she would have to do at the end of the semester, Maura decided to turn in her biology project one week early.

While she couldn't cure her fishes' mysterious infection, Maura was able to *alleviate* their suffering somewhat by treating the tank with antibiotics.

amicable (A-mi-ku-bl) (adjective) friendly.

Their formerly *amicable* relationship was changed after they had a huge and bitter argument.

Maura didn't like to mix African cichlids with South American cichlids in the same tank because their personalities were not *amicable*.

antagonistic (an-TA-gu-NIS-tik) (adjective) describes one who opposes another; hostile.

Because her fish aggressively established territories within their tanks, they were *antagonistic* towards other fish that entered those areas.

Because the two sides disagreed so completely about the conservation issue, the discussion became hotly *antagonistic*.

Word Play   *protagonist, antagonist,* and *deuteragonist*

We often think of the *protagonist* in a book or movie as "the good guy" and the *antagonist* as "the bad guy," but this isn't entirely accurate. Ancient Greek theater was often presented as a contest or *agon*, so the first actor in a play was referred to as the *protagonist* (prot = first + contestant) and the second actor would be referred to as the *deuteragonist* (*deuteros* = second + contestant) or as the *antagonist* (anti = against or opponent + contestant), depending on his role. Regardless of whether the lead character was good or evil, he was—and still is—the *protagonist*.

---

assiduously (uh-SIJ-wus-lee) (adverb) describes doing something carefully and consistently; diligently.

Although she normally did not take as much care with her homework as she did with her tanks, Maura worked *assiduously* on group projects so that she wouldn't let her classmates down.

When making a nest in the gravel to impress his mate, the cichlid would *assiduously* pick up aquarium stones in his mouth and then spit them out elsewhere in the tank for hours on end.

bellicose (BE-li-kos) (adjective) describes someone who is quick to anger; war-like; violent.

> While Maura's fish in her mixed tank of cichlids could be territorial and a little rough, she kept her most *bellicose* fish in their own tanks.

> Maura watched her fishes' behavior carefully; if one spread out his fins to look bigger and made his colors intensify, she knew he was getting in a *bellicose* mood and she needed to intervene in the tank.

brawl (BRAWL) (noun) 1. a loud or disorganized fistfight. 2. a noisy argument or fight. (plural: brawls)

> One male in her Lake Malawi tank had such a tendency to start *brawls* that Maura had to move him into a tank by himself for the safety of the others.

> While not likely to get involved in a *brawl* over it, Maura was passionate about her fish and defended her fishes' behavior hotly when cichlid aggression was criticized.

captivated (KAP-ti-vay-ted) (adjective) describes being attracted with a feeling of strong emotion; to be charmed.

> Not usually interested in plants, the artist in Nguyen was *captivated* by the pattern of the petals on an unusual flower he found.

> To be polite, Maura pretended to be *captivated* by other people's pets but she was really only interested in her own fish.

churlish (CHUR-lish) (adjective) behaving like someone with no manners; rude.

> Although it was *churlish*, Maura often expressed her disdain for more common tropical fish in front of her friends who kept them.

> Maura had a favorite Mozambique cichlid that was fun to watch in the tank but had, unfortunately, a tendency to be *churlish* with the other fish.

effervescent (EH-fur-VE-snt) (adjective) 1. to be filled with, or giving off, bubbles (as in a carbonated drink). 2. describes someone who is bouncy and excited.

> A healthy fish tank usually has an air tube from which *effervescent* bubbles of air flow up through the water to the surface.

> Maura bounced around the house all day, *effervescent* in her excitement about her brother's new fish tank.

hostility (hah-STI-lu-tee) (noun) a feeling of ill will or anger, normally directed at an enemy. (plural: hostilities)

> She felt *hostility* toward anyone who would choose to eat fish.

After several days of *hostility*, Maura decided to separate the two enemy fish and put them in separate tanks.

implacable (im-PLA-ku-bl) (adjective) describes someone whose anger or firm opinion cannot be reduced or changed by persuasion.

Maura's stance on eating fish was *implacable*: no fish at any time.

Maura tried to convince her teacher to accept her project in two stages—one part on time, the other part three days later—so that she could complete the behavior experiment on her fish, but the teacher was *implacable* as far as flexible due dates was concerned.

inhibit (in-HI-but) (verb) to hold something back; to reduce one's desire to do something.

Keeping her fish well-fed seemed to *inhibit* some of their aggressive tendencies.

The teacher's unwillingness to extend the due date to accommodate Maura's experiment *inhibited* Maura's desire to work very hard on the project.

jeopardize (JE-per-dyz) (verb) to place in danger; to risk something.

Maura monitored the water quality in her fish tanks very carefully so as not to *jeopardize* the good health of her fish.

Unwilling to *jeopardize* her strong grade in Biology class, Maura modified her experiment to fit the assignment's due date.

judiciously (joo-DI-shus-lee) (adverb) with care and prudent consideration.

She adjusted the pH of the tank's water *judiciously* so as not to over-correct and, possibly, harm her fish.

Maura acted *judiciously* when she agreed to her teacher's project due dates.

knack (NAK) (noun) a natural talent for something. (plural: This word, defined in this way, is not used in the plural.)

Some of her fish seemed to have a *knack* for "home decoration;" when building nests in the gravel they rearranged all of the plants and small rocks in the tank.

Maura seemed to have a *knack* for successfully breeding some of the more sensitive types of cichlids.

mitigate (MI-tu-gayt) (verb) to lessen the bad effects of something; to help something become milder or less intense.

> To *mitigate* the tendency of her tank water to become too warm in the summer, Maura had a small air conditioner in her tank room.

> Maura occasionally moved a dominant male out of his usual tank to help *mitigate* a growing problem with aggressive behavior in that tank.

Similar Sounds   ***inhibit* vs. *inhabit***

Inhibit is a verb that means "to hold something back," and *inhabit* is a verb that means "to live (in a particular place)." So, it might *inhibit* someone's actions if he *inhabited* a dangerous neighborhood.

---

mock (MOK) 1. (adjective) imitation; counterfeit. 2. (verb) to make fun of something or someone; to treat with ridicule or contempt.

> The younger fish sometimes staged *mock* battles, much as do kittens and puppies, to play at what they would do seriously as adults.

> Some of the girls at school *mocked* Maura's obsession with fish as silly and unfeminine, but Maura tried not to let that bother her.

mollify (MAH-lu-fie) (verb) to lessen someone's feelings of anger or resentment; to soothe.

> The fact that Maura made money by selling her fish to local pet shops helped to *mollify* her hurt feelings.

> The fish's aggressive tendencies were *mollified* by the addition of three more females to the tank at the same time the new male was introduced.

pacific (pu-SI-fik) (adjective) calm; tranquil.

> Don't think Maura only appreciated her rough-and-tumble fish; her more pacific varieties were just as precious to her.

> Most people who looked at Maura's tanks didn't see the elaborate social system at work in each fish community; all they appreciated was the *pacific* and hypnotic effect of watching the fish swim around.

pallid (PA-lud) (adjective) very pale, often from fright or illness; dull-colored or lacking intensity of color.

> The newcomer to the tank looked *pallid* for almost a w
> became more comfortable in his surroundings.

Maura bred her fish for attractive color as well as health. If she had some that were unusually *pallid*, she made a point to sell them rather than breed them.

penchant (PEN-chunt) (noun) a strong liking for something; a particular attraction or talent for something. (plural: This word is not usually used in the plural.)

Maura's careful monitoring and observation of her own fish translated itself into a penchant for careful work during biology lab experiments.

Without a particular *penchant* for business, Maura didn't always make the best financial decisions when selling her fish to shrewd pet shop owners.

rift (RIFT) 1. (noun) a break or gap in a natural geological formation or in a relationship. 2. (adjective) describes such a break or gap.

Maura and Chani used to be close friends until some mysterious argument caused a *rift* between them.

The *rift* lakes in Africa are so-called because of a natural shift in the land mass that has set them at different heights.

scorn (SKORN) 1. (verb) to criticize someone cruelly and with contempt. 2. (noun) the expression of disdain or contempt toward someone or something.

Maura *scorned* those people who used professional tank cleaning services; she preferred to tend to her fish herself.

You could see the *scorn* in Maura's eyes when she came across a salesperson in a pet shop who didn't know the African cichlid varieties very well.

Quick Match 28

Match each word to its definition.

1. ____	implacable	A.	describes one who opposes another
2. ____	abstain	B.	describes someone who is bouncy and excited
3. ____	mock	C.	a particular attraction or talent for something
4. ____	accumulate	D.	to lessen the pain or difficulty of something
5. ____	pacific	E.	an expression of disdain or contempt
6. ____	alleviate	F.	a feeling of ill will or anger
7. ____	inhibit	G.	to hold back from doing something by choice
8. ____	amicable	H.	with care and prudent consideration
9. ____	mollify	I.	a break or gap in the earth or in a relationship
10. ____	antagonistic	J.	friendly
11. ____	penchant	K.	describes someone quick to anger; war-like
12. ____	assiduously	L.	imitation, counterfeit; to treat with ridicule
13. ____	knack	M.	to gather together or pile up; to increase
14. ____	bellicose	N.	to soothe
15. ____	judiciously	O.	describes one whose opinion can't be changed
16. ____	brawl	P.	to reduce one's desire to do something; hold back
17. ____	rift	Q.	to do something carefully and consistently
18. ____	captivated	R.	calm, tranquil
19. ____	pallid	S.	a loud or disorganized fistfight; to fight noisily
20. ____	churlish	T.	to place in danger; to risk something
21. ____	scorn	U.	to lessen the bad effects of something
22. ____	effervescent	V.	behaving like someone with no manners; rude
23. ____	mitigate	W.	very pale; lacking intensity of color
24. ____	hostility	X.	a natural talent for something
25. ____	jeopardize	Y.	describes being attracted with a feeling of strong emotion

Sentence Completions 28

Choose the proper word or pair of words for each of the sentences below.

1. Her calm and _____ manner in the midst of the emergency was helpful to all concerned.

    (a) bellicose   (b) implacable   (c) pallid   (d) pacific   (e) effervescent

2. With his _____ for animals and his interest in research, he would make a terrific marine biologist.

    (a) scorn   (b) brawl   (c) penchant   (d) rift   (e) hostility

3. The unruly tourists were _____ and _____ to the park ranger even though she asked them nicely to obey the rules.

    (a) scornful . . . effervescent   (b) churlish . . . antagonistic
    (c) assiduous . . . pallid   (d) inhibited . . . captivated
    (e) pacific . . . amicable

4. Afraid that the project might be _____ by the lack of harmony in the group, she worked hard to _____ the anger the team members felt.

    (a) captivated . . . scorn   (b) jeopardized . . . mollify
    (c) mitigated . . . inhibit   (d) accumulated . . . pacify
    (e) alleviated . . . mock

5. The dominant fish's _____ manner made it unsafe for other fish in the tank; indeed, he often started _____ with the other males for no apparent reason.

    (a) bellicose . . . brawls   (b) pallid . . . knacks   (c) amicable . . . rifts
    (d) churlish . . . inhibitions   (e) mock . . . penchants

Chapter 29: Conserving Interest

Because of his interest in Isabelle, Nguyen had joined a local *conservation* group and found, to his surprise, that it was a gathering of *jovial* and *vivacious* citizens. He had expected every meeting to be an *ordeal* of suffering through the dull conversations of *sedate* and *phlegmatic* bores, *punctuated* by stolen quick and sunny chats with Isabelle herself. Certainly there were a few *killjoys* whose purpose seemed solely to *foretell* doom and the destruction of all living things, but they were in the *minority*. Nguyen and Isabelle both found themselves drawn to the *optimistic* crowd that was *infused* with a sense of purpose in relation to environmental issues. Rather than *harangue* about the *follies* of near-sighted governmental policies, this group chose to take action and try to persuade others of the seriousness of *hazardous* waste dump sites and the value of natural wetlands. They seemed *impervious* to *pessimism* and *devoted* to the *mammoth* task of improving all aspects of the local environment.

Trying to avoid letting Isabelle know *overtly* that he attended the meetings only on her account, Nguyen joined a committee to which she did not belong. He was an *obliging* committee member, performing whatever task was asked of him. He once spent a weekend in the woods with his dad counting various *nocturnal* moths for the group. Another time, worried about the *paucity* of *migrating* hawks in their county, the group asked Nguyen to help with a local *census* of birds of prey. As a *neophyte* naturalist, Nguyen felt lucky to be taking part in these projects.

census (SENT-sus) (noun) a periodic, official count of those in a particular population. (plural: This word is not usually used in the plural.)

> Nguyen and his family moved to the neighborhood just after the government did its official *census*, so they won't be included in government statistics of the area until the next one.

> Every year in December the Audubon Society holds its national Christmas Bird Count, a *census* of birds in particular areas of the country at that precise time.

conservation (KAHNT-sur-VAY-shun) (noun) the act of preserving something from loss or damage (now usually applied to issues regarding the natural environment). (plural: This word is not usually used in the plural.)

> The *conservation* of the health of our national waterways includes efforts to clean local streams that run into major waterways.

> Some might say my cat is lazy since she sleeps about twenty hours a day; I prefer to say that she is involved in energy *conservation*!

folly (FAH-lee) (noun) a silly mistake; something that shows a lack of judgment or careful thought. (plural: follies)

> One often excuses the *follies* of his or her past by explaining that people do silly things when they are young and inexperienced.

> In their haste to clean the fish tank before the party that night, they didn't see the *folly* of their ways until the tank was almost empty and they had no safe place to store the fish during the cleaning.

foretell (for-TEL) (verb) to speak of something that will happen in the future; to predict.

> Many conservationsts *foretell* great problems with our natural environment if individuals don't stop to think about little, everyday things they can do to help (for instance, recycling).

> I wonder how many scientists could have *foretold* how helpful the banning of DDT (a pesticide) would be in restoring bald eagle populations in the United States?

harangue (hu-RANG) (verb) to criticize or instruct someone forcefully and emotionally in speech or writing.

> I used to *harangue* my friends about issues in habitat conservation, but they didn't pay any attention to me until I calmed down and spoke to them as reasonable, intelligent human beings.

> A columnist in the local newspaper *harangued* the local politicians weekly for not taking firm stands on environmental issues.

hazardous (HA-zur-dus) (adjective) risky; dangerous.

> While counting hawks, Nguyen was careful to avoid *hazardous* situations such as tripping over loose rocks on the path while looking up at the sky.

> Certain chemicals that were once thought to be harmless when discharged into our rivers have been found to build up to *hazardous* levels in the water over time.

impervious (im-PUR-vee-us) (adjective) describes something that cannot be affected or penetrated by an outside factor.

> Isabelle was so devoted to her conservation efforts that she was *impervious* to criticism from those who did not take her interests as seriously as she did.

> The polluted creek was *impervious* to local efforts to try to clean it up.

infuse (in-FYOOZ) (verb) to soak something in water to extract certain properties (such as tea leaves in hot water to extract flavor or medicinal properties); to fill with something.

> He *infused* catnip leaves in hot water to make a tea. It tasted terrible, but this *infusion* did help him fall asleep.

> Despite himself, Nguyen became *infused* with enthusiasm over his role in the conservation society.

jovial (JO-vee-ul) (adjective) cheerful and friendly, usually in a way that includes a group of people.

> The host of the conservation meeting was *jovial* and included the newcomers in everything in a warm and friendly way.

> Normally *jovial*, Isabelle could become very cold with those who did not support her conservation efforts.

killjoy (KIL-joy) (noun) someone who ruins the fun for others or dampens their enthusiasm. (plural: killjoys)

> She and her boyfriend are such *killjoys* that no one wants to invite them to be on their committees.

> As the group's plans were getting bigger and bigger, Isabelle feared that they would never be able to make their plan work. She didn't want to be a *killjoy*, but she felt compelled to express her concerns.

mammoth (MA-muth) (adjective) very large.

> Educating the public about the need to conserve water seemed like a *mammoth* task to Isabelle.

> Lake Erie used to be much more polluted than it is now. It took a *mammoth* effort of both the U.S. and Canadian governments to save that lake.

Easy Errors   ***migrant, immigrant,*** **and** ***emigrant***

Someone who migrates (or regularly moves) from place to place is a *migrant* or nomad. Someone who leaves one's home country for another is an *emigrant* from his or her own country but an *immigrant* to his or her new country. So someone who moved permanently from Spain to the United States would be an *emigrant* from Spain and an *immigrant* to the United States.

migrating (MY-gray-ting) (adjective) describes someone or something that moves from one place to another, often seasonally.

> Some *migrating* birds travel great distances of thousands of miles from their winter grounds to their summer grounds each year; others only travel a relatively short distance of several hundred miles.

> I once had the privilege of seeing migrating monarch butterflies gathering to *fly* from Canada to Mexico for the winter. The branches of the trees around our house were literally drooping with the weight of them all!

minority (mu-NOR-uh-tee) (noun) a small group that is part of a larger group and is different in some way from the larger group. (plural: minorities)

> Serious environmentalists used to be a *minority* in this country but, over the years, many more people have become involved in conservation issues.

> Isabelle knew she was in the *minority*, but she had to disagree with the direction the discussion was going.

neophyte (NEE-uh-fyt) (noun) someone who is new to something; a trainee; a beginner. (plural: neophytes)

> At his first conservation meeting, Nguyen did not really understand what everyone was talking about and he was almost embarrassed at what a *neophyte* he was.

> The *neophyte* organization only had ten members but they expected to build up their membership as people heard about their activities.

nocturnal (nahk-TUR-nl) (adjective) most active or awake at night.

> Cats in the wild may be *nocturnal*, but my house cat has gradually resisted this tendency and adapted largely to my daytime schedule.

> During her summer holidays, Maura's schedule was much more *nocturnal* than usual; she went to bed at about 3 A.M. and got up around noon each day.

obliging (uh-BLYJ-ing) (adjective) very cooperative; happy to be of service.

> Anxious to do favors for Isabelle, Nguyen was extremely *obliging* every time she asked for his help.

> Once Nguyen became involved in the conservation society, his father was very supportive and *obliging*, often driving several members to the meeting each week.

optimistic (ahp-tuh-MIS-tik) (adjective) describes one who looks on the positive side of a situation; favoring the good in things over the bad; expecting things to go well.

> Nguyen is *optimistic* about his chances to get Isabelle to notice him.

> Maura has two pairs of fish that have not bred successfully recently, but she is *optimistic* that they will breed soon.

ordeal (or-DEEL) (noun) an extremely difficult or painful situation or experience. (plural: ordeals)

> When Isabelle was seriously ill last winter the true *ordeal* for her was not the disease itself but the fact that she could not go outside for three full weeks.

> Nguyen loved to read about arctic explorers and longed to visit the arctic himself; he did, however, have a pretty clear idea of the sorts of *ordeals* these explorers had to contend with in the bitter cold.

overtly (o-VERT-lee) (adverb) out in the open; publicly.

> *Overtly* supportive of the plan, Isabelle still had some secret doubts about how it would work.

> While he didn't enjoy being secretive about how he felt about Isabelle, Nguyen was worried that *overtly* declaring his affection would interfere with their growing friendship.

paucity (PAW-su-tee) (noun) a scarcity; a lack of something; a small amount or number of something. (plural: This word is not usually used in the plural.)

> With a *paucity* of cash in their account, it was difficult for the conservation group to do much work without trying to raise some money first.

> Although the group had a *paucity* of active members, they had a lot of community support for the work those few people were doing.

Pieces and Parts   *viv-*

Viv- comes from *vivere* (to live) and gives *vivacity* its liveliness in English. This root gives us a number of other words in English including *vivify* (to make something come alive), *vivid* (which describes something with lifelike images in the mind), and *viviparous* (which describes animals who bear their young alive instead of laying eggs).

pessimism (PE-su-mi-zum) (noun) the condition of looking on the negative side of a situation; a tendency to see the bad in things over the good; an expectation that things will go badly. (plural: This word is not used in the plural.)

> In a rare bout of *pessimism*, Isabelle declared that she could see no hope for their project's success.

> Maura was not normally given to *pessimism*, but she could not see how they could get everything done in time for Earth Day.

phlegmatic (fleg-MA-tik) (adjective) without excessive emotion; calm and practical (but a little boring).

> After Isabelle's pessimistic outburst, a more senior and phlegmatic member of the group calmly assured them all of the soundness of their plan.

> Those who had been in the group longer were more *phlegmatic* about what progress they might and might not be able to achieve than were the enthusiastic new recruits.

punctuate (PUNK-chu-wayt) (verb) 1. to put small marks in a printed text in order to direct a reader. 2. to emphasize something in a quick and direct way.

> The organization's brochure had to be reprinted; the editor forgot to *punctuate* the text and it was impossible to read.

> She *punctuated* the strong points in her speech by stabbing her right forefinger at the audience in a forceful way.

sedate (si-DAYT) (adjective) quiet and calm; calmly dignified.

> The president of the organization behaved in a very *sedate* manner during the debate, calmly responding to all criticisms.

> Most of the children were restless during the meeting, but one sedate little boy sat still in the back corner, imitating his father's calm manner.

vivacious (vu-VAY-shus) (adjective) lively; spirited.

> Isabelle charmed the older members of the group with her *vivacious* and animated spirit.

> Wishing the speaker were a little more *vivacious*, the audience struggled to stay awake throughout the long, monotonous speech.

Quick Match 29

Match each word to its definition.

1. ___	impervious	A.	a silly mistake that shows a lack of judgment
2. ___	neophyte	B.	preserving something from loss or damage
3. ___	folly	C.	risky, dangerous
4. ___	nocturnal	D.	very cooperative; happy to be of service
5. ___	vivacious	E.	an extremely difficult or painful experience
6. ___	paucity	F.	to emphasize in a quick and direct way
7. ___	conservation	G.	cannot be penetrated from outside
8. ___	migrating	H.	a negative point of view; expecting the worst
9. ___	harangue	I.	lively; spirited
10. ___	obliging	J.	without excessive emotion
11. ___	census	K.	a scarcity; a lack of something
12. ___	punctuate	L.	expecting things to go well; seeing the good
13. ___	hazardous	M.	cheerful and friendly
14. ___	overtly	N.	a trainee; a beginner
15. ___	foretell	O.	one who ruins the fun for others
16. ___	ordeal	P.	very large
17. ___	minority	Q.	describes something that moves, often seasonally
18. ___	phlegmatic	R.	a different, small group within a larger group
19. ___	killjoy	S.	a periodic official count of a population
20. ___	pessimism	T.	to predict
21. ___	sedate	U.	to criticize forcefully in a long speech
22. ___	mammoth	V.	to fill with something; to make a tea
23. ___	jovial	W.	calmly dignified; in a quiet manner
24. ___	optimistic	X.	most active or awake at night
25. ___	infuse	Y.	out in the open; publicly

Sentence Completions 29
Choose the proper word or pair of words for each of the sentences below.

1. Water is kept away from a duck's body by an oil the ducks preen through their feathers, making them _____ to water.

     (a) nocturnal   (b) impervious   (c) vivacious   (d) obliging   (e) phlegmatic

2. Documenting the human genome has been a _____ task, involving thousands of scientists and other specialists for years.

     (a) mammoth   (b) sedate   (c) hazardous   (d) nocturnal   (e) migrating

3. Usually his stuffy, _____ manner was boring and irritating, but during the emergency, his unemotional decisions were critical to everyone's safety.

     (a) pessimistic   (b) jovial   (c) phlegmatic   (d) overt   (e) obliging

4. The experienced researcher _____ the _____ at length over every little error or oversight the newcomer made.

     (a) punctuated . . . minority   (b) foretold . . . killjoy
     (c) infused . . . optimist   (d) harangued . . . neophyte   (e) obliged . . . folly

5. The _____ was confident that the _____ of interest was a temporary situation; more people would get involved soon, he thought.

     (a) pessimist . . . minority   (b) killjoy . . . mammoth
     (c) optimist . . . paucity   (d) neophyte . . . ordeal   (e) census . . . infusion

Chapter 30: Acting Locally

The more Isabelle and Nguyen *associated* with the conservation group, the more they realized that they needed to be doing something *significant* in their own neighborhood. They decided to start with a recycling *endeavor* at their school, and branch out into other projects later. Nguyen put several *partitioned* barrels in the cafeteria for student use, with separate sections for glass bottles, soft drink cans, and plastic waste. (These separations were as *stringently* enforced as possible.) *Simultaneously*, Isabelle *petitioned* the teachers to have *receptacles* in their classrooms for recyclable paper. As their best friend, Maura *rallied* a group of students to help with weekly collection of recyclables and also approached a *philanthropic* organization for money to help them pay for the classroom receptacles.

The project was more easily *initiated* than maintained. Despite their plastic gloves, student volunteers were *timid* about *scavenging* through a week's worth of lunch waste in preparation for taking things to the recycling center; the more indolent students had a tendency to throw trash as well as recyclables into the bins and that created quite a mess. As well, the sorters had to *scrutinize* every item to be sure it was properly sorted since the recycling center was *scrupulous* about not taking any improperly sorted materials. Nevertheless, Isabelle, Nguyen, and Maura were *tenacious* and *relentless*, increasing the *surveillance* of the recycle bins during lunch hour to prevent further *breaches* of the rules and *cajoling* the *apathetic* students into caring about the project. Maura *chastised* the more *blatant malefactors* with a humor so charming that they were *compelled* to laugh—and participate with a smile.

apathetic (a-pu-THE-tik) (adjective) indifferent; describes someone who doesn't care about something; showing a lack of interest in something.

> It wasn't that a group of students was against what the conservationists were trying to do, they were simply *apathetic*.

> The *apathy* of many of those students was turned to support once Isabelle and Nguyen explained the benefits of recycling.

associate (uh-SO-shee-ayt) (verb) to spend time, or develop a relationship, with a particular person or group; to join or connect together.

> Maura was happy to *associate* with Nguyen and Isabelle and help them with their projects, but she was too busy to join the conservation group to which they belonged.

> Nguyen used to *associate* the idea of "boring" with "conservationist" until he began to spend more time with a group of environmentalists.

blatant (BLAY-tnt) (adjective) obvious in an unpleasant or pushy way.

> Some of the more enthusiastic conservationists sometimes grossly exaggerated the local environmental problems. These *blatant* exaggerations

worked against the efforts of the more balanced members to enlist the help of others in their cause.

Chris really thought that the whole recycling effort was a waste of time and, in protest, made a *blatant* gesture of throwing the wrong trash into the recycle bin.

breach (BREECH) (noun) 1. a break or accidental opening in a wall. 2. an obvious violation of manner or rules. (plural: breaches)

Maura's guest realized her *breach* in manners a few seconds too late after commenting to another that Maura's fish were big enough to make a nice lunch.

In an accidental *breach* of the rules, Isabelle absentmindedly tossed an aluminum can into the recycling bin for plastics.

cajole (ku-JOL) (verb) to persuade more with charm than with logic; to wheedle.

Maura really had to *cajole* the school administration into letting her approach an outside charity for help with recycling expenses.

Isabelle had *cajoled* Maura and Nguyen into supporting her in her conservation efforts and she really appreciated their enthusiastic help.

chastise (chas-TYZ) (verb) to criticize someone's behavior severely.

Nguyen was more likely to try to persuade someone gently to behave properly; it was not in his nature to *chastise*.

When Isabelle *chastised* people for ignoring the recycling bins, they just got annoyed. When Maura turned on her charm, they were happy to help.

compel (kum-PEL) (verb) to force someone to do something.

While unwilling to actually *compel* anyone to cooperate, Isabelle still wished the school would help her team enforce the recycling rules.

As she saw it, there were so many strong reasons that would compel someone to recycle, that it shouldn't be difficult to get thinking human beings to participate in the program.

Easy Errors   *compel* **vs.** *impel*

Compel is a verb that means "to force someone to do something" whereas *impel* is a verb that means "to persuade or urge someone to do something." So if I am a stubborn person, I may respond better if someone tries to *impel* me to do something by using moral arguments rather than trying to *compel* me to do something by making threats against me.

endeavor (in-DE-ver) 1. (noun) a planned project, effort, or expedition; a task that takes effort and commitment to complete. (plural: endeavors) 2. (verb) to try hard at something.

> While a noble *endeavor*, a recycling project in a large school is a lot of work!

> "I shall *endeavor* to do what you ask," he said, "but I can't guarantee the results."

initiate (i-NI-shee-ayt) (verb) to begin an action or project.

> When Nguyen first met Isabelle, he was shy about talking to her; she had to *initiate* their first conversation.

> Many think that environmentalism is a product of the 1970s era, but an awareness of conservation issues was *initiated* much earlier than that.

malefactor (MA-lu-fak-tur) (noun) someone who does bad things; a criminal. (plural: malefactors)

> Some *malefactor* dumped a load of used tires into the creek behind the school and Nguyen's cleanup committee spent two weekends hauling them out and taking them to the dump.

> Picking wildflowers can make one an accidental *malefactor* if one of those flowers happens to be an endangered species.

partition (par-TI-shun) 1. (verb) to divide into sections. 2. (noun) a divider between areas or rooms. (plural: partitions)

> They tried to *partition* the work evenly but, inevitably, one committee had more to do than the others.

> To study an area of the forest in a scientific manner, one must first divide the forest floor into sections using low *partitions* to indicate different research areas.

petition (pu-TI-shun) 1. (verb) to ask for official action on an issue. 2. (noun) a list of signatures of people who support a certain political or social point of view, with the purpose of persuading public officials to act in their interests. (plural: petitions)

> They *petitioned* the local government to establish a new park.

> Isabelle signed the *petition* in support of the new park.

philanthropic (fi-lun-THRAH-pik) (adjective) describes a person or organization that donates money (and/or volunteer hours) for the good of society; describes charity work.

> One of the local *philanthropic* groups was excited to be able to help students make a difference in their community.

> Not all *philanthropic* groups can afford to support all good causes; they usually choose a specialized area—education, homelessness, the environment—and focus their efforts in that one area.

rally (RA-lee) 1. (verb) to gather together a group to support a project or idea. 2. (noun) a public gathering of supporters for a cause or idea. (plural: rallies)

> At a student council meeting, Isabelle gave a speech to *rally* support for the recycling project.

> Nguyen attended a *rally* in support of a local political candidate so that he could hear that candidate's views on conservation.

receptacle (ri-SEP-ti-kul) (noun) a container in which people keep things or into which they throw things (often used to mean a wastebasket or garbage can). (plural: receptacles)

> Maura kept her fish food in a sealed *receptacle* to protect it from the cat.

> Throwing trash into a waste *receptacle* when out in public is a great help in keeping our streets clean.

relentless (ri-LENT-lus) (adjective) without pause or stop; determined to carry an idea or project to the end; persistent.

> Determined to make a difference in her local environment, Isabelle was *relentless* in her attempts to make the recycling project work.

> The conservation group was *relentless* and persistent in reminding their local political representatives of the importance of their concerns.

scavenge (SKA-vunj) (verb) to look for valuables or food by sorting through unrelated material.

> Crows love to *scavenge*, searching the ground for tidbits to eat as they fly.

> Isabelle and Maura *scavenged* dozens of cardboard boxes to use for classroom paper recycling until the new receptacles were delivered.

scrupulous (SKROO-pyu-lus) (adjective) very careful and precise about rules and/or cleanliness; painstaking.

> After sorting the recyclables each week, the team members were *scrupulous* about scrubbing their hands clean.

At the recycling center, the attendants were *scrupulous* about weighing the recyclables precisely to give the students the exact credit they deserved for their work each week.

scrutinize (SKROO-tu-nyz) (verb) to examine closely and critically.

The accountant was hired to *scrutinize* the financial records of the conservation group very carefully to try to find ways for them to save money.

Before he worked on the hawk census, Nguyen had to spend hours carefully *scrutinizing* pictures of various kinds of hawks since it can be difficult to tell one variety from another, especially in flight.

Pieces and Parts   phile- or phil-

The suffix *-phile* describes someone who has a love or a strong affinity for something, such as a *bibliophile* (someone who loves books) or an *Anglophile* (someone who admires things that are British). *Philanthropist* is made up of *phil-* (love of) and *anthro* (man) and refers to a person who contributes to the good of mankind, often financially.

---

significant (sig-NI-fi-kunt) (adjective) important or meaningful; a fairly large amount of something.

Despite solid arguments on both sides, there may not be a *significant* environmental difference between using paper or plastic bags for one's groceries.

As the recycling program improved, Nguyen saw that it could become a *significant* fund-raising activity for their conservation efforts.

simultaneously (sy-mul-TAY-nee-us-lee) (adverb) at the same time.

During lunch, with Nguyen watching one recycling barrel and Maura *simultaneously* watching another, the odds of items being put in the proper barrels increased greatly.

With the recycling project taking so much time, Isabelle and Nguyen worried that they might not have enough volunteers to *simultaneously* launch other conservation projects at the school.

stringently (STRIN-junt-lee) (adverb) done according to very precise and meticulous standards; strictly done.

Obeying their standards *stringently*, the recycling center once rejected a whole bin of suitable paper because they found some staples in it.

On Friday afternoons, the team had to follow their after-school timetable *stringently* to have enough time to gather, sort, and deliver materials to the recycling center before its closing time.

surveillance (sur-VAY-lunts) (noun) the action of watching a person or a group of people very carefully (usually in expectation of their doing something suspicious or inappropriate). (plural: This word is not usually used in the plural.)

One of Isabelle's committee's tasks was to do regular *surveillance* of the creeks and rivers in the county to monitor the level of pollutants.

Once most of the students became comfortable with the recycling system at school, the level of *surveillance* could be reduced and the team members could eat their lunches in peace.

tenacious (tu-NAY-shus) (adjective) determined to stay with a project until it is done; committed to a particular point of view.

Nguyen and his dad were committed to the moth census they did, *tenacious* in their shared belief of the value of moths to the ecosystem.

Equally *tenacious*, though, were the mosquitoes that had the two of them slapping their arms and faces all night.

timid (TI-mud) (adjective) slightly afraid, unwilling, hesitant (often from a lack of self-confidence).

At first a little *timid* about volunteering for projects, Isabelle felt more confident after she got to know the members of the group better.

Some people in the conservation group were *timid* about doing field work, either because of a fear of snakes or a lack of self-confidence.

Quick Match 30

Match each word to its definition.

1. ____	malefactor	A.	indifferent; showing a lack of interest
2. ____	associate	B.	describes one that donates for public good
3. ____	receptacle	C.	to begin an action or project
4. ____	timid	D.	to ask for official action on an issue
5. ____	scavenge	E.	important or meaningful
6. ____	initiate	F.	to persuade someone with charm; wheedle
7. ____	scrupulous	G.	someone who does bad things; a criminal
8. ____	apathetic	H.	to divide into sections or the divider itself
9. ____	rally	I.	to examine closely and critically
10. ____	breach	J.	slightly afraid, unwilling, hesitant
11. ____	partition	K.	to force someone to do something
12. ____	scrutinize	L.	to gather together a group to support an idea
13. ____	blatant	M.	to join or connect together
14. ____	philanthropic	N.	painstaking; careful and precise
15. ____	relentless	O.	the act of watching a person or group carefully
16. ____	simultaneously	P.	a task that takes effort and commitment
17. ____	chastise	Q.	without pause or stop; persistent
18. ____	surveillance	R.	determined to stay with a project to end
19. ____	significant	S.	a break in a wall; breaking a rule
20. ____	endeavor	T.	at the same time
21. ____	petition	U.	strictly done; done precisely, meticulously
22. ____	cajole	V.	to look for food by sorting through material
23. ____	tenacious	W.	to criticize someone's behavior severely
24. ____	stringently	X.	a container in which to keep or throw things
25. ____	compel	Y.	obvious in an unpleasant or pushy way

Sentence Completions 30

Choose the proper word or pair of words for each of the sentences below.

1. _____ honest, Isabelle had to admit that she did not have statistical information with her that supported the statements she had just made.

    (a) Timidly   (b) Scrupulously   (c) Relentlessly   (d) Simultaneously
    (e) Apathetically

2. The conservation group _____ the town council for help in setting up a recycling system for the community.

    (a) partitioned   (b) scrutinized   (c) petitioned   (d) breached
    (e) chastised

3. _____ in her attempts to establish the recycling program, Isabelle found that Chris was equally _____ in efforts to try to stop it.

    (a) Tenacious . . . relentless   (b) Stringent . . . timid
    (c) Apathetic . . . scrupulous   (d) Cajoling . . . compelled
    (e) Simultaneous . . . blatant

4. In a(n) _____ attempt to reverse positive public opinion on the new park, the mayor _____ groups of people from out of town who were opposed to the project and brought them to a town meeting.

    (a) timid . . . scavenged   (b) apathetic . . . petitioned
    (c) scrupulous . . . breached   (d) significant . . . associated
    (e) blatant . . . rallied

5. When the initial donation from the _____ organization ran out, Maura had to _____ for funds from a variety of local organizations to continue to support their recycling effort.

    (a) associate . . . chastise   (b) surveillance . . . cajole
    (c) philanthropic . . . scavenge   (d) timid . . . petition
    (e) significant . . . endeavor

WRITING ACTIVITY: THE DAILY NATURALIST

Every morning John Caddy writes a poem about his observations of the natural world at that moment. It is sort of his morning exercises and meditation all rolled into one. Some of his poems are short and some are long, but each one captures a thought that connects him to nature every day.

I encourage you to do the same and, as a further challenge, I want you to use your newly-acquired vocabulary in the process. Read this simple example to get you motivated.

May 14
She bumbles into every window, hovers
before openings, crawls into cracks again, again,
until her palace place is found.
She is urgent and profound, for
within her abdomen, dynasties are quickening.
These sisters are no ordinary wasps.
They are young queens of May,
dangling gawky legs before us
until they find their place to lay.

Instead of waiting until tomorrow morning, why not start right now? Look out of your window, be still within yourself, and create!

SECTION 7: THE GREAT CELL PHONE CAPER

Learning Style: The Logical/Mathematical Learner

Are you the one who sees patterns and relationships that other people miss? Do you like to figure things out—math problems, logic puzzles, strategy games? When others read an endless, wordy explanation, do you long for a nice, well-constructed chart or graph to pull all that information together? Are you the one who always questions, always asks for the data to back up what someone says, is always ready to solve a problem through reason and logic? When others need help with math or science, do they think of you first?

If you have answered "yes" to several of the above, this is one of your stronger intelligences.

Possible Approaches

- **Make a Chart.** Make a parts-of-speech chart. On the chart, place each vocabulary word in its proper box by part of speech. Then, adjust the word's form so that each box has a correct variation of that word:

Nouns	Verbs	Adjectives	Adverbs
denial	*deny*	*denied*	*deniably*
intelligence	—	*intelligent*	*intelligently*
interrogation	*interrogate*	*interrogatory*	*interrogatively*
strain	*strain*	*strained*	—

- **Make a Word Line.** List each vocabulary word on the equivalent of a number line, with negative words where negative numbers would go, neutral words in the zero position, and positive words where positive numbers would go. For example:

negative	neutral	positive
heinous	*mull*	*avidly*

$$\xleftarrow{\hspace{2cm}} \underset{\substack{| \\ 0}}{} \xrightarrow{\hspace{2cm}}$$

−ve　　　　　　0　　　　　　+ve

- **Categorize Words.** Categorize your words numerically or logically in some way to make learning them easier. For instance, in this book, each chapter's words are listed alphabetically. If that is not the best categorization technique for you, try listing the words by least number of letters to most and learning them in that order. Another option would be to learn them grouped by parts of speech.

- **Break Down Word Parts.** Many mathematical thinkers are more comfortable learning about anything by approaching its component parts; in other words, what basic elements make up the compound you are trying to understand? For vocabulary, that means looking at roots, stems, and etymologies. For example:

veritable = *verité* (French = "true") + *-able* ("liable" or "fit for")

heinous = *haïne* (Old French = "hate") + *-ous* ("full of")

interrogation = *inter* (Latin = "between") + *rogare* (Latin = "to ask") + *-ation* ("condition" or "act of")

While this technique may not be useful for all words that you study, since the meanings of roots and words evolve over time, it is an excellent window into the way language works. As well, with some practice you will find certain roots turning up repeatedly. Once you recognize those common roots, they can help you take apart new words and figure them out even if you do not have a dictionary handy!

Chapter 31: The Eager Detective

The first Bian heard about the *heinous* crime, she was in study hall. The *susurrus* she barely heard among the guys behind her was about a group *interrogation* in last period's gym class. She *strained* her ears to hear better: not quite, no, close, they're saying . . . "cell phone"?

What was so *vitally* important about <u>that</u>?

After class she managed to *corner* Levon briefly outside of their math classroom and question him about his study hall conversation.

"Oh, that," he said. "Well, a bunch of us were talking in the library, near the study *carrels*, you know: Jake, me, Sammi, Nishandra, Ogun—really, I guess almost everyone was there. Anyway, Nishandra looked down and went 'Hey, where's my cell phone?' and Ogun laughed and said 'Don't you know you're not supposed to have one on at school?' and she said . . . ."

"Can't you *encapsulate* this?" Bian *insisted*. There wasn't much time before class.

"Oh, yeah. The *gist* of it is that the Dean of Students thought one of us stole Nishandra's phone. He came to the gym right after we left the library to *ferret* out the problem by *rifling* through our gym lockers and asking us about it. Hey, listen, I've got to get to class."

"Yeah, me too," said Bian absently, *mulling* over this *intelligence*.

Bian was a mystery *buff*, voraciously *devouring* mystery novels and *avidly* watching all the old mystery TV shows from the 1970s and 1980s. Now, finally, a *veritable* mystery had landed on her own doorstep and she wasn't about to let it go unsolved. She was in a good position to *launch* her investigation since Levon had already revealed a list of *likely* suspects. She also knew the *layout* of the crime scene; she *presumed* the *misdemeanor* had taken place in the library.

So, it was time to tackle the tough question: who had *absconded* with Nishandra's cell phone?

abscond (ab-SKAHND) (verb) to leave a place secretly and in haste, often to hide from arrest or harm.

> To give herself time to think quietly about a problem, Bian would *abscond* with a box of cookies and hide herself in a tree in the yard to avoid interruptions or household chores.

> When Bian asked friends to watch old TV shows with her, she often would find they had *absconded* before she could get an answer from them.

avidly (A-vud-lee) (adverb) enthusiastically or keenly interested.

> There was a book store in town that specialized in mysteries and Bian would visit often, *avidly* reading the latest novels.

> Nishandra was very sociable and spoke *avidly* on all kinds of subjects with her large circle of friends.

buff (BUF) (noun) a fan who knows a great deal about a particular favorite subject. (plural: buffs)

> Bian's friends found it odd that she was a mystery *buff* and yet had little or no interest in complicated riddles. The two seemed related to them.

> Levon was a history *buff* and he and Bian could have long conversations about true-life mysteries that they read about in history class.

carrel (KER-ul) (noun) a small, private study desk in a library with high sides to protect one's privacy while studying. (plural: carrels)

> While Bian preferred to read in the privacy of a study *carrel*, Nishandra preferred a table where she could study with a group of friends.

> Bian had a favorite *carrel* to work at in the library.

corner (KOR-nur) (verb) to trap; to manage to get someone into a corner for conversation or confrontation.

> The Dean of Students *cornered* a group of students in the gym to ask them about the theft of Nishandra's cell phone.

> Nishandra *cornered* her friend Sammi to ask if Sammi had taken the phone as a joke.

devour (di-VOWR) (verb) to eat quickly and eagerly; to eat greedily; to enjoy greatly.

> Bian *devoured* her lunch in a hurry that day, anxious to get started on her investigation.

> For every mystery she *devoured*, Bian would find three more at the library that she wanted to read.

encaspsulate (in-KAP-su-layt) (verb) to give a brief summary.

> The history teacher asked the class to *encapsulate* the events of the U.S. Civil War in a one-page summary.

> Bian respected anyone who could delete unnecessary information from a story and *encapsulate* its essence clearly and directly.

ferret (out) (FER-ut) (verb) to discover and reveal thorough searching.

> Bian was convinced she could *ferret out* the details of this case.

> Nishandra tried to *ferret out* who had her phone, but she wasn't successful.

gist (JIST) (noun) the main idea; the most critical element. (plural: This word is not usually used in the plural.)

> To the Dean of Students, the *gist* of the problem was that there was a thief on campus.

> The *gist* of the issue to Bian was that she finally had a chance to use her powers of logic to solve a community problem.

heinous (HAY-nus) (adjective) particularly bad or worthy of blame (usually used in reference to one's behavior).

> She knew it was an exaggeration to refer to this crime as *"heinous"* but Bian had always wanted to be able to use that word.

> It would be, however, a *heinous* behavior for a trusted friend to be stealing things from others.

Pieces and Parts   *en-*

En- as a prefix means "cause to make (something)." For example, *encapsulate* is to make something into a capsule. *En-* can also mean "put on." For example, *encircle* is to put a circle around something.

---

insist (in-SIST) (verb) to state firmly and without compromise, to refuse to give in.

> Nishandra continued to *insist* that she had had the phone during lunch that day.

> The Dean of Students *insisted* on searching the lockers immediately, before the thief had a chance to put the cell phone in a hiding place.

intelligence (in-TE-luh-junts) (noun) 1. secret information that has been gathered. 2. one's capacity for learning and understanding. (plural: intelligences)

> Bian knew she didn't have access to all of the *intelligence* available to the Dean of Students, but she still felt she would be able to solve the mystery.

> She was depending on her natural *intelligence*, as well as her knowledge of the criminal mind, to help her in this case.

interrogation (in-ter-uh-GAY-shun) (noun) the act of questioning someone formally or officially, often in relation to some wrongdoing. (plural: interrogations)

> While the Dean of Students did question the students about the case, it was not at all as forceful as a true *interrogation*.

> Bian tried to keep her *interrogations* on the level of friendly conversations so that her "suspects" wouldn't know she was gathering information.

launch (LAWNCH) (verb) to start something going; to begin a new venture.

> The Dean of Students decided to *launch* his investigation a week earlier when textbooks and a calculator were stolen from a locked locker.

> Her math teacher *launched* a new topic in class that day, but Bian was so involved in her case that she wasn't even paying attention to her favorite subject.

layout (LAY-owt) (noun) a formal plan or arrangement, usually for a room or printed page. (plural: layouts)

> The *layout* of the library was open and airy and that made it difficult to hide anything.

> Bian began to keep careful notes on the case, including a hand-drawn *layout* of the crime scene.

likely (LY-klee) (adjective) probable; apt; such as might well be true.

> With all this attention, it was not *likely* that someone would confess to the crime now.

> The Dean of Students was more *likely* to solve the case than Bian was, but she was not discouraged.

misdemeanor (mis-di-MEE-nur) (noun) a minor crime. (plural: misdemeanors)

> While the theft of a cell phone might seem to be merely a *misdemeanor*, the Dean of Students took any dishonesty very seriously.

> While there was not so much as a *misdemeanor* on Bian's record, she knew that even good kids get into trouble now and then.

mull (MUL) (verb) to think something over; to ponder.

> Bian *mulled* over this problem when she should have been paying attention in class.

> The Dean of Students was *mulling* over the theft even as he was dealing with other issues.

presume (pri-ZOOM) (verb) to believe something to be true since there is no proof to say it isn't.

> Bian *presumed* that someone in the group had, perhaps mistakenly, put the phone in his or her pocket.

> Nishandra *presumed* that someone had taken the phone as a joke.

rifle (RY-ful) (verb) to actively and physically search for something; to search actively with a plan to steal something.

> The pattern of the previous thefts seemed to be someone taking advantage of an opportunity to *rifle* through a locker or desk when the owner wasn't looking.

> As he and the Athletic Director *rifled* through the gym lockers, the Dean of students had a sinking feeling that the phone was not there.

Easy Errors   *-able* and *-ible*

Knowing whether an adjective form ends in *–able* or *–ible* can be very confusing, especially since magazines and newspapers often get these wrong! Some words, such as *collectable* (*collectible*) are acceptable in either spelling but that is unusual. The safest course of action is to look the word up in your dictionary. The more common of the two suffixes is *–able* so if there is no dictionary around, use that form until you have a chance to check it out.

---

strain (STRAYN) (verb) to push almost beyond the best of one's physical ability to achieve a goal.

> Although her hearing was good, Bian had to *strain* her ears to hear her classmates behind her.

> Bian *strained* her mind to think creatively about this mystery.

susurrus (soo-SUR-russ) (noun) soft whispering or rustling sounds.

> Usually the students had to be quieted during study hall so Bian was surprised that day at the quiet *susurrus* of their voices.

> On the way to school that day, Levon had enjoyed the soft *susurrus* of the autumn leaves as he shuffled his feet in them.

veritable (VER-uh-tuh-bl) (adjective) real, true, genuine.

> To Bian it was all a *veritable* mystery but to others the loss of the cell phone was no more than a mild annoyance.

> Levon was a *veritable* genius in science and math but his attitude was so relaxed that many didn't realize it.

vitally (VY-t-lee) (adverb) necessarily, critically.

> It was *vitally* important to the Dean of Students to solve this theft problem.

> Nishandra felt it was *vitally* important to get her phone back because she had to call her mom to pick her up after sports practice was finished that day.

voraciously (vo-RAY-shus-lee) (adverb) in a ravenous or greedy manner; with a great appetite.

> Nishandra approached breakfast and lunch in a balanced way but after a long school day and a vigorous sports practice, she often ate *voraciously* at dinner.

> Levon read science and technology magazines *voraciously* to keep up with all the latest theories and electronic equipment advances.

Quick Match 31

Match each word to its definition.

1. ___	gist	A.	a formal plan for a room or printed page
2. ___	voraciously	B.	secret information that has been gathered
3. ___	abscond	C.	to give a brief summary
4. ___	vitally	D.	probable; apt
5. ___	heinous	E.	to trap someone for conversation
6. ___	avidly	F.	to think something over; to ponder
7. ___	veritable	G.	to state firmly and without compromise
8. ___	insist	H.	in a ravenous or greedy manner; with great appetite
9. ___	buff	I.	the art of questioning someone formally or officially
10. ___	susurrus	J.	a minor crime
11. ___	intelligence	K.	to leave a place secretly and in haste
12. ___	carrel	L.	to actively and physically search for something
13. ___	strain	M.	to discover and reveal through searching
14. ___	interrogation	N.	enthusiastically or keenly interested
15. ___	corner	O.	to believe something to be true
16. ___	rifle	P.	a fan who knows a lot about a favorite subject
17. ___	launch	Q.	particularly bad or worthy of blame
18. ___	devour	R.	necessarily, critically
19. ___	presume	S.	a small, private study desk in a library
20. ___	layout	T.	to start something going; to begin a new venture
21. ___	encapsulate	U.	soft whispering or rustling sounds
22. ___	mull	V.	to eat quickly and eagerly
23. ___	likely	W.	real, true, genuine
24. ___	ferret	X.	the main idea; the most critical element
25. ___	misdemeanor	Y.	to push almost beyond the best of one's physical ability to achieve a goal

Sentence Completions 31
Choose the proper word or pair of words for each of the sentences below.

1. Distracted by the case, Bian was not as organized as usual and she had to _____ through all of the papers in her binder to find her science homework.

    (a) insist   (b) presume   (c) strain   (d) encapsulate   (e) rifle

2. A good detective gives himself or herself time to _____ over a case, thinking about it from as many angles as possible.

    (a) ferret   (b) corner   (c) insist   (d) mull   (e) rifle

3. It was a(n) _____ haystack in which one needed to find a needle to try to solve a case with so many suspects and so many differing accounts of what happened!

    (a) heinous   (b) vital   (c) veritable   (d) avid   (e) buff

4. The guilty party had decided to _____ to escape questioning before the _____ had actually been reported.

    (a) devour . . . intelligence   (b) presume . . . gist   (c) launch . . . layout
    (d) insist . . . interrogation   (e) abscond . . . misdemeanor

5. The _____ of quiet voices whispering in the library did not disturb the student working alone at a study _____.

    (a) intelligence . . . layout   (b) susurrus . . . carrel
    (c) veritable . . . interrogation   (d) launch . . . misdemeanor
    (e) gist . . . encapsulate

Chapter 32: On the Case

All discussions for the rest of the day and on the bus that afternoon *revolved* around the "Great Cell Phone *Caper*." Bian had *conversed* with most of the *principals* by the end of the day and, while there was *consensus* on a number of facts, several issues remained *inconclusive*. Ogun had been the easiest to question, saying what he knew in his usual *ingenuous* fashion. He actually remembered seeing the phone on the library table but couldn't remember how or when it had been removed. Nishandra was a *scatterbrain* that afternoon, with her attention *diverted* by *multitudinous* issues; she wasn't much help to Bian but she didn't seem to mind Bian's involvement. Bian had already spoken to Levon and he didn't have much to add in an *encore* interview. Sammi gave a *cogent chronicle* of the events as she remembered them. She *unequivocally* recalled Nishandra making a phone call during lunch but couldn't say that she had noticed the phone on the library table. She added *sagely* that Nishandra was *renowned* for her habit of misplacing her personal belongings on a regular basis.

The great *enigma* of the afternoon was Jake, who denied everything it was possible to *deny*. Was he with the group in the library? No, well, yes, but not for long. Did he know anything about the phone? Had he seen it? Had he taken it as a joke? No, no, NO! He left Bian in a *huff* and she was at an *impasse*, confused about what to do next. Jake's manner had *heightened* her interest rather than *quelled* it as he had hoped. She knew enough about investigations from her reading and TV watching to know that the obvious suspect is not necessarily the *perpetrator* of the crime, but it was difficult not to suspect Jake of some *wrongdoing* since he had been so *curt* with her.

The big news came at the end of the day. The cell phone had been found in Nishandra's locker.

caper (KAY-pur) (noun) a prank; an illegal plan, especially to steal something. (plural: capers)

> However this case worked out, Bian was certain it was a crime of opportunity not a planned *caper*.

> Every year the seniors planned some sort of *caper* or practical joke on campus to draw attention to themselves just before graduation.

chronicle (KRAH-ni-kul) (noun) a detailed personal report of an event or situation; an oral or written account of an historical event. (plural: chronicles)

> Bian was careful to keep a written *chronicle* of all of her interviews related to the phone's disappearance.

> Not only interested in novels and TV, Bian read factual *chronicles* of past crimes and the real-life detectives who solved them.

cogent (KO-junt) (adjective) describes a clear and logical argument that appeals directly to one's reason.

> Bian made a persuasive and *cogent* argument in favor of the Dean of Students sharing evidence with her in the solving of the case, but the Dean felt that that might be a breach of confidentiality and gently refused.

> Bian could create no *cogent* argument for the logic of stealing someone else's cell phone.

consensus (kun-SEN-sus) (noun) an opinion or course of action agreed to by a group of people. (plural: This word is not usually used in the plural.)

> Once the phone was found, the *consensus* among the students was to leave the mystery alone.

> The *consensus* of the school community, though, was that stealing was wrong because it was a betrayal of friendship and trust.

converse (kun-VERS) (verb) an exchange of words with another person or persons; to talk.

> Bian was happy to *converse* with others to try to find the solution, but she wondered how she could solve the case with no physical evidence or eyewitnesses.

> On her way to classes, Bian *conversed* about the case with whomever would talk to her about it.

curt (KURT) (adjective) terse; describes speaking so briefly as to sound rude.

> His *curt* manner made the detective suspicious.

> Jake's usually manner of communication was to be *curt*, so it was difficult to know if he were being rude out of guilt or out of habit.

Pieces and Parts   *chron-* or *chrono-*

Chron- or *chrono-* is from Greek and has to do with time. We use this root for the words *chronological* (the order in which things happen in time), *chronic* (lasting for a long period of time), and *chronicle* (an account of an historical event in time).

---

deny (di-NY) (verb) to refuse an idea, to contradict; to refuse to accept responsibility for words or actions attributed to you; to reject.

> Bian couldn't *deny* that her suspicions about Jake were based on emotion rather than the logic on which she so prided herself.

> Levon was helpful but *denied* seeing the phone on the library table.

divert (di-VURT) (verb) to draw away from a focus of attention or a certain direction.

> Hoping to trick her suspects into revealing more, Bian practiced speaking casually to them to *divert* their attention from the case.

> Determined to solve the school theft problem, the Dean of Students *diverted* some of his time reserved for record keeping into patrolling the school more often.

encore (AHN-kor) (adjective) an extra performance given because of an audience's demand (usually expressed through cheering or excessive applause); a repeated action.

> The Dean of Students was hoping to prevent an *encore* performance of the thief.

> Bian planned to conduct follow-up, *encore* interviews with each of those involved in the case.

enigma (ih-NIG-muh) (noun) something or someone mysterious and/or puzzling. (plural: enigmas)

> Jake seemed almost more of an *enigma* than the case itself.

> The case was an *enigma* in that the thief stole something and then, strangely, returned it almost immediately. Was this a thief who only needed to make a phone call?

heighten (HY-tn) (verb) to increase the intensity (of something).

> Bian feared she would find it hard to *heighten* interest in the case once the phone had been found.

> The Dean of Students *heightened* security somewhat by insisting that students use their locks on their lockers.

huff (HUF) (noun) an episode of indignation or annoyance, usually caused by an insult or a perceived insult. (plural: This word is not usually used in the plural.)

> Nishandra had been in a bit of a *huff* to think that someone would steal her phone.

> It was unusual for Levon to get into a *huff* since he was so easy-going and even-tempered.

impasse (IM-pas) (noun) a situation in which opposing forces or a dead end make it impossible to move forward and/or solve a problem. (plural: This word is not usually used in the plural.)

> Bian felt at an *impasse* when the Dean of Students refused to share information about the case with her.

Bian had reached an *impasse* with Jake and knew she would have to approach the case from a different angle to solve it.

inconclusive (in-kun-KLOO-siv) (adjective) unable to reach a final understanding in which no doubt remains; not decisive.

> The results of both Bian's and the Dean of Student's investigations were still *inconclusive*.

> The link between Nishandra's missing phone and any other thefts on campus was *inconclusive*.

ingenuous (in-JEN-yu-wus) (adjective) openly honest and straightforward; unsophisticated and naïve.

> After thinking about how evasive Jake had been, Bian was grateful for Ogun's *ingenuous* attitude.

> When Sammi had been new to the school, she had felt a bit awkward and *ingenuous*.

multitudinous (mul-tuh-TOOD-nus) (adjective) many; in great numbers.

> There were *multitudinous* possibilities in this case but Bian had to admit that none of the possibilities she could think of made any sense to her.

> Despite the *multitudinous* mysteries she had read, Bian couldn't think of a similar situation to draw on to help her with her investigation.

Easy Errors   ***consensus* vs. *census***

A consensus is "an opinion or course of action agreed to by a group of people" and a census is "a periodic, official count of those in a particular population." The words are from two different roots: *consensus* comes from *consentire* (to feel together, to agree), but *census* comes from *censere* (to appraise). They may sound similar, but these are two words that are totally different!

---

perpetrator (PUR-puh-tray-tur) (noun) one who commits an act (often, a crime). (plural: perpetrators)

> The *perpetrator* of this crime was clearly very clever.

> Bian's secret wish was to discover the *perpetrator* before the Dean of Students.

principal (PRIN-suh-puhl) (noun) the most important person involved in a situation; the leader who presides over a group, particularly used for leaders of schools. (plural: principals)

> The *principals* in this case were those who had been in the library with Nishandra (and her phone).

The school *principal* was anxious to have the school thefts stop as well.

quell (KWEL) (verb) to quiet, to put to rest (sometimes by force).

> The Dean of Students hoped that the recovery of the phone would *quell* some of the wild rumors floating around the school.

> Bian couldn't *quell* the hope in her heart that she would be the one to solve this case.

renowned (ri-NOWND) (adjective) famous; publicly known and honored.

> Although Nishandra wasn't locally famous, she was *renowned* within the school for her good nature and her tendency to lose things.

> Bian kept up with the news on several nationally *renowned* detectives across the United States.

revolve (ri-VAHLV) (verb) to center on or focus on; to rotate around.

> Most of Bian's school day *revolved* around classes and grades so she was glad of a little distraction from the ordinary.

> The solution of this case *revolved* around everyone's willingness to participate and offer honest testimony.

sagely (SAYJ-lee) (adverb) wisely; with calm and wise good sense.

> Sammi was *sagely* aware of her friend's shortcomings as well as her virtues.

> When Bian started to get excited about the case, her math teacher *sagely* recommended that she slow down and think things through carefully.

scatterbrain (SKA-tur-brayn) (noun) one whose mind jumps from one idea to another without much order or planning; someone who is disorganized in thought. (plural: scatterbrains)

> Nishandra had a tendency to be a *scatterbrain*, but she did well in school despite the lack of consistent focus.

> Because of her logical mind, Bian had never been a *scatterbrain* and had trouble communicating with people who thought that way.

unequivocally (un-i-KWI-vu-kuh-lee) (adverb) without any doubt or chance of misunderstanding.

> Bian was *unequivocally* committed to solving this crime no matter how long it might take.

> Sammi and Ogun were *unequivocally* certain that they had reported the events of the day to Bian exactly as they had happened.

wrongdoing (RAWNG-doo-ing) (noun) illegal or immoral act or acts. (plural: This word is not usually used in the plural.)

> Bian wondered of what *wrongdoing* Jake was guilty if not this one since he seemed to be guilty by nature.

> Most *wrongdoing* seems to fall into two categories: doing wrong to yourself and doing wrong to others.

Quick Match 32

Match each word to its definition.

1. ___	ingenuous	A.	to talk
2. ___	curt	B.	extra performance given due to audience demand
3. ___	multitudinous	C.	openly honest and straightforward
4. ___	deny	D.	to quiet, to put to rest (sometimes by force)
5. ___	converse	E.	not decisive
6. ___	perpetrator	F.	course of action agreed to by a group of people
7. ___	divert	G.	famous; publicly known and honored
8. ___	principal	H.	describes a clear argument that appeals to reason
9. ___	encore	I.	many; in great numbers
10. ___	consensus	J.	something (or someone) mysterious or puzzling
11. ___	quell	K.	an episode of indignation or annoyance
12. ___	enigma	L.	someone who is disorganized in thought
13. ___	renowned	M.	terse; speaking so briefly as to sound rude
14. ___	cogent	N.	one who commits an act (often, a crime)
15. ___	revolve	O.	a prank; an illegal plan, especially to steal
16. ___	heighten	P.	the most important person involved in a situation
17. ___	chronicle	Q.	to center on or focus on; to rotate around
18. ___	sagely	R.	dead end making it impossible to move forward
19. ___	huff	S.	without any doubt or chance of misunderstanding
20. ___	scatterbrain	T.	a detailed personal report of an event or situation
21. ___	impasse	U.	illegal or immoral act or acts
22. ___	caper	V.	wisely; with calm and wise good sense
23. ___	unequivocally	W.	to refuse an idea, to contradict
24. ___	inconclusive	X.	to increase the intensity (of something)
25. ___	wrongdoing	Y.	to draw away from a focus of attention

Sentence Completions 32

Choose the proper word or pair of words for each of the sentences below.

1. Even an amateur detective tries to _____ naturally with each suspect so that no one realizes that he or she is actually suspected of the crime.

   (a) encore   (b) deny   (c) converse   (d) quell   (e) revolve

2. Often, a detective's first interview with each suspect is _____ and the detective must speak to people again to find gaps in their stories and reach reasonable conclusions.

   (a) inconclusive   (b) revolved   (c) multitudinous   (d) ingenuous
   (e) renowned

3. A good detective keeps a careful _____ of all evidence gathered and people interviewed in the process of solving a case.

   (a) enigma   (b) encore   (c) chronicle   (d) principal   (e) impasse

4. Bian's favorite TV detective was the _____ Sherlock Holmes who _____ used flawless logic and reasoning to solve his cases.

   (a) scatterbrained . . . unequivocally   (b) renowned . . . sagely
   (c) enigma . . . conversely   (d) ingenuous . . . inconclusively
   (e) curt . . . deniably

5. Sometimes the true _____ of the crime will try to _____ attention from himself or herself by blaming someone who is innocent of the crime.

   (a) principal . . . converse   (b) scatterbrain . . . quell
   (c) perpetrator . . . divert   (d) consensus . . . deny   (e) caper . . . heighten

Chapter 33: A Lively Imagination

One would have thought that the *reclamation* of the phone would end the investigation, but Bian still felt that a clear resolution of the mystery was *imperative*. Nishandra was *steadfast* in her *attestation* that she hadn't seen the phone in her locker earlier. As well, the Dean of Students was trying to get to the bottom of a *rash* of *petty* thefts on campus; he felt this theft might be a breakthrough in cracking that mystery. Bian knew that if this case were related to the other thefts in some way, an *illumination* of the details might prove *indispensable*. *Nescient* of the motivations of those involved, she found herself wondering what they might be thinking . . . .

* * *

"Maybe I was too *candid*," she thought, *perturbed* with herself. "She's one of my best friends, and if what I said to Bian gets back to her the wrong way, she could *misconstrue* it. Of course, it's absolutely true—she couldn't *refute* that—but it might hurt her feelings. It's not like I *instigated* this whole investigation-thing; I'm just trying to help. If she were to get angry, it would be *unwarranted*—she knows we're friends."

* * *

"Of course I'm the first one to be *castigated*," he though *wrathfully*. "Everyone is more ready to *denounce* me than to try to figure out what really happened. A couple of small issues and everybody gets touchy with me. I was only borrowing that book from Tricia last year and that got all blown out of *proportion*; it wasn't like I was *appropriating* it for good. Sure, I may have looked over at Kai's work to get a good answer to impress Dr. Farley, but it's not like it was a major grade or anything. It's lucky nobody knows about that thing with Nisa or they'd all *embellish* that one for sure as well! You have to be *resourceful* to make it in this world and these other people won't admit that everyone has to look out for himself. Besides, none of this really matters, it's not *crucial*—it's only school. When I think about . . . ."

* * *

Realizing her lack of attention in class, Bian *roused* herself out of her daydream and forced herself back to the subject at hand. She wondered just how accurate her *reveries* might be . . . .

appropriate (uh-PRO-pree-ayt) (verb) to take or use something of someone else's, often without permission.

> Bian was not likely ever to *appropriate* something that didn't belong to her.

> Bian wondered if whoever had *appropriated* the phone had also realized that he or she would be totally unable to use it once the theft were discovered.

attestation (a-tes-TAY-shun) (noun) a statement that affirms that something is absolutely true or correct. (plural: attestations)

> Jake's *attestation* of innocence hadn't sounded very convincing to Bian.

> The *attestation* from Sammi of Nishandra's forgetfulness supported information that Bian already knew.

candid (KAN-dud) (adjective) straightforward; honest and direct in one's expression of thought or ideas.

> Sammi had been *candid* but kind when discussing Nishandra.

> Bian was *candid* with the Dean of Students and disappointed that the Dean couldn't be that straightforward with her.

castigate (KAS-tuh-gayt) (verb) to punish or criticize strongly.

> If this theft were an isolated incident, the student involved would not be likely to be *castigated* too severely.

> The Dean would be more likely to *castigate* a student for a dishonest act than for an unwise choice.

crucial (KROO-shul) (adjective) critical; of utmost importance.

> Bian daydreamed about discovering the *crucial* piece of information that would make the whole case come together.

> To the Dean of Students, it was *crucial* to be firm but fair.

denounce (di-NOWNS) (verb) to accuse openly of evil behavior or character.

> Bian's daydream was right in at least one way: people were ready to *denounce* Jake before bringing all of the facts together.

> The Dean didn't want to have to *denounce* anyone. He was hoping for a quiet, low-key resolution to this issue.

Pieces and Parts   -tion

The suffix *-tion* signals a noun. So, since *castigate* means to punish or criticize strongly, *castigation* would then be the action of punishing or criticizing someone strongly. Just so, *denunciation* becomes an open accusation of someone (from *denounce*) and *refutation* is the communicated evidence that shows something is untrue or inaccurate (from *refute*).

---

embellish (im-BE-lish) (verb) to decorate in a fancy way or to make more elaborate.

> Bian felt that if Jake were truly guilty, he would be more likely to *embellish* his story to cover himself than to tell a simple story.

Nishandra had *embellished* her phone with a new cover only two days before the theft.

illumination (ih-loo-muh-NAY-shun) (noun) the process of shedding light on something, physically or spiritually. (plural: illuminations)

The *illumination* of her special talents in math and logic had come about for Bian in third grade.

An *illumination* of the facts of this case might lend greater understanding to other situations on campus.

imperative (im-PER-uh-tiv) (adjective) describes something that must be done immediately; critically important; obligatory.

The Dean of Students felt is was *imperative* to act swiftly and effectively in cases such as these.

Bian longed to work on the case every night, but it was *imperative* that she get her homework done as well.

indispensable (in-di-SPEN-suh-bl) (adjective) required; essential; cannot be left out.

Bian found her friendships with most of the people involved to be *indispensable* to her investigation.

As she continued to conduct repeated interviews about the case, Bian found her notebook *indispensable* for helping her keep track of information.

instigate (in-STUH-gayt) (verb) to start or encourage trouble or activity; to urge (someone) to do something.

Would someone be likely to *instigate* another such prank?

The Dean wondered if someone had *instigated* another to take the phone as a joke.

misconstrue (mis-KUN-stroo) (verb) to misinterpret the meaning of words or a situation.

Bian would be careful not to say anything that Nishandra might *misconstrue*.

Nishandra had *misconstrued* someone's words in the past and felt insulted when no insult had been intended.

nescient (NE-shunt) (adjective) ignorant.

Sammi was *nescient* of Bian's sensitivity in this matter.

Because the Dean of Students was handling the situation, the principal was *nescient* of any details of the case.

perturbed (pur-TURBD) (adjective) emotionally very anxious or disturbed.

Jake was *perturbed* by all of the negative attention he was getting.

The Dean was *perturbed* by the series of thefts on campus.

petty (PEH-tee) (adjective) minor; not worth one's attention; trivial.

No detail was too *petty* for Bian to ignore it in her ongoing investigation.

There were some *petty* quarrels between Nishandra and a few others but they seemed to have no connection to the theft.

proportion (pruh-POR-shun) (noun) the relationship of the parts of something to the whole thing. (plural: proportions)

A large *proportion* of the thefts on campus was likely to be solved but it might take a lot of time.

Bian felt that the amount of time she was spending in researching this case was in *proportion* with the importance of settling the matter.

rash (RASH) (noun) many instances of a particular event in a short period of time. (plural: rashes)

A *rash* of thefts might mean a single person stealing a lot of things, or a group of people in which each person only stole one thing.

The teachers all hoped for a *rash* of instances of all of the students completing their homework on time!

reclamation (re-kluh-MAY-shun) (noun) to bring back to its proper location or course of action. (plural: reclamations)

Bian's role as detective was also a *reclamation* of her reputation as a clear and logical thinker.

The Dean hoped that solving this problem would be a *reclamation* of the school as a place of honesty and trust.

Easy Errors   *lose* vs. *loose*

It is unusual for anyone to mix up the pronunciations of these two words when speaking, but the spelling seems elusive to many. To *lose* (LOOZ) something is to misplace it. If something is *loose* (LUCE), it is no longer confined where it should be. So, if your dog gets *loose*, there is a risk that you will *lose* the animal.

refute (ri-FYOOT) (verb) to prove that something is untrue or inaccurate through argument and evidence.

> Jake longed to *refute* everyone's suspicions but there was no firm proof of his innocence.

> There was also no evidence to *refute* the popular theory that the phone had been stolen.

resourceful (ri-SORS-ful) (adjective) describes using only those materials, people, or skills that are available to solve a problem creatively or imaginatively.

> Because Bian had no physical evidence (such as fingerprints) from the crime scene, she would need to be intellectually *resourceful* in solving this matter.

> The Dean of Students was known for being *resourceful* in the use of student sources in the resolution of problems.

reverie (RE-vuh-ree) (noun) daydream. (plural: reveries)

> The Dean of Students indulged in a *reverie* in which he counseled a student kindly and all of the student's problems melted away.

> A practical person who didn't daydream much, Bian nevertheless had a favorite *reverie* in which she solved seemingly impossible cases for a major metropolitan police force—perhaps even Scotland Yard in England!

rouse (ROWZ) (verb) to bring out of sleep or a quiet emotional state such as depression; to excite action in someone.

> Levon was so relaxed in life that it took a lot to *rouse* him to anger.

> When the phone was first missing, Nishandra had been anxious to *rouse* others to actively search for it with her.

steadfast (STED-fast) (adjective) consistently and dependably loyal.

> Once her friendship was earned, Sammi was a *steadfast* friend for life.

> Ogun's reputation for *steadfast* honesty meant that his version of what had happened in the library was exactly as it happened.

unwarranted (un-WOR-unt-ed) (adjective) done without good sense or reason; without justification.

> Bian worried that her suspicion of Jake might be *unwarranted*.

> The main problem with this case was that taking the phone seemed totally *unwarranted* as far as logic was concerned.

wrathfully (RATH-fuh-lee) (adverb) with great anger.

> Bian didn't know for sure if Jake was reacting *wrathfully* to everyone's suspicions.

> Nishandra spoke *wrathfully* when she first reported the missing phone to the Dean of Students.

Quick Match 33

Match each word to its definition.

1. ___	indispensable	A.	to excite action in someone
2. ___	refute	B.	required; essential; cannot be left out
3. ___	imperative	C.	emotionally very anxious or disturbed
4. ___	reclamation	D.	to punish or criticize strongly
5. ___	illumination	E.	minor; not worth one's attention; trivial
6. ___	wrathfully	F.	to start or encourage trouble or activity
7. ___	rash	G.	straightforward; honest and direct
8. ___	embellish	H.	daydream
9. ___	proportion	I.	to misinterpret the meaning of words
10. ___	denounce	J.	prove that something is untrue through evidence
11. ___	unwarranted	K.	consistently and dependably loyal
12. ___	petty	L.	critical; of utmost importance
13. ___	crucial	M.	appropriate relationship of parts to whole
14. ___	perturbed	N.	to take or use something of someone else's
15. ___	castigate	O.	describes solving a problem creatively or imaginatively
16. ___	steadfast	P.	to accuse openly of evil behavior or character
17. ___	nescient	Q.	needing to be done immediately
18. ___	candid	R.	done without good sense or reason
19. ___	rouse	S.	affirms that something is absolutely true
20. ___	misconstrue	T.	ignorant
21. ___	attestation	U.	to bring back to its proper location
22. ___	reverie	V.	to decorate in a fancy way
23. ___	instigate	W.	with great anger
24. ___	appropriate	X.	the act of shedding light on something
25. ___	resourceful	Y.	many instances in a short period of time

Sentence Completions 33

Choose the proper word or pair of words for each of the sentences below.

1. Once when Bian's father went to get into his car, he found that someone had
    _____ all four of his tires and left the car supported only on concrete blocks!

    (a) embellished   (b) appropriated   (c) instigated   (d) perturbed
    (e) castigated

2. The _____ of solved crimes in relation to all crimes is not as high as TV
    detective and police shows would lead us all to believe.

    (a) attestation   (b) illumination   (c) proportion   (d) reclamation
    (e) rash

3. Sometimes the true criminal isn't the one who actually commits the crime but
    the one who _____ the crime by convincing another to do it.

    (a) embellishes   (b) perturbs   (c) instigates   (d) illuminates
    (e) denounces

4. If people are wrongly accused of a crime, they are likely to _____ the accuser
    forcibly and _____.

    (a) denounce . . . wrathfully   (b) refute . . . resourcefully
    (c) rouse . . . rashly   (d) embellish . . . crucially
    (e) appropriate . . . steadfastly

5. If someone is straightforward and _____ when being questioned, it is very
    difficult to misunderstand or _____ what they have said.

    (a) rash . . . refute   (b) imperative . . . rouse   (c) perturbed . . . instigate
    (d) candid . . . misconstrue   (e) indispensable . . . embellish

Chapter 34: Dead End?

Bian decided it was tougher to catch a *miscreant* if the crime was no longer in effect. Although the solution was still *shrouded* in mystery, the actual return of the phone had *dampened* most people's interest in the incident. She and the Dean of Students were the only ones still trying to *reconstruct* the details of the case. By the second day, Nishandra herself would no longer *cooperate* in the investigation.

"Everyone thinks I am *colluding* with the Dean of Students to get them into trouble," Nishandra *lamented* to Sammi. "Jake is holding me totally *incommunicado*; he won't even talk to me on the phone. Even Levon *resents* me, and Ogun says he expected me to be more *magnanimous* about the whole thing!"

Bian couldn't *feign* ignorance of this growing problem. She hated the idea that she was creating a *schism* in her class, but she was *inexorable* in her drive to tie up all the loose ends of this affair. Because of Jake's *notoriety* as someone who would never tell the truth if a lie would do, she hesitated to declare him *inculpable* even as she realized he had no motive and no evidence against him. The Dean of Students may have been *skeptical* about Jake's part in this as well but maintained a *prudent* silence with Bian.

On another front, Bian felt that Sammi's *hypothesis* that Nishandra might simply have forgotten that she had put her phone in her locker *belied* Sammi's own testimony that Nishandra had used the phone at lunch (also *substantiated* by Ogun's *profession* that he had seen the phone on the library table after that). No, she was *assured* within herself that the phone had been in the library as stated. Bian had even done a physical search of the area itself, *poking* around on her hands and knees under the table and *rummaging* under the bookcases nearby. Evidence was *conspicuous* by its absence: she found nothing.

assure (uh-SHOOR) (verb) to convince; to tell someone something with complete confidence.

> Bian *assured* the Dean of Students that she would not reveal what he told her, but he still couldn't compromise another's trust that way.

> Nishandra tried to *assure* her friends that she was not the one still pushing for this investigation.

belie (bi-LY) (verb) to contradict; to show to be untrue or inaccurate.

> Levon's easy-going manner served to *belie* his passion for knowledge.

> Jake's history as a liar *belied* his declaration of innocence.

collude (kuh-LOOD) (verb) to be in a plot together; to conspire.

> Bian wasn't looking for a conspiracy. How could one effectively *collude* with another to steal a phone that was unpredictably left on a table?

> No one really thought that Nishandra was *colluding* with the Dean of Students, but they were irritated that she wouldn't seem to leave the theft of her phone alone.

conspicuous (kun-SPI-kyu-wus) (adjective) very showy or noticeable; obvious.

> To let everyone know her phone was recovered, Nishandra was *conspicuous* in carrying it around the next day.

> Bian tried not to be *conspicuous* as she investigated the theft.

cooperate (ko-AH-puh-rayt) (verb) to work together amicably for a common goal.

> Nishandra didn't want to *cooperate* further with the investigation once her phone was returned.

> Sammi had *cooperated* with Bian because she respected Bian's ability to solve problems logically.

Pieces and Parts
co-

Co- as a prefix means "with" or "together." *Collude*, then, is to "conspire together" and *cooperate* is to "operate together." Other words that use this prefix are *collaborate* (to work together), *colleague* (someone you work with), and *collate* (to arrange together in proper order).

---

dampen (DAM-pun) (verb) to reduce one's interest in something; to cause to hold back.

> Even the Dean of Students was unable to *dampen* Bian's enthusiasm for the case after the phone was found.

> Nishandra *dampened* Bian's interest slightly when she worried aloud about the tension in the class over the incident.

feign (FAYN) (verb) to pretend; to give a false impression.

> Bian didn't have to *feign* sincerity about being sorry for the tension in the class; she was truly concerned about it.

> Jake *feigned* unconcern when he believed people suspected him of stealing Nishandra's phone.

hypothesis (hy-PAH-thuh-ses) (noun) a reasonable theory based on (usually) incomplete information that is designed to be tested further. (plural: hypotheses)

> Bian's working *hypothesis* was that Jake had picked up the phone, thought better of stealing it, and had returned it to Nishandra's open locker.

> Despite her own testimony to the contrary, Sammi's *hypothesis* was that, somehow, Nishandra had forgotten that she had put the phone in her locker herself.

incommunicado (in-kuh-myoo-nuh-KAH-doe) (adjective) without the ability to communicate with others.

> Nishandra was such a social animal that holding her *incommunicado* was one of the greatest punishments one could inflict on her.

> Because he was angry with his classmates, Jake was holding himself *incommunicado* for a few days until he got over his hurt feelings.

inculpable (in-KUL-puh-bl) (adjective) not guilty; without blame.

> Someone who didn't know Nishandra suggested to Bian that she had lied about the lost phone, but Bian knew Nishandra was *inculpable* of that charge.

> Although Ogun was the only one other than Nishandra to have noticed the phone on the library table, he was thought *inculpable* of the crime by all because of his reputation of honesty.

inexorable (ih-NEKS-ruh-bl) (adjective) cannot be persuaded or begged to change one's mind; singleminded.

> The Dean of Students was *inexorable* in his quest to solve the problem of these petty robberies on campus.

> Not even Nishandra could convince Bian to drop her *inexorable* determination to solve this matter.

lament (luh-MENT) (verb) to express sadness, regret, or grief; to mourn.

> She may have enjoyed most of her classes, but Bian *lamented* having to attend them while she was trying to solve a crime.

> Jake *lamented* the negative side of his reputation privately but never let anyone else know how he really felt about it.

magnanimous (mag-NA-nuh-mus) (adjective) describes forgiving someone or something generously and with no hard feelings.

> Ogun was universally *magnanimous* when forgiving someone for a wrong done to him.

> It was typical of Nishandra to be *magnanimous* as well which made Ogun's charge against her all the more difficult for her to take.

miscreant (MIS-kree-unt) (noun) a criminal or a villain. (plural: miscreants)

> Who were the *miscreants* who were creating a climate of mistrust on campus by stealing?

> Bian knew from her reading that many *miscreants* passed as fine, worthy citizens most of the time.

notoriety (no-tuh-RY-uh-tee) (noun) a state of being famous for being bad; an infamous reputation. (plural: This word is not usually used in the plural.)

> Jake's *notoriety* was putting him in a bad light in this situation.

> Even if Jake hadn't taken the phone, it didn't erase his *notoriety* or the possibility that he might be related to the other thefts on campus.

poke (POKE) (verb) to look around an area in an undirected way.

> Ogun asked Levon if he thought it were appropriate for Bian to *poke* around in other people's business.

> When she was younger, Bian had enjoyed *poking* through old cupboards in the house, making up her own mystery stories about items she found.

profession (pruh-FE-shun) (noun) a statement of truth or belief. (plural: professions)

> A *profession* of faith in the basic honesty of most human beings was the approach the Dean of Students took to his work.

> Ogun didn't have to make a *profession* of his honesty because people already accepted that about him.

prudent (PROO-dnt) (adjective) cautious; using common sense and being careful about one's behavior.

> When Ogun became unhappy with her, Bian decided to be a little more *prudent* and a little less energetic in her investigation.

> Bian felt it wasn't *prudent* for a detective to share his or her theories of the crime until after it had been solved.

reconstruct (ree-kun-STRUKT) (verb) to put together again or rebuild.

> Bian was able to *reconstruct* most of the elements of what had happened that afternoon.

> Every time an element of her theory was disproved, Bian had to *reconstruct* her evidence into a new theory.

resent (ri-ZENT) (verb) to feel angry and/or indignant at real or imagined insults or wrongs done.

> Sammi hoped that Nishandra would not *resent* her honesty with Bian.

> A small part of Bian *resented* that the others were not as involved in solving the case as she was.

rummage (RUH-mij) (verb) to search thoroughly and energetically by handling items.

> Nishandra hadn't even had to *rummage* through her locker to find her cell phone; it was sitting in plain sight on top of her books.

> Bian *rummaged* under the bookcase in the library and found two combs, three crumpled papers, and a collection of pens but no hard evidence.

Easy Errors   ***hypo-* vs. *hyper-***

Hypo- means "under or less than," whereas *hyper-* means "over or greater than." A *hypothesis*, then, is the foundation theory upon which work is based. A *hypodermic* needle—*hypo* (under) + *dermis* (skin)—is designed to deliver medicine below or under the skin. *Hyperactive* means more active than usual and *hyperbole* is an expression that exaggerates to make a point.

---

schism (SI-zum) (noun) a rift between two groups or people who were formerly close; discord. (plural: schisms)

> Bian hoped she wasn't creating a permanent *schism* within the class.

> Nishandra realized that the *schism* between her and Jake would be healed as soon as the case was solved.

shrouded (SHROWD-ed) (adjective) protected and hidden.

> The solution was *shrouded* from Bian but she had no doubt that she would get to the truth.

> Jake's true feelings were *shrouded* behind his outward attitude of unconcern.

skeptical (SKEP-ti-kul) (adjective) showing a lack of faith in information presented; an attitude of disbelief or doubt.

> The Dean of Students was *skeptical* of Jake's supposed innocence, but he had no firm evidence against him.

> Nishandra was *skeptical* of Bian's ability to solve this mystery.

substantiate (sub-STAN-shee-ayt) (verb) to support with evidence.

> Bian did not have the evidence to *substantiate* any of her theories.

> Eyewitness testimony *substantiated* Nishandra's use of the phone over lunch that day.

Quick Match 34

Match each word to its definition.

1. ___	inexorable	A.	to feel angry and/or indignant
2. ___	assure	B.	a statement of truth or belief
3. ___	rummage	C.	describes forgiving generously and with no hard feelings
4. ___	lament	D.	a rift between two who were formerly close
5. ___	belie	E.	not guilty; without blame
6. ___	magnanimous	F.	to be in a plot together; to conspire
7. ___	collude	G.	to put together again or rebuild
8. ___	schism	H.	to pretend; to give a false impression
9. ___	miscreant	I.	to search thoroughly and energetically
10. ___	conspicuous	J.	to look around an area in an undirected way
11. ___	notoriety	K.	to reduce one's interest in something
12. ___	cooperate	L.	describes using common sense and being careful
13. ___	shrouded	M.	protected and hidden
14. ___	poke	N.	to contradict; to show to be untrue or inaccurate
15. ___	dampen	O.	a criminal or a villain
16. ___	profession	P.	very showy or noticeable; obvious
17. ___	feign	Q.	the state of being famous for being bad
18. ___	skeptical	R.	to tell someone something without any doubt
19. ___	prudent	S.	without the ability to communicate with others
20. ___	hypothesis	T.	to support with evidence
21. ___	reconstruct	U.	to work together amicably for a common goal
22. ___	incommunicado	V.	to express sadness, regret, or grief; to mourn
23. ___	substantiate	W.	reasonable theory from incomplete information
24. ___	resent	X.	cannot be persuaded to change one's mind
25. ___	inculpable	Y.	an attitude of disbelief or doubt

Sentence Completions 34

Choose the proper word or pair of words for each of the sentences below.

1. Columbo, an old TV detective, had a sleepy and relaxed manner that _____ his sharp intellect and strong deductive abilities.

   (a) poked   (b) lamented   (c) resented   (d) belied   (e) colluded

2. A professional criminal is careful to blend into a crowd and not seem to be too noticeable and _____ .

   (a) prudent   (b) magnanimous   (c) cooperative   (d) shrouded
   (e) conspicuous

3. The _____ of Jesse James, Billy the Kid, and Bonnie and Clyde has lived on long after these criminals' deaths.

   (a) notoriety   (b) hypothesis   (c) schism   (d) miscreant   (e) belie

4. Some criminals _____ innocence very well and one cannot always be sure that they are as _____ as they may seem.

   (a) belie . . . incommunicado   (b) lament . . . magnanimous
   (c) feign . . . inculpable   (d) poke . . . prudent   (e) resent . . . conspicuous

5. It is smart to be _____ of any _____ of honesty from a stranger since one never knows the truth.

   (a) incommunicado . . . notoriety   (b) skeptical . . . profession
   (c) inexorable . . . lament   (d) inculpable . . . magnanimous
   (e) conspicuous . . . schism

Chapter 35: All Is Revealed

Reading in the library, Bian had *resorted* to sitting in the *environs* of the crime on the *supposition* that an inspiration would come to her in that place. It *irked* her that the case continued to *evade* solution.

"Some detective I am," she *opined* to herself in *chagrin*. "I can't even get to the bottom of a crime that has solved itself!"

Involved in her own *morose* thoughts, she almost didn't look up at Amber who had *tarried* beside her to say hello.

"What's been going on?" asked Amber. "I was at my aunt's funeral for a couple of days."

"Oh, I heard about that. My *condolences*," said Bian sympathetically. "Were you two very close?"

"Actually, no," *granted* Amber. "I barely knew her, but my mom is still pretty upset. Say, did Nishandra get her cell phone back?"

Bian was taken *aback*; how did Amber know about that?

"Oh," replied Amber *airily*, "I found it on the floor under this table the other day. I knew it was Nishandra's so I *stowed* it in her locker before my mom picked me up to drive to my uncle's. She never locks that stupid locker and I was afraid someone else might *pilfer* it. She got it back, right?"

Bian explained the entire *fiasco* to Amber before everyone had to *vacate* the library for a school-wide assembly.

Bian's natural *resilience* took over now that she had a full explanation, but she also felt somewhat *swindled*. In the first place, this "crime" was no such thing and clearly had no *relevance* to the pattern of thefts that *plagued* the Dean of Students. In the second place, it was ending in a way she *detested*: a solution from totally outside of the evidence she had *garnered*. She knew a good novel or TV plot would never have *incorporated* such a weak *denouement*. Maybe her disappointment wasn't in mysteries, though, but in life itself. The world is not always complicated, she realized. Sometimes life is just, well, *mundane*.

(take) aback (uh-BAK) (adverb) to startle or surprise.

> Amber's surprise involvement in the case took Bian *aback*.

> Nishandra would probably be taken *aback*, too, once it was all explained to her.

airily (AYR-uh-lee) (adverb) with a light, unconcerned attitude.

> When it was explained to Nishandra, she replied *airily* that she didn't really care as long as her phone was back.

> Bian covered her disappointment by speaking *airily* about the case to her mother that evening when she got home.

chagrin (shu-GRIN) (noun) a feeling of mental or emotional discomfort because of embarrassment at a character flaw (often in oneself) or a mistake. (plural: This word is not usually used in the plural.)

> To his *chagrin*, the Dean of Students realized he had been following the wrong case to solve the theft problems.

> Bian's mother recognized her disappointment and, to Bian's *chagrin*, sympathized with her.

condolences (kun-DO-lun-sez) (noun) an expression of sympathetic sadness to someone who has suffered a loss. (plural: This word is usually used in the plural.)

> The Dean of Students expressed his *condolences* to Amber on the death of her aunt.

> Amber's advisor offered her *condolences* to Amber's mother as well.

denouement (day-noo-MAH) (noun) the end result of a sequence of events; in literature, the explanations and clarifications that take place after the climax of the story. (plural: denouements)

> The *denouement* of the affair was more satisfying than expected because everyone was relieved that no one in the class had been a thief.

> The class discussed the details of the *denouement* for the whole day, making Amber a bit of a celebrity in the process.

detest (di-TEST) (verb) to hate (something or someone) intensely.

> Nishandra had grown to *detest* the stress in the class, so she was happy that the case was solved.

> As much as she *detested* the weak ending of her first mystery, Bian was happy to have had a chance to be a real detective.

environs (in-VY-runs) (noun) the surrounding area of a place. (plural: This word is usually used in the plural.)

> The students smiled about the case every time they were in the *environs* of the famous library table where it all happened.

> A few months later, Bian heard that the story had gone beyond the *environs* of her own school and others at neighboring schools had heard about it.

evade (i-VAYD) (verb) to escape or avoid something negative through cleverness.

> Bian was unable to *evade* good-natured jokes about her temporary role as a detective.

Jake *evaded* part of his past notoriety by emphasizing how he had been wrongly accused in this instance.

fiasco (fee-AS-koe) (noun) an unsuccessful event or sequence of events; a total failure. (plural: fiascos)

While Bian considered the entire affair a *fiasco*, her friends and classmates thought it had been fun to work through the mystery for a few days.

It was indeed a *fiasco* for the Dean of Students who had hoped to solve a series of problems with a single investigation.

Easy Errors   *imply* and *infer*

The simplest way to explain the difference between these two words is to imagine a conversation. The speaker hints at something without saying it directly (he *implies* an idea) and the listener picks up what she thinks the idea is without stating it directly (she *infers* the speaker's meaning). The speaker is always the one to *imply* and the listener is always the one to *infer*.

---

garner (GAHR-nur) (verb) to gather and keep.

With a sigh and a bit of a smile, Bian threw out all of the evidence she had worked so hard to *garner*.

Because of this case, Bian *garnered* a reputation as an organized and systematic investigator.

grant (GRANT) (verb) to admit or acknowledge.

Bian had to *grant* that she had been a bit overly enthusiastic in her investigation.

The Dean of Students *granted* to the principal that he was a little disappointed not to be on the right track with the theft problem.

incorporate (in-KOR-puh-rayt) (verb) to cause to combine or put together parts into a whole.

Bian decided to *incorporate* her real-life detective experiences into a project on "Mysteries in History" with Levon.

To prevent another loss of her cell phone, Nishandra *incorporated* a new habit into her routine: she always put the phone in her book bag as soon as she was finished using it.

irk (URK) (verb) to irritate or annoy.

It *irked* Jake that his being innocent in this case didn't totally eliminate his reputation for dishonesty.

While it *irked* Bian that the mystery had fallen flat, she was pleased that Nishandra had her phone back.

mundane (mun-DAYN) (adjective) commonplace; typical of the world.

Soon everyone was back into the *mundane* cycle of classes and homework.

Bian had to admit that a *mundane* solution to the case had always been more likely than a wildly dramatic one like those in her novels.

opine (o-PYN) (verb) to state or believe (something) from one's own point of view.

The Dean of Students *opined* that Bian would make a good administrator some day because of her detective skills.

Nishandra *opined* that she had never believed someone had actually stolen her phone.

pilfer (PIL-fur) (verb) to steal something small or a small amount of something.

No one in the class dared to *pilfer* even a carrot stick from a classmate's lunch for the next six months because they didn't want another investigation.

Bian *pilfered* a pen from her sister's backpack to complete her homework.

plague (PLAYG) (verb) to annoy repeatedly.

After her sister found out about the pen, she *plagued* Bian about it for days.

Bian had *plagued* everyone with questions for days so they were relieved when the case was solved.

relevance (RE-luh-vuns) (noun) the relationship of something outside of a situation to the matter currently at hand or under consideration.

Bian began to wonder about the *relevance* of mystery novels to everyday life.

Levon was finding the *relevance* of detective work to an historian's job to be very interesting.

resilience (ri-ZIL-yuns) (noun) the ability to quickly recover one's usual positive state after being temporarily brought down by something negative (such as illness or bad luck). (plural: resiliences)

Bian bounced back with natural *resilience* after her disappointment.

It took the class a few days to recover its *resilience* after all the tension over the case.

resort (ri-ZORT) (verb) to go frequently or by habit to a particular place or idea.

Bian had to *resort* to math and science again as ways for her to keep her logic and reasoning skills sharp.

She *resorted* to her old idea that no good mysteries would come her way until she was a real detective.

Pieces and Parts   ***re-***

Re- as a prefix means "again" or "new." *Resilience* is a noun that means "the state of having bounced back" and *resort*—*re-* (again) + *sortir* (go out)—means "to return to a particular habit or idea." This prefix is used extensively to indicate repetition in such words as *repeat, rewire, restructure, renew,* and *reappear.*

---

stow (STOE) (verb) to store something away safely or in a tidy way for future use.

Nishandra resolved to *stow* her phone carefully in her book bag from now on.

Nishandra *stowed* away this experience to remind herself to check all possibilities the next time before saying something had been stolen.

supposition (suh-puh-ZI-shun) (noun) an assumption; an opinion arrived at with insufficient evidence. (plural: suppositions)

Her immediate *supposition* that Jake had been guilty made Bian feel very uncomfortable now.

The Dean of Student's *supposition* that the thefts had been related was now called into question.

swindled (SWIN-dld) (adjective) cheated; lost or obtained through fraud or illegal means.

Bian felt *swindled* of her dream when she was unable to solve her first case.

No one was *swindled* of his or her good name over this affair although Jake tried to argue that he had been.

tarry (TER-ee) (verb) to linger; to wait or delay in leaving.

Amber couldn't *tarry* long after after classes because she had practice.

Bian *tarried* at school long enough that afternoon to be sure that the Dean of Students had heard the whole story.

vacate (VAY-kayt) (verb) to empty an area of people or occupants; to give up (something or someplace) by leaving it.

Almost everyone *vacated* the school that afternoon to go to the big game.

Bian wondered to herself if it was time to *vacate* her role as an amateur detective and wait until she could be trained as a true professional.

Quick Match 35
Match each word to its definition.

1. ___	fiasco	A.	a feeling of mental or emotional discomfort
2. ___	relevance	B.	a total failure
3. ___	evade	C.	to state or believe from one's own point of view
4. ___	plague	D.	commonplace; typical of the world
5. ___	resilience	E.	to store away safely for future use
6. ___	environs	F.	to avoid something negative through cleverness
7. ___	pilfer	G.	an opinion arrived at with insufficient evidence
8. ___	resort	H.	the relationship of something outside of a situation to the matter currently at hand
9. ___	detest	I.	with a light, unconcerned attitude
10. ___	opine	J.	to steal something small
11. ___	stow	K.	an expression of sympathetic sadness
12. ___	denouement	L.	to annoy repeatedly
13. ___	mundane	M.	to irritate or annoy
14. ___	supposition	N.	to gather and keep
15. ___	condolences	O.	the ability to recover one's positive state quickly
16. ___	irk	P.	to linger; to wait or delay in leaving
17. ___	swindled	Q.	to admit or acknowledge
18. ___	chagrin	R.	to go frequently to a particular place or idea
19. ___	incorporate	S.	the end result of a sequence of events
20. ___	tarry	T.	to startle or surprise
21. ___	airily	U.	to empty an area of people or occupants
22. ___	grant	V.	the surrounding area of a place
23. ___	vacate	W.	lost or obtained through fraud or illegal means
24. ___	(take) aback	X.	to combine or put together parts into a whole
25. ___	garner	Y.	to hate (something or someone) intensely

Sentence Completions 35

Choose the proper word or pair of words for each of the sentences below.

1. Despite the fact that the cell phone case didn't shed any light on other thefts, the Dean of Students had to _____ that it had been entertaining to watch Bian at work.

     (a) grant   (b) incorporate   (c) garner   (d) detest   (e) tarry

2. A good mystery novel always contains facts and information that have no true _____ to the case so that the reader can try to figure out what is and is not truly important.

     (a) environs   (b) supposition   (c) chagrin   (d) relevance   (e) condolences

3. Although the _____ of the case was disappointing, the actual investigation had been fun.

     (a) condolences   (b) chagrin   (c) environs   (d) denouement   (e) resilience

4. As soon as Bian _____ a chair in the library, someone at the next table _____ it for a friend to use.

     (a) opined . . . swindled   (b) stowed . . . granted   (c) detested . . . garnered
     (d) tarried . . . resorted   (e) vacated . . . pilfered

5. Bian tried to _____ the commonplace and _____ in life by reading about an exciting and glamorous world of mysteries.

     (a) evade . . . mundane   (b) aback . . . swindled   (c) garner . . . supposition
     (d) grant . . . denouement   (e) pilfer . . . fiasco

WRITING ACTIVITY

The Butler Did It!

Why anyone wouldn't love vocabulary lessons is puzzling to me. To find the *perfect* word to express one's *precise* thoughts—ah, it is a beautiful thing! That another human being would find this exploration irksome is one of life's *great mysteries*.

Speaking of *great mysteries*, we should write one of our own!

Using as many words from this section as possible, complete the mystery started below:

He—or it?—was slinking across the exquisitely tended lawn of the huge estate, ducking behind the blooming banks of rhododendrons in the pale light of a waning gibbous moon. Estrella, determined to find the reprehensible culprit who had so heinously . . . .

Make it daring, make it fun, make it mysterious! Enjoy!

SECTION 8: AN ARTIST AND HIS DOG

Learning Style: The Visual/Spatial Learner

If you prefer to approach your world through pictures and images, diagrams and maps, one of your primary intelligences is likely that of the Visual/Spatial learner.

Do you routinely notice not only of the color of an item but also its texture? Is art in any of its manifestations—drawing, painting, sculpting, creating—a driving force in your life? Are you the one who pulls out the diagram of an item you are assembling rather than check the written instructions first? Do you find that you are the picture puzzle champion in your family and always the first one to be elected when a map needs to be read? If you have answered "yes" to several of the above, this is one of your stronger intelligences.

Possible Approaches

- **Draw a Simple Picture.** The simplest and most effective process to help you retain vocabulary words is to draw a picture to illustrate a word. Remember that your picture doesn't have to make sense to anyone but you!

- **Picture a Movie.** Create pictures or movies in your mind of vocabulary words in action. Make them silly or outrageous and, so, memorable.

- **Create a Cartoon.** Draw a cartoon for the words that you find most difficult; this will help you remember them. If you already have a favorite cartoon character, use him or her to demonstrate the word on paper for you. Or you can use your own invented characters. Peter, a friend of mine from high school, used to draw cartoon characters in the form of gourds (yes, the squash and pumpkin kind) with arms, legs, and silly facial expressions: certainly memorable images! Try using *your* imagination to come up with your own cast of vocabulary-helping characters.

- **Create a Map.** Draw a map of this section's vocabulary journey. For each natural or manmade landmark on the map, name it with a vocabulary word from this section. Write a quick history of this "place" with a definition or sentence using this word in the legend of the map.

  - **Variation.** To make your map even more interesting and useful, you might want to use different parts of speech for different kinds of landmarks. Try color-coding nouns as blue, and then name all rivers and bodies of water with noun names. Make adjectives green, and then perhaps all mountains can be named for adjectives. With verbs as red, you might want to name all buildings or man-made objects with verb

305

names. Adverbs can be yellow, so fields of different flowering crops could be named for adverbs. These are just suggestions; be sure to make your map your own to help you remember in your own way.

- **Create Graphic Organizers.** Create a triangle and a rectangle side by side. In the pyramid, list the vocabulary words, shortest to longest from top to bottom to make the triangular shape clear. In the rectangle beside the triangle, write the definition (or a sentence using the vocabulary word) on the same line as it appears in the triangle. These graphic organizers will help you remember your words.

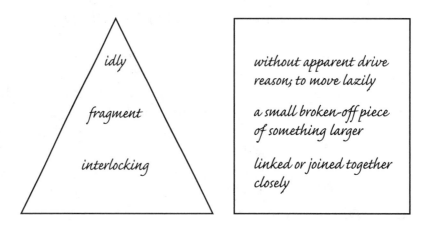

- **Variation.** Put all of this information in a three-dimensional box.

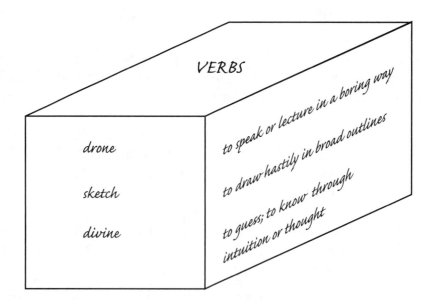

- **Create Flashcards.** Cut flashcards in wild or geometric shapes and write the vocabulary word on one side and its definition on the other. Again, it will help keep these words straight in your mind if you color code your cards: blue for nouns; green for adjectives; red for verbs; and yellow for adverbs. If a word is used as more than a single part of speech (for instance, "discourse" may be used as a noun or a verb) make a separate card for each part of speech in its proper color.

  - **Variation.** To make your flashcards even more memorable, follow the shape of the card when you write your vocabulary word on it and do the same on the back with the definition. Don't be afraid to put more than one word on the same card (but be sure all words on a single card are the same part of speech for color-coding reasons). For twenty-five words, for instance, you might put up to five words and definitions on a single card and use five or more cards in different shapes and colors to help you remember the words more individually. Here's an example:

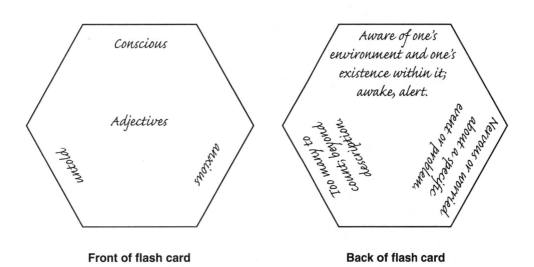

Front of flash card   **Back of flash card**

Chapter 36: The Spark

Bron *slumped* in his desk, *sketching interlocking* circles and triangles in the left *margin* of his loose-leaf notebook paper. It was history class—again. Although Mr. Jenkins could occasionally *drone* on for what seemed like hours, today he was *animated*, enthusiastic about his topic. Bron rolled his eyes at his buddy Arkady to *underscore* his boredom, and Kai looked *askance* at the two of them before returning his attention to taking notes. Bron couldn't *divine* why Kai found history so *rewarding*. What could even *remotely* interest him about events that happened *untold* years before? Bron returned to his *doodles*.

Idly wondering if he should begin drawing on the right side of the margin as well as on the left, Bron gradually became *conscious* of something interesting *emanating* from Mr. Jenkins. He and another student were *discoursing* about a Newfoundland dog. A Newfoundland dog? A *fragment* of memory *nudged* Bron's mind: *reminiscences* of a beach vacation from when he was barely five years old and a gigantic dog on that beach. The dog had been *frantic*—why? Yeah, yeah, the kid in the water—the dog was *anxious* about the kid in the water. No tragedies had *ensued*, and Bron had found himself almost face-to-face with this huge and gentle dog, *embracing* him fearlessly and burying his face in the thick fur of the dog's *withers*. Bron began to sketch this dog on his page. Wait, why was Mr. Jenkins talking about dogs? Lewis and Clark had a Newfoundland on their expedition with them? To Bron, history was beginning to get interesting.

animated (A-ni-may-tud) (adjective) lively, active.

> Bron was usually quiet in manner, but Arkady would get really *animated* when talking about something that excited him.

> It was hard for Kai not to be *animated* when talking about the search for the northwest passage from the Atlantic to the Pacific because he was fascinated by arctic explorers.

anxious (ANK-shus) (adjective) nervous, worried; also, worried or nervous about a specific event or problem.

> Many people's dogs get *anxious* and pace back and forth if they think their owners might be in danger.

> Bron seldom took notes in any class, so he was likely to get a bit *anxious* before a test since he seldom had a clear idea of what might be on it.

askance (uh-SKANS) (adverb) showing irritation or distrust; describes looking at someone sideways.

> Kai may have been irritated with Bron and Arkady in class, but occasionally Bron looked *askance* at him, too, because of his interest in all things historical.

> Arkady had developed a talent for seeming to pay attention in class when he was really looking *askance* at Bron from the corner of his eye to see what Bron was drawing.

conscious (KAHNT-shus) (adjective) being aware of one's environment and one's own existence within that environment; awake, alert.

> While Bron didn't really sleep during class, he sometimes drifted away in thought until he wasn't *conscious* of what was really happening.

> Bron was *conscious* of his lack of involvement in class and sometimes he wished he could be more interested because that might relieve his boredom.

discourse (DIS-kors) (noun) conversation; expression or a specific discussion in speech or writing. (plural: discourses)

> Bron had heard Ms. Patel and Mr. Rinehart *discourse* at length over lunch on their differing opinions of the writing of Charlotte Brontë.

> One history class discussion that interested Bron grew out of three really committed students' *discourse* about the morality of the westward expansion of the pioneers.

divine (du-VYN) (verb) to guess; to know through one's own intuition or thought.

> Kai seemed able to *divine* exactly what a teacher wanted for every assignment given.

> Unlike some others in art class, Bron could *divine* the precise angle of a line in his work to make a drawing come alive.

> ### *Easy Errors*   ***conscious* vs. *conscience***
>
> *Conscious* is an adjective that means "awake and alert" and *conscience* is a noun that refers to "one's inner sense of what is right and what is wrong." One, therefore, needs to be *conscious* of one's *conscience* to make moral and ethical decisions.

---

doodle (DOO-dl) (noun) random scribbles and drawings made while bored or to keep oneself occupied during another activity, such as a meeting or a class. (plural: doodles)

> At the end of each school year, Bron's mom would sort through some of his schoolwork from the previous year and save some of his more promising *doodles* with his other more formal artwork.

> Arkady enjoyed Bron's *doodles* and felt they helped Bron pay more attention in class than he would have otherwise.

drone (DRONE) (verb) to make a low, humming noise that is ongoing and monotonous; to speak or lecture in a boring way.

> The air conditioner in the computer room sometimes *droned* louder than the hum of the computers themselves.

> Mr. Jenkins didn't always *drone* in class when he lectured; he could be quite interesting.

emanate (EH-mu-nayt) (verb) to send something forth from someone or something; to send out a force, light, or energy.

> The heat that *emanated* from the sun through the classroom windows sometimes made even Kai a little sleepy during class.

> Although Bron was usually quiet, enthusiasm *emanated* from him when he talked about drawing and photographic techniques.

embrace (im-BRAYS) (verb) to show affection by holding in one's arms; to enthusiastically take in an idea or set of values for oneself.

> Bron's college-aged sister returned to visit the school once and excitedly *embraced* Bron when she saw him in the hall.

> In art history class, Bron was enchanted by the paintings of the French Impressionists and, for a while, *embraced* their style in his own work.

ensue (in-SOO) (verb) to occur as a result or consequence of something else.

> The advanced art class was always noisy at the beginning, but as the students became focused on their art, silence would *ensue*.

> Arkady and his sister disagreed on politics a great deal and noisy arguments often *ensued* after they listened to the news together.

fragment (FRAG-ment) (noun) a small piece of something larger, often a piece that has broken off or is one of a number of broken pieces. (plural: fragments)

> It was just a *fragment* of the story of the explorations of Lewis and Clark that caught Bron's imagination that afternoon.

> To learn to draw in three dimensions, the art teacher often had the students draw actual *fragments* of broken pottery because of their interesting angles and curves.

frantic (FRAN-tik) (adjective) describes an agitated emotional state, usually caused by fear, frustration, or being rushed; frenzied.

> Arkady would often be *frantic* if he lost something he needed, whereas Bron would normally stay cool and calm in most situations.

> The *frantic* pace of rushing from one class to the next, five days a week, would sometimes wear Bron out.

idly (EYD-lee) (adverb) without any apparent drive or reason; to move lazily.

> At the end of class, Bron would glance *idly* at the front board to see if the teacher had posted any homework for the next class.

> Since he had a study hall the next period, Arkady walked *idly* through the courtyard, unworried about being late.

interlocking (in-tur-LAHK-ing) (adjective) linked or joined together closely.

> As a child, Bron had really enjoyed picture puzzles and the interesting shapes of their *interlocking* pieces.

> Kai probably enjoyed school because he could see *interlocking* ideas from one subject to the next, whereas many saw each school subject as unconnected to any other.

margin (MAR-jun) (noun) the border around the outside of a printed page where there is no printing. (plural: margins)

> Bron could figure out the required one-inch *margin* around his paintings in class without ever having to measure; he just knew by looking.

> Kai liked to write notes to himself in the left *margin* of his loose leaf paper while he took down the teachers' words on the main body of the page.

nudge (NUJ) (verb) to bump someone or something slightly, whether figuratively or literally, especially as a way to send a message.

> The teachers knew Bron was willing to work, but they still had to *nudge* him a bit to keep him on track with his homework.

> After class, Arkady *nudged* Bron as Ming walked by. Bron ignored him.

reminiscence (re-mu-NI-snts) (noun) a memory; the process of remembering certain situations or memories. (plural: reminiscences)

> When his aunts and uncles got to their childhood *reminiscences* at a family reunion, Bron would usually take his camera and try out interesting shots of their animated faces.

> One of his favorite *reminiscences* was a story his mother would tell about him as a baby.

remotely (ri-MOT-lee) (adverb) slightly; not an immediate possibility.

> Bron was not even *remotely* interested in Ming, but Arkady knew that she admired Bron.

> Arkady was only *remotely* interested in art, but he did admire his friend's talent.

Easy Errors   *idle* and *idol*

If *idle* is an adjective that describes someone who has "little or nothing to do," and *idol* is a noun that means "an image or statue that is an object of worship," then one might say, "In some religious traditions, artists are kept so busy creating *idols* that they have no *idle* time to relax."

rewarding (ri-WOR-ding) (adjective) describes an action or experience that is valued more because of the satisfaction it gives than by any other payment or profit.

> Bron did some personally *rewarding* volunteer work with a children's art project downtown.

> Mr. Jenkins thought teaching was *rewarding*, but sometimes he worried that he wasn't reaching the hearts of all of his students.

sketch (SKECH) (verb) to hastily draw (or write) the initial broad outlines of a work of art (or a written work) in preparation for filling in the details later.

> Bron always had a small pad of paper with him so that he could be prepared to *sketch* anything that caught his eye.

> Mr. Jenkins liked to *sketch* his ideas out on paper first before presenting them to the class.

slump (SLUMP) (verb) to sit or stand casually with back bent; to slouch.

> Arkady knew that although Bron liked to *slump* in his seat, that didn't always mean he wasn't paying attention.

> Tired, Bron would *slump* in his chair at the end of each school day.

underscore (UN-der-skor) (verb) to emphasize.

> To *underscore* its importance, Mr. Jenkins spent several class periods discussing the Lewis and Clark expedition.

> The art teacher was *underscoring* the difference in mood that color can make when he had the students sketch the same still life in both color and black and white.

untold (un-TOLD) (adjective) not counted or too many to count; beyond description.

> As a child, the *untold* stars in the night sky inspired Bron to do a series of drawings of the solar system.

> The Lewis and Clark expedition faced *untold* hardships before returning home.

withers (WI-thurz) (noun) The high part of the back (between the shoulder blades) of a horse, dog, or other large four-footed animal. (plural: This word, defined in this way, is always used in the plural.)

> After hugging him, Bron had thrown his arm over the *withers* of the large dog and walked with him down the beach all those years ago.

> Drawing horses was always a challenge for Bron, and he never could get the proportions of the horse correct from the *withers* to the hoof.

Quick Match 36

Match each word to its definition.

1. ____ withers
2. ____ remotely
3. ____ animated
4. ____ divine
5. ____ ensue
6. ____ untold
7. ____ reminiscence
8. ____ anxious
9. ____ fragment
10. ____ doodle
11. ____ underscore
12. ____ nudge
13. ____ askance
14. ____ frantic

15. ____ drone
16. ____ slump
17. ____ margin
18. ____ conscious
19. ____ idly
20. ____ emanate
21. ____ sketch

22. ____ interlocking
23. ____ discourse
24. ____ embrace
25. ____ rewarding

A. conversation
B. to speak or lecture in a boring way
C. to bump someone slightly
D. random scribbles and drawings
E. the process of remembering certain things
F. to occur as a result of something else
G. awake, alert; aware of one's environment
H. beyond description; too many to count
I. border around the outside of a printed page
J. showing irritation or distrust; looking sideways
K. slightly
L. to sit or stand casually with back bent; slouch
M. to send out a force, light, or energy
N. to enthusiastically take in a set of values or ideas
O. the high part of an animal's back
P. lively, active
Q. to emphasize
R. a small broken-off piece of something larger
S. linked or joined together closely
T. nervous, worried
U. describes an experience valued more for its satisfaction
V. frenzied; an agitated emotional state
W. to draw hastily in broad outlines
X. to guess; to know through intuition or thought
Y. without apparent drive or reason; to move lazily

Sentence Completions 36
Choose the proper word or pair of words for each of the sentences below.

1. The art survey course covered art from the time of cave paintings _____ years ago right up to the present day.

    (a) animated   (b) interlocking   (c) untold   (d) fragmented   (e) marginal

2. The students were not even _____ interested in visiting the art museum until they actually got there and were enchanted by the wonderful paintings on display.

    (a) remotely   (b) frantically   (c) consciously   (d) interlocking
    (e) rewardingly

3. The teacher tried to _____ the importance of Renaissance art by emphasizing the great artists who worked at the time.

    (a) nudge   (b) ensue   (c) fragment   (d) emanate   (e) underscore

4. It was important for the art students to _____ the different styles of earlier artists by trying to _____ in those styles as part of their learning process.

    (a) drone . . . nudge   (b) emanate . . . divine   (c) doodle . . . ensue
    (d) embrace . . . sketch   (e) reminisce . . . slump

5. Most of the students were _____ about the upcoming test and looked _____ at the one classmate who was whistling and unconcerned about it.

    (a) animated . . . idly   (b) anxious . . . askance   (c) conscious . . . remotely
    (d) frantic . . . rewarding   (e) interlocking . . . underscore

Chapter 37: And What It Lit

Shirking his PowerPoint assignment *momentarily* in computer class, Bron hit the Internet to find pictures of, and *statistics* about, Newfoundland dogs. A Web site described the two acceptable colors for this dog: a black and white and a pure black. Searching his memory, Bron *conjured* up an image of a pure black dog from the beach; fine, that part of the memory fit. He read on. Originally *indigenous* to Newfoundland, the Web site said that the dogs are great in the water and actually have slightly *webbed* toes. As to size, Bron was *thunderstruck* to read that the dogs grow to weigh between 120 and 150 pounds; this dog truly was as *colossal* as his five-year-old mind remembered! Hurriedly sketching a dog from a *grainy* Internet photo, Bron was a little frustrated by the lack of *discernable* detail in the picture, knowing he was going to need a better model from which to work if he was going to be able to draw these creatures. Bron glanced up in time to see Mr. Carrothers *strolling* toward his computer station. As the teacher *elevated* an eyebrow in question, Bron *hastily* returned to his assignment.

That weekend found Bron at the home of a local Newfoundland dog breeder, *encircled* (and almost *engulfed*) by a *writhing horde* of good-sized puppies. *Lunging* at him in *ersatz* aggression and *gnawing* on everything available with little, sharp teeth, the puppies were both *excruciating* and *endearing* at the same time. Laughing helplessly, he *perceived* that he would never be able to sketch the puppies while *accessible* to them. With regret, he watched the breeder herd them back into their *runs*. Bron then found a comfortable spot to sit so he could sketch them as they played and napped.

accessible (ik-SE-suh-bl) (adjective) easy to get to; easy to use.

> Bron was surprised to find a Newfoundland breeder *accessible* to him.

> Both Mr. Carrothers, the computer teacher, and Ms. Patel, one of the art teachers, made themselves *accessible* to students for extra help on a regular basis during the week.

colossal (ku-LAH-sul) (adjective) huge, gigantic; so large that it induces awe.

> Bron often left his homework undone from day to day until he had a *colossal* stack that he had to get done all in one night.

> When Arkady had first seen his new high school, it had seemed *colossal* to him. He has become comfortable with its size over time, though.

conjure (KAHN-jur) (verb) to create, as if by magic; to imagine or to bring to one's mind.

> When Bron had one of his huge stacks of homework to do, he often wished he could *conjure* up a genie to do it for him.

> Some people had trouble imagining what they might produce in art class, but Bron could almost always *conjure* up a very clear image of what he wanted to create.

discernable (di-SURN-abl) (adjective) able to be seen; distinguished with the eyes or with the mind; recognizable as being different.

> Bron drew one really dark piece in charcoal on paper in which two dangerous-looking figures were barely *discernable* in the gloomy background.

> Once he became familiar with the French Impressionists, Bron found the differences in style among various artists easily *discernable*.

elevate (EH-lv-vayt) (verb) to raise up; to move to a higher level.

> Arkady claims that Bron's artistic skills *elevate* the teachers' expectations for all of the rest of them on projects that involve art.

> Ms. Patel had wanted to *elevate* Bron to the advanced photography class when he was only in his first year of high school.

encircled (in-SUR-kl) (adjective) surrounded on all sides.

> Sometimes Kai felt *encircled* by people who didn't care about school at all.

> Although Bron was a bit of a loner, he still felt that he was *encircled* by a community that would support him if he had the need.

Word Play   *colossal*

This adjective comes from the name of one of the great wonders of the ancient world, a statue of Apollo referred to as the Colossus of Rhodes. This was a bronze statue over one hundred feet in height that was erected at the harbor of the city of Rhodes in the Greek islands around 280 BCE. *Colossal* takes its meaning from the size of this huge statue.

---

endearing (in-DEER-ing) (adjective) charming; something or someone that inspires affection.

> Arkady's sister had an *endearing* habit of chewing on her bottom lip when she was lost in thought.

> Many students found Ms. Patel *endearing* because of her unfailing enthusiastic encouragement of them in their artistic efforts.

engulfed (en-GULFD) (adjective) completely covered; overwhelmed; swallowed up completely.

> Excessive homework *engulfed* Kai now and then because he set such high standards for himself.

> High levels of nervousness regularly *engulfed* the school on the days leading up to an SAT test date.

ersatz (ER-sats) (adjective) describes something that is a substitute or an imitation of something else. (Often implies that the substitute is of lower quality than the original.)

> When Bron was younger, he used to complete paint-by-number craft kits but later gave them up and referred to them as "*ersatz* art."

> When Arkady first received a ribbon for being a "participant" in a competition, he laughingly called it his "*ersatz* award."

excruciating (ik-SKROO-shee-ay-ting) (adjective) extremely painful; agonizing.

> Puppies' teeth are tiny and so sharp that they can cause *excruciating* pain even when they just playfully nibble on someone.

> Bron found the embarrassment almost *excruciating* every time Arkady teased him about Ming's affection for him.

gnaw (NAW) (verb) to chew on something over a period of time with one's teeth (or, metaphorically, with one's mind).

> The Newfoundland puppies liked to *gnaw* on a variety of chew toys, to Bron's great entertainment.

> After art class one day, Bron had a question *gnawing* at him for days about how best to approach a design project he was working on.

grainy (GRAY-nee) (adjective) unclear or indistinct in details (in describing an image or photograph).

> For effect, Bron enlarged his photo so many times that all one could really see were the *grainy* dots that had made up the original image.

> Bron enjoyed looking at old, *grainy* snapshots of his grandparents as children.

hastily (HAY-stu-lee) (adverb) quickly and (often) somewhat carelessly or thoughtlessly done.

> Pulling together information *hastily* just after Mr. Carrothers' class, Bron found the address of a local Newfoundland breeder.

> Arkady wrote down the history assignment too *hastily* and had to call Bron later to confirm what it actually was.

horde (HORD) (noun) a large crowd, usually of people. (plural: hordes)

> Bron avoided the mall because he didn't really like to be around *hordes* of people.

> It seemed to Bron as though there were a *horde* of people at the school art show but it really wasn't as crowded as he thought.

indigenous (in-DI-ju-nus) (adjective) native to a particular area or environment.

> For biology class, the teacher assigned Bron a year-long project of doing watercolors of local *indigenous* species of plants and animals.

> Kai's father worked as a gardener and his great dream was to open a landscaping nursery that sold only *indigenous* species of trees and shrubs.

lunge (LUNJ) (verb) to suddenly move forward; to make a sudden forward thrusting movement with one's body or with a sword or other weapon.

> Arkady tripped with his lunch tray, and Bron managed to *lunge* forward to grab it just in time to prevent everything from crashing to the floor.

> Bron's dog *lunged* at the stick Bron was carrying just before the boy tossed it for her to chase.

momentarily (mo-mun-TER-uh-lee) (adverb) for a short period of time.

> When Bron emerged from his occasional daydreams in class, he was sometimes *momentarily* confused about where he was.

> Ms. Patel was *momentarily* held up in a meeting before class one day, so her students just went ahead and picked up their work where they had left off in the last class.

perceive (pur-SEEV) (verb) to understand or become aware of something through the senses, most particularly through sight or hearing.

> Art history class was interesting to Bron because he could *perceive* a lot about the values of people of different periods of history based on their art.

> Arkady could *perceive* nothing unusual about Bron's growing interest in Newfoundlands.

run (RUN) (noun) an outdoor, man-made enclosed space to give domesticated animals a chance to exercise without risking escape. (plural: runs)

> The Newfoundland breeder had built several *runs* for the puppies that were covered to protect the animals from rain.

> Bron preferred seeing the puppies in *runs* to seeing them in cages because they so clearly needed room to tumble and play.

Easy Errors   *lay* and *lie*

In the infinitive form, *to lie* means for a person *to lie* down (I had a headache so I wanted *to lie* down) and *to lay* is a verb that requires an object, that is, one must *lay* (something) down (I wanted *to lay* down my hairbrush but there was no room on the counter). The confusion comes in the past tense, when *to lay* becomes *laid* (I *laid* down my hairbrush) and *to lie* becomes *lay* (I felt so ill I *lay* down all afternoon).

---

shirk (SHURK) (verb) to avoid an assigned task or work (also implies laziness).

> Bron didn't mean to *shirk* his computer assignment; he just had something else he wanted to work on.

> Bron often *shirked* his household chores not from laziness but because he would get distracted by something else and forget about them.

statistics (stu-TIS-tiks) (noun) numerical information that has been gathered and analyzed [in the case above of the dog breed, these data have been gathered to show an average size of the dog plus standard, expected characteristics of the breed]. (plural: This word, defined in this way, is always used in the plural.)

> The Newfoundland's breed *statistics* confirmed Bron's memory of a very large dog.

> Arkady's favorite class was *statistics* because he liked gathering and analyzing his own data to prevent his being influenced so much by other people's conclusions.

stroll (STROLE) (verb) to walk in a relaxed, leisurely way.

> To think through his art projects, Bron would sometimes *stroll* for hours up and down the streets of his neighborhood.

> After sketching the puppies, Bron *strolled* over to a run which housed a much older dog.

thunderstruck (THUN-dr-struk) (adjective) hit by sudden surprise or astonishment.

> When she first saw his artwork, Ms. Patel was *thunderstruck* by Bron's work and his potential to do even better.

> Bron may have been initially *thunderstruck* by the adult size of the Newfoundlands, but looking now at the puppies' feet, he would have known instinctively that those puppies would grow up to be big animals.

webbed (WEBD) (adjective) describes the flat connections of skin between toes that, when the toes are stretched out, help form a slight paddle that aids in the ability to swim.

> It was odd to Bron to think that both a duck and a dog might have *webbed* feet.

> Of course the *webbed* toes would help the Newfoundland swim more efficiently.

writhe (RYTHE) (verb) to move in a twisted or contorted way due to pain, embarrassment, or struggle; to squirm.

> When Bron tried to pick up and hold a puppy, it would *writhe* out of his grasp to chase a new imagined enemy.

> Tenderhearted Bron wouldn't even step on a wasp on the sidewalk because he couldn't stand to see the creature *writhe* in pain.

Quick Match 37

Match each word to its definition.

1. ___ momentarily	A.	native to a particular area or environment
2. ___ accessible	B.	numerical information
3. ___ endearing	C.	to chew on something with one's teeth
4. ___ engulf	D.	a large crowd, usually of people
5. ___ writhe	E.	hit by sudden surprise or astonishment
6. ___ lunge	F.	surrounded on all sides
7. ___ colossal	G.	to avoid an assigned task or work
8. ___ encircled	H.	charming; something that inspires affection
9. ___ ersatz	I.	a relaxed, leisurely walk
10. ___ webbed	J.	able to be seen with the eyes or the mind
11. ___ perceive	K.	an outdoor, man-made enclosure for animals
12. ___ indigenous	L.	quickly and (often) somewhat carelessly done
13. ___ elevate	M.	to create, as if by magic
14. ___ excruciating	N.	describes an image that is unclear in details
15. ___ thunderstruck	O.	describes connections of skin between toes
16. ___ run	P.	to completely cover; to overwhelm
17. ___ horde	Q.	to understand something through the senses
18. ___ discernable	R.	huge, gigantic; so big it inspires awe
19. ___ gnaw	S.	extremely painful; agonizing
20. ___ stroll	T.	to make a sudden forward thrusting movement
21. ___ shirk	U.	to raise up; to move to a higher level
22. ___ hastily	V.	to squirm; to move in a twisted way
23. ___ conjure	W.	substituted or imitating something else
24. ___ grainy	X.	easy to get to or easy to use
25. ___ statistics	Y.	for a short period of time

Sentence Completions 37

Choose the proper word or pair of words for each of the sentences below.

1. Judging between the fake Rembrandt painting and the real one, there were so few _____ differences that it took a true expert to identify the fake.

   (a) endearing   (b) elevated   (c) discernable   (d) grainy   (e) encircled

2. Unable to afford original artwork, she hung up a(n) _____ Picasso in her living room.

   (a) thunderstruck   (b) ersatz   (c) endearing   (d) discernable   (e) colossal

3. Sometimes painting what is _____ to one's own environment is not as productive as going to a totally new place with new plants and animals.

   (a) ersatz   (b) excruciating   (c) webbed   (d) colossal   (e) indigenous

4. Even a leisurely _____ down a familiar street can allow a true artistic eye to _____ the familiar in an all-new way.

   (a) conjure . . . elevate   (b) lunge . . . shirk   (c) horde . . . encircle
   (d) stroll . . . perceive   (e) engulf . . . discern

5. _____ blinded by the flashbulb, the subject jumped when her picture was taken and that made the resulting image a little blurred and _____ when enlarged and developed.

   (a) Excruciatingly . . . webbed   (b) Discernibly . . . endearing
   (c) Momentarily . . . grainy   (d) Hastily . . . indigenous
   (e) Thunderstruck . . . writhed

Chapter 38: He's Everywhere!

If one can have a two-dimensional *mascot*, then Bron had one in "Newf." There were drawings of Newfoundlands in his school notes, on the message pad by the phone, on paper napkins—if there was paper available, there was Newf, in all possible *bearings* and *aspects*. Originally *unsettled* by Bron's *obsession*, his parents first began to get weary of *ubiquitous* dog pictures but, finally, were *entertained* by them. They had been waiting for Bron to become *passionate* about something, particularly in his art, but this was a totally *unforeseen development*, to say the least.

Newf became Bron's eyes during class lectures: How would Newf *respond* to this new Native American tribe that Lewis and Clark met? How would Newf *visualize* chemistry problems? How would Newf *formulate* an opinion in an essay? Bron's notes became windows into Newf's *psyche* and, *ironically*, more useful for study since they featured pictures of Newf *contemplating* Bron's school work. Bron began to keep notes that looked like *chaotic*, random facts circled in bubbles around Newf's head, but as he continued, the bubbles came to be much more *structured* and logical in their patterns. Arrows *zigzagged* from one bubble of information to another as Newf, in various *postures*, tried to catch them with his teeth or *cuff* them with a giant paw. No longer *slouching* in his desk, Bron *wielded* his pencil quickly and *capably* as he kept Newf entertained. Bron had never before noticed how much new information *streamed* by him in class every day and he was determined to see what he—and Newf—could do with it.

aspect (AS-pekt) (noun) a particular body attitude or facial expression. (plural: aspects)

> Because it was more difficult to do well, Bron liked to draw Newf from unusual *aspects*, such as from above or below, instead of from the side.

> No matter what his body attitude might be, Newf's facial *aspect* was always gentle and pleasant.

bearing (BAYR-ing) (noun) poise; the individual and personal conduct and posture of a particular person. (plural: bearings)

> Bron might have drawn Newf in all kinds of poses, but in each one, the dog had the *bearing* of a champion.

> Arkady had the *bearing* of a relaxed, casual person but he was actually very serious about his work.

capably (KAY-puh-blee) (adverb) done with ability, efficiency, and skill.

> Kai's schoolwork was always done *capably* and with care.

> Arkady had always drawn maps and geometric figures very *capably*, but fine art was difficult for him.

chaotic (kay-AH-tic) (adjective) without order; jumbled; confused.

> Although Ms. Patel's art class seemed *chaotic* at times, creative work was definitely being done in that room!

> Before having Newf to help him organize his thoughts, Bron's approach to writing notes in class had been *chaotic* and inefficient.

contemplate (KAHN-tum-playt) (verb) to think about carefully and in detail; to ponder.

> Bron began to *contemplate* the big ideas introduced in class with more attention to detail.

> While Bron became immersed in his drawings, Arkady *contemplated* the change in his friend's school work.

cuff (KUFF) (verb) to hit or slap, usually lightly.

> When they were studying together and Bron got distracted by his drawings, Arkady would *cuff* him good-naturedly in the shoulder to get his attention.

> Bron had seen his own dog *cuff* a stick as it lay motionless on the ground, so he tried to sketch Newf doing the same thing.

development (di-VEL-up-munt) (noun) a change or growth in circumstances; the natural evolution of a live being or a situation; the process of growth and maturation. (plural: developments)

> Having Bron pay attention in class was a new *development* for several of his teachers.

> Sketching the dogs at the breeder's gave Bron a chance to notice the differences in the breed at various stages of *development*.

entertain (EN-tur-TAYN) (verb) to perform for another in a way that pleases them; to amuse.

> Arkady liked to *entertain* his friends with outrageous (and slightly exaggerated) stories of his old school.

> The puppies' antics *entertained* Bron enormously.

formulate (FOR-myoo-layt) (verb) to create or invent.

> Bron's parents wanted to *formulate* a way for Bron to have an outlet for his art and also a way to make a living in the world after he graduated.

> While Bron was drawing Newf, he was also *formulating* a new way to take notes during class.

ironically (EYE-RON-i-klee) (adverb) in a way that goes in opposition to an anticipated direction; a way of expressing an idea with words that strictly mean its opposite.

> Mr. Jenkins, who was strict about how his students should record their notes, was, *ironically*, supportive of Bron's work with Newf.

> Bron, *ironically*, was not usually fond of big dogs.

mascot (MAS-kaht) (noun) an animal or an object that is considered good luck and is used as a symbol for a person, team, or organization. (plural: mascots)

> Kai drew a bear on his history notebook because it was the *mascot* of his favorite football team.

> Some of the girls had key chains with little stuffed *mascots* attached to them on their school backpacks.

Easy Errors   less **and** fewer

The rule for using *less* or *fewer* when describing any noun comes down to whether or not you can count the items you are describing. If it can be counted (a "count noun") then you use *fewer* (*fewer* trees, *fewer* hats, *fewer* people) but if it can't be counted (a "non-count noun") then you must use *less* (*less* smoke, *less* rice, *less* grass in the lawn). Be aware of how an idea is expressed. *Rice* is a non-count noun, but in the phrase *grains of rice*, *grains* is a count noun. That would provide this correct sentence: "She had *fewer* grains of rice in her bowl although it appeared that he had *less* rice in his bowl than she had in hers."

---

obsession (ah-SE-shun) (noun) a fixed compulsion or preoccupation with a particular idea or activity; excessive commitment to a particular idea or activity. (plural: obsessions)

> Arkady was amused by Newf but didn't think Bron had an *obsession* about the breed.

> Arkady himself had an *obsession* with state politics and seldom missed a chance to criticize the current governor.

passionate (PA-shu-nut) (adjective) under the influence of powerful emotion, usually anger, joy, or desire.

> Bron was careful not to irritate Arkady too much because his friend was *passionate* and unreasonable when angry.

> Bron couldn't decide if he were more *passionate* about painting with acrylics or watercolors.

posture (PAHS-chur) (noun) the attitude, position, or pose of a body. (plural: postures)

> Bron's *posture* in his desk wasn't as slumped as it used to be.

Kai had an upright *posture* which made him seem taller than he really was.

psyche (SY-kee) (noun) the soul or spirit of a being. (plural: psyches)

Bron knew that his drawing had no real soul, but he imagined a *psyche* and personality for Newf that became very real to him.

To Bron, his own *psyche* felt connected to those of artists all over the world, both living and dead.

respond (ri-SPAHND) (verb) to do something in answer to a stimulus, either in action or words; to reply.

Sometimes, when Arkady asked him a question, Bron would *respond* as though he were Newf himself looking at the situation from the outside.

The teachers *responded* favorably to Bron's increased note taking.

slouch (SLOWCH) (verb) not walking, standing, or sitting up straight; to walk, sit, or stand without using the energy to straighten one's back; to droop.

When he was late to class, Bron would *slouch* into the room, trying to seem as small and insignificant as possible so as not to be noticed.

At the end of the week, Kai *slouched* in his desk, exhausted from all of the work he had done.

stream (STREEM) (verb) to flow as would water.

Ideas on positions in which to draw Newf would constantly *stream* through Bron's mind.

Bron stayed away from the mall because he didn't like people *streaming* all around him all day.

Word Play   *week* and *weak*

If *week* is a noun that means "a period of seven days in a row," and *weak* is an adjective that means "lacking strength," you could tell this old joke if you find chocolate essential to your daily existence: Seven days without chocolate makes one *weak/week*.

---

structured (STRUK-churd) (adjective) in an orderly fashion; very organized.

Ms. Patel's class seemed free-form but it was actually carefully *structured* to allow for maximum creativity within a necessary amount of order.

Kai thrived in a very *structured* environment.

ubiquitous (yoo-BI-kwu-tus) (adjective) seeming to be everywhere; seeming to be all around all the time.

> To Bron, distractions had been *ubiquitous* until Newf helped him focus his thoughts.

> However *ubiquitous* Newf was becoming, Bron didn't neglect his other art projects.

unforeseen (UN-for-SEEN) (adjective) not predicted or expected.

> One *unforeseen* aspect of his work with Newf was that Bron began to go through pencils at an alarming rate.

> Bron's interest in drawing dogs may have been *unforeseen*, but his continuing interest in art was predictable—and welcome.

unsettled (un-SE-tld) (adjective) upset emotionally; disrupted; uneasy.

> Once during class when Ms. Patel had to gently remind Bron to draw something other than Newf, even he was a little *unsettled* by the ferocity of his interest.

> Bron was also a bit *unsettled* by Ming's interest in him because she was a nice girl and he didn't want to hurt her feelings.

visualize (VI-zhu-wi-lyz) (verb) to form an image in one's mind; to see in one's mind's eye.

> Arkady could clearly *visualize* what he wanted to draw, but he didn't have Bron's talent for putting that idea on paper.

> Ms. Patel felt that Bron's ability to *visualize* exactly what he wanted his finished product to look like was his strongest tool in art class.

wield (WEELD) (verb) to exercise the power of something with skill and ease.

> Although Bron could *wield* pencils, paintbrushes, and charcoal with skill, he was less successful working in three-dimensional art forms, such as sculpture.

> Mr. Jenkins *wielded* his authority in class in such a way that students tended to obey him without question.

zigzag (ZIG-zag) (verb) to move back and forth in an erratic fashion or in a course that alternates sharp right and left turns at an angle.

> Bron's thoughts during class did, in fact, *zigzag* as much as his notes implied.

> The puppies had dashed and *zigzagged* about in their runs as they attacked their siblings.

Quick Match 38

Match each word to its definition.

1. ____ mascot
2. ____ cuff
3. ____ respond
4. ____ zigzag
5. ____ aspect
6. ____ obsession
7. ____ development
8. ____ slouch
9. ____ wield
10. ____ bearing
11. ____ passionate
12. ____ entertain
13. ____ stream
14. ____ visualize
15. ____ capably
16. ____ posture
17. ____ formulate
18. ____ structured
19. ____ unsettled
20. ____ ubiquitous
21. ____ psyche
22. ____ ironically
23. ____ chaotic
24. ____ unforeseen
25. ____ contemplate

A.   done with ability, efficiency, and skill

B.   to do something in answer to a stimulus

C.   a good-luck symbol for a person, team, or group

D.   without order; jumbled; confused

E.   upset emotionally; disrupted; uneasy

F.   the soul or spirit of a being

G.   to think about carefully and in detail; to ponder

H.   to hit or slap, usually lightly

I.   to droop; not sitting up straight

J.   in a way that goes opposite original expectations

K.   the attitude, position, or pose of a body

L.   a course that alternates sharp right and left turns

M.   poise; someone's individual conduct and posture

N.   to flow, as would water

O.   the process of growth and maturation

P.   in an orderly fashion; very organized

Q.   to exercise the power of something with skill

R.   a particular body or facial expression

S.   not predicted or expected

T.   to form an image in one's mind

U.   to amuse; to perform pleasingly for another

V.   seeming to be everywhere

W.   a fixed compulsion with a particular idea

X.   under the influence of a powerful emotion

Y.   to create or invent

Sentence Completions 38

Choose the proper word or pair of words for each of the sentences below.

1. The _____ of acrylic paints made painting at home easier for hobbyists because cleanup is less messy than with traditional oil paints.

    (a) obsession   (b) aspect   (c) bearing   (d) entertainment
    (e) development

2. She could _____ in her mind's eye a very successful future as an artist, but she wasn't sure how to go about making that dream become a reality.

    (a) wield   (b) slouch   (c) visualize   (d) contemplate   (e) obsess

3. When rudely and loudly challenged about his beliefs about art, Bron didn't know how to _____ politely.

    (a) respond   (b) contemplate   (c) stream   (d) entertain   (e) formulate

4. This was the home of a true artist: the entire house was _____ with clothes and leftover food everywhere, but the studio area itself was tidy and very _____.

    (a) ubiquitous . . . unforeseen   (b) unsettled . . . streamed
    (c) visualized . . . zigzagged   (d) chaotic . . . structured
    (e) wielded . . . passionate

5. The artist's manner was oddly stiff; her _____ was very straight and her _____ was very formal.

    (a) obsession . . . unforeseen   (b) posture . . . bearing   (c) psyche . . . slouch
    (d) mascot . . . development   (e) aspect . . . formulate

Chapter 39: A Day of Surprises

Kai approached Bron one Monday.

"Hey, Bron, I missed a couple of days last week. Could I borrow your history notes?"

Bron was *astounded*. No one ever borrowed his notes, most particularly someone like Kai who was a note-taking *fanatic*. He had to know why.

"Well," said Kai, *flushing*, "I'm going to borrow Davonna's notes too, but I've seen what you've been doing in class. I think you catch some *overriding themes* with your *bizarre* system that she and I sometimes miss by writing down the *entirety* of what we hear. With that term test coming up, I want to be sure I get it all."

Bron agreed, with a mental note to remember to *ransack* his locker over lunch to *exhume* those notes; putting things in order in a binder wasn't really a strength for him.

Notes found and delivered, the surprises continued over lunch as Pia asked Bron if she could sit with him. A pretty *senior* wanted to eat lunch with him? In shock once again, he just nodded and *gestured* to the bench facing him. Leaning over the lunch tray, she came right to the point.

"You know I'm *editor* of the school paper? Well, we need to make it a lot more *insightful*. Jess had really made it her own paper last year, what with the *horoscopes* and gossip columns she added, but now that she's *graduated*, I need to put my own *mark* on it. I think you're just what we need. We need political cartoons."

Now he was just *puzzled*. He wasn't a political cartoonist.

"Don't tell me that!" Pia laughed *dismissively*. "You draw, and you draw dogs like our school team's mascot. All we need is someone to come up with the words for that dog to say—and I've already got someone for that job, someone who can do all the *satire* and *cynicism* we need."

Pia totally *disregarded* Bron as he tried to *convince* her that Newfoundlands looked nothing like *Huskies*, which their school team was named for. She just waved away his *reservations* and promised to send him a *ghostwriter* for Newf.

astounded (uh-STOWN-dud) (adjective) extremely surprised and bewildered; astonished.

> Bron was *astounded* by the fact that Newf was attracting so much attention.

> Arkady was *astounded* (and not a little jealous) that someone like Pia wanted to eat lunch with Bron.

bizarre (bu-ZAR) (adjective) very odd; very different from the expected or the usual in manner, behavior, dress, or opinions.

> Bron's note-taking strategy may have been *bizarre*, but it was attracting positive attention.

Arkady and Bron never discussed politics both because Bron was not very interested and because Arkady had a reputation for having some *bizarre* and unusual opinions.

convince (kun-VINTS) (verb) to persuade someone of something using logic and argument.

> Pia didn't quite *convince* Bron that he was really what she needed for the newspaper.

> Someone else—the mysterious writer perhaps—had *convinced* Pia that political cartoons would make the school newspaper more interesting.

cynicism (SI-nuh-si-zum) (noun) a mocking attitude characterized by meanness of spirit, bitterness, and scorn; comments that express this kind of attitude. (Cynicisms are often used to comment on extremes of social behavior or governmental policy.) (plural: cynicisms)

> *Cynicism* that stings but does not also carry a social lesson within it usually just sounds mean.

> One must balance hope with *cynicism* or else one gets the feeling that nothing can be done to change the bad things in society.

dismissively (dis-MI-siv-lee) (adverb) describes turning away from someone with little regard or with indifference to his or her value.

> Because of her higher status as a senior, Pia felt comfortable treating Bron's concerns *dismissively*.

> At first, Bron was tempted to treat Pia's suggestion *dismissively*, but the more he thought about political cartooning, the more interested he became.

> ### *Easy Errors*   *bizarre* vs. *bazaar*
>
> *Bizarre* is an adjective that describes something "very odd" but a *bazaar* is totally different. A *bazaar* is a marketplace where one can buy items, or a fundraising sale, usually at a religious center or school. So, one might find "a *bizarre* knitted potholder at the school *bazaar* last week."

---

disregard (dis-ri-GARD) (verb) to ignore; to treat someone without proper respect or attention.

> The artist in Bron was determined not to let Pia *disregard* the fact that Newf was <u>not</u> a husky.

> It was becoming impossible for Bron to *disregard* the growing interest in Newf.

editor (EH-du-tur) (noun) one who corrects, revises, adapts, or modifies written text; one who chooses certain texts for publication in particular instances. (plural: editors)

> As *editor* of the school newspaper, Pia had a responsibility to represent the school not only fairly but also in an entertaining fashion.

> Bron wasn't sure he wanted an *editor* or anyone else putting words into Newf's mouth.

entirety (in-TY-ru-tee) (noun) something in a completed and final form; a whole. (plural: entireties)

> Kai and Davonna both wrote very quickly and tried to get down the *entirety* of what each teacher said during lectures.

> Bron was a bit confused about just what the *entirety* of this deal with Pia would involve.

exhume (ig-ZOOM) (verb) 1. to dig up something that has been buried in the earth, usually from a grave. 2. to bring to light something that has been lost or obscured.

> In history class, Bron was studying how scientists worked to *exhume* mummies from graves in Egypt so that they could study the process of mummification.

> His experiences with Newf had *exhumed* a playfulness in Bron's art that he hadn't enjoyed for a number of years.

fanatic (fu-NA-tik) (noun) someone committed to a particular cause or idea in an extreme, unreasoning way. (plural: fanatics)

> Other students considered Bron a dog *fanatic* but he didn't see himself that way at all.

> Kai may have been a bit of a *fanatic* about his notes, but that didn't mean he wasn't open to new ideas and new approaches.

flush (FLUSH) (verb) to blush; to have one's face turn red from embarrassment or fever.

> Ming would *flush* beet-red every time she saw Bron in the hallway between classes.

> Kai *flushed* when talking to Bron because he was afraid telling Bron the truth about why he wanted to borrow his notes might hurt his feelings.

gesture (JES-chur) (verb) to motion with one's hands or body to help express an idea, with or without spoken language.

> Bron particularly liked drawing Newf in positions that showed him *gesturing* toward something else on the page.

When Kai looked so embarrassed, Bron *gestured* with his hand to indicate that Kai shouldn't worry about it.

ghostwriter (GOST-ryt-er) (noun) one who writes text on behalf of someone else who gets the credit for the work. (plural: ghostwriters)

Bron was a little confused and wondered if the *ghostwriter* would actually be writing on his behalf or Newf's.

The idea of a *ghostwriter* had never occurred to Bron before; it felt a little like cheating.

graduate (GRA-ju-wayt) (verb) to receive an academic diploma for having finished a course of study successfully.

Once Bron had finished with his "dog phase," Bron's parents were hoping he would *graduate* to drawing something a little more serious.

Bron wanted to go to art school after he *graduated*.

horoscope (HOR-uh-skop) (noun) a forecast of a person's future based on birth date, time, and place, as well as the position of the stars and planets in the universe at the time of birth. (plural: horoscopes)

Pia had kept the *horoscopes* in the school newspaper because there was a serious astrologer in eleventh grade who wanted to continue to write them.

Arkady secretly consulted his *horoscope* daily on the Internet, but he wouldn't admit that to Bron.

husky (HUS-kee) 1. (noun) a breed of dog bred for pulling sleds in cold climate. (plural: huskies) 2. (adjective) heavy, strong, muscular.

Despite what most people think, *huskies* are not the only dogs that are good at pulling sleds.

The school team was known as the *Huskies* not only because the dog makes a good mascot but because the name makes the team sound strong and formidable.

Word Play
horoscope and *astrology*

Horoscope—*hora* (hour) + *-skopos* (watching)—literally means the art of "watching the hours" and judging one's future accordingly. *Astrology*—*astro* (star) + *logos* (treating of or speaking of)—has to do with the study of the stars for determining one's future. This is an old art form and belief system that is still popular today. *Astronomy*, despite the common root with *astrology*, is a different art—*astro* (star) + *nomos* (naming or arranging)—which studies the elements of the cosmos for scientific reasons.

insightful (in-SYT-ful) (adjective) describes the ability to use one's intuition effectively in trying to understand hidden aspects of a person, problem, or situation.

> Pia was actually more *insightful* than her discussion with Bron made her seem.

> Bron was becoming attracted to the idea of Newf being able to "say" *insightful* and clever things in a public forum like the newspaper.

mark (MARK) (noun) an imprint or some kind of personal identifier put on something to show its origin or ownership.

> Pia wanted to contribute something original to the newspaper, something that would put her *mark* on it and, perhaps, still be in the paper after she left the school.

> As his own *mark* as the artist, Bron started drawing his initials into the swirls of Newf's fur when he drew him.

overriding (O-vur-RYD-ing) (adjective) more important (than others mentioned).

> Bron's *overriding* objection to being in the paper was that he really had no interest in politics.

> Pia's *overriding* interest in getting Newf into the paper was to increase the number of readers each issue.

puzzled (PUH-zuld) (adjective) mentally confused; to be baffled by a particular problem or issue.

> Bron was *puzzled* at Newf's popularity.

> Pia was a little *puzzled* why Bron hadn't immediately accepted the honor of being on the newspaper staff.

ransack (RAN-sak) (verb) to plunder; to search through or examine thoroughly.

> In way of research, Bron *ransacked* his father's bookcase that night looking for a collection of political cartoons he had seen there before.

> Pia had been *ransacking* her brain for ways to improve the paper when the ghostwriter came to her about Newf.

reservations (re-zur-VAY-shunz) (noun) objections based on factual information that places limitations on certain conclusions; doubts. (plural: This word, defined in this way, is always used in the plural.)

> Although Pia had had some *reservations* at first about putting in biased political cartoons, the ghostwriter convinced her that they would be written from different political viewpoints.

While Mr. Jenkins had some *reservations* about Bron drawing during class, he could see that the boy was paying more attention than usual as he did so.

satire (SA-tyr) (noun) stinging wit and irony, usually in print form, used to attack human weakness and folly. (plural: satires)

Pia became really excited about the idea of having *satire* and political discourse in the paper because she felt it would get students talking.

People had occasionally written short pieces of *satire* for the newspaper, but Pia felt that a cartoon would get the message across faster to more readers.

senior (SEE-nyur) (noun) a student in the fourth and final year of study in high school (i.e., twelfth grade); also a fourth-year undergraduate student in college in the American school system. (plural: seniors)

It is common for students below *seniors* to know who the *seniors* are, but less common for the *seniors* to know the underclassmen.

Arkady was very sociable and seldom had any idea of whether he was chatting with a *senior* or someone from his own grade.

theme (THEEM) (noun) an organizing idea that serves to connect different ideas and events in conversation or writing. (plural: themes)

Pia could see that the cartoons could also follow certain *themes*, such as homelessness or poverty, that the paper might be focusing on from time to time.

Another one of Pia's common *themes* was trying to get people involved in school life, and inviting Bron to draw for the paper was also inviting him to do just that.

Quick Match 39

Match each word to its definition.

1. ___	ghostwriter	A.	to dig up something from a grave
2. ___	entirety	B.	describes ignoring someone or something; not respectfully
3. ___	theme	C.	baffled by a problem; mentally confused
4. ___	dismissively	D.	one who corrects, revises, or chooses written text
5. ___	astounded	E.	breed of dog bred for work and cold conditions
6. ___	graduate	F.	one committed to something in an extreme way
7. ___	senior	G.	a fourth-year student in a four-year program
8. ___	horoscope	H.	to turn away from someone with indifference
9. ___	disregard	I.	to plunder; to examine or search thoroughly
10. ___	gesture	J.	something in complete and final form; whole
11. ___	satire	K.	describes using intuition well to see hidden aspects
12. ___	husky	L.	to blush; to turn red from fever or embarrassment
13. ___	cynicism	M.	a forecast of one's future based on the stars
14. ___	flush	N.	objections based on facts; doubts
15. ___	reservations	O.	extremely surprised and bewildered; astonished
16. ___	insightful	P.	to motion with body or hands to express an idea
17. ___	convince	Q.	to receive an academic diploma
18. ___	fanatic	R.	more important (than others mentioned)
19. ___	ransack	S.	very different from the expected; odd
20. ___	mark	T.	an organizing idea for connecting differences
21. ___	bizarre	U.	one who writes a text without getting credit
22. ___	exhume	V.	stinging wit and irony, usually in print form
23. ___	puzzled	W.	a mocking, bitter, and scornful attitude
24. ___	editor	X.	a personal identifier which shows origin
25. ___	overriding	Y.	to persuade someone to believe something

Sentence Completions 39

Choose the proper word or pair of words for each of the sentences below.

1. The student submitted a painting to a competition at the county fair and was surprised and pleased that the judge's comments proved to be both _____ and helpful.

    (a) insightful   (b) puzzled   (c) dismissive   (d) cynical   (e) satirical

2. Some art collectors have _____ about buying art from unknown artists, but being willing to take a chance on a new talent can make one's collection much more valuable later if those artists become famous.

    (a) editor   (b) satire   (c) senior   (d) reservations   (e) cynicism

3. Although Bron spoke as persuasively as he could, he was unable to _____ his art teacher that a local artist he admired was as visionary as he thought.

    (a) disregard   (b) flush   (c) ransack   (d) exhume   (e) convince

4. Fond of more traditional art, he was _____ by nonobjective art of simple lines and angles and found it _____ that others thought it was stimulating and exciting.

    (a) astounded . . . exhuming   (b) insightful . . . cynical
    (c) puzzled . . . bizarre   (d) convinced . . . satire
    (e) ransacked . . . graduated

5. A(n) _____ about art projects, her _____ goal was to do the best she could on them no matter what else she had to neglect (including her other homework).

    (a) husky . . . flush   (b) theme . . . insightful   (c) ghostwriter . . . senior
    (d) editor . . . bizarre   (e) fanatic . . . overriding

Chapter 40: New Directions

*S*idling up to his locker after last period that day was Marisha, Arkady's little sister.

"What's up?" asked Bron, *thrusting* his math textbook *forcefully* into the locker to prevent a potential *avalanche* of stray books and papers from hitting them both.

"Well, uh," Marisha *floundered*, "I'm, uh, Newf's ghostwriter."

Bron stopped *abruptly*, and really <u>looked</u> at her—truly a day of surprises.

"I was expecting a senior," he said *reprovingly*. "Why didn't you come directly to me, instead of going through Pia? Arkady's one of my best friends. Besides, what do you know about *social commentary* or political cartooning?"

"I figured you would *overlook* me before hearing me out since I'm 'just the little sister,'" Marisha *retorted*, annoyed at his *tone*. "I thought a little mystery coming from Pia might *tantalize* you and make you *reflect* on cartooning as a possibility. Besides that, you should know about my political commentary already. Don't you listen to Arkady and me in the car? Don't you read my *column* in the school paper?"

When Bron *confessed* that he didn't really listen to their more *heated* discussions and he hadn't ever read the school newspaper, Marisha was *exasperated* with him.

"Now you have to hear me out!" she declared.

Hear her out he did and, *by degrees*, Bron was convinced that with her words and his artwork, they could have a lot of fun and help *liven* up the school paper a bit. Marisha had strong opinions but an even stronger sense of the *absurd* in society, so she was willing to write the occasional text that went slightly against her own politics if the joke was good.

Working with Marisha, Bron was forced into discussing politics and gradually became more aware of the political and social issues of his day as he and Newf *addressed* them artistically each issue.

As the weeks went by, the cartoon was attracting a steadily growing *circle* of admirers. The more *biting* the satire, the more often Newf appeared *anonymously* posted on school bulletin boards and quoted in letters to the editor. Newf's image continued to *grace* most of Bron's school notes, but since his grades were going up and everyone liked Newf, Bron didn't have to defend his "bizarre system" of note taking anymore. School, Bron decided, was getting a little better every day.

abruptly (uh-BRUPT-lee) (adverb) suddenly and without warning.

> When Arkady sneezed *abruptly* in the middle of the history test, everyone jumped.

> Because of Newf, Bron's low-key school life changed *abruptly* to one of discussion and interaction.

absurd (ub-SURD) (adjective) describes something so ridiculous that it doesn't relate to common sense or logic.

> Marisha found it *absurd* that anyone might not pay attention to what the government was doing "on their behalf."

> What was happening to Bron would have been *absurd* if it hadn't been true—he certainly had not intended for Newf to become a campus sensation.

address (uh-DRES) (verb) to focus attention on something; to deal with (something).

> Marisha wanted to *address* every social problem she could think of each issue, and sometimes Bron had to hold her back a bit.

> Arkady spoke to Bron privately when he and his sister disagreed on an issue; he would try to get Bron to *address* that issue from his own point of view.

anonymously (uh-NAH-nuh-mus-lee) (adverb) done without credit; in a manner that withholds a person's name.

> Marisha thought it would be more mysterious to write *anonymously* for the cartoon, but Bron insisted that her name be included.

> Someone sent in a donation to the school newspaper *anonymously* and included a note saying that the donation was because of Newf.

avalanche (A-vuh-lanch) (noun) 1. a heavy slide of snow or rock down a mountainside. 2. an overwhelming amount of something. (plural: avalanches)

> When it was a slow news week on campus, Bron sometimes wished for an *avalanche* or a hurricane or <u>something</u> so that he would have something interesting to draw.

> Although the newspaper didn't receive an *avalanche* of mail, there was a significant increase in the number of letters to the editor.

biting (BY-ting) (adjective) harsh or stinging.

> The letters to the editor that disagreed with Newf (or Marisha or Bron) could be quite *biting* in their criticism of the cartoon.

> After an issue when Newf made a particularly *biting* comment about someone or something, a reader would always write in and complain that Newf was "too nice" to say something like that.

circle (SUR-kul) (noun) a group of people who share a common interest or point of view. (plural: circles)

> Bron's *circle* of friends widened as he did the cartoon, and he found he enjoyed people more than he had thought before.

There was still a strong *circle* of people on campus who were artists and Bron continued to be involved in that group.

Easy Errors   ***weather* and *whether***

If *weather* is "the pattern of atmospheric conditions involving rain, snow, wind, sunshine, etc." and *whether* is used to "offer alternatives and options," one could decide "*whether* or not to go to the beach based on the *weather* that day."

---

column (KAH-lum) (noun) an article that appears in a journal, newspaper, or magazine on a regular basis, usually by the same author. (plural: columns)

> Marisha continued to write her *column* because it was a forum for her to express her ideas more fully than she could in a cartoon.

> Pia offered Arkady a *column* as well, since the siblings disagreed about almost everything and that would add balance to the newspaper's discussions.

commentary (KAH-mun-ter-ee) (noun) an opinionated discussion, interpretation, or review of a subject. (plural: commentaries)

> Arkady considered accepting Pia's offer of doing a regular *commentary*, but he decided that he didn't want to commit to writing that much each week.

> Arkady found that he could offer important *commentary* on an occasional basis by writing letters to the editor.

confess (kun-FES) (verb) to admit one's guilt in a matter or event.

> Marisha was openly biased in her political views and did not feel the need to *confess* that that might be a fault in her column.

> Bron *confessed* to Arkady that he sometimes felt that he had betrayed Newf by drawing him publicly.

(by) degrees (di-GREEZ) (adverb) describes doing something in small bits or steps at a time; gradually.

> *By degrees*, Newf seemed to take on a certain personality and there were just some comments that didn't sound right coming from his mouth, no matter how often Marisha reworked the language.

> Marisha was hoping that, *by degrees*, she would get Bron more involved politically.

exasperated (ig-ZAS-pu-rayt-ed) (adjective) very impatient or annoyed; angry in a frustrated way.

> Marisha would get *exasperated* with Bron occasionally, but he was so naturally calm that he never got annoyed with her.

> If the team couldn't think of anything to cartoon near the issue deadline, Pia would get *exasperated* with them and tell them just to "write something funny" instead.

flounder (FLOWN-dur) (verb) to move or act in a clumsy or ungainly fashion.

> At first, Bron's drawing seemed to *flounder* a bit, but as he gained experience, he gained confidence.

> Bron still *floundered* somewhat around Ming, although he was beginning to like her a bit himself.

forcefully (FORS-fu-lee) (adverb) with great strength or thrust.

> Bron would rather shove his books back into his locker *forcefully* than take the time to tidy up the locker.

> Bron began to listen to Arkady and Marisha when they argued *forcefully* on certain issues and found he often had an opinion now, too.

grace (GRAYS) (verb) to adorn; to give honor or favor to.

> The prom committee approached Bron to ask if Newf could *grace* their invitations to the prom this year.

> Newf had already *graced* the programs for several school shows and pep rallies by this time.

heated (HEE-tud) (adjective) highly emotional, usually with anger.

> Arkady would often start the more *heated* discussions with his sister after he read what Newf had to say in the school paper.

> Although Bron avoided being a part of any *heated* argument, he did occasionally like to listen to the two points of view from a safe distance.

liven (LY-vun) (verb) to fill with energy and spirit.

> Pia thought that Newf would really *liven* up the newspaper.

> Bron's widening perspective *livened* up his own fine art considerably as he began unconsciously to work with bolder colors and lines.

reflect (ri-FLEKT) (verb) to think about something carefully and seriously.

> Bron found he had less time to *reflect* on his art before producing it because he was now so busy with Marisha and the paper.

Sometimes Marisha and Bron disagreed on the message of a cartoon, and each had to *reflect* on whether or not it should be printed.

reprovingly (ri-PROO-ving-lee) (adverb) expressing disapproval; finding fault.

Once Bron was called to the vice-principal's office to be spoken to *reprovingly* about his tardiness to school, but the interview ended with the vice-principal laughing over a Newf-ism he had particularly enjoyed.

When Bron wanted to draw something light and funny, Marisha spoke to him *reprovingly* about all of the social issues they really should be addressing instead.

retort (ri-TORT) (verb) to reply, especially in a witty or clever way; a counterargument.

Newf's cartoon twice *retorted* directly to a letter to the editor that had been received during the week.

Once when Arkady was arguing with Marisha, she *retorted* that she "didn't wish to have a battle of wits with an unarmed man."

sidle (SY-dl) (verb) to move forward sideways or in small, mincing steps so as to be unnoticeable.

Normally cool and confident, Marisha *sidled* up to Bron to break the news to him in what seemed to be a shy fashion. She just wasn't sure how supportive he would be of having a ghostwriter for Newf.

During Homecoming, Bron looked to his right and was surprised to see that Ming had quietly *sidled* up next to him to watch the game.

social (SO-shul) (adjective) having to do with communities; describes issues of human welfare within communities.

Bron began to be invited to more *social* gatherings than ever before although he was still somewhat unwilling to be in crowds.

Arkady decided to act as Bron's *social* secretary and helped him to decide what events to go to.

tantalize (TAN-tuh-lyz) (verb) to tempt someone with something that may not be available.

Marisha continued to inspire Bron by trying to *tantalize* him with the thought that he could make a living doing political cartoons and spend his free time doing his fine art.

Marisha was interested in essay contests for students, and the scholarship money they promised to their winners *tantalized* her immensely.

> **Word Play**   *tantalize*
>
> This word comes to us from the name of an evil-doer in Greek mythology, Tantalus. After his death, Tantalus was punished in the Underworld by being made to stand in chin-deep water under a branch laden with beautiful fruit. He was always desperately hungry and thirsty, but every time he tried to pick the fruit, it moved out of his reach and every time he bent his head to drink the water, it flowed away from his mouth. He remained tempted and *tantalized* by the food and drink for all eternity but was never able to satisfy his hunger or thirst.

thrust (THRUST) (verb) to push forward suddenly and with force.

> Being *thrust* into the center of attention was unusual, not to mention uncomfortable, for Bron.

> Newf's wit also caused Marisha to be *thrust* into the limelight as writer, although she had originally planned on being an anonymous ghost-writer.

tone (TON) (noun) a quality of sound (pitch) in a person's voice; a quality of word choice in a written work from which one can derive the author's attitude or opinion. (plural: tones)

> If Newf's *tone* was particularly stinging in one issue, they tried to make him a little more relaxed and funny in the next.

> Bron's irritated *tone* of voice at the beginning of their partnership really angered Marisha, but they managed to work it out and create a terrific working relationship.

Quick Match 40

Match each word to its definition.

1. ____	reflect	A.	in a manner that expresses disapproval, finds fault
2. ____	(by) degrees	B.	having to do with communities
3. ____	tone	C.	a dangerous or heavy slide of snow or rock
4. ____	liven	D.	an opinionated discussion or review
5. ____	absurd	E.	to move forward sideways or unnoticeably
6. ____	thrust	F.	in a manner which withholds a person's name
7. ____	biting	G.	to reply, especially in a witty or clever way
8. ____	heated	H.	to move or act in a clumsy or ungainly fashion
9. ____	tantalize	I.	harsh or stinging
10. ____	abruptly	J.	to think about something carefully and seriously
11. ____	grace	K.	a quality of sound (pitch) in a person's voice
12. ____	social	L.	to focus attention on something; to deal with it
13. ____	circle	M.	article that appears regularly in a journal
14. ____	address	N.	to fill with energy and spirit
15. ____	sidle	O.	a group of people who share a common interest
16. ____	forcefully	P.	very impatient or annoyed; angry in frustration
17. ____	column	Q.	to admit one's guilt in a matter or event
18. ____	retort	R.	to adorn; to give honor or favor to
19. ____	anonymously	S.	with great strength or thrust
20. ____	reprovingly	T.	suddenly and without warning
21. ____	commentary	U.	to tempt someone with something unavailable
22. ____	flounder	V.	ridiculous and without common sense
23. ____	avalanche	W.	highly emotional, usually with anger
24. ____	exasperated	X.	gradually; to do something in small steps
25. ____	confess	Y.	to push forward suddenly and with force

Sentence Completions 40

Choose the proper word or pair of words for each of the sentences below.

1. The art student _____ up to the famous painter shyly to ask for an autograph.

   (a) confessed   (b) sidled   (c) reflected   (d) heated   (e) by degrees

2. The artist was irritated and _____ with the art critic who totally misunderstood her work.

   (a) absurd   (b) anonymous   (c) social   (d) floundered   (e) exasperated

3. When the new art museum was about to open, several issues needed to be _____, such as what the museum hours and the admittance fees would be.

   (a) reflected   (b) addressed   (c) sidled   (d) exasperated   (e) confessed

4. Each week, the editorial _____ in the local newspaper offered an opinionated _____ on current state and federal political decisions.

   (a) retort . . . circle   (b) address . . . tone   (c) column . . . commentary
   (d) confession . . . avalanche   (e) thrust . . . biting

5. The art patron gave her donation _____ because she did not wish to have her name _____ the public list of donors posted by the museum.

   (a) reprovingly . . . tantalize   (b) abruptly . . . liven
   (c) by degrees . . . address   (d) forcefully . . . reflect
   (e) anonymously . . . grace

WRITING ACTIVITY

Creative Advertising Copy

We all know that most of us are far too clever and aware of the advertising world to be seduced into buying something simply based on its carefully crafted description—aren't we?

Maybe the only reason the rest of us can resist the lure of retail is because YOU are not the one writing the advertising copy. If you wrote the descriptions of these wonderful consumer products ("The lucky buyer will be *thunderstruck* to discover how the spirit of beauty *emanates* from this necklace, enticing her *psyche* . . . ") how could the rest of us possibly resist buying (and buying and buying and buying . . . .)?

Using as many of this section's words as possible, you are to write absolutely irresistible copy on the retail item of your choice: entice us, reel us in, compel us to buy your product. You are welcome to write sales material for one product or several. Try consulting the mail-order catalog of your choice for inspiration.

Appendix 1: Parts of Speech Chart

One of the beauties of the English language is its wonderful flexibility! Once you recognize and understand one specific word, you often know several others because a word can have multiple forms. Your new word could have a noun form, an adjective form, a verb form, and/or an adverb form[1] that you can now use. We like to call these groupings "word families."

The following chart shows some of the word families with vocabulary from this book. The chart doesn't cover every word form possible in English; it's up to you to fill in any missing pieces!

Noun Form	Verb Form	Adjective Form	Adverb Form
			(take) **aback**
abnormality	abnormalize	abnormal	**abnormally**
abortion	abort	**abortive**	abortively
abruptness		abrupt	**abruptly**
absconder	**abscond**		
absentmindedness		**absentminded**	absentmindedly
abstention	**abstain**	abstaining	
absurdity		**absurd**	absurdly
abundance		abundant	abundantly
academics		academic	academically
accessibility	access	**accessible**	accessibly
accommodation	accommodate	**accommodating**	accommodatingly
accomplice			
accountability		**accountable**	accountably
accumulation	accumulate	accumulative	accumulatively
acknowledgement	**acknowledge**	acknowledged	
acquaintance	acquaint	**acquainted**	
acquiescence	acquiesce	acquiescent	
actuality	actualize		actually
adamancy		**adamant**	adamantly
addressee	**address**	addressable	
adjacency		**adjacent**	adjacently
adroitness		adroit	**adroitly**
advantage	advantage	advantaged	advantageously
adversary		adversarial	
affability		**affable**	affably
affinity		affinitive	
affirmation	**affirm**	affirmative	affirmably
aficionado			
aggravation	aggravate	aggravated	aggravatingly

[1]Just as a quick review, a "noun" is the name of a person, place, thing, or idea (*Bill*, *Philadelphia*, *neighborhood*, *joke*, *honor*). A "verb" shows action (He *runs*) or a state of being (He *is*). An adjective modifies a noun (*red* truck; *careful* writer). An adverb modifies a verb, adjective, or another adverb (run *fast*; *highly* educated person; run *very* fast).

Noun Form	Verb Form	Adjective Form	Adverb Form
aggressor	aggress	**aggressive**	aggressively
		aghast	
agony	**agonize**	agonized	agonizingly
aimlessness		**aimless**	aimlessly
airiness		airy	**airily**
aisle		aisled	
alarm	alarm	alarming	**alarmingly**
alertness	**alert**	alert	alertly
alleviator	**alleviate**	alleviated	
allocation	**allocate**	allocable	
alteration	**alter**	alterable	alterably
amateur		amateurish	amateurishly
ambidextrousness		**ambidextrous**	ambidextrously
amenability		**amenable**	amenably
amendment	**amend**	amendatory	
amiability		**amiable**	amiably
amicability		**amicable**	amicably
amorousness		**amorous**	amorously
animation	animate	**animated**	animatedly
announcement	announce	announced	
annual	annualize	**annual**	annually
anonymity		anonymous	**anonymously**
antagonist	antagonize	**antagonistic**	antagonistically
anticipation	anticipate	anticipatory	
anxiety		**anxious**	anxiously
apathy		**apathetic**	apathetically
apology	apologize	apologetic	**apologetically**
	appall	**appalling**	
appeal	**appeal**	appealing	appealingly
applause	**applaud**	applaudable	applaudably
apportionment	**apportion**		
appraisal	appraise	appraised	**appraisingly**
appreciation	appreciate	**appreciative**	appreciatively
apprehension	apprehend	apprehensive	apprehensively
approbation	approbate	approbative	
appropriation	**appropriate**	appropriative	
aquarium		**aquatic**	aquatically
articulation	**articulate**	articulated	articulately
ascertainableness	**ascertain**	ascertainable	ascertainably
			askance
aspect			
assembly	assemble	assembled	
assent	assent	assenting	assentingly
assertion	**assert**	assertible	
assessment	assess	assessed	
asset			
assiduousness		assiduous	**assiduously**
association	**associate**	associated	
assumption		assumptive	assumptively
assurance	**assure**	assured	
	astound	**astounded**	astoundingly
astuteness		**astute**	astutely
attestation	attest	attested	

Noun Form	Verb Form	Adjective Form	Adverb Form
attire	attire	attired	
attitude	attitudinize	attitudinal	
audition	**audition**	auditioning	
auditorium			
auditor	audit	**auditory**	auditorily
augmentation	**augment**	augmentable	
auspiciousness		**auspicious**	auspiciously
availability	avail	available	availably
avalanche	avalanche		
averment	**aver**	averable	
	avert	avertable	
avidity		avid	**avidly**
avowal	**avow**	avowable	avowably
		awash	awash
awkwardness		**awkward**	awkwardly
badger	**badger**	badgering	
bafflement	baffle	**baffled**	
balker	**balk**	balky	
banter	banter	bantering	banteringly
beam	**beam**	beaming	
bearing			
	befuddle	**befuddled**	
belier	**belie**	belied	
bellicosity		**bellicose**	bellicosely
bewilderment	**bewilder**	bewildered	bewilderingly
biter	bite	**biting**	bitingly
bizarreness		**bizarre**	bizarrely
blancher	**blanch**	blanched	
blatancy		**blatant**	blatantly
		bleary-eyed	
blitheness		**blithe**	blithely
blunder	blunder	blundering	blunderingly
boisterousness		**boisterous**	boisterously
bolster	**bolster**	bolstered	
boom	**boom**	booming	
boon			
bound	**bound**	bounded	
brainstorm	**brainstorm**	brainstormed	
brawl	**brawl**	brawling	brawlingly
breach	breach	breached	
breathlessness		breathless	**breathlessly**
briskness		**brisk**	briskly
broacher	**broach**	broached	
broadcaster	**broadcast**	broadcasting	
buff			
		buoyant	**buoyantly**
	burgeon	**burgeoning**	
cacophony		**cacophonous**	cacophonously
cajoler	**cajole**	cajoling	cajolingly
calamity		calamitous	calamitously
callousness		**callous**	callously
callowness		**callow**	
campaign	**campaign**	campaigning	

Noun Form	Verb Form	Adjective Form	Adverb Form
candor		**candid**	candidly
candidate			
capableness		capable	**capably**
caper			
	capsize	capsized	
captivation	**captivate**	captivating	
carrel			
cast	cast	**cast**	
castigator	**castigate**	castigated	
catalog	catalog	cataloged	
catastrophe		**catastrophic**	catastrophically
	catch off-guard		
category	categorize	categorical	categorically
caution	caution	**cautious**	cautiously
caveat			
census			
certainty			
certifier	certify	**certified**	certifiably
chagrin		chagrined	
challenge	**challenge**	challenging	
chaos		**chaotic**	chaotically
characterization	characterize	characteristic	characteristically
chasm		chasmal	
chastener	chasten	**chastened**	
chastiser	**chastise**	chastisable	
chauffeur	**chauffeur**	chauffeured	
checklist		checklisted	
chider	**chide**	chided	chidingly
choppiness		**choppy**	choppily
choreography	**choreograph**	choreographed	choreographically
chortler	**chortle**	chortled	
chronicle	chronicle	chronicled	
chronology		**chronological**	chronologically
churlishness		**churlish**	churlishly
circler	**circle**	circled	
	cite	citable	
clamorousness		**clamorous**	clamorously
clarifier	**clarify**	clarified	
clash	**clash**	clashed	
clientele			
cogency		**cogent**	cogently
cognition		**cognizant**	
coincidence	coincide	coincidental	coincidentally
collaborator	**collaborate**	collaborative	collaboratively
collapse	**collapse**	collapsible	
collectivity	collectivize	**collective**	collectively
collision	**collide**	colliding	
collusion	**collude**	colluded	
		colossal	colossally
column		columnar	
combustion		combustible	combustibly
commentary	commentate	commentarial	
commission		commissioned	

Noun Form	Verb Form	Adjective Form	Adverb Form
compeller	**compel**	compellable	compellably
competency		**competent**	competently
complexity		**complex**	complexly
compliance	comply	compliant	compliantly
component		componential	
concession	**concede**		concededly
conception	**conceive**	conceivable	conceivably
conclusion	conclude	conclusive	conclusively
		concurrent	**concurrently**
condolences	condole	condolent	
conference	**confer**	conferring	
confession	**confess**	confessing	confessedly
confidence	**confide**	**confident**	confidently
confoundedness	**confound**	confounded	confoundedly
congeniality		congenial	congeniality
conjecture	**conjecture**	conjectural	
	conjoin	**conjoint**	conjointly
conjunction		conjunctional	conjunctionally
conjuror	**conjure**	conjured	
conscientiousness		**conscientious**	conscientiously
consciousness		**conscious**	consciously
consensus			
conservation	conserve	conservational	
consignment	**consign**	consignable	
conspicuousness		**conspicuous**	conspicuously
contemplation	**contemplate**	contemplated	
contention	**contend**	**contentious**	contentiously
continuation	continue	continuous	**continually**
contradiction	**contradict**	contradictory	contradictorily
contribution	**contribute**	contributive	contributively
contrition		**contrite**	contritely
conversation	**converse**	conversant	
convincer	**convince**	convincing	convincingly
convolution	convolve	**convoluted**	convolutedly
cooperation	**cooperate**	cooperative	cooperatively
coordination	**coordinate**	coordinated	coordinatedly
cordiality		cordial	**cordially**
core	core	cored	
corner	**corner**	cornered	
correspondent	correspond	**corresponding**	correspondingly
courtesy		courteous	**courteously**
covertness		covert	**covertly**
crank	**crank**	cranked	
credence			
creditor	**credit**	creditable	creditably
crestfallenness		**crestfallen**	crestfallenly
criticism	criticize	criticizing	critically
critique	**critique**	critiquing	
crony			
		crucial	crucially
cruise	**cruise**	cruising	
crypticness		cryptic	**cryptically**
cue	**cue**	cued	

Noun Form	Verb Form	Adjective Form	Adverb Form
cuff	**cuff**	cuffed	
cull	**cull**	culled	
cultivation	**cultivate**	cultivating	
curb	**curb**	curbed	
curriculum		curricular	curricularly
cursoriness		**cursory**	cursorily
curtness		**curt**	curtly
cutthroat		**cutthroat**	
cynicism		cynical	cynically
	dampen	dampened	
deception	deceive	deceptive	deceptively
decision	decide	**decided**	decidedly
declaration	**declare**	declarable	
decliner	**decline**	declinable	
defense	defend	defensive	**defensively**
deference	**defer**	deferred	deferentially
deftness		**deft**	deftly
			(by) degrees
dejection		dejected	dejectedly
		deleterious	
deliberation	**deliberate**	deliberate	deliberately
delineation	delineate	delineative	
delver	**delve**	delving	
demoralization	demoralize	**demoralizing**	
denouement			
denunciation	**denounce**	denounced	
denial	**deny**	denied	
despair	**despair**	despairing	despairingly
despondency	despond	despondent	**despondently**
determination	**determine**	determined	determinedly
detestation	**detest**	detestable	detestably
development	develop	developmental	developmentally
deviousness		**devious**	deviously
devourer	**devour**	devoured	devouringly
dilemma		dilemmatic	
direction	**direct**	directed	directly
disadvantage		disadvantaged	disadvantageously
disaster		**disastrous**	disastrously
discard	discard	**discarded**	
discernment	discern	**discernable**	discernibly
disclosure	**disclose**	disclosable	
discomfiture	**discomfit**	discomfited	
discomfort	discomfort	discomfortable	discomfortingly
discordance		**discordant**	discordantly
discount	discount	discounted	
discourse	discourse	discoursing	
discreetness		discreet	**discreetly**
dismay		dismayed	dismayingly
dismission		dismissive	**dismissively**
disparagement	**disparage**	disparaged	disparagingly
disparateness		**disparate**	disparately
dispute	dispute	disputable	disputably
disquiet		**disquieting**	disquietingly

Noun Form	Verb Form	Adjective Form	Adverb Form
disregard	**disregard**	disregarded	
dissatisfaction	**dissatisfy**	dissatisfied	dissatisfiedly
dissection	**dissect**	dissected	
distinction		**distinct**	distinctly
	distinguish	distinguished	distinguishably
distraction	distract	**distracted**	distractedly
		distraught	
diversion	**divert**	diverting	divertingly
divinity	**divine**	divine	divinely
doggedness		dogged	**doggedly**
doodle	doodle	doodled	
		downcast	
draft	draft	drafted	
drone	**drone**	droning	
dubiousness		**dubious**	dubiously
ease	ease	easier	easily
eavesdropper	**eavesdrop**	eavesdropped	
edibility		**edible**	
editor	edit	edited	editorially
effervescence	effervesce	**effervescent**	effervescently
egotism		egotistical	egotistically
elation		elated	elatedly
elevation	**elevate**	elevated	
elicitation	**elicit**	eliciting	
emanation	**emanate**	emanative	
embellishment	**embellish**	embellished	
	embolden	emboldened	
embrace	**embrace**	embraceable	
	empathize	**empathetic**	empathetically
encapsulation	**encapsulate**	encapsulated	
encirclement	**encircle**	encircling	
encore		encore	
encounter	**encounter**	encountered	
endearment	endear	**endearing**	endearingly
endeavor	endeavor	endeavorial	
energizer	energize	**energized**	
engagement	**engage**	engaging	engagingly
engrossment	**engross**	engrossing	
engulfment	**engulf**	engulfed	
enigma		enigmatic	enigmatically
enlightenment	**enlighten**	enlightened	
enrollment	**enroll**	**enrolled**	
		ensue	ensuing
entailment	**entail**		
entertainment	entertain	**entertained**	entertainingly
enthrallment	**enthrall**	enthralling	enthrallingly
enthusiasm	**enthuse**	enthusiastic	enthusiastically
entirety		entire	entirely
entr'acte			
entreaty	**entreat**	entreated	entreatingly
entry	enter		
environs			
envy	envy	**envious**	enviously

Noun Form	Verb Form	Adjective Form	Adverb Form
equitableness		equitable	**equitably**
		ersatz	
eschewal	**eschew**	eschewed	
escort	**escort**	escorted	
eternity	eternalize	eternal	eternally
evasion	**evade**	evadable	
event		eventual	**eventually**
exaggeration	**exaggerate**	exaggerated	exaggeratedly
exasperation	exasperate	**exasperated**	exasperatedly
excruciation	excruciate	**excruciating**	excruciatingly
excursion			
exhaustion	**exhaust**	exhaustive	exhaustively
exhumation	**exhume**	exhumed	
expansion	**expand**	expandable	
expectancy	expect	expectant	**expectantly**
expeditor	expedite	expeditious	**expeditiously**
explication	explicate	explicative	explicatively
explicitness		**explicit**	explicitly
		extracurricular	extracurricularly
exuberance		**exuberant**	exuberantly
factor	factor	factoring	
faculty			
falterer	**falter**	faltering	falteringly
fanatic		fanatical	fanatically
fancy	fancy	fancied	fancily
fathom	**fathom**		
fatigue	**fatigue**	fatigued	
	favor	favorite	favorably
fecklessness		**feckless**	fecklessly
	feign	feigned	
	ferret (out)		
fetidness		**fetid**	fetidly
fiasco			
fibber	**fib**		
fiddler	**fiddle**		
file	**file**	filing	
finalization	**finalize**	finalized	
flagger	**flag**	flagging	flaggingly
flounderer	**flounder**	floundering	
flourish	flourish	flourishing	
flusher	**flush**	flushed	
follies			
following	follow	followed	
forcefulness	force	forceful	**forcefully**
foreteller	**foretell**	foretelling	
forlornness		**forlorn**	forlornly
format	format	formatted	
formulation	**formulate**	formulated	
forthcoming		**forthcoming**	
forum			
foyer			
fragment	fragment	fragmented	fragmentally
frankness		frank	**frankly**

Noun Form	Verb Form	Adjective Form	Adverb Form
franticness		**frantic**	frantically
fretfulness	**fret**	fretful	fretfully
fruition			
fruitlessness		**fruitless**	fruitlessly
fulfillment	**fulfill**	fulfilling	
fume	**fume**	fumed	
funnel	**funnel**	funneled	
furnishings	**furnish**	furnished	
garner	**garner**	garnered	
garrulousness		**garrulous**	garrulously
gauge	**gauge**		
generation	**generate**	generated	
germination	germinate	germinating	
gesticulation	**gesticulate**	gesticulative	
gesture	**gesture**	gestured	gesturally
ghostwriter	ghostwrite	ghostwritten	
gist			
glare	glare	**glaring**	glaringly
glibness		glib	glibly
glimmer	glimmer	**glimmering**	
gloom		**gloomy**	gloomily
gnawer	**gnaw**	gnawed	
good-naturedness		good-natured	**good-naturedly**
grace	**grace**	graceful	gracefully
graduate	**graduate**	graduated	
graininess		**grainy**	
grantor	**grant**	granted	
gratification	gratify	**gratified**	gratifyingly
gravity	gravitate	grave	
grounds		grounded	
grudge		grudging	**grudgingly**
		grueling	gruelingly
guard	guard	**guarded**	guardedly
		halting	**haltingly**
		hands-on	
haphazardness		**haphazard**	haphazardly
harangue	**harangue**	harangued	
hastiness		hasty	**hastily**
hazard	hazard	**hazardous**	hazardously
	hearten	heartened	
heat		**heated**	heatedly
		hectic	hectically
heed	**heed**	heeded	
height	**heighten**	heightened	
heinousness		**heinous**	heinously
hilarity		**hilarious**	hilariously
hindrance	**hinder**	hindered	
horde			
horoscope			
hostility		hostile	hostilely
house	house	housed	
huff	huff	huffy	huffily
hurriedness	hurry	hurried	**hurriedly**

Noun Form	Verb Form	Adjective Form	Adverb Form
husky		husky	huskily
hypothesis	hypothesize	hypothesized	hypothetically
ice		icy	**icily**
identification	**identify**	identifiable	identifiably
idleness	idle	idle	**idly**
ignorance	**ignorant**		ignorantly
illumination	illuminate	illuminating	illuminatingly
	imbue	imbued	
immersion	**immerse**	immersed	
	impart	imparted	
impasse		impassable	impassably
impeccability		**impeccable**	impeccably
impediment	**impede**	impedimentary	
imperativeness		**imperative**	imperatively
imperviousness		**impervious**	imperviously
impetus			
implacability		**implacable**	implacably
impression	**impress**	impressive	impressibly
improvisation	**improvise**	improvised	
impulsiveness		**impulsively**	impulsively
	inch	inching	
incident		incidental	incidentally
		incommunicado	
incomprehensibleness		**incomprehensible**	incomprehensibly
inconclusiveness		**inconclusive**	inconclusively
incorporation	**incorporate**	incorporated	
inculpation	inculpate	**inculpable**	
independence		independent	**independently**
indication	**indicate**	indicated	indicatively
indifference		indifferent	**indifferently**
indigenousness		**indigenous**	indigenously
indignation		**indignant**	indignantly
indispensableness		**indispensable**	indispensably
individuality	individuate	**individual**	individually
indolence		**indolent**	indolently
indulgence	**indulge**	indulging	indulgently
inexorableness		**inexorable**	inexorably
infection	infect	**infectious**	infectiously
infusion	**infuse**	infusible	
ingenuousness		**ingenuous**	ingenuously
inhibition	**inhibit**	inhibited	
initialness		**initial**	initially
initiation	**initiate**	initiatory	
innocence		**innocent**	innocently
innocuousness		**innocuous**	innocuously
innovation	innovate	**innovative**	innovatively
inoffensiveness		**inoffensive**	inoffensively
input			
insatiability		**insatiable**	insatiably
insight		**insightful**	insightfully
insincerity		insincere	insincerely
insistence	**insist**	insisting	insistently
instigation	**instigate**	instigated	

Noun Form	Verb Form	Adjective Form	Adverb Form
intelligence		intelligent	intelligently
intention		intentional	**intentionally**
interference	**interfere**	interferential	
interjection	**interject**	interjectional	interjectionally
interlock	interlock	**interlocking**	
interminability		**interminable**	interminably
	intermingle	**intermingled**	
interpretation	**interpret**	interpreted	interpretability
interrogation	interrogate	interrogational	
interspersion	**intersperse**	interspersed	interspersedly
intervention	**intervene**	intervened	
intimation	**intimate**	intimated	intimately
intrigue	intrigue	intriguing	intriguingly
intrusion	intrude	intrusive	intrusively
intuition	intuit	intuitive	**intuitively**
inundation	**inundate**	inundated	
involvement	involve	involved	involvedly
irksomeness	**irk**	irksome	irksomely
irony		ironic	**ironically**
jabber	**jabber**	jabbered	
jeopardy	**jeopardize**	jeopardized	
jettison	**jettison**	jettisoned	
jitters	jitter	jittered	
joviality		**jovial**	jovially
jubilance		**jubilant**	jubilantly
judiciousness		judicious	**judiciously**
juncture			
juxtaposition	**juxtapose**	juxtaposed	
keenness		**keen**	keenly
kill-joy			
knack			
		laconic	laconically
lament	**lament**	lamented	lamentably
		latter	latterly
launch	**launch**	launch	
layout			
laxness		**lax**	laxly
		likely	likely
limitation	limit	limited	
lingerer	**linger**	lingered	lingeringly
literariness		**literary**	literarily
	liven	livened	
loathing	**loathe**	loathsome	loathingly
lock	**lock**	locked	
logistics		logistical	logistically
lounge	lounge	lounged	
lowliness		**lowly**	lowly
lucidity		**lucid**	lucidly
lunge	**lunge**	lunged	
lyrics		lyrical	lyrically
magnanimity		**magnanimous**	magnanimously
malefactor			
malice		**malicious**	maliciously

Noun Form	Verb Form	Adjective Form	Adverb Form
malodor		**malodorous**	malodorously
		mammoth	
mandate	mandate	**mandatory**	mandatorily
maneuver	**maneuver**	maneuvered	
manipulation	**manipulate**	manipulated	manipulatively
manuscript			
margin	margin	marginal	marginally
mark	**mark**	marked	
marketing	market	marketing	
martialism		**martial**	martially
mascot			
materialization	**materialize**	materialized	
meagerness		**meager**	meagerly
meanderer	**meander**	meandering	meanderingly
measure	measure	**measured**	measurably
meddler	**meddle**	meddlesome	meddlesomely
medley			
meekness		meek	**meekly**
melancholy		**melancholy**	melancholily
mellifluousness		**mellifluous**	mellifluously
melodiousness		**melodious**	melodiously
mentor	mentor	mentored	
meticulousness		**meticulous**	meticulously
migration	migrate	**migrating**	
mindfulness		**mindful**	mindfully
		minuscule	
minority			
	misconstrue	misconstrued	
miscreant		miscreant	
misdemeanor			
misgivings			
mission	missionize	missional	
mitigation	**mitigate**	mitigated	
mobilization	**mobilize**	mobilized	
mockery	mock	**mock**	mockingly
modesty		**modest**	modestly
mollifier	**mollify**	mollified	mollifyingly
moment		momentary	**momentarily**
	mull	mulled	
multitude		**multitudinous**	multitudinously
mundaneness		**mundane**	mundanely
muse	**muse**	mused	musingly
myriad		**myriad**	
mystification	mystify	mystified	mystifyingly
naïveté		**naïve**	naïvely
nascence		**nascent**	
necessitation	**necessitate**	necessitative	
neophyte			
nescience		**nescient**	
			nevertheless
		nocturnal	nocturnally
noisomeness		**noisome**	noisomely
notedness	**note**	noted	notedly

Noun Form	Verb Form	Adjective Form	Adverb Form
notion		notional	notionally
notoriety		notorious	notoriously
nudge	**nudge**	nudged	
numerousness		**numerous**	numerously
nurturer	**nurture**	nurturing	
obdurateness		**obdurate**	obdurately
obligingness	oblige	**obliging**	obligingly
obscurity	obscure	**obscure**	obscurely
obsession	obsess	obsessive	obsessively
obstinateness		obstinate	**obstinately**
offense	**offend**	offended	offensively
ominousness		**ominous**	ominously
		onboard	
opinion	**opine**	opined	
opposition	oppose	**opposing**	opposingly
optimism		**optimistic**	optimistically
option	option	optional	optionally
orchestration	**orchestrate**	orchestrated	
ordeal			
organization	organize	**organizational**	organizationally
outline	**outline**	outlined	
	outweigh	outweighed	
		overall	overall
overkill		**overkill**	
override	override	**overriding**	overridingly
overtness		overt	**overtly**
pacification	pacify	**pacific**	pacifically
painstaking		**painstaking**	painstakingly
pallor		**pallid**	pallidly
palpability		**palpable**	palpably
par	par	parred	
paraphernalia			
partition	partition	partition	
passion		**passionate**	passionately
patriot		**patriotic**	patriotically
patrol	**patrol**	patrolled	
paucity			
penchant			
penultimate		**penultimate**	penultimately
perception	**perceive**	**perceptive**	perceptibly
perfunctoriness		perfunctory	**perfunctorily**
periphery		peripheral	**peripherally**
perpetrator	perpetrate	perpetrated	
perplexity	perplex	**perplexed**	perplexingly
persistence	persist	persistent	persistently
perspiration	perspire	perspiring	
persuasion	**persuade**	persuaded	persuasively
perturbation	**perturb**	perturbed	
perusal	**peruse**	perused	
pessimism		pessimistic	pessimistically
petition	petition	petitioned	
pettiness		**petty**	pettily
phase	phase	phased	

Noun Form	Verb Form	Adjective Form	Adverb Form
philanthropy		**philanthropic**	philanthropically
phlegm		**phlegmatic**	phlegmatically
physics		physical	physically
piece	**piece**	pieced	
pilferage	**pilfer**	pilfered	
pique	pique	piqued	
plague	**plague**	plagued	
plodder	plod	**plodding**	ploddingly
poke	**poke**	poked	
ponderer	**ponder**	pondered	
posture	**pose**	posturing	
potential		potential	potentially
potpourri			
precedence	precede	**preceding**	
precision		precise	precisely
predilection			
preliminary		**preliminary**	preliminarily
preoccupation	preoccupy	**preoccupied**	
pressure	**pressure**	pressured	
presumption	**presume**	presumed	presumably
preternaturalness		**preternatural**	preternaturally
prevarication	prevaricate	prevaricated	
principal		principal	principally
principle		principled	
priority	prioritize	**prior**	
proceeds			
process	process	processed	
proffer	**proffer**	proffered	
profession	profess	professed	professedly
professionalism		professional	professionally
proficiency		**proficient**	proficiently
promotion	**promote**	promotable	
proportion	proportion	proportioned	proportionally
proposal	**propose**	prepositional	propositional
protester	**protest**	protested	protestingly
prowess			
prudence		**prudent**	prudently
psyche			
publicity	**publicize**	publicized	
punctiliousness		**punctilious**	punctiliously
punctuation	**punctuate**	punctuated	
puzzlement	puzzle	**puzzled**	
quandary			
quagmire			
	quell	quelled	
query	**query**	queried	
quintessence		**quintessential**	quintessentially
rally	**rally**	rallied	
randomness	randomize	**random**	randomly
ransacker	**ransack**	ransacked	
rash		rash	rashly
ravenousness		**ravenous**	ravenously
reason	**reason**	reasonable	reasonably

Noun Form	Verb Form	Adjective Form	Adverb Form
recalcitrance		**recalcitrant**	
receptacle			
reclamation	reclaim	reclaimed	
recognition	**recognize**	recognized	recognizably
recollection	**recollect**	recollected	recollectively
reconsideration	**reconsider**	reconsidered	
reconstruction	**reconstruct**	reconstructed	
recruitment	**recruit**	recruited	
redemption	redeem	redemptory	
reflection	**reflect**	reflected	
refutation	**refute**	refutable	refutably
regret	**regret**	regretted	
reiteration	**reiterate**	reiterated	reiteratively
rejoinder	**rejoin**	rejoined	
relentlessness	relent	**relentless**	relentlessly
relevance		relevant	relevantly
reluctance	reluct	reluctant	**reluctantly**
reliance	**rely**	reliable	reliably
reminiscence	reminisce	reminisced	reminiscently
remorse		**remorseful**	remorsefully
remote		remote	**remotely**
rendezvous	rendezvous	rendezvoused	
renege	**renege**	reneged	
renown		**renowned**	
repentance	repent	repentant	repentantly
repertoire			
reproof	reprove	reproved	**reprovingly**
rescindment	**rescind**	rescinded	
resentment	**resent**	resented	resentfully
reservations	reserve	reserved	reservedly
resilience		resilient	resiliently
resolution	**resolve**	resolute	**resolutely**
resort	resort		
resourcefulness		**resourceful**	resourcefully
respectiveness		**respective**	respectively
respite	respite	respited	
response	**respond**	responded	
restoration	**restore**	restored	
	retort	retorted	
retreat	**retreat**	retreated	
retrospect	retrospect	retrospective	retrospectively
revel	**revel**		
reverberation	**reverberate**	reverberated	
reverie			
revolution	**revolve**	revolved	
reward	reward	**rewarding**	
rifler	**rifle**	rifled	
rift	rift	**rift**	
roamer	**roam**	roaming	
role			
rouse	**rouse**	roused	
ruefulness	rue	rueful	**ruefully**
rummage	**rummage**	rummaged	

Noun Form	Verb Form	Adjective Form	Adverb Form
run			
sageness		sage	**sagely**
salvage	**salvage**	salvageable	
satire	satirize	satirical	satirically
saunter	**saunter**	sauntered	
savory	**savor**	savored	
scan	**scan**	scanned	
scatterbrain		scatterbrained	
scavenger	**scavenge**	scavenged	
scheme	**scheme**	schemed	
schism		schismatic	schismatically
scorn	scorn	scornful	scornfully
scout	**scout**	scouted	
scruple		**scrupulous**	scrupulously
scrutiny	**scrutinize**	scrutinized	scrutinizingly
seamlessness			**seamlessly**
security	secure	**secure**	securely
sedateness	sedate	**sedate**	sedately
	seethe	**seething**	
		self-appointed	
self-assurance		**self-assured**	self-assuredly
self-evidence		**self-evident**	self-evidently
senior		**senior**	
sensitiveness	**sense**	**sensitive**	sensitively
sentiment		**sentimental**	sentimentally
settle	**settle**	settled	
shepherd	**shepherd**	shepherded	
shirker	**shirk**	shirked	
showcase	**showcase**	showcased	
shroud	shroud	**shrouded**	
shrug	**shrug**	shrugged	
sibling			
		sidelong	sidelong
sideswipe	**sideswipe**	sideswiped	
sidle	**sidle**	sidled	sidlingly
sigh	sigh	sighed	
signal	signal	signaled	signally
significance	signify	**significant**	significantly
simultaneity		simultaneous	**simultaneously**
	single (out)		
singularness		singular	**singularly**
sizeableness		**sizeable**	sizably
skeptic		**skeptical**	skeptically
sketch	**sketch**	sketched	
slacker	**slacken**	slack	slackly
slate	**slate**	slated	
slouchiness	**slouch**	slouched	slouchily
sluggishness		**sluggish**	sluggishly
slump	**slump**	slumped	
slyness		**sly**	slyly
smirk	**smirk**	smirked	smirkily
smugness		smug	**smugly**
snicker	**snicker**	snickered	snickeringly

Noun Form	Verb Form	Adjective Form	Adverb Form
snideness		**snide**	snidely
soberness	sober	**sober**	soberly
society		**social**	socially
solicitation	**solicit**	solicited	
solidification	**solidify**	solidified	
		sole	**solely**
solitary		**solitary**	solitarily
solo	solo	**solo**	solo
soother	**soothe**	soothed	soothingly
sophistication	sophisticate	**sophisticated**	sophisticatedly
			sotto voce
sower	**sow**	sown	
speculation	speculate	speculative	**speculatively**
		spent	
spirit		**spirited**	
sponsor	sponsor	sponsorial	
sputterer	**sputter**	sputtering	sputtery
stage	**stage**	staged	
stammerer	**stammer**	stammered	
	stamp	stamped	
stance			
statistics		statistical	statistically
staunchness		**staunch**	staunchly
steadfastness		**steadfast**	steadfastly
	steel		
stock	**stock**	stocked	
stowage	**stow**	stowed	
straightforwardness		**straightforward**	straightforwardly
strain	**strain**	strained	
stream	**stream**	streamed	
	stricken	**strickened**	
stride	**stride**	striding	
stringency		**stringent**	stringently
stroller	**stroll**	strolled	
structure		**structured**	
stumble	**stumble**	stumbled	stumblingly
	stun	**stunned**	
	stymie	**stymied**	
submission	submit	submissive	submissively
subsequence		subsequent	**subsequently**
subsidization	**subsidize**	subsidized	
substantiation	**substantiate**	substantiated	
substantialness		**substantial**	substantially
subtlety		**subtle**	subtly
succession	succeed	succeeded	
suitable	**suit**	suited	suitably
sullenness		**sullen**	sullenly
supposition	suppose	suppositional	suppositionally
surface	**surface**	surfaced	
surrender	**surrender**	surrendered	
susurrus		susurrant	
surveillance	surveil		
survey	survey	surveyed	

Noun Form	Verb Form	Adjective Form	Adverb Form
suspect	**suspect**	suspected	
suspicion		**suspicious**	suspiciously
swindler	swindle	**swindled**	
synopsis	synopsize	synoptic	synoptically
table	**table**	tabled	
taciturnity		**taciturn**	taciturnly
tactility		**tactile**	tactilely
taint	**taint**	tainted	
tangent		tangential	tangentially
tangle	**tangle**	tangly	
tantalizer	**tantalize**	tantalized	
tardiness		**tardy**	tardily
tarry	**tarry**	tarried	
tedium		tedious	tediously
temperament		**temperamental**	temperamentally
tenacity		**tenacious**	tenaciously
tension		tense	tensely
tentativeness		**tentative**	tentatively
term		termed	
terseness		**terse**	tersely
		testy	**testily**
	thaw	thawed	
theme		thematic	thematically
theory	**theorize**	theorized	
thicket			
thingamajig			
thrust	**thrust**	thrusting	
		thunderstruck	
timidity		**timid**	timidly
tinkerer	**tinker**	tinkered	
tirade			
toll	toll	tolled	
tone		toned	
	trail (off)		
traipse	**traipse**		
trend	trend	**trendiest**	
trepidation			
trickle	**trickle**	trickled	
trio			
triteness		**trite**	tritely
triumph	triumph	triumphant	**triumphantly**
troupe		trouped	
turmoil			
twinge		twinged	
ubiquitous		**ubiquitous**	ubiquitously
ultimatum			
		unbeknown	
undercurrent			
underhandedness		**underhanded**	underhandedly
	underscore	underscored	
	undertake	undertaken	
unearthliness	**unearth**	unearthed	unearthly
		unequivocal	**unequivocally**

Noun Form	Verb Form	Adjective Form	Adverb Form
		unforced	
		unforeseen	unforeseen
		unintelligible	unintelligibly
universality		**universal**	universally
unjustness		**unjust**	unjustly
unlikeliness		**unlikely**	
		unorthodox	
unpredictability		**unpredictable**	unpredictably
		unruffled	
unsettlement	unsettle	**unsettled**	unsettlingly
		untold	
		unwarranted	unwarrantably
unwieldiness		**unwieldy**	unwieldily
		unwitting	**unwittingly**
uproariousness		uproarious	**uproariously**
urgency	urge	urgent	**urgently**
vacation	**vacate**	vacated	
vagueness		vague	**vaguely**
			(in) vain
vehemence		vehement	**vehemently**
veracity		veracious	veraciously
veritableness		**veritable**	veritably
versatility		versatile	
viability		**viable**	viably
vigor		vigorous	**vigorously**
vintage		**vintage**	
visibility		visible	**visibly**
visuality	**visualize**	visual	visually
vitalness		vital	**vitally**
vivacity		**vivacious**	vivaciously
vocalness	vocalize	**vocal**	vocally
vocation		vocational	vocationally
vociferousness		vociferous	**vociferously**
voice	**voice**	voiced	
volatility		**volatile**	
voraciousness		voracious	**voraciously**
	vouch	vouched	
	waft	wafting	
wariness		**wary**	warily
webbing		webbed	
		well-groomed	
wheedler	**wheedle**	wheedled	
whim			
wholeheartedness		wholehearted	**wholeheartedly**
wield	**wield**	wielded	
	wilt	wilted	
wince	**wince**		
winnower	**winnow**	winnowed	
withers			
woebegoneness		**woebegone**	
wordlessness		wordless	**wordlessly**
workforce			
wrangler	**wrangle**	wrangled	

Noun Form	Verb Form	Adjective Form	Adverb Form
wrathfulness		wrathful	**wrathfully**
wrestler	**wrestle**	wrestled	
writhe	**writhe**	writhing	
wrongdoing			
yield	**yield**	yielding	yieldingly
zest	zest	zestful	zestfully
zigzag	**zigzag**	zigzag	zigzag

Appendix 2: Word List

A

(take) aback
abnormally
abortive
abruptly
abscond
absentminded
abstain
absurd
abundance
academics
accessible
accommodating
accomplice
accountable
accumulate
acknowledge
acquainted
acquiescence
actuality
adamant
address
adjacent
adroitly
advantage
adversary
affable
affinity
affirm
aficionado
aggravation
aggressive
aghast
agonize
aimless
airily
aisle
alarmingly
alert
alleviate
allocate
alter
amateur
ambidextrous
amenable
amend
amiable
amicable
amorous
animated
announcement

annual
anonymously
antagonistic
anticipation
anxious
apathetic
apologetically
appalling
appeal
applaud
apportion
appraisingly
appreciative
apprehension
approbation
appropriate
aquatic
articulate
ascertain
askance
aspect
assembly
assent
assert
assessment
asset
assiduously
associate
assumption
assure
astounded
astute
attestation
attire
attitude
audition
auditorium
auditory
augment
auspicious
availability
avalanche
aver
avert
avidly
avow
awash
awkward

B

badger

baffled
balk
banter
beam
bearing
befuddled
belie
bellicose
bewilder
biting
bizarre
blanch
blatant
bleary-eyed
blithe
blunder
boisterous
bolster
boom
boon
bound
brainstorm
brawl
breach
breathlessly
brisk
broach
broadcast
buff
buoyantly
burgeoning

C

cacophonous
cajole
calamity
callous
callow
campaign
candid
candidate
capably
caper
capsize
captivated
carrel
cast
castigate
catalog
catastrophic
catch off-guard

category
cautious
caveat
census
certainty
certified
chagrin
challenge
chaotic
characterization
chasm
chastened
chastise
chauffeur
checklist
chide
choppy
choreograph
chortle
chronicle
chronological
churlish
circle
cite
clamorous
clarify
clash
clientele
cogent
cognizant
coincidence
collaborate
collapse
collective
collide
collude
colossal
column
combustion
commentary
commission
compel
competent
complex
compliance
component
concede
conceive
conclusion
concurrently
condolences

367

confer
confess
confide
confident
confound
congeniality
conjectured
conjoint
conjunction
conjure
conscientious
conscious
consensus
conservation
consign
conspicuous
contemplate
contend
contentious
continually
contradict
contribute
contrite
converse
convince
convoluted
cooperate
coordinate
cordially
core
corner
corresponding
courteously
covertly
crank
credence
credit
crestfallen
criticism
critique
crony
crucial
cruise
cryptically
cue
cuff
cull
cultivate
curb
curriculum
cursory
curt
cutthroat
cynicism

D
dampen
deception
decided
declare
decline
defensively
defer
deft
(by) degrees
dejection
deleterious
deliberate
delineation
delve
demoralizing
denouement
denounce
deny
despair
despondently
determine
detest
development
devious
devour
dilemma
direct
disadvantage
disastrous
discarded
discernable
disclose
discomfit
discomfort
discordant
discount
discourse
discreetly
dismay
dismissively
disparage
disparate
dispute
disquieting
disregard
dissatisfy
dissect
distinct
distinguish
distracted
distraught
divert
divine
doggedly

doodle
downcast
draft
drone
dubious

E
ease
eavesdrop
edible
editor
effervescent
egotism
elation
elevate
elicit
emanate
embellish
embolden
embrace
empathetic
encapsulate
encircled
encore
encounter
endearing
endeavor
energized
engage
engross
engulfed
enigma
enlighten
enroll
ensue
entail
entertained
enthrall
enthuse
entirety
entr'acte
entreat
entry
envious
environs
equitably
ersatz
eschew
escort
eternity
evade
eventually
exaggerate
exasperated
excruciating

excursion
exhaust
exhume
expand
expectantly
expeditiously
explication
explicit
extracurricular
exuberant

F
factor
faculty
falter
fanatic
fancy
fathom
fatigue
favor
feckless
feign
ferret (out)
fetid
fiasco
fib
fiddle
file
finalize
flag
flounder
flourish
flush
folly
following
forcefully
foretell
forlorn
format
formulate
forthcoming
forum
foyer
fragment
frankly
frantic
fret
fruition
fruitless
fulfill
fume
funnel
furnish

G

garner
garrulous
gauge
generate
germination
gesticulate
gesture
ghostwriter
gist
glaring
glibness
glimmering
gloomy
gnaw
good-naturedly
grace
graduate
grainy
grant
gratification
gratified
gravity
grounds
grudgingly
grueling
guarded

H

haltingly
hands-on
haphazard
harangue
hastily
hazardous
hearten
heated
hectic
heed
heighten
heinous
hilarious
hinder
horde
horoscope
hostility
house
huff
hurriedly
husky
hypothesis

I

icily
identify

idly
ignorant
illumination
imbue
immerse
impart
impasse
impeccable
impede
imperative
impervious
impetus
implacable
impress
improvise
impulsively
inch
incident
incommunicado
incomprehensible
inconclusive
incorporate
inculpable
independently
indicate
indifference
indifferently
indigenous
indignant
indispensable
individual
indolent
indulge
inexorable
infectious
infuse
ingenuous
inhibit
initial
initiate
innocent
innocuous
innovative
inoffensive
input
insatiable
insightful
insincerity
insist
instigate
intelligence
intentionally
interfere
interject
interlocking

interminable
intermingled
interpret
interrogation
intersperse
intervene
intimate
intrigue
intrusion
intuitively
inundate
involvement
irk
ironically

J

jabber
jeopardize
jettison
jitters
jovial
jubilant
judiciously
juncture
juxtapose

K

keen
kill-joy
knack

L

laconic
lament
latter
launch
lax
layout
likely
limitation
linger
literary
liven
loathe
lock
logistics
lounge
lowly
lucid
lunge
lyrics

M

magnanimous

malefactor
malicious
malodorous
mammoth
mandatory
maneuver
manipulate
manuscript
margin
mark
marketing
martial
mascot
materialize
meager
meander
measured
meddle
medley
meekly
melancholy
mellifluous
melodious
mentor
meticulous
migrating
mindful
minority
minuscule
misconstrue
miscreant
misdemeanor
misgivings
mission
mitigate
mobilize
mock
modest
mollified
momentarily
mull
multitudinous
mundane
muse
myriad
mystification

N

naïve
nascent
necessitate
neophyte
nescient
nevertheless
nocturnal

noisome
note
notion
notoriety
nudge
numerous
nurture

O

obdurate
obliging
obscure
obsession
obstinately
offend
ominous
onboard
opine
opposing
optimistic
option
orchestrate
ordeal
organizational
outline
outweigh
overall
overkill
overriding
overtly

P

pacific
painstaking
pallid
palpable
par
paraphernalia
partition
passionate
patriotic
patrol
paucity
penchant
penultimate
perceive
perceptive
perfunctorily
peripherally
perpetrator
perplexed
persistence
perspiration
persuade
perturbed

peruse
pessimism
petition
petty
phase
philanthropic
phlegmatic
physics
piece
pilfer
pique
plague
plodding
poke
ponder
pose
posture
potential
potpourri
preceding
precision
predilection
preliminary
preoccupied
pressure
presume
preternatural
prevarication
principal
principle
prior
priority
proceeds
process
proffer
profession
professionalism
proficient
promote
proportion
propose
protest
prowess
prudent
psyche
publicize
punctilious
punctuate
puzzled

Q

quandary
quagmire
quell
query

quintessential

R

rally
random
ransack
rash
ravenous
reason
recalcitrant
receptacle
reclamation
recognize
recollect
reconsider
reconstruct
recruit
redemption
reflect
refute
regret
reiterate
rejoin
relentless
relevance
reluctantly
rely
reminiscence
remorseful
remotely
rendezvous
renege
renowned
repentance
repertoire
reprovingly
rescind
resent
reservations
resilience
resolutely
resolve
resort
resourceful
respective
respite
respond
restore
retort
retreat
retrospect
revel
reverberate
reverie
revolve

rewarding
rifle
rift
roam
role
rouse
ruefully
rummage
run

S

sagely
salvage
satire
saunter
savor
scan
scatterbrain
scavenge
scheme
schism
scorn
scout
scrupulous
scrutinize
seamlessly
secure
sedate
seething
self-appointed
self-assured
self-evident
senior
sense
sensitive
sentimental
settle
shepherd
shirk
showcase
shrouded
shrug
sibling
sidelong
sideswipe
sidle
sigh
signal
significant
simultaneously
single (out)
singularly
sizeable
skeptical
sketch

slacken
slate
slouch
sluggish
slump
sly
smirk
smugly
snicker
snide
sober
social
solicit
solidify
solely
solitary
solo
soothe
sophisticated
sotto voce
sow
speculatively
spent
spirited
sponsor
sputter
stage
stammer
stamp
stance
staunch
statistics
steadfast
steel
stock
stow
straightforward
strain
stream
stricken
stride
stringent
stroll
structured
stumble
stunned
stymied

submission
subsequently
subsidize
substantial
substantiate
subtle
succession
suit
sullen
supposition
surface
surrender
sursurrus
surveillance
survey
suspect
suspicious
swindled
synopsis

T

table
taciturn
tactile
taint
tangent
tangle
tantalize
tardy
tarry
tedium
temperamental
tenacious
tension
tentative
term
terse
testily
thaw
theme
theorize
thicket
thingamajig
thrust
thunderstruck
timid
tinker

tirade
toll
tone
trail (off)
traipse
trendiest
trepidation
trickle
trio
trite
triumphantly
troupe
turmoil
twinge

U

ubiquitous
ultimatum
unbeknown
undercurrent
underhanded
underscore
undertake
unearth
unequivocally
unforced
unforeseen
unintelligible
universal
unjust
unlikely
unorthodox
unpredictable
unruffled
unsettled
untold
unwarranted
unwieldy
unwittingly
uproariously
urgently

V

vacate
vaguely
(in) vain
vehemently

veracity
veritable
versatility
viable
vigorously
vintage
visibly
visualize
vitally
vivacious
vocal
vocation
vociferously
voice
volatile
voraciously
vouch

W

waft
wary
webbing
well-groomed
wheedle
whim
wholeheartedly
wield
wilt
wince
winnow
withers
woebegone
wordlessly
workforce
wrangle
wrathfully
wrestle
writhe
wrongdoing

Y
yield

Z

zest
zigzag

Appendix 3: Answer Key

Section 1: Life is a Symphony

Chapter 1: Falling Apart?

Quick Match 1
1. G
2. W
3. X
4. T
5. L
6. B
7. M
8. P
9. Q
10. S
11. D
12. H
13. O
14. C
15. E
16. U
17. V
18. I
19. K
20. F
21. Y
22. N
23. A
24. J
25. R

Sentence Completions 1
1. C
2. E
3. A
4. D
5. B

Chapter 2: Working It Out

Quick Match 2
1. S
2. W
3. R
4. O
5. C
6. V
7. U
8. T
9. H
10. P
11. E
12. M
13. A
14. F
15. L
16. G
17. J
18. X
19. Y
20. N
21. Q
22. I
23. D
24. K
25. B

Sentence Completions 2
1. D
2. C
3. E
4. D
5. B

Chapter 3: Feelin' Your Pain

Quick Match 3
1. T
2. N
3. V
4. S
5. P
6. H
7. R
8. B
9. Y
10. X
11. G
12. Q
13. W
14. D
15. J
16. I
17. U
18. L/C
19. K
20. F
21. C/L
22. M
23. A
24. E
25. O

Sentence Completions 3
1. D
2. C
3. B
4. C
5. A

Chapter 4: Secrets

Quick Match 4
1. X
2. K
3. G
4. O
5. J
6. A
7. I
8. C
9. S
10. V
11. R
12. Y
13. T
14. L
15. W
16. N
17. D
18. H
19. E
20. F
21. M
22. B
23. P
24. Q
25. U

Sentence Completions 4
1. C
2. A
3. E
4. E
5. B

Chapter 5: Starting Over?

Quick Match 5
1. W
2. U
3. Q
4. Y
5. X
6. C/K
7. T
8. O
9. H
10. N
11. G
12. V
13. K/C
14. D
15. L

16. I
17. J
18. F
19. E
20. M
21. B
22. A
23. S
24. P
25. R

Sentence Completions 5
1. E
2. C
3. D
4. D
5. B

Section 2: Touch and Talent

Chapter 6: Life Is a Kick

Quick Match 6
1. Y
2. I
3. M
4. O
5. V
6. S
7. X
8. B
9. T
10. F
11. Q
12. A
13. H
14. R
15. D
16. L
17. U
18. K
19. N
20. J

21. E
22. G
23. C
24. P
25. W

Sentence Completions 6
1. C
2. A
3. C
4. B
5. D

Chapter 7: Tinkering

Quick Match 7
1. K
2. O
3. G
4. N
5. Y
6. P
7. F
8. M
9. D
10. Q
11. C
12. A
13. T
14. W
15. S
16. L
17. I
18. U
19. B
20. V
21. J
22. H
23. X
24. R
25. E

Sentence Completions 7
1. E

2. A
3. C
4. B
5. E

Chapter 8: Discovering Oneself

Quick Match 8
1. H
2. N
3. K
4. T
5. A
6. X
7. B
8. U
9. Q
10. I
11. G
12. D
13. S
14. F
15. V
16. W
17. Y
18. O
19. C
20. P
21. M
22. E
23. R
24. L
25. J

Sentence Completions 8
1. D
2. E
3. C
4. A
5. B

Chapter 9: The Favor

Quick Match 9
1. J
2. V
3. Q
4. A
5. K
6. B
7. C
8. T
9. M
10. P
11. E
12. W
13. F
14. O
15. R
16. I
17. Y
18. L
19. D
20. H
21. X
22. U
23. G
24. N
25. S

Sentence Completions 9
1. D
2. E
3. D
4. C
5. A

Chapter 10: Its Result

Quick Match 10
1. F
2. M
3. Y
4. L
5. O

6. P

7. Q

8. V

9. J

10. X

11. H

12. W

13. B

14. T

15. R

16. A

17. G

18. U

19. E

20. S

21. C

22. D

23. I

24. K

25. N

Sentence Completions 10

1. B

2. A

3. C

4. B

5. C

Section 3: At the Mall

Chapter 11: A First Step

Quick Match 11

1. I

2. K

3. G

4. H

5. L

6. A

7. T

8. X

9. S

10. W

11. N

12. Y

13. O

14. R

15. U

16. E

17. C

18. D

19. M

20. F

21. J

22. Q

23. V

24. B

25. P

Sentence Completions 11

1. D

2. C

3. E

4. B

5. E

Chapter 12: In Training

Quick Match 12

1. P

2. K

3. U

4. B

5. N

6. J

7. T

8. V

9. D

10. G

11. F

12. C

13. H

14. E

15. Y

16. M

17. O

18. A

19. W

20. S

21. X

22. L

23. R

24. I

25. Q

Sentence Completions 12

1. B

2. C

3. A

4. D

5. B

Chapter 13: Watching Your Words

Quick Match 13

1. N

2. F

3. W

4. K

5. R

6. Y

7. J

8. P

9. B

10. U

11. E

12. A

13. O

14. D

15. X

16. H

17. G

18. T

19. V

20. C

21. M

22. I

23. S

24. Q

25. L

Sentence Completions 13

1. E

2. A

3. B

4. D

5. C

Chapter 14: Complications

Quick Match 14

1. F

2. T

3. R

4. W

5. I

6. V

7. Y

8. C

9. M

10. Q

11. X

12. H

13. G

14. B

15. S

16. K

17. E

18. J

19. P

20. D

21. L

22. A

23. N

24. O

25. U

Sentence Completions 14

1. C

2. E

3. C

4. B

5. A

Chapter 15: Some Answers

Quick Match 15
1. O
2. G
3. F
4. J
5. C
6. S
7. P
8. B
9. A
10. D
11. N
12. X
13. E
14. U
15. T
16. W
17. M
18. V
19. H
20. Y
21. R
22. K
23. L
24. Q
25. I

Sentence Completions 15
1. D
2. B
3. B
4. D
5. A

Section 4: Interiors

Chapter 16: The Dreaded Group Project

Quick Match 16
1. J
2. X
3. W
4. D
5. M
6. T
7. N
8. U
9. C
10. B
11. R
12. V
13. Q
14. I
15. F
16. G
17. H
18. L
19. Y
20. P
21. E
22. O
23. S
24. K
25. A

Sentence Completions 16
1. E
2. C
3. D
4. B
5. A

Chapter 17: Coming Together

Quick Match 17
1. M
2. L
3. Q
4. G
5. J
6. W
7. E
8. I
9. N
10. R
11. T
12. B
13. Y
14. X
15. K
16. U
17. D
18. S
19. F
20. O
21. V
22. C
23. P
24. A
25. H

Sentence Completions 17
1. E
2. A
3. C
4. A
5. C

Chapter 18: Three's a Crowd

Quick Match 18
1. Y
2. Q
3. J
4. H
5. B
6. A
7. D
8. C
9. N
10. L
11. T
12. M
13. F
14. W
15. U
16. K
17. X
18. I
19. P
20. O
21. R
22. S
23. E
24. G
25. V

Sentence Completions 18
1. D
2. B
3. C
4. E
5. B

Chapter 19: Disconnections

Quick Match 19
1. X
2. E
3. W
4. F
5. C
6. A
7. S
8. R
9. N
10. H
11. Y
12. J
13. L
14. K
15. M
16. G
17. V
18. B
19. I
20. D
21. P
22. U
23. O
24. T
25. Q

Sentence Completions 19
1. D
2. A
3. B
4. E
5. C

**Chapter 20:
Honoring
Differences**

Quick Match 20
1. D
2. K
3. J
4. W
5. G
6. C
7. I
8. N
9. F
10. L
11. T
12. S
13. B
14. X
15. Y
16. E
17. H
18. Q
19. R
20. O
21. M
22. U
23. A
24. P
25. V

Sentence Completions 20
1. B
2. D
3. C
4. D
5. B

Section 5:
Words,
Words,
Words!

**Chapter 21:
Sowing**

Quick Match 21
1. V
2. T
3. Y
4. X
5. M
6. K
7. N
8. L
9. C
10. H
11. Q
12. W
13. D
14. G
15. P
16. B
17. A
18. F
19. O
20. E
21. S
22. I
23. J
24. U
25. R

Sentence Completions 21
1. C
2. E
3. A
4. D
5. B

**Chapter 22:
Germination**

Quick Match 22
1. Y
2. U
3. K
4. Q
5. R
6. W
7. O
8. V
9. X
10. T
11. C
12. J
13. P
14. D
15. E
16. F
17. B
18. G
19. H
20. M
21. L
22. N
23. S
24. A
25. I

Sentence Completions 22
1. B
2. D
3. D
4. A
5. C

**Chapter 23:
Sprouting**

Quick Match 23
1. V
2. P
3. E
4. K
5. O

6. S
7. Y
8. W
9. Q
10. C
11. H
12. X
13. R
14. L
15. U
16. T
17. A
18. B
19. D
20. I
21. F
22. N
23. J
24. G
25. M

Sentence Completions 23
1. C
2. B
3. D
4. A
5. E

**Chapter 24:
Burgeoning**

Quick Match 24
1. R
2. F
3. W
4. I
5. O
6. L
7. B
8. J
9. M
10. A
11. D
12. Q
13. P
14. X

15. H
16. N
17. T
18. U
19. K
20. G
21. E
22. Y
23. C
24. S
25. V

Sentence Completions 24
1. B
2. E
3. A
4. C
5. D

Chapter 25: Fruition

Quick Match 25
1. N
2. Q
3. V
4. I
5. H
6. O
7. A
8. L
9. P
10. F
11. C
12. B
13. G
14. W
15. Y
16. S
17. T
18. X
19. K
20. D
21. E
22. R
23. M

24. J
25. U

Sentence Completions 25
1. C
2. B
3. E
4. B
5. A

Section 6: The Rhythm of the Earth

Chapter 26: Wild Child

Quick Match 26
1. M
2. J
3. U
4. I
5. A
6. T
7. S
8. H
9. C
10. F
11. N
12. Q
13. O/R
14. L
15. K
16. R/O
17. V
18. E
19. W
20. Y
21. X
22. B
23. P
24. G
25. D

Sentence Completions 26
1. C
2. E
3. D
4. C
5. B

Chapter 27: An Unhappy Plan

Quick Match 27
1. B
2. X
3. T
4. A
5. I
6. H
7. E
8. C
9. K
10. N
11. Y
12. R
13. F
14. V
15. M
16. D
17. S
18. G
19. J
20. P
21. Q
22. O
23. L
24. W
25. U

Sentence Completions 27
1. C
2. A
3. B
4. D
5. C

Chapter 28: Some Things Fishy

Quick Match 28
1. O
2. G
3. L
4. M
5. R
6. D
7. P
8. J
9. N
10. A
11. C
12. Q
13. X
14. K
15. H
16. S
17. I
18. Y
19. W
20. V
21. E
22. B
23. U
24. F
25. T

Sentence Completions 28
1. D
2. C
3. B
4. B
5. A

Chapter 29: Conserving Interest

Quick Match 29
1. G
2. N
3. A
4. X

5. I
6. K
7. B
8. Q
9. U
10. D
11. S
12. F
13. C
14. Y
15. T
16. E
17. R
18. J
19. O
20. H
21. W
22. P
23. M
24. L
25. V

Sentence Completions 29
1. B
2. A
3. C
4. D
5. C

Chapter 30: Acting Locally

Quick Match 30
1. G
2. M
3. X
4. J
5. V
6. C
7. N
8. A
9. L
10. S
11. H
12. I
13. Y

14. B
15. Q
16. T
17. W
18. O
19. E
20. P
21. D
22. F
23. R
24. U
25. K

Sentence Completions 30
1. B
2. C
3. A
4. E
5. C

Section 7: The Great Cell Phone Caper

Chapter 31: The Eager Detective

Quick Match 31
1. X
2. H
3. K
4. R
5. Q
6. N
7. W
8. G
9. P
10. U
11. B
12. S
13. Y
14. I
15. E
16. L
17. T
18. V

19. O
20. A
21. C
22. F
23. D
24. M
25. J

Sentence Completions 31
1. E
2. D
3. C
4. E
5. B

Chapter 32: On the Case

Quick Match 32
1. C
2. M
3. I
4. W
5. A
6. N
7. Y
8. P
9. B
10. F
11. D
12. J
13. G
14. H
15. Q
16. X
17. T
18. V
19. K
20. L
21. R
22. O
23. S
24. E
25. U

Sentence Completions 32
1. C
2. A
3. C
4. B
5. C

Chapter 33: A Lively Imagination

Quick Match 33
1. B
2. J
3. Q
4. U
5. X
6. W
7. Y
8. V
9. M
10. P
11. R
12. E
13. L
14. C
15. D
16. K
17. T
18. G
19. A
20. I
21. S
22. H
23. F
24. N
25. O

Sentence Completions 33
1. B
2. C
3. C
4. A
5. D

Chapter 34: Dead End?

Quick Match 34
1. X
2. R
3. I
4. V
5. N
6. C
7. F
8. D
9. O
10. P
11. Q
12. U
13. M
14. J
15. K
16. B
17. H
18. Y
19. L
20. W
21. G
22. S
23. T
24. A
25. E

Sentence Completions 34
1. D
2. E
3. A
4. C
5. B

Chapter 35: All Is Revealed

Quick Match 35
1. B
2. H
3. F
4. L
5. O
6. V
7. J
8. R
9. Y
10. C
11. E
12. S
13. D
14. G
15. K
16. M
17. W
18. A
19. X
20. P
21. I
22. Q
23. U
24. T
25. N

Sentence Completions 35
1. A
2. D
3. D
4. E
5. A

Section 8: An Artist and His Dog

Chapter 36: The Spark

Quick Match 36
1. O
2. K
3. P
4. X
5. F
6. H
7. E
8. T
9. R
10. D
11. Q
12. C
13. J
14. V
15. B
16. L
17. I
18. G
19. Y
20. M
21. W
22. S
23. A
24. N
25. U

Sentence Completions 36
1. C
2. A
3. E
4. D
5. B

Chapter 37: And What It Lit

Quick Match 37
1. Y
2. X
3. H
4. P
5. V
6. T
7. R
8. F
9. W
10. O
11. Q
12. A
13. U
14. S
15. E
16. K
17. D
18. J
19. C
20. I
21. G
22. L
23. M
24. N
25. B

Sentence Completions 37
1. C
2. B
3. E
4. D
5. C

Chapter 38: He's Everywhere!

Quick Match 38
1. C
2. H
3. B
4. L
5. R
6. W
7. O
8. I
9. Q
10. M
11. X
12. U
13. N
14. T
15. A
16. K
17. Y
18. P
19. E
20. V
21. F
22. J
23. D
24. S
25. G

Sentence Completions 38

1. E
2. C
3. A
4. D
5. B

Chapter 39: A Day of Surprises

Quick Match 39

1. U
2. J
3. T
4. B
5. O
6. Q
7. G
8. M
9. H
10. P
11. V
12. E
13. W
14. L
15. N
16. K
17. Y
18. F
19. I
20. X
21. S
22. A
23. C
24. D
25. R

Sentence Completions 39

1. A
2. D
3. E
4. C
5. E

Chapter 40: New Directions

Quick Match 40

1. J
2. X
3. K
4. N
5. V
6. Y
7. I
8. W
9. U
10. T
11. R
12. B
13. O
14. L
15. E
16. S
17. M
18. G
19. F
20. A
21. D
22. H
23. C
24. P
25. Q

Sentence Completions 40

1. B
2. E
3. B
4. C
5. E

Bibliography

Here is a very short list of useful books on vocabulary study and multiple intelligences.

Burchers, Sam, Max Burchers, and Bryan Burchers. *Vocabulary Cartoons II: Building an Educated Vocabulary with Sight and Sound Memory Aids.* Punta Gorda, FL: New Monic Books, 2000.

Darnell, Jane. *Rhyme Your Way to a Powerful Vocabulary.* New York: Henry Holt and Co., 1990.

Gardner, Howard. *The Disciplined Mind: Beyond Facts and Standardized Tests, the K-12 Education That Every Child Deserves.* New York: Penguin, 2000.

———. *Frames of Mind: The Theory of Multiple Intelligences.* New York: Basic Books, 1983.

Kagan, Spencer and Miguel Kagan. *Multiple Intelligences: The Complete MI Book.* San Clemente, CA: Kagan Cooperative Learning, 1998.

Mersand, Joseph and Francis Griffith. *Spelling the Easy Way, Second Edition.* New York: Barron's Educational Series, Inc., 1982.

Nicholson-Nelson, Kristen. *Developing Students' Multiple Intelligences.* New York: Scholastic Professional Books, 1998.

Silver, Harvey F., Richard W. Strong, and Matthew J. Perini. *So Each May Learn: Integrating Learning Styles and Multiple Intelligences.* Alexandria, VA: Association for Supervision and Curriculum Development, 2000.

Index

A

-able, 269
Accept, 37
Adding, 178
Aisle, 99
All right, 123
Alliteration, 2
Alright, 123
Altar, 158
Alter, 158
Annual, 178
Antagonist, 238
Appraise, 103
Apprise, 103
Ascent, 72
Assent, 72
Assonance, 1
Astrology, 333
Aud-, 180

B

Bazaar, 331
Bizarre, 331
Bodily/kinesthetic
    learner, 45
Broach, 142
Brooch, 142

C

Callous, 161
Callus, 161
Categorizing, 220
Census, 276
Chart, 263
Chron-, 274
Chrono-, 274
Cite, 20
Co-, 290
Colonel, 6
Colossal, 316
Comparatives, 91, 189

Compel, 254
Compound words, 79
Comprehensible, 231
Comprehensive, 231
Confidant, 109
Confident, 109
Conscience, 309
Conscious, 309
Consensus, 276
Continually, 115
Continuously, 115
Cred-, 167

D

Desert, 49
Dessert, 49
Deuteragonist, 238
Dis-, 64
Discreet, 134
Discrete, 134
Disregardless, 145
Draft, 13
Draught, 13

E

ei, 223
Elicit, 57
Emigrant, 247
En-, 267
Enthuse, 28
Eschew, 28
Evocation, 67
Ex-, 151
Except, 37
Explicit, 58

F

Fewer, 325
Flammable, 211
Flashcards, 307
Flotsam, 233

G

Graphic organizers, 306

H

Heteronyms, 125
Horoscope, 333
Hyper-, 293
Hypo-, 293

I

-ible, 269
Idle, 311
Idol, 311
ie, 223
I'll, 99
Illicit, 57
Immigrant, 247
Impel, 254
Implicit, 58
Imply, 298
Incidence, 117
Incidents, 117
Infer, 298
Inflammable, 211
-ing, 101
Inhabit, 241
Inhibit, 241
Inter-, 23
Interpersonal learner, 87
Intrapersonal learner, 131
Invocation, 67
Irregardless, 145
Isle, 99
Its, 169
It's, 169

J

Jetsam, 233